JEWISH WISDOM
IN THE HELLENISTIC AGE

THE OLD TESTAMENT LIBRARY

Editorial Advisory Board

John J. Collins

JEWISH WISDOM IN THE HELLENISTIC AGE

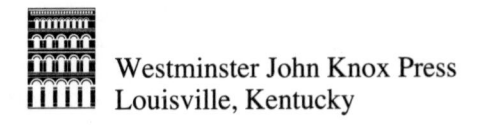

Westminster John Knox Press
Louisville, Kentucky

Book design by Jennifer K. Cox

First edition

Published by Westminster John Knox Press
Louisville, Kentucky

This book is printed on acid-free paper that meets the American National Standards Institute Z39.48 standard. ∞

PRINTED IN THE UNITED STATES OF AMERICA

97 98 99 00 01 02 03 04 05 06 — 10 9 8 7 6 5 4 3 2 1

Library of Congress Cataloging-in-Publication Data

Collins, John Joseph, date.
 Jewish wisdom in the Hellenistic age / John J. Collins. — 1st ed.
  p. cm. — (The Old Testament library)
 Includes bibliographical references and indexes.
 ISBN 0-664-22109-2
 1. Bible. O.T. Apocrypha. Ecclesiasticus—Criticism,
interpretation, etc. 2. Bible. O.T. Apocrypha. Wisdom of
Solomon—Criticism, interpretation, etc. 3. Pseudo-Phocylides—
Criticism and interpretation. 4. Wisdom—Biblical teaching.
5. Hellenism I. Title. II. Series.
 BS1765.2.C65 1997
 229′.306—dc21   97-20102

In memory of my father, John Collins
1912–1996

כי כאל לאיש כו אבוהי

4Q416 2. iii. 16

CONTENTS

ACKNOWLEDGMENTS

I wish to express my gratitude to Daniel J. Harrington, S.J., for graciously providing me with a copy of his manuscript on "Wisdom in the Dead Sea Scrolls" prior to publication; to Torleif Elgvin for giving me access to several unpublished articles on 4QSapiential Work A; and to Frederick Brenk, S.J., Gregory Sterling, and Gideon Bohak for bibliographic information on the status of the Jewish communities in Egypt. Shannon Burkes read the manuscript and made several helpful observations. Brenda Shaver prepared the bibliography and helped with the indexes.

ABBREVIATIONS

AB	Anchor Bible
ABD	D. N. Freedman, ed., *Anchor Bible Dictionary* (1992)
Anbib	Analecta biblica
ANET	J. B. Pritchard, ed., *Ancient Near Eastern Texts*
ANRW	H. Temporini and W. Haase, eds., *Aufstieg und Niedergang der römischen Welt* (1972–)
APOT	R. H. Charles, ed., *Apocrypha and Pseudepigrapha of the Old Testament*
ARW	*Archiv für Religionswissenschaft*
BAR	*Biblical Archaeologist Reader*
BETL	Bibliotheca ephemeridum theologicarum lovaniensium
BIB	*Biblica*
BibS	Biblische Studien (F: Freiburg; N: Neukirchen)
BN	*Biblische Notizen*
BTB	*Biblical Theology Bulletin*
BZ	*Biblische Zeitschrift*
BZAW	Beihefte zur *ZAW*
BZNW	Beihefte zur *ZNW*
CBQ	*Catholic Biblical Quarterly*
CBQMS	Catholic Biblical Quarterly Monograph Series
CIJ	Corpus Inscriptionum Judaicarum
CPJ	*Corpus Papyrorum Judaicarum*
CRINT	Compendia rerum iudaicarum ad novum testamentum
DBSup	*Dictionnaire de la Bible, Supplément*
DJD	*Discoveries in the Judaean Desert*
EncJud	*Encyclopaedia Judaica* (1971)
ETL	*Ephemerides theologicae lovanienses*
ExpTim	*Expository Times*
FOTL	The Forms of the Old Testament Literature
Fs.	Festschrift
HAT	Handbuch zum Alten Testament
HR	*History of Religions*

HTR	*Harvard Theological Review*
HUCA	*Hebrew Union College Annual*
Int	*Interpretation*
JAAR	*Journal of the American Academy of Religion*
JANESCU	*Journal of the Ancient Near Eastern Society of Columbia University*
JBL	*Journal of Biblical Literature*
JJS	*Journal of Jewish Studies*
JQR	*Jewish Quarterly Review*
JRE	*Journal of Religious Ethics*
JSHRZ	Jüdische Schriften aus hellenistisch-römischer Zeit
JSJ	*Journal for the Study of Judaism in the Persian, Hellenistic and Roman Periods*
JSOTSup	Journal for the Study of the Old Testament Supplement Series
JTS	*Journal of Theological Studies*
LCL	Loeb Classical Library
LD	Lectio divina
NovT	*Novum Testamentum*
NRT	*La nouvelle revue théologique*
NTS	*New Testament Studies*
OBO	Orbis biblicus et orientalis
OTL	Old Testament Library
OTP	J. H. Charlesworth, ed., *The Old Testament Pseudepigrapha*
OTS	*Oudtestamentische Studiën*
PEQ	*Palestine Exploration Quarterly*
PWRE	Pauly-Wissowa, *Real-Encyclopädie der classischen Altertumswissenschaft*
RAC	*Reallexikon für Antike und Christentum*
RB	*Revue biblique*
RevQ	*Revue de Qumran*
RHR	*Revue de l'histoire des religions*
RSR	*Recherches de science religieuse*
RTL	*Revue de théologie et de philosophie*
SBL	Society of Biblical Literature
SBLDS	SBL Dissertation Series
SBLMS	SBL Monograph Series
SBLSBS	SBL Sources for Biblical Study
SBLSP	SBL Seminar Papers
SCS	Septuagint and Cognate Studies
SVF	H. von Arnim, *Stoicorum Veterum Fragmenta* (1903–)

TDNT	G. Kittel and G. Friedrich, eds., *Theological Dictionary of the New Testament*
TLZ	*Theologische Literaturzeitung*
VT	*Vetus Testamentum*
VTSup	Vetus Testamentum, Supplements
WBC	World Biblical Commentary
WMANT	Wissenschaftliche Monographien zum Alten und Neuen Testament
WUNT	Wissenschaftliche Untersuchungen zum Neuen Testament
ZAW	*Zeitschrift für die alttestamentliche Wissenschaft*
ZNW	*Zeitschrift für die neutestamentliche Wissenschaft*
ZTK	*Zeitschrift für Theologie und Kirche*

Chapter 1.
Where Is Wisdom to Be Found?

The category of wisdom literature is identified in modern scholarship primarily with the books of Proverbs, Qoheleth, and Job in the Hebrew Bible, and the apocryphal or deuterocanonical books of Ben Sira (Ecclesiasticus) and the Wisdom of Solomon. The reason for the designation "wisdom literature" is simple enough: more than half the occurrences in the Hebrew Bible of the word *ḥokmāh,* wisdom, are found in Proverbs, Qoheleth, and Job,[1] while the Greek equivalent, *sophia,* is found more than a hundred times in Ben Sira and the Wisdom of Solomon.[2] Other wisdom literature from the ancient Near East is identified by analogy with these books. Like most traditional scholarly categories, however, "wisdom" is not identified by a systematic literary analysis, but is an impressionistic, intuitive grouping of books that seem to have something in common. Those who have attempted to define just what they have in common have found the task surprisingly difficult.[3] Wisdom literature has certain typical literary forms, such as the proverb and instruction, but it is itself a macro-genre that embraces several literary forms. In the Hebrew Bible, wisdom is characterized by a particular view of the world or theological perspective. That perspective, however, changes over time, and there is a vast difference between Qoheleth's view of the world and that of the Wisdom of Solomon.[4] Wisdom, in short, is a tradition, held together by certain family resemblances rather than by a constant essence. In this book we are concerned with a segment of that tradition, Jewish wisdom in the Hellenistic age, as

---

1. The word occurs in some form 318 times in the Hebrew Bible, and 183 of these occurrences are in the three wisdom books. See R. E. Murphy, "Wisdom in the OT," *ABD* 6 (1992) 920.

2. The root *soph-* in its various forms (noun, adjective, and verb) occurs almost a hundred times in Ben Sira alone. See A. A. DiLella, "The Meaning of Wisdom in Ben Sira," in L. G. Perdue, B. B. Scott, and W. J. Wiseman, eds., *In Search of Wisdom* (Louisville, Ky.: Westminster John Knox, 1993) 133.

3. R. N. Whybray, "Slippery Words. IV. Wisdom," *ExpTim* 89 (1978) 359–62; J. L. Crenshaw, "The Wisdom Literature," in D. A. Knight and G. M. Tucker, eds., *The Hebrew Bible and Its Modern Interpreters* (Philadelphia: Fortress, 1985) 369–407.

4. H. H. Schmid, *Wesen und Geschichte der Weisheit* (BZAW 101; Berlin: de Gruyter, 1966) was one of the first to draw attention to the diachronic aspects of wisdom literature in all its ancient Near Eastern manifestations.

represented primarily by Ben Sira and the Wisdom of Solomon. In order to understand these writings, however, it is necessary to have some grasp of the long tradition to which they were heirs and on which they built.

Wisdom in Proverbs

Anyone who reads the book of Proverbs in the context of the Hebrew Bible cannot fail to be struck by the contrast with the Torah and the Prophets. From a literary point of view, Proverbs is neither narrative nor law nor prophecy. Neither is it liturgical poetry such as we find in Psalms. The greater part of the book (chapters 10 to 30) is a collection of sentences that are sometimes strung together by catchwords or a common theme, but on the whole defy continuous reading. These sentences are either simple declarative statements, asserting that something is the case, or commands or prohibitions, which are sometimes, but not always, accompanied by explanatory statements.[5] In Proverbs 1–9 and again in chapter 31 we find longer, more developed instructions, which still contain a mixture of imperatives and declarative assertions. The direct, second-person form of address is characteristic of this material. Unlike the prophets, the sage does not address the nation as a whole but the individual person, typically "my son." The address is authoritative, but it has neither the force of law nor the vehemence of the prophetic oracle. The authority to which it lays claim is that of the accumulated wisdom of parents and tradition.[6] The typical sapiential attitude is articulated nicely by Bildad the Shuhite in the book of Job: "Inquire now of bygone generations, and consider what their ancestors have found; for we are but of yesterday, and we know nothing, for our days on earth are but a shadow" (Job 8:8–10).

The subject matter of Proverbs also stands in sharp contrast to most of the biblical tradition. The people of Israel and its history and destiny are not even mentioned. The focus here is on the life of the individual and the family. Nothing is said of a revelation in history or of mighty acts of deliverance from Egypt. Neither is there any mention of Moses or the covenantal law. The sage does not claim divine inspiration in the manner of a prophet, nor does he report visionary experiences. The subject matter is drawn from everyday life, and should in principle be accessible to anyone. One might speak of a revelation of wisdom in Proverbs, chapter 8, where wisdom is said to call out "on the heights, beside the way, at the crossroads." This revelation, however, does not require extraordinary experiences such as visions,

---

5. R. E. Murphy, *Wisdom Literature: Job, Proverbs, Ruth, Canticles, Ecclesiastes and Esther* (FOTL 13; Grand Rapids: Eerdmans, 1981) 4–6. G. von Rad, *Wisdom in Israel* (Nashville: Abingdon, 1972) 24–50, gives a more complete inventory of "the forms in which wisdom is expressed."

6. J. L. Crenshaw, "Wisdom and Authority: Sapiential Rhetoric and Its Warrants," in J. A. Emerton, ed., *Congress Volume: Vienna, 1980* (VTSup 32; Leiden: Brill, 1981) 10–29.

but rather the attentive observation of everyday experience and, above all, deference to tradition.

There has been a long-standing debate as to whether the wisdom tradition preserved in Proverbs was originally secular in character. Some scholars have drawn a sharp distinction between "old wisdom," which is "this-worldly and has no commitment to ethical values" and another strand that was "transformed through its subjection to distinctively Israelite religious and ethical insights."[7] There is an undeniable contrast between the hardheaded pragmatism of some sayings (e.g., 22:26–27: "Do not be one of those who give pledges, who become surety for debts. If you have nothing with which to pay, why should your bed be taken from under you?") and the doctrinaire pietism of others (e.g., 10:3: "The Lord does not let the righteous go hungry, but he thwarts the craving of the wicked"). Whether this contrast can be translated into a differentiation of stages, however, remains disputed. In the book as we have it "the rules of wisdom cover all areas of life from a perspective that is ultimately religious."[8] It is doubtful whether any literature from the ancient Near East can really be described as secular. But even if the pragmatic "old wisdom" also rests on religious suppositions, it is reasonable to suppose that the doctrinaire attitude of a saying like Prov. 10:3 represents a distinct redactional stage in the development of the collection. We shall certainly find that the later wisdom tradition was increasingly influenced by covenantal Yahwism. It is not unlikely that such influence can already be detected within the book of Proverbs.

On the whole, however, what is most striking about the book of Proverbs is its distinctiveness in the context of biblical Yahwism. There is, to be sure, coherence with the rest of the biblical tradition in significant respects.[9] Wisdom theology is creation theology, and is therefore based on a fundamental presupposition of Israelite religion.[10] There is an underlying similarity between proverbial wisdom and covenantal Yahwism insofar as both posit a system of retribution. Proverbial wisdom posits a chain of act and consequence,

---

7. W. McKane, *Prophets and Wise Men* (London: SCM, 1965) 15. Cf. H. Gressmann, "Die neugefundene Lehre des Amenemope und die vorexilische Spruchdichtung Israels," *ZAW* 41 (1924) 289–91; J. Fichtner, *Die altorientalische Weisheit in ihrer israelitischjüdischen Ausprägung* (BZAW 62; Berlin: de Gruyter, 1933) 13–59. The most elaborate defense of this distinction is found in the commentary of W. McKane, *Proverbs: A New Approach* (Philadelphia: Westminster, 1970). McKane argues that several terms that have a positive sense in "old wisdom" are evaluated negatively in the more overtly religious proverbs (pp. 17–18).

8. Murphy, "Wisdom in the OT," 922. See further idem, *The Tree of Life: An Exploration of Biblical Wisdom Literature* (New York: Doubleday, 1990).

9. J. J. Collins, "Proverbial Wisdom and the Yahwist Vision," *Semeia* 17 (1980) 1–17.

10. R. E. Murphy, "Wisdom and Creation," *JBL* 104 (1985) 3–11; L. G. Perdue, *Wisdom and Creation: The Theology of Wisdom Literature* (Nashville: Abingdon, 1994).

which is set in motion by the creator.[11] God is the guarantor of this system, but his role is like that of a midwife. No miraculous interference is needed. "Whoever sows injustice will reap calamity" (Prov. 22:8) just as surely as whoever sows the seed will reap the grain. Covenantal Yahwism also assumes that actions have their consequences, but it allows more scope for appeals to divine mercy, and its concern is with the conduct of the people as a whole rather than with the individual. Proverbial wisdom also allows for the unpredictability of divine freedom[12] (Prov. 16:1: "The plans of the mind belong to mortals, but the answer of the tongue is from the Lord"). Proverbs, however, has only a negligible place for prayer and sacrifice (e.g., 3:9; 12:2). The book is permeated by "the fear of the Lord," which is the beginning of wisdom (1:7). This attitude bespeaks a cautious, conservative attitude, which reveres tradition and is wary of human arrogance, but it does not require the specific beliefs and practices that characterize the religion of Israel in the Torah and the books of the Prophets.

The Setting of Proverbs

In view of the distinctive character of proverbial wisdom, the question arises how such a tradition arose and took root in ancient Israel. Some scholars argue that its origins are to be found in folk wisdom and that it was transmitted in the context of home education within the family.[13] The popular use of proverbs is often illustrated in biblical narratives (e.g., Judg. 8:2, 21 or Ezek. 18:2).[14] It is certainly plausible that some of the proverbs in the collection originated as popular sayings. Many of the proverbs are concerned with issues of family importance, such as finding a good wife (12:4; 14:1; 18:22; 19:13, 14; 21:9, 19), or the discipline of children and slaves (19:18; 20:20; 22:6, 15).[15] The typical wisdom instruction in Proverbs 1–9 is cast as the advice of a father to his son. It seems reasonable then to assume that some of

11. K. Koch, "Gibt es ein Vergeltungsdogma im Alten Testament?" *ZTK* 52 (1955) 1–42 (English translation: "Is There a Doctrine of Retribution in the Old Testament?" in J. L. Crenshaw, ed., *Theodicy in the Old Testament* (Philadelphia: Fortress, 1983) 57–87.

12. Von Rad, *Wisdom in Israel*, 96–110 ("The Limits of Wisdom").

13. E. Gerstenberger, *Wesen und Herkunft des sogennanten 'apodiktischen Rechts' im Alten Testament* (WMANT 20; Neukirchen-Vluyn: Neukirchener Verlag, 1965); C. R. Fontaine, *Traditional Sayings in the Old Testament: A Contextual Study* (Sheffield: Almond, 1982); idem, "The Sage in Family and Tribe," in J. G. Gammie and L. G. Perdue, eds., *The Sage in Israel and the Ancient Near East* (Winona Lake, Ind.: Eisenbrauns, 1990) 155–64; C. Westermann, *Roots of Wisdom* (Louisville, Ky.: Westminster John Knox, 1995).

14. Fontaine, *Traditional Sayings*, 76–86.

15. C. R. Fontaine, "Wisdom in Proverbs," in L. G. Perdue, B. B. Scott, and W. J. Wiseman, eds., *In Search of Wisdom: Essays in Memory of John G. Gammie* (Louisville, Ky.: Westminster John Knox, 1993) 102–3.

this material either originated in a family setting or was modeled on home instruction, and that the book of Proverbs served as a resource for education
within the household. It is difficult to believe, however, that the book as a
whole was compiled either as a record of or as a resource for home instruction. The collection of instructions and proverbs that make up the book is most
plausibly ascribed to a school setting.[16]

The book of Proverbs is attributed to King Solomon. No one would argue
that the book as we now have it comes from the time of Solomon, but many
scholars have held that the wisdom tradition had its origin in the time of
Solomon. The establishment of the monarchy created a need for scribes and
hence for schools attached to the court where scribes could be trained. The wisdom literature would then have developed in these scribal schools. This hypothesis derived support from the affinities between Israelite and Egyptian
wisdom literature. The publication of "The Teaching of Amenemope" in 1923
led to the discovery of close parallels between this work and Prov. 22:17–
23:11, and to the conclusion that the Hebrew text was modeled on the Egyptian.[17] The reign of Solomon was the most plausible occasion for extensive
Egyptian influence on Hebrew wisdom, although that influence might well
continue once the tradition had been established.

The Teaching of Amenemope stands in a long tradition of Egyptian instructional literature, stretching back to the Instruction of Ptah-hotep, which
some scholars date as early as the middle of the third millennium.[18] Other examples of the genre are attributed to Merikare (a pharaoh from the twenty-
second century B.C.E.);[19] Amenemhet (a pharaoh about 2000 B.C.E.); Duauf
(a treatise on the superiority of the scribe, preserved in copies from the nineteenth dynasty, 1320–1200 B.C.E., but possibly dating from the Middle Kingdom, 2150–1750 B.C.E.); and Ani (a parental instruction from the New Kingdom, 1580–1085 B.C.E.). The date of the Teaching of Amenemope is widely

---

16. H. J. Hermisson, *Studien zur Israelitischen Spruchweisheit* (WMANT 28; Neukirchen-
Vluyn: Neukirchener Verlag, 1968) 93 rightly argues that a popular origin cannot be assumed in
all cases, although the literate wisdom of the editors of Proverbs builds on the heritage of popular
wisdom.

17. E. A. Wallis Budge, *Facsimiles of Egyptian Hieratic Papyri in the British Museum with Descriptions, Summaries of Contents, Etc.* (2d Series; London: Harrison & Sons, 1923); P. Humbert,
Recherches sur les sources égyptiennes de la littérature sapientiale d'Israel (Mémoires de l'Université de Neuchatel 7; Neuchatel: Secrétariat de l'Université, 1929); G. E. Bryce, *A Legacy of
Wisdom: The Egyptian Contribution to the Wisdom of Israel* (Lewisburg, Pa.: Bucknell, 1979).

18. For the texts, see *ANET* 412–24. A helpful analysis can be found in McKane, *Proverbs,*
51–150. M. Lichtheim, *Ancient Egyptian Literature,* vol. 1 (Berkeley: Univ. of California Press,
1973) 7, favors a later date for the Instruction of Ptah-hotep, toward the end of the third millennium.

19. Several of these Instructions are thought to be pseudonymous, and so later in date than their
supposed authors.

disputed, but a date in the thirteenth or twelfth century seems likely.[20] Later examples of the Instruction genre, from the Hellenistic period, are found in the Teaching of Onchsheshonqy and Papyrus Insinger.[21] These instructions were written for the training of scribes and statesmen. Although these documents are typically cast as the instructions of fathers to their sons, they were copied in writing and learned by rote in Egyptian schools for more than two millennia. The existence of similar schools in Israel is often posited by analogy.[22]

In Egypt schools existed primarily to train courtiers and scribes for governmental service, but the Egyptian instructions extend to matters of human psychology and proper behavior. The kingdoms of Israel and Judah also had need of scribes, and the eventual production of the corpus of biblical literature shows that there was demand for scribes for religious purposes. The question is, how did these scribes receive their training? N. Whybray has sought to debunk the existence of a scribal class and hence also of scribal schools.[23] He then has to substitute the idea of an intellectual tradition among upperclass landowners, but it is difficult to imagine how such a tradition could be sustained without the institutional underpinning of a school tradition.[24] F. W. Golka argues that the scribal profession was hereditary, so that scribal instruction could be carried on adequately in a family setting.[25] Even in the story of Ahikar, a popular Near Eastern tale that is found in Aramaic in the fifth-century Jewish archive from Elephantine in the south of Egypt, we find that Ahikar instructs his nephew Nadin at home.[26] Nonetheless, it is difficult to be-

20. Bryce, *A Legacy of Wisdom,* 56; R. J. Williams, "The Sage in Egyptian Literature," in J. G. Gammie and L. G. Perdue, eds., *The Sage in Israel and the Ancient Near East* (Winona Lake, Ind.: Eisenbrauns, 1990) 23.

21. Williams, "The Sage in Egyptian Literature," 23; M. Lichtheim, *Late Egyptian Wisdom Literature in the International Context: A Study of Demotic Instructions* (OBO 52; Fribourg: Fribourg University, 1983).

22. See recently Nili Shupak, "The 'Sitz im Leben' of the Book of Proverbs in the Light of a Comparison of Biblical and Egyptian Wisdom Literature," *RB* 94 (1987) 98–119; idem, *Where Can Wisdom Be Found? The Sage's Language in the Bible and in Ancient Egyptian Literature* (OBO 130; Fribourg: Fribourg University, 1993). Shupak argues from the use of similar terminology for "instruction" in the Egyptian and Israelite wisdom literature, but there are also significant differences in the way the terms are used (e.g., Egyptian instructions are usually written, whereas the Hebrew *mûsār* refers to oral instruction).

23. N. Whybray, *The Intellectual Tradition in the Old Testament* (Berlin: de Gruyter, 1974) 33–43.

24. E. W. Heaton, *The School Tradition of the Old Testament* (Oxford: Oxford Univ. Press, 1994) 4, derides the notion of an "intellectual tradition" as "a residual concept" like the grin of the Cheshire cat.

25. F. W. Golka, "The Israelite Wisdom School or 'The Emperor's New Clothes,' " in idem, *The Leopard's Spots* (Edinburgh: T. & T. Clark, 1993) 11.

26. For the text see J. M. Lindenberger, *The Aramaic Proverbs of Ahiqar* (Baltimore: Johns Hopkins, 1983).

lieve that something as important for the state as the training of scribes was left entirely to family tradition in any Near Eastern kingdom in the first millennium B.C.E. There is room for debate as to when the kingdoms of Judah and Israel evolved to the point that they would need a scribal bureaucracy. It has been argued, on archaeological grounds, that this point was reached no earlier than the eighth century.[27] But it seems safe to say that there would have been need of scribal training in Jerusalem by the time of Hezekiah, at the end of the eighth century.

There has been a lively debate about the existence and distribution of schools in ancient Israel. The evidence for the preexilic period is very fragmentary. The classic study of A. Klostermann pointed to three texts.[28] Isaiah 28:9–13 has been read as a reflection of early instruction ("Whom will he teach knowledge, to whom will he explain the message? Those who are weaned from the breast? For it is precept upon precept, precept upon precept, line upon line, line upon line, here a little, there a little"). This text, however, is complicated by the reference to weaning. It would seem that "it is the parents . . . who are using baby-talk for the instruction of children of this age group."[29] In Isa. 50:4 the prophet says that "the Lord God has given me a trained tongue [literally, a tongue of those who are taught *lᵉšôn limmûdîm*], that I may know how to sustain the weary with a word." The objection that the reference here is to prophetic discipleship does not dispose of the evidence.[30] The point of the verse is to draw an analogy between prophetic discipleship and the training of pupils, and it suggests that at least in the exilic context the prophet was familiar with some kind of schooling. The third text, Prov. 22:17–21, was regarded by Klostermann as a teacher's farewell discourse to his pupil. It was subsequently shown to be dependent on the Egyptian Instruction of Amenemope. F. W. Golka argued that it therefore lost its evidentiary value for ancient Israel.[31] One might argue to the contrary, that the evidentiary value is increased. The copying of an Egyptian wisdom book in Jerusalem is surely more likely to have taken place in a school setting than in the context of family-based instruction. In short, while the textual evidence is meager, it cannot be dismissed entirely. Isaiah 50 dates from the exilic period. The date of Proverbs 22 is unknown, but it need be no earlier than the time of Hezekiah (cf. Prov. 25:1).

---

27. D. W. Jamieson-Drake, *Scribes and Schools in Monarchic Judah* (Sheffield: Almond, 1991) 138–39.

28. A. Klostermann, "Schulwesen im alten Israel," *Theologische Studien Th. Zahn* (Leipzig: Deichert, 1908) 193–232.

29. Golka, "The Israelite Wisdom School or 'The Emperor's New Clothes,'" in idem, *The Leopard's Spots* (Edinburgh: Clark, 1993) 6.

30. The objection is raised by Golka, ibid., 8.

31. Ibid., 5–6.

The archaeological evidence for educational practice has been collected primarily by A. Lemaire.[32] It consists of ostraka from the eighth and seventh centuries B.C.E., inscribed with letters that are best explained as abcedaries, or schoolboy exercises in drawing the alphabet. The most notable ostraka are from Lachish. Others are found at Kadesh-Barnea, Kuntilat-Ajrud, Arad, and a number of other sites.[33] Some of the evidence admits of different explanations. Large letters and poor drawings may be due to poor eyesight rather than to beginning students, and even a beginning student does not necessarily presuppose the existence of a school. The consistency of Israelite paleography, however, suggests that writing was taught systematically in accordance with recognized standards, and this again favors the existence of schools (whether the ostraka are thought to derive from such schools or not).

After Josiah's reform, and especially after the Babylonian exile, scribes often became associated with the book of the Law, which acquired increasing importance in Second Temple Judaism. Second Chronicles 17:7–9 claims that King Jehoshaphat sent officials "to teach in the cities of Judah. . . . They taught in Judah, having the book of the law of the Lord with them; they went around through all the cities of Judah and taught among the people." The historical value of this passage is questionable. It is more likely to reflect a practice of the Second Temple period than the time of Jehoshaphat, but it may only reflect the ideals of the Chronicler. The Chronicler further tells us that "some of the Levites were scribes." We also read of "Levites who taught the people" in Neh. 8:9. In the view of the Chronicler, at least, the Levites were responsible for teaching the people the Torah. Already the blessing of Moses in Deuteronomy 33 says of the children of Moses: "They teach Jacob your ordinances and Israel your law" (v. 10). Priests and Levites appear repeatedly as authoritative teachers in Second Temple literature, notably in the Dead Sea Scrolls (1QS 5:2; CD 14:6b–8; 13:2–4; 1QSb 3:22–27). In the Second Temple period, literacy was required for this function, and while not all Levites were scribes we can probably infer the existence of schools associated with the Temple. The copying of sacred literature and the production of learned psalms also suggest that the realms of the temple cult and the sages were often interrelated.[34] There is minimal reference to the cult, however, in the classic wisdom books of

---

32. A. Lemaire, *Les écoles et la formation de la Bible dans l'ancien Israel* (Göttingen: Vandenhoeck & Ruprecht, 1981); idem, "The Sage in School and Temple," in J. G. Gammie and L. G. Perdue, eds., *The Sage in Israel and the Ancient Near East* (Winona Lake, Ind.: Eisenbrauns, 1990) 165–81.

33. Lemaire, *Les écoles,* 7–33; J. L. Crenshaw, "Education in Ancient Israel," *JBL* 104 (1985) 605–6. Jamieson-Drake, *Scribes and Schools,* 147–48, argues that the sites where writing was found were related to, or dependent on, Jerusalem in various ways and that the training of scribes would have been done in Jerusalem, but the latter inference seems to be gratuitous.

34. L. G. Perdue, *Wisdom and Cult* (SBLDS 30; Missoula, Mont.: Scholars, 1977) 360–61.

Proverbs, Job, and Qoheleth. It would seem that some scribal schools flourished independently of the cult down to the Hellenistic period.

One section of the book of Proverbs is introduced as "other proverbs of Solomon that the men of Hezekiah copied" (25:1). There is no apparent reason why "the men of Hezekiah" should be introduced here unless they actually had some role in collecting the material. The reference strengthens the association of Proverbs with the royal court. The "men of Hezekiah" are not said to compose these Proverbs. They may have collected popular sayings and shaped them for their purposes. The reign of Hezekiah marks a relatively late point in the history of the monarchy (after the fall of the northern kingdom). The reference shows, however, that proverbial wisdom was at that time the object of royal patronage.

The book of Proverbs as we have it is not a manual of instruction for young diplomats at the royal court. Relatively few of its sayings address concerns peculiar to the court.[35] It is primarily a book of religious and ethical instruction, which presents wisdom as a religious disposition. Its purpose is stated in the opening verses:

> For learning about wisdom and instruction,
>   for understanding and words of insight,
> for gaining instruction in wise dealing,
>   righteousness, justice, and equity;
> to teach shrewdness to the simple,
>   knowledge and prudence to the young.
> (Prov. 1:2–4)

This is intellectual training with a moral purpose. The wise person acquires skill in understanding proverbs and riddles (1:5–6), but also acknowledges that "the fear of the Lord is the beginning of knowledge" (1:7). Even the adaptation of the teaching of Amenemope in Prov. 22:17–23:11, which represents an older stage of the wisdom tradition, has a moral purpose: "to show you what is right and true, so that you may give a true answer to those who sent you" (22:21), although in that case it may be argued that the primary concern is "to prepare messengers to represent wealthy clients effectively."[36] In Proverbs 1, however, the religious and moral purpose is primary, and it is this passage that characterizes the book as a whole. The neglect of specifically Israelite traditions is all the more remarkable in view of this explicitly religious character. We must infer that the wisdom schools of the early Second Temple period had their own traditions, and only slowly came to adopt the Jewish Scriptures as part of their curriculum.

35. J. L. Crenshaw, "The Sage in Proverbs," in Gammie and Perdue, eds., *The Sage*, 210.
36. Ibid., 207. Crenshaw notes that the images of the older passage derive primarily from human anatomy (ears, heart, belly, lips), whereas those of Proverbs 1 consist of intellectual abstractions.

The Worldview of Proverbs

The wisdom tradition embodied in the book of Proverbs has its own distinctive worldview. In the words of James Crenshaw, "that way of looking at things begins with humans as the fundamental point of orientation. It asks what is good for men and women and it believes that all essential answers can be learned in experience, pregnant with signs about reality itself."[37] It has a strongly this-worldly character and views claims of supernatural revelation with skepticism: "Who has gone up to heaven and come down?" asks Agur, son of Jakeh, in Prov. 30:4. Proverbs is devoid of eschatological expectation, envisaging neither cosmic transformation nor reward or punishment after death.[38] The teaching embodied in the book is essentially conservative. It is an ethic of caution, which lacks the fire and passion of the Hebrew prophets. The status quo is simply given; there is no thought of overthrowing it. Proverbs is also profoundly patriarchal.[39] All issues are seen from the male point of view. The prostitute, or "loose woman," symbolizes all the danger that lurks in wait for the innocent youth. It would not be fair to label the authors of Proverbs misogynist. The figures of the seductress in Proverbs 7 and the foolish woman in 9:13–18 are balanced by the portrayal of Wisdom as a female in chapter 8 and in 9:1–6.[40] It is true, however, that everything is viewed from the male point of view. Even the "capable wife" of Proverbs 31 is praised chiefly for the help she gives her husband and the honor he receives on her account. Nonetheless, the ethic of Proverbs also has its positive aspects. It is grounded in creation, and views human beings simply as creatures of one God, without regard to ethnic origin or cultic affiliation. The pragmatic tone of many of the Proverbs provides a refreshing realism that measures actions by their effects rather than by the intentions of their agents. This sapiential worldview is shared, with some modifications, by Job and Qoheleth. We shall find, however, that it undergoes profound transformations in the Hellenistic age.

Wisdom Personified

From a theological point of view, the outstanding contribution of the book of Proverbs is that it inaugurated a line of speculation about Wisdom, personified as a female. The classic passage is in Proverbs 8. God created (or ac-

---

37. J. L. Crenshaw, *Old Testament Wisdom: An Introduction* (Atlanta: John Knox, 1981) 18.

38. B. Vawter, "Intimations of Immortality and the Old Testament," *JBL* 91 (1972) 158–71 (= idem, *The Path of Wisdom* [Wilmington: Glazier, 1986] 140–60).

39. See Carol A. Newsom, "Women and the Discourse of Patriarchal Wisdom: A Study of Proverbs 1–9," in Peggy L. Day, ed., *Gender and Difference in Ancient Israel* (Minneapolis: Fortress, 1989) 142–60.

40. Cf. C. Camp, "Woman Wisdom as Root Metaphor: A Theological Consideration," in K. G. Hoglund et al., eds., *The Listening Heart: Essays in Wisdom and the Psalms in Honor of Roland E. Murphy, O. Carm.* (JSOTSup 58; Sheffield: Almond, 1987) 45–76.

quired) Wisdom as the beginning of his way, the first of his works of old (8:22). Whether Wisdom herself is part of God's creation is open to question. The Hebrew verb *qānāh*, which is usually translated "created" in this passage, usually means "to acquire."[41] The following verses speak of Wisdom's being brought forth, so she is not supposed to be eternal. She is not explicitly said to have been brought forth by God, but the text does not suggest any other source from which she might have originated. In any case, Wisdom is clearly prior to the rest of creation. She accompanied God in the work of creation, and presumably informed that work. Now she cries out to people at the crossroad and the city gate and promises that whoever follows her way will attain true life. The source of this imagery, and its meaning, have been debated extensively.[42] There is probably some influence from the Egyptian concept of Maat, which embodies truth, justice, and world order.[43] Maat is the daughter of the creator god Re and escorts him through the heavens.[44] In the biblical context, this wisdom is most often understood as an attribute of Yahweh (cf. Prov. 3:19: "The Lord by wisdom founded the earth").[45] Von Rad protests that wisdom "has no divine status, nor is it a hypostasized attribute of Yahweh; it is rather something created by Yahweh and assigned to its proper function. Although clearly differentiated from the whole of creation, it is an entity which belongs in the world, even if it is the first of the works of creation, the creature above all creatures."[46] He goes on to speak of the self-revelation of creation. In fact, the peculiarity of wisdom is that it is both an attribute of God and an aspect of creation. It is the mode of God's presence in the world, but it is also something in which human beings can participate.

The great wisdom poem in Proverbs 8 may be divided into three sections. Verses 1–21 present the call of wisdom. Wisdom professes to be better than gold and silver, and to be the power by which kings reign. This call can be understood on a fairly simple level as the proclamation of the wisdom *teacher,* recruiting students at the city gate. It is an advertisement for wisdom, concluding with the benefits it has to offer: riches and honor, and righteousness that is better than silver and gold.

41. B. Vawter, "Proverbs 8:22: Wisdom and Creation," *JBL* 99 (1980) 205–16. The LXX translates *ektise* "created."

42. B. Lang, *Frau Weisheit* (Düsseldorf: Patmos, 1975) 147–76.

43. Von Rad, *Wisdom in Israel,* 153; C. Kayatz, *Studien zu Proverbien 1–9* (Neukirchen-Vluyn: Neukirchener Verlag, 1966) 76–119. B. Lang, *Wisdom and the Book of Proverbs: An Israelite Goddess Redefined* (New York: Pilgrim, 1986) 115–20, argues that Wisdom is an actual goddess, patroness of education.

44. See G. Englund, "Gods as a Frame of Reference: On Thinking and Concepts of Thought in Ancient Egypt," in idem, ed., *The Religion of the Ancient Egyptians: Cognitive Structures and Popular Expressions* (Stockholm: Almqvist & Wiksell, 1989) 23.

45. R. N. Whybray, *Wisdom in Proverbs* (London: SCM, 1965) 78.

46. Von Rad, *Wisdom in Israel,* 153–54.

Verses 22–31, however, claim for wisdom a status that goes far beyond the experience of the wisdom teacher. It existed before earth, and it was God's accomplice in the work of creation. The link with creation is also explicit in 3:19, and is fundamental to the worldview of Proverbs. Since the world was created with wisdom, it is amenable to understanding. There is an order in creation, waiting to be discovered. This order is implicit in the proverbial material of Proverbs 10–31. It underlies the quest for analogies and the predictability of consequences. The theology of Proverbs is creation-based, and in that sense it may be termed a precedent for natural theology.[47] The self-revelation of creation, however, is in no way opposed to divine revelation. It is the same wisdom of God that is being revealed in either case. Moreover, all the wisdom literature acknowledges the limits of human understanding, and these limits are emphasized in Job and Qoheleth. But while Proverbs acknowledges limits, its approach to wisdom is positive and optimistic.

The final section, vv. 32–36, reverts to the direct address of the first section. Again, the benefits of wisdom are emphasized, summarized here as "life," by which is meant not life after death but the fullness of life in the present. The same promise is found in Prov. 3:16–18, where wisdom is called a tree of life. The poem couples this promise with a threat: "He who misses me injures himself; all who hate me love death" (v. 36). This warning is reinforced in the chapters that surround this poem. Both Proverbs 7 and chapter 9 warn against the attraction of the "strange" or loose woman. While a practical warning against adultery is no doubt intended, this figure is also clearly an antitype to Lady Wisdom in chapter 8. The contrast between wisdom and folly is sharpened by representing both as female figures in chapter 9. Hence the somewhat hyperbolic conclusion to the description of the seductress in Proverbs 7: "Her house is the way to Sheol, going down to the chambers of death." Here again, the issue is not physical death, but the loss of true fulfillment in life.[48]

The use of female imagery, in texts where the implied readers are clearly male, facilitates another aspect of the presentation of wisdom. It is tinged with eroticism, some of it reflected from the negative eroticism associated with the adulteress. Wisdom loves those who love her (8:17) and lays out her feast for those who seek her (9:1–6). This manner of presenting wisdom, and the preoccupation of Proverbs 1–9 with sexual imagery, can be seen as motivational rhetoric, but there is more to it than that. The pursuit of wisdom is depicted as being as all-consuming as the pursuit of love. It should engage the student's entire being. This ideal of intellectual love is only hinted at in Proverbs. We will find it further developed in the later tradition.

47. J. J. Collins, "The Biblical Precedent for Natural Theology," *JAAR* 45/1 Supplement B (1977) 35–67; J. Barr, *Biblical Faith and Natural Theology* (Oxford: Clarendon, 1993) 90–92.
48. See further G. von Rad, "Life and Death in the OT," *TDNT* 2 (1964) 843–49.

Side by side with this attractive presentation of Lady Wisdom, however, there is a persistent reminder that "fear of the Lord is the beginning of wisdom" (1:7; 9:10). This disposition entails turning from evil (Prov. 3:7) and seeking wisdom (2:1–5). More specifically, we are told in Prov. 8:13: "The fear of the Lord is hatred of evil. Pride and arrogance and the way of evil and perverted speech I hate." It is a humble and respectful attitude, which is docile before teachers and tradition, and is not unduly self-reliant or innovative. It is ultimately the willingness to accept the kind of instruction that is offered throughout the book of Proverbs.

Before we turn to Ben Sira and the wisdom teaching of the Hellenistic age, there are two developments in the tradition to be noted. The first is the rise of skeptical wisdom in Job and Qoheleth, and the second is the rapprochement between wisdom instruction and the temple cult with its related scriptures.

Job and Qoheleth

The date of Job is quite uncertain. The book may well be older than the final redaction of Proverbs.[49] It represents a reaction, however, against the more dogmatic doctrine of retribution found in one stratum of Proverbs.[50] This doctrine is articulated in the book by the friends of Job: "Think now, who that was innocent ever perished? or where were the upright cut off" (Job 4:7). But the reader knows, from the prologue of the book, that Job is innocent. At the end of the book, the friends are told that "you have not spoken of me what is right, as my servant Job has" (42:7), although Job has angrily declared that God "destroys both the blameless and the wicked" and "mocks at the calamity of the innocent" (9:22–23). But neither is Job's anger vindicated. When God addresses him from the whirlwind, it is to make the point that Job's grievances are of little account in comparison with all the works of creation. Job's humbled response, "See, I am of small account" (40:4), is precisely right. The God of Job is the creator of all, just as surely as the God of Proverbs. But the lesson of Job is that no one has the right to call the creator to account.

The contrast between Job and Proverbs can be seen clearly by contrasting the great wisdom poem in Job 28 with its counterpart in Proverbs 8. While Wisdom in Proverbs can be encountered in the city gate, in Job it is hidden, and only God knows the way. For Proverbs, the fear of the Lord is the beginning

---

49. On the difficulty of establishing a date, see N. C. Habel, *The Book of Job* (Philadelphia: Westminster, 1985) 40–42. Habel grants only that the book is no earlier than the sixth century B.C.E., on linguistic grounds.

50. For recent scholarship on Job see L. G. Perdue, *Wisdom in Revolt: Metaphorical Theology in the Book of Job* (JSOTSup 112; Sheffield: Sheffield Academic Press, 1991), and L. G. Perdue and W. C. Gilpin, eds., *The Voice from the Whirlwind: Interpreting the Book of Job* (Nashville: Abingdon, 1992).

of wisdom, the predisposition necessary for gaining understanding. In Job "the fear of the Lord *is* wisdom" (italics added) for humankind. Life is mysterious, and past human understanding. The appropriate human response is to resign oneself to the will of God, as Job eventually does at the end of the book.

The book of Job is remote from Proverbs in style and literary form. It stands as a reaction to certain aspects of traditional wisdom rather than as an example of school wisdom itself. Qoheleth is also distinctive in form, insofar as it consists primarily of personal observations and reflections rather than compendia of traditional teaching, as in Proverbs. But we are told in the epilogue to the book that "besides being wise, Qoheleth also taught the people knowledge, weighing and studying and arranging many proverbs" (Qoh. 12:9). From this it would seem that the author was a teacher and a practitioner of school wisdom, even if his book has a personal rather than a traditional character.[51]

Qoheleth also rejects the facile dogma of retribution that prevails in the final edition of Proverbs.[52] For him, the one verifiable end of human life is death. He is caustic on the subject of an afterlife, which was probably gaining ground in apocalyptic circles by the time Qoheleth wrote in the Hellenistic period:[53] "For the fate of humans and the fate of animals is the same; as one dies, so dies the other. They all have the same breath, and humans have no advantage over the animals, for all is vanity. All go to one place; all are from the dust, and all turn to dust again. Who knows whether the human spirit goes upward and the spirit of animals goes downward to the earth?" (Qoh. 3:19–21). Qoheleth shares with Ben Sira a preoccupation with death that is not found in the older wisdom literature, and must reflect in some way the new circumstances of the Hellenistic age.[54] Qoheleth resembles Job insofar as both books submit the wisdom of tradition to the judgment of personal experience. Job, however, does not set out to investigate wisdom. His critique of tradition is forced upon him by sudden calamity. Qoheleth, in contrast, systematically makes trial of wisdom and madness and folly (2:12). Even though it is not clear that Qoheleth had read Greek philosophy or been influenced by any specific philosopher, Michael Fox has astutely remarked that "he does, however, incorporate the

51. We must reckon, however, with the possibility that the author of the epilogue is presenting Qoheleth in his own likeness. On the epilogist as a member of the class of the sages see R. E. Murphy, "The Sage in Ecclesiastes and Ecclesiastes the Sage," in Gammie and Perdue, eds., *The Sage,* 264.

52. See the comments of R. E. Murphy, *Ecclesiastes* (WBC 23; Dallas: Word, 1992) lxvi. Murphy, however, underestimates the sense of crisis in Qoheleth and the sharpness of its break with tradition. He views the crisis as merely an instance of "the mysterious ways of the Lord."

53. On the setting of Qoheleth in the Hellenistic age see J. L. Crenshaw, *Ecclesiastes* (Philadelphia: Westminster, 1987) 49–50.

54. J. L. Crenshaw, "The Shadow of Death in Qoheleth," in John G. Gammie, ed., *Israelite Wisdom: Theological and Literary Essays in Honor of Samuel Terrien* (Missoula, Mont.: Scholars, 1978) 205–16.

fundamental tenet of Greek philosophy—the autonomy of individual reason, which is to say, the belief that individuals can and should proceed with their own observations and reasoning powers on a quest for knowledge and that this may lead to discovery of truths previously unknown."[55]

The Greek spirit of inquiry also left some mark on Ben Sira, but on the whole we shall find that the later sage is much closer in spirit to Proverbs than he is to Qoheleth. The turn to skepticism in Job and Qoheleth has relatively little impact on the subsequent wisdom tradition. Instead we shall find a renewed confidence in divine retribution, even though Ben Sira is hard-pressed to defend and explain it and the Wisdom of Solomon breaks radically with both Proverbs and Ben Sira by basing its hope on a belief in immortality.

The Rapprochement
with the Torah

While the wisdom tradition maintains its distinct identity, and refrains from overt appeal to the traditions of Israel, down to the time of Qoheleth, we should not think that the sages were isolated from the rest of Jewish society. Proverbial wisdom was not the exclusive property of the schools, and so we should expect to find some parallels between Proverbs and other biblical books. One important locus of such parallels is the book of Deuteronomy, as has been shown above all by Moshe Weinfeld.[56] The fact that the laws of Deuteronomy draw on popular wisdom at some points is not surprising. What is more noteworthy is the fact that the book as a whole is presented, by a redactor,[57] as a kind of wisdom: "I now teach you statutes and ordinances for you to observe in the land that you are about to enter and occupy. You must observe them diligently, for this will show your wisdom and discernment to the peoples, who, when they hear all these statutes, will say, 'Surely this great nation is a wise and discerning people!'" (Deut. 4:5–6). The wisdom of Deuteronomy is inevitably different from that of Proverbs, since it is addressed to the nation and has the force of law, and since it appeals to a particular divine revelation. But the sapiential terminology is significant: "The commandments are seen as the intensification and consummation of something found among all peoples,

---

55. M. V. Fox, "Wisdom in Qoheleth," in Perdue et al., eds., *In Search of Wisdom*, 123. See also his earlier discussion in *Qoheleth and His Contradictions* (JSOTSup 71; Sheffield: Sheffield Academic Press, 1989) 79–120. The case for more extensive dependence on Greek philosophy has been argued by R. Braun, *Kohelet und die frühhellenistische Popularphilosophie* (BZAW 130; Berlin: de Gruyter, 1973).

56. M. Weinfeld, *Deuteronomy and the Deuteronomistic School* (Oxford: Oxford Univ. Press, 1972); *Deuteronomy* (AB 5; New York: Doubleday, 1991) 62–65.

57. On the place of Deuteronomy 4 in the redaction of the book, see J. D. Levenson, "Who Inserted the Book of the Torah?" *HTR* 68 (1975) 203–33.

Wisdom."[58] To anticipate later categories, the revealed law is the supreme expression of the natural law. The same equation of the Torah with wisdom is found in Ezra, where King Artaxerxes refers interchangeably to "the law of your God, which is in your hand" (7:14) or "the wisdom of your God which is in your hand" (7:25).

The construal of the Torah as wisdom is also in evidence in the Psalter, most explicitly in Psalms 1, 19, and 119.[59] Psalm 1 draws a familiar contrast between the righteous and the wicked, but adds that the righteous man finds his delight in the Torah of the Lord, on which he meditates day and night.[60] The reference to the Torah may be an insertion here, but if so it was probably added by the editor of the Psalter.[61] As the opening psalm in the collection, Psalm 1 sets the tone for what follows, and suggests that the Psalter should be read in the light of the Torah as a source of wisdom.[62] Psalm 119 also has an impact on the collection as a whole, because of its sheer length. Here again, language usually associated with wisdom is applied to the Law (e.g., v. 66: "Teach me good judgment and knowledge, for in your commandments have I trusted").[63] In Psalm 19B the decrees of the Lord make the simple wise and enlighten the eyes (Ps. 19:7–8).

At least some of these psalms appear to be didactic poems, which inculcate a kind of wisdom derived from the Law of the Lord, or the Torah.[64] Moreover, Leo Perdue has shown that several wisdom psalms, including Psalms 1 and 19B, are built around proverbial sayings, which suggests that the psalmists combined the wisdom derived from the Torah with the more traditional prover-

58. J. D. Levenson, "The Theologies of Commandment in Biblical Israel," *HTR* 73 (1980) 26.

59. On these psalms see J. L. Mays, "The Place of the Torah-Psalms in the Psalter," *JBL* 106 (1987) 3–12.

60. Cf. Ps. 112:1: "Happy are those who fear the Lord, who greatly delight in his commandments."

61. Perdue, *Wisdom and Cult,* 270–71. This verse has no parallel in the second strophe and is syntactically awkward. Perdue comments: "This insertion was made probably by a pious scribe of Torah similar to the picture we have drawn of Sirach who wishes to emphasize that the one who is truly righteous will find guidance for his life in the meditation on Torah."

62. Cf. G. H. Wilson, *The Editing of the Hebrew Psalter* (SBLDS 76; Chico, Calif.: Scholars, 1985) 143: "The placement of Ps 1 as an introduction to the whole Psalter . . . offers the reader a pair of 'hermeneutical spectacles' through which to view the contents." See also A. R. Ceresko, "The Sage in the Psalms," in Gammie and Perdue, eds., *The Sage,* 220–21.

63. See further J. P. M. van der Ploeg, "Le Psaume 119 et la sagesse," in M. Gilbert, ed., *La Sagesse de l'Ancien Testament* (BETL 51; Louvain: Leuven Univ. Press, 1979) 82–87.

64. See R. E. Murphy, "A Consideration of the Classification, 'Wisdom Psalms,'" *Congress Volume, Bonn 1962* (VTSup 9; Leiden: Brill, 1963) 156–67; Perdue, *Wisdom and Cult,* 261–343. The wisdom psalms constitute a broader category than the Torah psalms. Murphy lists Pss. 1, 32, 34, 37, 49, 112, 128. See also J. Luyten, "Psalm 73 and Wisdom," in Gilbert, ed., *La Sagesse de l'Ancien Testament,* 59–81.

bial instruction.[65] We do not know the settings for which these poems were composed. Some scholars argue that "wisdom psalms . . . were not composed and used strictly in a private or educational setting that was foreign to the cult" but "in reality were liturgical pieces from the very beginning."[66] In this view, these psalms had their *Sitz im Leben* in the synagogue, where they would still have served in part a didactic purpose. Others distinguish between poems "used to teach literature and ideology to young schoolboys" (e.g., Psalm 1) and others intended for use in the cult (e.g., Pss. 19; 119).[67] It has been suggested that they derive from schools associated with the Temple,[68] but while this is not implausible, the very existence of these schools is hypothetical, and we do not know how such schools would relate to those of Qoheleth or Ben Sira. The Torah figures prominently in the wisdom instruction of Ben Sira. Presumably, different wisdom teachers in the Hellenistic period could focus on different material and have their own distinctive emphases. We learn from the Torah psalms of the Psalter that Ben Sira was not alone in regarding the Torah as source of wisdom. If such a sapiential construal of the Torah was widespread, it was inevitable that this body of literature would also be integrated into the curriculum of at least some traditional wisdom schools.

The Emergence of
"Canonical" Scripture

The growing importance of the Torah for wisdom instruction is related to the emergence in the Hellenistic period of an authoritative corpus of Hebrew scriptures, which would much later be formalized as a canon. The formation of the Hebrew canon was a lengthy process, which can be traced back to the promulgation of "the book of the law" in the reform of Josiah (621 B.C.E.).[69] Ezra is often credited with giving the Torah, or Pentateuch, its final shape. The books of

---

65. Perdue, *Wisdom and Cult*, 269–99. For the "central proverbs" cf. Ps. 1:6 ("the Lord watches over the way of the righteous") and Ps. 19:10 ("More to be desired are they [the ordinances] than gold, even much fine gold; sweeter also than honey and drippings of the honeycomb").

66. E. Gerstenberger, *Psalms* (FOTL 14; Grand Rapids: Eerdmans, 1988) 1.20. Cf. S. Mowinckel, "Psalms and Wisdom," in *Wisdom in Israel and the Ancient Near East* (Fs. H. H. Rowley; VTSup 3; Leiden: Brill, 1955) 205–44, and H. Ludin Jansen, *Die spätjüdische Psalmendichtung: Ihr Entstehungskreis und ihr 'Sitz im Leben'* (Oslo: Dybwad, 1937).

67. Perdue, *Cult and Wisdom*, 268. W. Soll, *Psalm 119: Matrix, Form, and Setting* (CBQMS 23; Washington: Catholic Biblical Association, 1991) 115–25, argues that "Psalm 119 displays no signs of didactic intent," although its author was evidently a learned man. Murphy does not include either Ps. 119 or Ps. 19 in the category "wisdom psalms."

68. Perdue, *Cult and Wisdom*.

69. S. Z. Leiman, *The Canonization of Hebrew Scripture: The Talmudic and Midrashic Evidence* (Hamden, Conn.: Archon, 1976) 32.

Ezra and Nehemiah, however, make no mention of the Day of Atonement, although Nehemiah 8 describes the liturgical observances of the seventh month, especially the Feast of Booths. The omission indicates that the Pentateuch had not yet reached its final form, although Ezra presupposes other priestly laws, and must have had something close to the Torah as we know it.[70] The prophetic corpus took shape somewhere in the Persian or early Hellenistic period.

The first clear witness to a canon, in the sense of an accepted corpus of authoritative scripture, is found in the prologue to Ben Sira. The prologue was written by Sirach's grandson, who had migrated to Egypt in 132 B.C.E., in the thirty-eighth year of Euergetes II. The prologue was written sometime later, possibly after the death of that king in 117 B.C.E.[71] It begins with the following statement: "Many great teachings have been given to us through the Law and the Prophets and the others that followed them, and for these we should praise Israel for instruction and wisdom. . . . So my grandfather Jesus, who had devoted himself especially to the reading of the Law and Prophets and the other books of our ancestors, and had acquired considerable proficiency in them, was himself also led to write something pertaining to instruction and wisdom."

It has been widely assumed that this statement implies a tripartite canon, but in fact it is not at all clear that "the other books of our ancestors" constitute a canonical category. They are simply "other traditional writings." The category is open-ended and, according to the grandson, Sirach himself felt free to contribute to it. It is also uncertain which writings were classified as prophetic. Sirach knew all the prophets of the Hebrew Bible, and refers to the Twelve as such. In his review of Israelite history in the "Praise of the Fathers," however, it is not apparent that he makes any distinction between the prophetic books and Nehemiah. In the New Testament period, David was often regarded as a prophet and the Psalms as prophecy (e.g., Acts 2:30). Daniel, too, is often identified as a prophet in antiquity.[72] In short we cannot tell just how much material was categorized under "the Prophets" in Ben Sira's time.[73] There is in Sirach what we might call a "canon consciousness" with respect to the Torah, but there is no sense of a closed canon beyond the books of Moses. The same can be said of Philo in the first century C.E.[74]

There is ample evidence for the authority of certain scriptures in the first

70. J. Blenkinsopp, *Ezra-Nehemiah. A Commentary* (OTL; Philadelphia: Westminster, 1988) 157, 291.

71. R. Smend, *Die Weisheit des Jesus Sirach erklärt* (Berlin: Reimer, 1906) 3–4; P. W. Skehan and A. A. DiLella, *The Wisdom of Ben Sira* (AB 39; New York: Doubleday, 1987) 134.

72. K. Koch, "Is Daniel Also Among the Prophets?" *Int* 39 (1985) 117–30.

73. J. Barton, *Oracles of God: Perceptions of Ancient Prophecy in Israel after the Exile* (Oxford: Oxford Univ. Press, 1986) 48.

74. Leiman, *The Canonization of Hebrew Scripture*, 31.

century B.C.E., in the Dead Sea Scrolls.[75] The most explicit comment on the authoritative writings of the day is found in the so-called Halakic Letter, 4QMMT. This document is addressed to a religious leader of Israel, most probably a High Priest, and it sets out the reasons why the community had separated itself from the majority of the people. It appeals to the leader to consider the validity of the sectarian interpretation of scripture: "We have [written] to you so that you may study (carefully) the book of Moses and the books of the Prophets and [the writings of] David [and the events of] ages past."[76] The statement refers to the familiar categories of the Law and the Prophets. David was widely regarded as a prophet, but he is singled out as the author of a special category (Psalms). These were the scriptures that were presumed to be common to all Jews.[77]

The evidence of the Dead Sea Scrolls overwhelmingly supports the view that the Torah preserved by the Masoretes was already known and recognized as authoritative at Qumran, and that the proto-Masoretic form of the text was dominant.[78] Nonetheless, we must recognize that even though the Torah and the Prophets were accepted as authoritative by the second century B.C.E., the authoritative text had not yet been definitively established and there was some variation as to what constituted the authoritative scripture. Consequently it is reasonable to ask whether the Torah in the Hellenistic period was necessarily the same as the text we now have. Philip Davies has argued that "Ben Sira does not know the five books that now constitute the Pentateuch in their now canonical form. He is more knowledgeable of Adam and Enoch than the modern reader of Genesis would be; he may well be ignorant of Genesis 2–3 and seems not to have heard of either Ezra or of Joseph's exploits in Egypt. It is as clear that Ben Sira does not regard this literature as what might now be termed 'scripture.' He does not cite proof texts from the literature, nor does he exegete passages from it."[79] We shall have occasion in the following chapters to examine

75. J. J. Collins, "Before the Canon: Scriptures in Second Temple Judaism," in J. L. Mays, D. L. Petersen, and K. H. Richards, eds., *Old Testament Interpretation* (Nashville: Abingdon, 1995) 225–41.

76. E. Qimron and J. Strugnell, *Qumran Cave 4. V. Miqṣat Maʿaśe HaTorah* (DJD 10; Oxford: Clarendon, 1994) 59.

77. Suggestions that a reference to Chronicles, and so to the rest of the Writings, should be restored here seem improbable (contra E. E. Ellis, *The Old Testament in Early Christianity* [WUNT 54; Tübingen: Mohr, 1991]) 10. Chronicles is barely attested at Qumran, and there is no evidence that it enjoyed any special authority.

78. The dominance of the proto-Masoretic text is defended by L. Schiffman, *Reclaiming the Dead Sea Scrolls* (New York: The Jewish Publication Society, 1994) 161–80. In my view, Schiffman exaggerates the conformity of the Scrolls to later Jewish tradition, but he is right that the proto-Masoretic text is by far the most widely attested.

79. P. R. Davies, "Scenes from the Early History of Judaism," in D. V. Edelman, ed., *The Triumph of Elohim: From Yahwisms to Judaisms* (Kampen: Kok, 1995) 170. Cf. his *In Search of Ancient Israel* (JSOTSup 148; Sheffield: Sheffield Academic Press, 1992) 140–41.

Ben Sira's relationship to what we know as the canonical Torah. He certainly knew traditions that have not been incorporated in the Hebrew Bible, and his allusions to the Pentateuchal material are sometimes surprising. Nonetheless, Davies's conclusions seem more radical than the evidence permits. He argues that the "book of the covenant of the Most High" in Sirach 24 is Deuteronomy rather than the Pentateuch, but there are transparent allusions to Genesis and Exodus in Sir. 24:3–4 ("I came forth from the mouth of the Most High and covered the earth like a mist. I dwelt in the highest heaven and my throne was in a pillar of cloud."[80] Ignorance of Genesis 2–3 is difficult to maintain in view of such passages as Sir. 15:14; 17:7; and 25:24. It is easier to suppose that Ben Sira knew the text that has come down to us, but interpreted it freely, than to posit a variant text that is not attested, even among the diverse texts found at Qumran. In the following chapters we shall assume that Ben Sira knew the Torah essentially in the form preserved by the Masoretes. The controversy, however, should alert us to the fact that even when wisdom is closely identified with the Torah it is never simply a literalist reproduction of a canonical text.

Nonetheless, the emergence of an authoritative scripture as a recognized source of wisdom in Jewish education is perhaps the most obvious factor that differentiates the wisdom of Ben Sira and later sapiential writers from that of their biblical predecessors. It was not the only factor, however. We now turn to consider the more general influence of the *Zeitgeist* of the Hellenistic age.

---

80. On the allusions in Sirach 24 see G. T. Sheppard, *Wisdom as a Hermeneutical Construct* (BZAW 151; Berlin: de Gruyter, 1980) 19–71.

PART ONE.
HEBREW WISDOM

Chapter 2.
Ben Sira in His Hellenistic Context

The book of Ben Sira is exceptional among the ancient Jewish wisdom writings in disclosing the name of the actual author, Jeshua ben Eleazar ben Sira.[1] The approximate date of composition is also disclosed by the grandson's preface to the Greek translation. The grandson, we are told, arrived in Egypt in the thirty-eighth year of King Euergetes. The reference can only be to Ptolemy VII Euergetes II (Physcon), and the date of arrival is 132 B.C.E. The translation was completed some years later, probably after the death of Euergetes in 117 B.C.E. If we assume that the grandson was an adult when he moved to Egypt, and that the grandfather's prime was about half a century earlier, we may infer that Ben Sira's book was compiled somewhere in the first quarter of the second century B.C.E. Since it claims to present accumulated wisdom, it can scarcely be the work of a young man. Consequently, a date toward the end of that period is likely. The glowing praise of the High Priest Simon in chapter 50 suggests that he was a contemporary of Ben Sira, although the eulogy was probably written after his death. Simon II was High Priest from 219 to 196 B.C.E. The book shows no awareness of the upheavals of the time of Antiochus IV Epiphanes (175–164). (The only possible reflection of these events is found in the prayer in chapter 36, but this is so alien to the thought world of Ben Sira that it must be regarded as a secondary addition, possibly from the Maccabean period).

Ben Sira was evidently a scribe, and he provides a eulogistic account of his way of life in Sir. 39:1–11. In his view, the ideal scribe is a man of piety, devoted to the study of the Law and to prayer, but also concerned with the wisdom of all the ancients. He also appears before rulers and travels in foreign lands. The book concludes with a quasi-autobiographical poem (51:13–30), in which the author refers to travels in his youth and invites the uneducated "to lodge in my house of instruction." The first part (vv. 13–20) of this poem is

---

1. The author of the book is identified in MS B from the Cairo Geniza as "Simon son of Jeshua son of Eleazar son of Sira" (51:30; cf. 50:27). No other source identifies the author as Simon. The name is probably introduced by mistake, because of the praise of the High Priest Simon in chap. 50. The author's grandson, who translated the book into Greek, refers to his illustrious ancestor as "my grandfather Jesus." See P. W. Skehan and A. A. DiLella, *The Wisdom of Ben Sira* (AB 39; New York: Doubleday, 1987) 3–4.

found independently in the Psalms Scroll from Qumran Cave 11, and its authenticity as a composition of Ben Sira is disputed.[2] Regardless of the authenticity of this passage, however, it is likely that the author of this book was a teacher and that the book preserves a sample of one kind of instruction offered to the youth of Jerusalem in the period before the Maccabean revolt.

Ben Sira wrote in an era of transition, not only for Judaism but for the entire Near East. The conquests of Alexander the Great had changed the face of the region. Greek replaced Aramaic as the lingua franca of trade and commerce, and the landscape was dotted with new cities with Greek names and Greek institutions. In Palestine alone there were some thirty Greek towns, mainly on the coast, around the Sea of Tiberias, and in Transjordan.[3] The impact of these settlements, and of Hellenistic culture in general, on Jerusalem and Judea is greatly disputed. There were no Greek settlements in Judea itself. Even in places where there were Greek colonies, the degree of Hellenization was often quite superficial. The colonists were not drawn from the Greek intelligentsia, but from the lower strata of society, and they came not to spread Greek culture but to make a living. These settlers were influenced by the local culture just as much as they influenced it. Nonetheless, even if Hellenistic influence did not produce a genuinely Greek culture in the Near East, it did modify the traditional local cultures in various ways.[4]

The impact of Hellenistic culture may be considered under two headings. First, there is the cultural influence on the ethos of a country mediated by social and material changes. Second, there is the formal culture, reflected in education and literature.

Social and Material Changes

Throughout the third century B.C.E., Palestine was under the rule of the Ptolemies. When it passed into Seleucid control at the beginning of the second century, Antiochus III issued a proclamation confirming the right of the Jews to live according to their ancestral laws (Josephus, *Ant.* 12.142, 150). In so doing he was merely continuing the arrangement that had been in place under the Ptolemies, and under the Persians before them. It would be a mistake, however, to think that Judea was immune to cultural change throughout this period.

2. J. A. Sanders, *The Psalms Scroll of Qumrân Cave 11 (11QPsª)* (*DJD*4; Oxford: Clarendon, 1965) 79–85. See, however, Skehan and DiLella, *The Wisdom of Ben Sira,* 576–80, who defend its autobiographical character.

3. V. Tcherikover, *Hellenistic Civilization and the Jews* (New York: Atheneum, 1970) 90–116; E. Schürer, *The History of the Jewish People in the Age of Jesus Christ* (rev. and ed. G. Vermes, F. Millar, and M. Black; Edinburgh: T. & T. Clark, 1979) 2.85–183.

4. See in general M. Hengel, *Judaism and Hellenism* (Philadelphia: Fortress, 1974) 1.1–175; A. Kuhrt and S. Sherwin-White, *Hellenism in the East* (Berkeley: Univ. of California, 1987).

The most fundamental changes ushered in by the Hellenistic era were in the domain of commerce.[5] Several factors contributed to increased productivity and prosperity. One was the general use of coined money, in place of the more cumbersome barter in kind. Another was improved technology. Ben Sira bears witness to the new foot-powered potter's wheel, which replaced the traditional hand-turned instrument (Sir. 38:29), and also to the variety of arts and crafts practiced in Jerusalem in his time. The main novelty of the Hellenistic age, however, lay in the increase of trade. The Ptolemaic empire was a tightly organized moneymaking machine. By a conception that was quite un-Greek, the whole kingdom was regarded as the personal estate of the king, and this allowed a high degree of centralized supervision and direction of commercial activity. The primary source of wealth was agriculture, especially the production of wheat. The Ptolemaic administration sought to maximize this asset not merely by exploiting the land but by improving methods of cultivation. By farming out the land and other sources of wealth, it allowed scope for entrepreneurs to make their own fortunes. In Palestine and Syria, where the population was not as uniform or as submissive as it was in Egypt, much power remained in the hands of the local aristocracy. The Ptolemies drained off much of the wealth by taxation, but at least the intermediary classes experienced a significant rise in their standard of living under Greek rule. The increase in foreign trade in the third century B.C.E. is attested by many stamped jars from Rhodes and other parts of the Aegean from this period that are found throughout Palestine.

Our main source of information about commercial life in Palestine in the Ptolemaic era comes from the Zeno papyri, supplemented by an important papyrus from Vienna.[6] Zeno was a subordinate of the finance minister (*dioiketes*) Apollonius under Ptolemy II Philadelphus. Zeno's major charge was the management of a large estate that Apollonius had received from the king in the Faiyûm, near Philadelphia, but before he was given this charge he undertook several missions for Apollonius. In the course of such a mission, he spent more than a year in Palestine, from late 260 to early 258 B.C.E. The correspondence preserved in his archive, which was discovered in 1915, throws considerable light on society in Palestine and Transjordan at the time. There is no mention of a governor. Tcherikover suggests that Palestine was under the direct supervision of the *dioiketes* in Alexandria. There were, however, a large number of officials, at various levels, charged with supervision of the local economy. Apollonius also had an estate, by royal grant, at Bet Anat in Galilee.

One of the more interesting aspects of Zeno's correspondence concerns the prominence of local, native chieftains. We read of a cleruchy, a colony of

---

5. Hengel, *Judaism and Hellenism*, 1.6–57; E. J. Bickerman, *The Jews in the Greek Age* (Cambridge, Mass.: Harvard Univ. Press, 1988) 69–80.
6. Tcherikover, *Hellenistic Civilization*, 60.

soldiers, in Transjordan, under the command of one Tobiah, whose family history can be traced from the time of Nehemiah down to the Maccabean revolt. Various people refer to themselves as Tobiah's people, and the region is known as Tobiah's land. At this time, the Ptolemies still refused to assign high posts in Egypt to the natives, but in Syria and Palestine they bowed to necessity and worked through the local leaders. The papyri mention several other prominent and powerful people who were not holders of official positions, including one Jeddous, who drove off Zeno's officials by force.[7] Tobiah was presumably a Yahwist (in view of his name), but he evidently did whatever was necessary in the service of the Egyptians. His use of the epistolary formula "many thanks to the gods" (CPJ 4) has aroused much comment, but may not be very significant. The letters were written by secretaries, and in any case both Hebrew and Aramaic use plural nouns for God (*'elōhîm, 'elāhîn*).

Trade between Syria and Egypt was dominated by the royal officials. Major imports, such as wheat and olive oil, were carefully supervised and heavily taxed. There were fewer restrictions on trade in slaves. No slaves were exported from Egypt, but they were frequently imported from Syria and Palestine. Slave trade was not, of course, an innovation of the Hellenistic era. The Samaria papyri from Wâdi Dâliyeh, which date from the half-century before the coming of Alexander, include several contracts for the sale of slaves.[8] The international trade, however, seems to have grown in the Hellenistic period. The prophet Joel complains that Tyre, Sidon, and Philistia "have sold the people of Judah and Jerusalem to the Greeks, removing them far from their own border" (Joel 3:6). Such trade may have begun before the coming of Alexander, but it flourished under Ptolemaic rule. We also find slaves sent as presents, including four young slaves sent by Tobiah to Apollonius (*CPJ* 4–5). Slave traffic included the trade of *paidiskai,* or young serving maids, sometimes used as prostitutes. The demand for slaves was such that Ptolemy Philadelphus had to issue a decree (preserved in the Vienna papyrus) to prohibit attempts to enslave free men and women in Syria.

The slave-trade highlights the essential ambiguity of commercial prosperity. The success of some was built on the misery of others. In the words of Tcherikover, the Ptolemaic empire "offered a broad field for the activities of unscrupulous people from Egypt, and also perhaps of people locally born, who took no thought of morality or of another law."[9]

---

7. Ibid., 65.
8. F. M. Cross, "Papyri of the Fourth Century B.C. from Dâliyeh," in D. N. Freedman and J. C. Greenfield, eds., *New Directions in Biblical Archaeology* (New York: Doubleday, 1969) 41–62.
9. Tcherikover, *Hellenistic Civilization,* 69.

The Tobiads

A parade example of such people is provided by the story of the Tobiad family preserved in Josephus (*Ant.* 12.154–234).[10] The story takes its point of departure from an incident in the high priesthood of Onias (most probably Onias II, about 240 B.C.E.). Onias allegedly refused to pay the customary tribute of twenty talents of silver to the Ptolemaic king, who responded by threatening to divide Jerusalem into cleruchies and settle it with his soldiers. Joseph, son of Tobiah (of the Zeno correspondence) and nephew of the High Priest, came forward and saved the day by entertaining the envoy lavishly. He then borrowed money from friends in Samaria, went to Egypt, and won over the Ptolemy. He outbid all others for the right to farm the taxes for Coele-Syria, Phoenicia, Judea, and Samaria, by offering double what his rivals offered. He proceeded to raise the taxes by force. When he met with resistance at Ashkelon, he had twenty of the leading citizens put to death and confiscated their property. He subdued Scythopolis by similar means. He secured his position by sending presents to everyone who was powerful at court.

The episode of the taxes is sufficient to render paradoxical the statement of Josephus that Joseph had a reputation for uprightness (*Ant.* 12.161). The story goes on to cast further doubt on his character. Allegedly, while on a visit to Alexandria with his brother and niece, he fell in love with a dancing girl. His brother, alarmed lest Joseph sin by sleeping with a foreigner, substituted his own daughter. Eventually Joseph married his niece and begot a son Hyrcanus. This son, in turn, won the favor of the Ptolemy by lavish and outrageous behavior, but he was forced to withdraw to Transjordan because of tensions with his brothers.

The tale of the Tobiads is a colorful narrative, which has the character of legend rather than critical history. Even if the details of the story are not reliable, it gives a vivid picture of the kind of society that flourished in Ptolemaic Palestine. Josephus professes admiration for Joseph, son of Tobiah, "who had been an excellent and high-minded man and had brought the Jewish people from poverty and a state of weakness to more splendid opportunities of life during the twenty-two years when he controlled the taxes" (*Ant.* 12.224). The splendid opportunities enjoyed by some, however, were bought at the expense of others. They were enjoyed primarily by the wealthy families of the Jewish aristocracy. It was in these families that Hellenism made its initial impact.

Not all the Jewish upper class were as ruthless as the Tobiads. Qoheleth paints the following picture of a leisured gentleman of Jerusalem:

10. Tcherikover, *Hellenistic Civilization,* 126–36. Further pertinent extracts from Tcherikover's book can be found in M. E. Stone and D. Satran, eds., *Emerging Judaism: Studies on the Fourth and Third Centuries B.C.E.* (Minneapolis: Fortress, 1989) 77–99. See also Hengel, *Judaism and Hellenism,* 1.267–72.

I built for myself houses, I planted for myself vineyards. I made for myself gardens and parks and I planted there fruit trees of every variety. I made for myself pools of water from which to irrigate a forest sprouting with trees. I bought male and female slaves, and their children became my slaves. I also had much cattle, oxen, and sheep, more than all who preceded me in Jerusalem. I collected for myself both silver and gold, as well as the treasure of kings and of provincial rulers; I had for myself male and female singers, also the delights of men—a mistress, many mistresses. I increased greatly, more than all who preceded me in Jerusalem.[11]

Qoheleth's hypothetical career is characteristic of the era in several respects: the use of technology (irrigation), the exploitation of slaves, and the unabashed pursuit of pleasure. We are not told how Qoheleth acquired his wealth. There is no admission of violent methods such as those employed by the Tobiads. Of course, Qoheleth's account cannot be taken at face value as autobiography, since the author assumes a royal persona in Qoh. 1:12, thereby circumventing the need to explain his wealth. While the picture he paints is idealized, however, it is an idealization based on the experience of the Hellenistic age.

How relevant is the intrigue and luxury of the Tobiads to the book of Ben Sira? Quite relevant. The clearest window that Ben Sira opens on contemporary events is found in his praise, in Sir. 50:1–21, of the High Priest Simon II, "the leader of his kindred, glory of his people." Simon was the High Priest who welcomed Antiochus III into Jerusalem and presided over the transfer of Jerusalem from Ptolemaic to Seleucid control. In appreciation of the welcome he was given, Antiochus promised to help restore the city, which had been damaged by the war, and to provide provisions for the sacrifices (*Ant.* 12.139–40). Ben Sira begins by praising the High Priest for his building accomplishments: "In his life he repaired the house, and in his time he fortified the temple." He goes on to extol the splendor of his performance on the altar. The whole passage has a Hellenistic ring to it, because of its emphasis on spectacle as the way to win glory.

Ben Sira emphasizes the cultic role of Simon, but gives little indication of his politics or his culture. Yet this man was the son of Onias II and first cousin of Joseph the Tobiad. His son, Onias III, who is also credited with great piety by 2 Maccabees, sought refuge in a pagan temple when his life was in danger (2 Macc. 4:33). The same Onias allowed Hyrcanus the Tobiad to use the Jerusalem Temple as a safe-deposit bank (2 Macc. 3:11). Simon's younger son, Jason, was the prime mover in the Hellenistic reform in Jerusalem in the time

---

11. Qoh. 2:4–9, trans. J. Crenshaw, *Ecclesiastes* (Philadelphia: Westminster, 1987) 69. S. Applebaum, "Jewish Urban Communities and Greek Influences," in *Judaea in Hellenistic and Roman Times* (Leiden: Brill, 1989) 31–32, reads the disputed phrase *šiddāh wĕšidôt*, "a mistress, many mistresses," as male and female paramours, following the Greek, "a male wine-pourer and female wine-pourers." He argues that Greek readers, at least, would see a reference to homosexuality here.

of Antiochus IV Epiphanes. The household of Simon can hardly have been a bastion of traditional values. Yet Simon did uphold the right of the Jews to live in accordance with ancestral law, even if this necessarily imposed some limits on trade with Gentiles. (For example, a decree of Antiochus recorded in *Ant.* 12.146 prohibits the introduction of "animals forbidden to the Jews" into Jerusalem.)

Ben Sira as Social Critic

Tcherikover and Hengel have depicted Ben Sira as the champion of traditional Judaism against the new Hellenistic ethos. Tcherikover notes the sage's delight in travel (34:12; 51:13), and finds here a "widening of the intellectual horizon" representative of the new generation. Nonetheless, he insists that "Ben Sira returned to Jerusalem the orthodox Jew he had been before" and "fought against the spirit of Greek civilization all his life."[12] In part, this judgment concerns Ben Sira's attitude toward Greek philosophy, to which we will return later. For the present, let us consider his social teaching and see whether it has what Hengel has called an "apologetic-polemical" character.[13]

The difficulty here lies in distinguishing between the traditional verities of wisdom literature and remarks that are targeted against specific contemporary abuses. Sirach has a lengthy reflection on relations between rich and poor in chapter 13. When he says that "a rich person will exploit you if you can be of use to him, but if you are in need he will abandon you" (13:4), he is echoing an age-old observation. Compare the comments on the inequity of rich and poor in Prov. 14:20; Qoh. 9:16; and Sayings of Ahikar 55. The danger of indiscreet indulgence at the table of a rich man is noted persistently in Egyptian wisdom literature[14] and in Proverbs (23:1–3). Sirach, however, describes the antagonism between rich and poor more sharply than is customary in traditional wisdom literature:

> What does a wolf have in common with a lamb?
>   No more has a sinner with the devout.
> What peace is there between a hyena and a dog?
>   And what peace between the rich and the poor?
> Wild asses in the wilderness are the prey of lions;
>   likewise the poor are feeding grounds for the rich.
>
> (13:17–19)

We are reminded of the jibe of the court jester when Hyrcanus, son of Joseph the Tobiad, was at dinner with King Ptolemy: "My lord, do you see the bones

---

12. Tcherikover, *Hellenistic Civilization,* 143–44.
13. Hengel, *Judaism and Hellenism,* 1.138.
14. Instruction of Ani, *ANET* 412; Instruction of Amen-em-opet 23, *ANET* 424.

lying before Hyrcanus? From this you may guess that his father has stripped
all Syria in the same way as Hyrcanus has left these bones bare of meat" (*Ant.*
12.212).

But while Sirach observes this state of affairs, his tone remains detached. A
similar situation is reflected in the Epistle of Enoch (*1 Enoch* 94–105), which
may have been written about the same time.[15] But the tone of Enoch is very
different:

> Woe to you who acquire silver and gold, but not in righteousness, and say, we
> have become very rich and have possessions and have acquired everything that
> we desired. . . . Like water your life will flow away, for your riches will not stay
> with you, but will quickly go up from you; for you acquired everything in iniq-
> uity, and you will be given over to a great curse.
>
> (*1 Enoch* 97:8–10)

Sirach stops well short of cursing the rich, even if he disapproves of their actions. The difference in tone reflects the different social locations of the authors
of the two works. Ben Sira made his living by instructing the well-to-do. The
Epistle of Enoch is the work of social outsiders.[16]

Sirach's attitude to the wealthy is perhaps best summed up in chapter 31.
After noting that "one who loves gold will not be justified" and that "it is a
stumbling block to those who are avid for it," Sirach continues: "Blessed is the
rich person who is found blameless, and who does not go after gold. Who is
he, that we may praise him? . . . Who has had the power to transgress and did
not transgress and to do evil and did not do it?" (Sir. 31: 8–10). Such a person
is hard to find, but Sirach has not given up on the ideal. In another passage,
which is directly applicable to the Hellenistic context, the sage opines:

> A merchant can hardly keep from wrongdoing,
>   nor is a tradesman innocent of sin.
> Many have committed sin for gain,
>   and those who seek to get rich will avert their eyes.
> As a stake is driven firmly into a fissure between stones,
>   so sin is wedged in between selling and buying.
> If a person is not steadfast in the fear of the Lord,
>   his house will be quickly overthrown.
>
> (26:29–27:3)

---

15. G. W. Nickelsburg, *Jewish Literature between the Bible and the Mishnah* (Philadelphia:
Fortress, 1981) 150.

16. See the comments of R. A. Argall, *1 Enoch and Sirach: A Comparative Literary and Conceptual Analysis of the Themes of Revelation, Creation and Judgment* (Atlanta: Scholars, 1995)
252–54. Argall also notes that Sirach's theology does not allow him to threaten the rich with eternal damnation.

Even though sin is endemic to commerce, Sirach does not repudiate all commercial activity. It is not incompatible with the fear of the Lord, although the right combination is rare. Moreover, we may have here an echo of the professional snobbery of the scribe, such as we find in the discussion of the trades in chapters 38–39.

Mention of the "fear of the Lord" brings us to the heart of Sirach's critique of the ethos of his day. The positive implications of this notion will concern us later. For the present, it is safe to say that such people as the Tobiads, or the Hellenistic reformers of the next generation, were not characterized by "fear of the Lord." On this level, there was a real gulf between the traditional mores of the Semitic peoples and the new ethos introduced by the Greeks. Bickerman observes astutely:

> When an oriental subject appeared before an oriental despot, even if he were in the king's favor, he became like Nehemiah, "very afraid." . . . The situation was very different in Ptolemaic Egypt. Here another Joseph, a man from Jerusalem, comes to Alexandria and happens to meet the king's chariot in the street; a courtier mentions his name to King Ptolemy, who greets the newcomer and seats him in his carriage beside his queen. Joseph tells a few jokes and is invited to the royal table."[17]

Ben Sira was deeply imbued with a traditional "ethic of caution."[18] Insofar as Hellenism is associated with the brash entrepreneurial ethos of the Tobiads, Ben Sira was indeed opposed to it. But this did not mean that he was opposed to Hellenistic culture, or even Hellenistic commerce, if it could be combined with the traditional, reverential fear of the Lord.

Any discussion of Sirach's attitude to Hellenistic mores must bear in mind the social location of the sage.[19] Unlike Qoheleth's idealized, royal persona, the typical scribe was not independently wealthy. Yet his way of life required a degree of leisure that was not available to craftsmen and artisans, as Sirach makes very clear in 38:24: "The wisdom of the scribe depends on the opportunity of leisure; only the one who has little business can become wise." The scribe belonged to the retainer class, which served the needs of the governing class and included such professions as soldier, educator, and bureaucrat.[20] The glory of the scribe is to serve among the great and appear before rulers (39:4). To please the great is a mark of good sense, and those who please the great are even said to atone for injustice (20:28). Sirach also warns against seeking high office and against being partial to the powerful (7:6), but his reflection on the

17. Bickerman, *The Jews in the Greek Age,* 80.
18. J. T. Sanders, "Ben Sira's Ethics of Caution," *HUCA* 50 (1979) 73–106.
19. R. Gordis, "The Social Background of Wisdom Literature," *HUCA* 18 (1943/44) 77–118.
20. A. J. Saldarini, *Pharisees, Scribes and Sadducees in Palestinian Society* (Wilmington: Glazier, 1988) 313.

various professions in chapters 38–39 makes clear where his own ambitions lie. Craftsmen are disparaged because

> they are not sought out for the council of the people,
>   nor do they attain eminence in the public assembly.
> They do not sit in the judge's seat,
>   nor do they understand the decisions of the courts;
> they cannot expound discipline or judgment,
>   and they are not found among the rulers.
>   (38:32–33)

The person who aspires to serve the great, as Ben Sira does, is not well positioned for the role of social critic. It is to his credit that he speaks out against the abuse of wealth, but he is no radical polemicist.

Banquets and the Hellenistic Ethos

Indicative of Ben Sira's embedment in Hellenistic social mores is the inclusion of a treatise on behavior at banquets in 31:12–32:13.[21] Behavior at banquets is a theme of Egyptian literature from an early time, and is treated in the Instruction of Ptah-hotep, the Instruction of Kagemni, and the Instruction of Amenemope.[22] The latter work was probably the source for Prov. 23:1–3. Sirach's instruction follows the same pattern (cf. also Sir. 13:8–13). The advice is directed toward someone who is inexperienced in such matters, and is likely to be excited by the abundance of food. Sirach counsels moderation, and this is in accordance both with age-old Near Eastern wisdom and with Hellenistic philosophy.[23] Sirach goes beyond Proverbs in recommending vomiting as a relief from distress caused by overeating (31:21). This advice does not imply the Roman custom of using an emetic so that one could then eat more, but is simply practical advice to relieve distress. The need for such advice, however, is not reflected in the older wisdom literature.

Dinner parties were much more common in the Hellenistic world than they had been in the ancient Near East (cf. the passing reference to banquets in 2 Macc. 2:27, which assumes familiarity with the practice). They were also a source of prestige for the hosts. In the Hellenistic banquet, the main course was followed by wine drinking and entertainment, but this was also the custom in the ancient Near East. (Compare Esth. 5:6 and Dan. 5:1–2, which are set in the

---

21. O. Wischmeyer, *Die Kultur des Buches Jesus Sirach* (Berlin: de Gruyter, 1995) 106–9.

22. J. T. Sanders, *Ben Sira and Demotic Wisdom* (Chico, Calif.: Scholars, 1983) 67.

23. Compare the Sayings of Pseudo-Phocylides 69: "Eat and drink in moderation." For Greek parallels see P. W. Van der Horst, *The Sayings of Pseudo-Phocylides* (Leiden: Brill, 1978) 160–61.

Persian and Babylonian periods, but, at least in the case of Daniel 5, date from the Hellenistic era.)[24] Wine drinking was a problem long before the Hellenistic period. Isaiah taunts those who are "heroes in drinking wine and valiant in mixing drink" (Isa. 5:22), and Amos complains of the drinking of the women of Samaria (Amos 4:1). Proverbs paints an amusing picture of drunkenness (23:29–35), but is invariably negative on the subject (cf. also 20:1; 31:4–5). Sirach is more positive, and proclaims wine to be "life" to humans. (Cf. Ps. 104:15; 1 Tim. 5:23.) He is no less cautionary than Proverbs on the danger of excess, but he recognizes the inadvisability of reproaching a person who is inebriated. The dangers of intoxication at a banquet take on extreme forms in 1 Macc. 16:15–16 (where Simon Maccabee and his sons are murdered in a drunken state) and Judith 13:2–8 (where the heroine beheads the drunken Holofernes).

In Sir. 32:1–13, Sirach addresses in turn the conduct appropriate to the banquet master, the elder guests, and the younger guests. The position of banquet master or symposiarch reflects the Hellenistic context of this discussion. This person had the responsibility of arranging seating and ensuring good service. Since this was an honorary position, there was danger of self-importance (32:1). Sirach acknowledges that older guests have the right to speak, but he urges moderation. He discourages speech making by the younger guests. His preference is that people simply enjoy the music. In contrast, in Plato's *Symposium* (176E) the flute girl is dismissed so that the company can concentrate on philosophical discussion. The Greek text of Sir. 9:14–16 (but not the Hebrew) seems to imply that the righteous should discuss the Torah on such occasions, but chapter 31 envisages a social situation where all the company is not necessarily righteous. The well-educated person should also know how to behave in an urbane manner in such a setting. Sirach, characteristically, concludes the section with an exhortation to piety, but it was also customary at Greek banquets to pour a libation and sing a chant to the gods (cf. Plato's *Symposium* 176).

Sirach's evident familiarity with, and acceptance of, Hellenistic banquets shows that he was no zealous opponent of Hellenistic culture as such. The conflict that runs through his ethical reflection is not between Greek and Jew but between arrogance and temerity on the one hand and humility and caution on the other. The fact that Hellenistic culture seemed to promote arrogance and temerity was not a reason to reject all aspects of it out of hand. A sweeping rejection of Hellenism, or of the Hellenized mores of the upper class, was scarcely a possibility for someone in Ben Sira's social location.

---

24. On the Greek banquet see D. E. Smith and H. Taussig, *Many Tables: The Eucharist in the New Testament and Liturgy Today* (Philadelphia: Trinity, 1990) 21–35.

Honor and Shame

Another feature of Ben Sira's ethos that may have been influenced by the Hellenistic context is the great importance that he attaches to honor and shame, which have long been identified as core concerns of Hellenic society.[25] Such concerns are not absent from the Hebrew Bible; think, for example, of the action of Dinah's brothers against Shechem in Genesis 34 or of the complaint of Job in Job 31. Yet there is a marked increase in the frequency of terms relating to honor and shame in Ben Sira in comparison with earlier Hebrew literature.[26] Honor and shame were pivotal values in Greek society. Homer's epics are dominated by the warrior's search for honor. In the Hellenistic world people gained honor by their benefactions to their cities. Honor and shame were very much at stake in sexual relations. A man was shamed by the loss of chastity on the part of a woman under his control. The pursuit of honor was sometimes criticized by Hellenistic philosophers, especially Epicureans and Cynics, but such criticism had little impact on popular culture.[27]

The subject of honor and shame comes up several times in Ben Sira (3:1–6; 4:20–31; 10:19–25; 20:21–23). There is an extended discussion in 41:14–42:8. This section is given a title, "Instruction about Shame," in the Hebrew MS B. In general, Sirach seeks to retain the categories of honor and shame, but he also seeks to modify them. The catalog of things of which one should be ashamed gives considerable prominence to sexual offenses, even when they only involve gazing (9:1–9). All forms of lawbreaking are disapproved, but shame also extends to bad manners at table and lack of graciousness (41:19). The Torah heads the list of things of which one should not be ashamed. In this respect, Sirach tries to adapt the categories of Hellenistic culture to the values of Hebrew tradition. Inevitably, he also modifies the tradition in doing this. Moreover, as we shall see when we consider Sirach's views on family ethics, he retains a conventional code of patriarchal control that is quite in accordance with Hellenistic values of honor and shame. Here again,

25. E. R. Dodds, *The Greeks and the Irrational* (Berkeley: Univ. of California Press, 1951) 28–63.

26. C. Muenchow, "Dust and Dirt in Job 42:6," *JBL* 108 (1989) 603, counts 277 occurrences of roots meaning shame in the Hebrew Bible. C. Camp, "Understanding a Patriarchy: Women in Second Century Jerusalem through the Eyes of Ben Sira," in A. J. Levine, ed., *"Women like This,": New Perspectives on Jewish Women in the Greco-Roman World* (Atlanta: Scholars, 1991) 5, finds 52 occurrences of Greek equivalents of words for shame in Ben Sira alone, a significantly higher concentration.

27. For a concise overview and bibliography of the study of honor and shame in the Hellenistic world, see H. Moxnes, "Honor and Shame," *BTB* 23 (1993) 167–76. See further D. G. Gilmore, ed., *Honor and Shame and the Unity of the Mediterranean* (Washington, D.C.: American Anthropological Association, 1987).

there is no question of a simple choice between Hellenism and traditional Jewish values. There were features of the Hellenistic ethos of which Sirach did not approve, especially in the area of sexual morality, but other features were so much part of his cultural context that he would never have perceived them as foreign.

Education and Literature

H. I. Marrou has characterized Hellenistic culture as "a civilization of *paideia*."[28] The Greeks built schools wherever they went. There was also a measure of higher education attached to the gymnasium, and some places had institutes of research and higher learning, such as the Mouseion of Alexandria. In Jerusalem, however, the first gymnasium was built after 175 B.C.E., most probably after Sirach's time, and the impact of Hellenistic education in the Ptolemaic period is uncertain.

Schools in
Second Temple Judaism

We have regrettably little information about Jewish education before the Maccabean revolt. Universal schooling was not introduced until Hasmonean times. There are two legends on the subject.[29] The Jerusalem Talmud says that Simeon ben Shetach, who was president of the sanhedrin during the reign of Alexander Jannaeus (103–76 B.C.E.), ordained that children go to school (*j. Kethuboth* 8.32c). The Babylonian Talmud has a more detailed tradition:

> Verily the name of that man is to be blessed, Joshua ben Gamala, for but for him the Torah would have been forgotten from Israel. For at first if a child had a father, his father taught him, and if he had no father he did not learn at all. . . . They then made an ordinance that teachers of children should be appointed in Jerusalem. . . . Even so, however, if a child had a father, the father would take him up to Jerusalem and have him taught there; and if not, he would not go up to learn there. They, therefore, ordained that teachers should be appointed in each prefecture, and that boys should enter school at the age of sixteen or seventeen. They did so; and if the teacher punished them, they used to rebel and leave the school. At length Joshua ben Gamala came and ordained that teachers of young children should be appointed in each district and each town and that children should enter school at the age of six or seven.
>
> (*b. Baba Bathra* 21a)

---

28. H. I. Marrou, *A History of Education in Antiquity* (London: Sheed & Ward, 1956) 95.

29. S. Safrai, "Education and the Study of the Torah," in S. Safrai and M. Stern, eds., *The Jewish People in the First Century* (CRINT 1/2; Assen: Van Gorcum, 1976) 947–48.

Joshua ben Gamala functioned as High Priest during the last years of the
Temple (63–65 C.E.).[30] It would seem that the Jewish educational system developed gradually, and that universal education became the norm only at the
very end of the Second Temple period. Riesner has noted that sixteen or sev-
enteen is surprisingly late as an age for starting school in the period before
Joshua ben Gamala. This was approximately the age of the ephebes in the
Greek gymnasium. Riesner speculates that the first Torah-centered schools in
Jerusalem may have been developed in reaction to Jason's gymnasium.[31] They
could also have been developed as a counterpart to that phase of Greek education in the time of Alexander Jannaeus or later. It seems clear, however, that
there was no system of public education in Jerusalem in Ben Sira's time.[32]

Ben Sira's School

Most scholars cite Sir. 51:23 as the earliest clear reference to a school in a
Jewish text: "Draw near to me, you who are uneducated, and lodge in my house
of instruction [bêt midrāšî]."[33] This statement is found in the acrostic poem that
concludes the book. The same poem is found, in part, in the Psalms Scroll from
Qumran Cave 11, where it is placed between Psalm 138 and the "Apostrophe
to Zion." (Only vv. 11–17 and the last two words of the poem are preserved at
Qumran.) Most scholars read this poem as autobiographical, but Ben Sira's authorship has been questioned in view of the inclusion of the poem in the Psalms
Scroll.[34] Moreover, the reference to the house of instruction could be taken as
metaphorical—cf. Prov. 9:1, where Wisdom builds her house.[35] Even the
metaphor of a house of instruction, however, assumes that the phenomenon was
familiar to the reader. Even if the poem was not Sirach's own composition, it
must be taken to reflect the realities of the time. The Hebrew text from the Cairo
Geniza (MS B) also includes mention of a yeshivah in v. 29. The Greek has a
reference to God's mercy at this point, however, and since the Hebrew text is
medieval it is open to suspicion of late modification. There can be little doubt,
in any case, that the institution of the bêt midrash was known in Jerusalem in

30. On the problems of the identification, see R. Riesner, *Jesus als Lehrer* (Tübingen: Mohr,
1981) 201–5.
31. Ibid., 206.
32. On the rabbinic school system, see H. L. Strack and G. Stemberger, *Introduction to the Talmud and Midrash* (Edinburgh: T. & T. Clark, 1991) 9–16; Safrai, "Education and the Study of the
Torah," 945–70.
33. See, e.g., J. L. Crenshaw, "Education in Ancient Israel," *JBL* 104 (1985) 601; E. W. Heaton,
The School Tradition of the Old Testament (Oxford: Oxford Univ. Press, 1994) 1–23.
34. See note 2 above. For an account of the debate see H. Stadelmann, *Ben Sira als Schriftgelehrter* (Tübingen: Mohr, 1980) 30–33.
35. Wischmeyer, *Die Kultur des Buches Jesus Sirachs,* 175–76, insists that the reference is
metaphorical.

Sirach's time, and that it forms the setting of the sage's own teaching. The instructional character of Sirach is shown especially in his use of the paradigmatic instructional form of address: "Listen to the reproof of your father, O children" (3:1) and the intermittent address to "my son," especially in the early chapters (Sir. 2:1; 3:17; 4:1; 6:23, etc.). By the time of Sirach, this form of address is stereotypical, but it signals that Sirach stands in the tradition of Proverbs, and more broadly in the long line of Near Eastern, primarily Egyptian, instructional treatises that stretches back to the third millenium.

H. Stadelmann has argued that Sirach, as scribe and teacher, must have belonged to the priestly class.[36] He draws a specific analogy with Ezra, who was both priest and scribe. But Ezra is notoriously absent from Ben Sira's "Praise of the Fathers," and however this is to be explained it should caution us against casting Ben Sira in the likeness of Ezra. Ben Sira clearly affirms the authority of the priesthood with respect to teaching the Torah. Moses gave Aaron "authority and statutes and judgments to teach Jacob the testimonies and to enlighten Israel with his law" (45:17). The praise of Simon the Just in chapter 50 shows that Sirach was close to the circles of the High Priest and in no way opposed to the priesthood. He urges his readers to revere the priests and give them their portion (7:29–31) and he supports the offering of sacrifices (34:21–35:13). Neither these passages nor any other part of the book, however, gives any hint that Ben Sira was himself a priest. His deference toward the priesthood can be explained by supposing that he depended on the patronage of the High Priest. While his attention to sacrifices is without precedent in the biblical wisdom books, he still gives only a small fraction of his space to priestly concerns. He ignores the cultic and dietary laws of Leviticus. Moreover, despite his explicit identification of Wisdom with the Torah in 24:23, Ben Sira does not expound the Law directly. He is a wisdom teacher, who makes extensive use of the Torah, but he makes no pretense of authoritative interpretation of the kind that he reserves to the priesthood.

Priests and Levites were not the only teachers in Second Temple Judaism. The most obvious precedents for Sirach are found in the books of Proverbs and Qoheleth. The epilogue to the book of Qoheleth claims that the sage "taught the people knowledge." We can hardly imagine Qoheleth as a Levite teaching the Torah. His teaching is exceptional in the wisdom tradition in its appeal to personal experience. Presumably, he had a private school and took on pupils who sought him out. Many scholars also posit a school setting for Proverbs, or at least for Proverbs 1–9 and for the whole book as it was transmitted in the Second Temple period.[37] The rhetorical situation of a father addressing his son

---

36. Stadelmann, *Ben Sira als Schriftgelehrter,* 25.

37. B. Lang, "Schule und Unterricht in Israel," in M. Gilbert, ed., *La Sagesse de l'Ancien Testament* (Louvain: Leuven University Press, 1990) 192–99.

is a convention inherited from the Egyptian instructions, and can be taken as metaphorical for the relationship of teacher and student. (References to the mother's teaching in 1:8 and 6:20 do not lend themselves so easily to metaphorical explanation, but there is no reason why a school instruction should not affirm the authority of both parents.) A school setting is clearly implied in Prov. 5:12–13, where the errant youth laments: "Oh, how I hated discipline, and my heart despised reproof! I did not listen to the voice of my teachers [*mōray*] or incline my ear to my instructors [*mĕlammĕday*]." The developed poetic instructions of Proverbs 1–9 are more plausibly explained as a product of school instruction than of home-based education.

When we speak of schools in this context, we mean simply a relationship between a teacher and some number of students who are not his actual children. We know nothing of the circumstances in which teaching took place. Proverbs 8 has Wisdom cry out at the crossroads and the city gate, inviting people to come and receive instruction.[38] The wisdom poem at the end of Ben Sira's book also calls out for pupils. On several occasions Sirach speaks of the need to pursue wisdom, but in 6:34–37 he gives more practical advice: "Stand in the company of the elders. Who is wise? Attach yourself to such a one. Be ready to listen to every godly discourse, and let no wise proverbs escape you. If you see an intelligent person, rise early to visit him; let your foot wear out his doorstep." What this passage suggests is a tutorial relationship rather than a formal course of study. The wisdom school of Ben Sira may have had the character of a group tutorial.[39]

In this respect, there is at least a limited analogy between the Jewish wisdom school in the Second Temple period and the Greek philosophical schools that developed about the same time. The great originators of private schools of higher learning in classical Greece were the Sophists. In the words of H. I. Marrou: "They did not open any schools—in the institutional sense of that word. Their method, not unlike that of early times, might be described as collective tutoring. They gathered round the youths entrusted to their care and undertook their entire training."[40] The Sophists, like Wisdom, had to go out into the highways and byways in search of students. By the Hellenistic period, Greek philosophy had become a more technical discipline, and the various philosophical "schools" had developed into virtual sects with their own doctrines. Judaism in Ben Sira's time had nothing to compare with the developed philosophical schools of the Stoics and Epicureans. The analogy extends only to the phenomenon of individual teachers' going out in search of students and offering to instruct them in the ways of wisdom.

38. Cf. Prov. 1:20–21; Lang, "Schule und Unterricht," 200–201.
39. Wischmeyer, *Die Kultur,* 177 also concludes that Ben Sira had "a private wisdom school," and was not part of any official system of education.
40. Marrou, *A History of Education,* 49.

The kind of instruction provided by Proverbs and Qoheleth is by no means secular, but neither is it based on the Torah or directed to the needs of a priestly class. It represents a different tradition in education from the kind of instruction in the Torah that is attributed to the Levites in Chronicles. Proverbs includes a certain amount of practical wisdom (e.g., 22:17–23:11) that stands in the tradition of Egyptian court wisdom. Practical issues recede, however, in Proverbs 1–9 and in Qoheleth. (They come to the fore again in Ben Sira.) Qoheleth represents a highly personal, existential search for what is good in life. Proverbs 1–9 emphasizes moral instruction and the pursuit of Wisdom, which is given a personal, feminine form. Here again there is a limited analogy with Greek philosophy, which was also the pursuit of wisdom, in its cognitive and moral dimensions. It is not impossible that the Jewish wisdom books have been influenced, if only indirectly, by Greek philosophy. Such influence has often been posited in the case of Qoheleth,[41] and has recently been suggested in the case of Proverbs by Michael Fox, who underlines the novelty of Proverbs in equating wisdom with virtue.[42] The analogy is admittedly limited. The pursuit of wisdom, as evidenced in Proverbs 1–9 or in Qoheleth is a philosophical undertaking, however modest it may be in comparison to Plato or Aristotle. It is an attempt to arrive at an understanding of life without recourse to prophetic revelation or miraculous divine intervention, and simultaneously to determine what is good for humanity. It may be that this was a parallel development to Greek philosophy, and not influenced by it to any significant degree, but it represented a new departure over against the traditional scribal wisdom of the ancient Near East.

Greek and Egyptian Wisdom in Ben Sira

It does not, of course, follow that the curriculum taught by a Jewish teacher like Ben Sira was at all influenced by Hellenistic philosophy. The core of Sirach's teaching is still traditional Near Eastern wisdom material. Much of it can be read as an elaboration of the teaching of Proverbs. Sirach had some acquaintance with Greek literature and philosophy, but he never refers to a Greek book, or indeed to any nonbiblical book, by name. The extent of his acquaintance with Greek literature is disputed. Middendorp has claimed to identify approximately a hundred passages in which Sirach is indebted to Greek

41. R. Braun, *Kohelet und die frühhellenistische Popularphilosophie* (BZAW 130; Berlin: de Gruyter, 1973).
42. M. Fox, "Wisdom in Proverbs," a paper read to the International Organisation for the Study of the Old Testament at Cambridge (July 1995).

literature,[43] but his arguments have not withstood scholarly criticism.[44] In many cases Middendorp's argument consists of finding a Greek passage that expresses a sentiment similar to something that is also attested in biblical tradition. It is generally accepted that Sir. 14:18, which compares the generations of humanity to the leaves of a tree, echoes Homer's *Iliad* 6.146–49 ("People come and go as leaves year by year upon the trees"), but the sentiment was probably proverbial by the Hellenistic age, and does not require any extensive acquaintance with Homer. The Greek author most frequently echoed by Sirach is the gnomic poet Theognis, whose subject matter often parallels that of the Jewish sage. So Sir. 6:10 ("There is a friend who is a table-friend, but he is not to be found in the day of affliction") echoes a doublet from Theognis 115–16/643–44: "Many become comrades dear beside the bowl, but few in a grave matter." Or again Sir. 6:15, "A faithful friend is beyond price, and his worth cannot be weighed," parallels Theognis 77–78, "A trusty man is to be reckoned against gold and silver." The parallels are not restricted to the theme of friendship, but touch on various aspects of practical wisdom. (E.g., Sir. 10:6a: "Requite not evil to thy neighbor for every wrong" echoes Theognis 325: "If a man grow always angry at a friend's offence . . .")[45] It is not surprising that the non-Jewish work with which Sirach has most parallels is the Egyptian Instruction of Phibis, preserved in Papyrus Insinger.[46] These include the example of the productive little bee (Sir. 11:3; P. Insinger 25:3), a hundred years as the upper limit of human life (Sir. 18:9; P. Insinger 27:21) and catalogs of vices and virtues of women.[47] Most striking is the fact that both Phibis and Sirach have sections on filial piety near the beginning of their books and hymns to God the creator near the end. Sirach's attraction to the works of Theognis and Phibis is obvious: they too are works of traditional wisdom, which elaborate on many issues that receive only cursory treatment in Proverbs. Ben Sira's acquaintance with Egyptian wisdom literature is further shown by the similarity between Sir. 38:24–39:11 and the Maxims of Duauf, or the Satire on the Trades, even though the Jewish sage adapted his model freely.[48] Sirach also appears to have a smattering of Greek philosophy, espe-

---

43. Th. Middendorp, *Die Stellung Jesu Ben Siras zwischen Judentum und Hellenismus* (Leiden: Brill, 1973).

44. J. T. Sanders, *Ben Sira and Demotic Wisdom* (Chico, Calif.: Scholars, 1983); H. V. Kieweler, *Ben Sira zwischen Judentum und Hellenismus* (Frankfurt am Main: Lang, 1992).

45. See further J. T. Sanders, *Ben Sira and Demotic Wisdom*, 29–38.

46. Ibid., 61–101. On Papyrus Insinger see M. Lichtheim, *Late Egyptian Wisdom Literature in the International Context: A Study of Demotic Instructions* (OBO 52; Göttingen: Vandenhoeck & Ruprecht, 1983) 107–234.

47. Sanders, *Ben Sira and Demotic Wisdom*, 71, 98.

48. O. Rickenbacher, *Weisheitsperikopen bei Ben Sira* (Göttingen: Vandenhoeck & Ruprecht, 1973) 176–96. For the Maxims of Duauf see *ANET*, 432–34.

cially Stoicism, to which we will return when we consider his views of God and nature and the question of theodicy. It is unlikely, however, that Sirach had ever studied with a Stoic philosopher or that he had any real understanding of the system. There was no center of Stoic philosophy in Judea such as could be found in Alexandria.[49] The instruction that Sirach himself imparted is presumably represented fairly enough by his book.

It must be said that Hellenistic literature had made only a very modest impression in Judea at the time Sirach wrote. There was, by this time, a flourishing Jewish literature in Greek in Alexandria. Such authors as Demetrius the chronographer, Ezekiel the tragedian, and the historian Artapanus can all be dated plausibly before the Maccabean revolt.[50] It is significant, however, that Martin Hengel, in his review of Hellenism in Palestine before the Maccabean revolt, cannot point to a single Jewish author who wrote in Greek.[51] The first such author was Eupolemus, who was active about the time of the revolt. It must have been possible to learn Greek in Jerusalem in Sirach's time. People needed it for business and diplomacy. But the contrast between Jerusalem, which was still a Semitic-speaking city, and the situation in the Diaspora is remarkable.

Hellenistic education and philosophy, then, had some impact on Judean intellectuals in Sirach's day, but that impact was modest. There is no evidence that Sirach, or anyone else for that matter, actively opposed Greek philosophy in this period, or saw it as a threat. There was no need to oppose it, as it was not being promoted. The main innovation of Sirach in the tradition of the Jewish wisdom school was in the prominence he gave to the Torah of Moses. Some people argue that Sirach's identification of the Law with wisdom was intended to counter the claims of Greek philosophy, but this seems unlikely. Nowhere in Sirach do we find any explicit polemic against Greek wisdom. The Jewish Law was the nearest thing to a philosophical system of which Sirach had any mastery. His objective in incorporating the Torah into his wisdom teaching was simply to integrate the traditions at his disposal. The objective was constructive rather than apologetic. We shall consider this constructive enterprise in more detail in the following chapter.

49. According to Diogenes Laertius 7.185, Ptolemy Philadelphus, in the middle of the third century B.C.E., invited Cleanthes to come to Alexandria or to send someone else. Cleanthes's pupil, Sphaerus, accepted the invitation. D. Winston, "Theodicy in Ben Sira and Stoic Philosophy," in R. Link-Salinger, ed., *Of Scholars, Savants, and Their Texts* (New York: Lang, 1989) 240.

50. See J. J. Collins, *Between Athens and Jerusalem: Jewish Identity in the Hellenistic Diaspora* (New York: Crossroad, 1983) 27–38, 207–11.

51. Hengel, *Judaism and Hellenism*, 1.88–102.

Chapter 3.
Wisdom and the Law

Of all the pre-Mishnaic writings that were eventually excluded from the Hebrew canon, the book of Ben Sira was the most widely used. Fragments found
at Qumran and Masada confirm that it was widely known in antiquity. (Nothing about it was especially congenial either to the Essenes of Qumran or to
the Zealots.) Although its use was reputedly banned by R. Akiba, it was ven-
erated by many rabbis in the subsequent generations. Verses from the book
are often cited as popular proverbs, and it is also often cited by name.[1] Nevertheless, the Hebrew text was eventually lost. In Christian circles, the status of the book was ambiguous, like that of the other Apocrypha. On the one
hand it was widely cited, and included in some canonical lists. On the other
hand some authorities, most notably St. Jerome, limited the canonical scriptures to those found in the Hebrew Bible.[2] Unlike the Hebrew text, however,
the Greek and Latin versions of Sirach were transmitted continuously with
the other scriptures.

The Text of Ben Sira

The textual history of Ben Sira's book is exceptionally complicated.[3] We
know from the grandson's prologue that the book was composed in Hebrew,
but it has not survived intact in the original language. For many centuries the
Hebrew text was known only from rabbinic citations. At the end of the nineteenth century, however, several fragments were found at Cambridge Univer-

---

1. S. Schechter, "The Quotations from Ecclesiasticus in Rabbinic Literature," *JQR* 3 (1890–91)
682–706; S. Leiman, *The Canonization of Hebrew Scripture: The Talmudic and Midrashic Evidence* (Hamden, Conn.: Archon, 1976) 92–102.

2. G. H. Box and W. O. E. Oesterley, "Sirach," in *APOT* 1. 298–303.

3. See A. A. DiLella, *The Hebrew Text of Sirach* (The Hague: Mouton, 1966); H. P. Rüger, *Text
und Textform im Hebräischen Sirach* (BZAW 112; Berlin: de Gruyter, 1970); B. G. Wright, *No
Small Difference: Sirach's Relationship to Its Hebrew Parent Text* (SCS 26; Atlanta: Scholars,
1989).

sity, in the collection of manuscripts recovered from the Cairo Geniza.[4] These fragments represented four distinct manuscripts—A, B, C, and D. More leaves of MSS B and C were discovered later. Fragments of another manuscript (MS E) were discovered in the Adler Geniza collection at the Jewish Theological Seminary in New York, and yet another (MS F) at Cambridge.[5] All these Geniza fragments, which include most of chapters 3 to 16 and fragments of chapters 18 to 36, are of medieval origin. The Dead Sea Scrolls yielded further, much older, fragments, from around the turn of the era. Two fragments from Cave 2 (2Q18) contain only four complete words and some letters from chapter 6,[6] but the Psalms Scroll from Cave 11 contains Sir. 51:13–20, and the last two words of verse 30b.[7] Then twenty-six leather fragments were found at Masada.[8] These dated to the first century C.E. and contained portions of chapters 39 to 44. In all, about 68 percent of the book is now extant in Hebrew. For a time, some scholars expressed doubts about the Hebrew text preserved in the medieval Geniza fragments and entertained the possibility that it might have been retranslated from Syriac. The Masada fragments, however, confirmed the antiquity of Geniza MS B and indirectly enhanced the credibility of the other fragments. The present consensus is that the Geniza fragments faithfully preserve a text from antiquity.

The Hebrew fragments bear witness to two textual recensions.[9] The second recension is distinguished from the first primarily by additions (e.g., 15:14b, 15c). These passages can be recognized as secondary because they are not found in the primary manuscripts of the Greek translation, and in some cases the variations between the recensions are reflected in overlapping Hebrew fragments. There is also a second Greek recension, which expands the text in a way similar to the second Hebrew recension.[10] The second Greek recension is also reflected in the Old Latin. One of the distinctive features of this recension is the belief in eternal life and judgment after death. The textual situation is further complicated by the fact that the Greek text is poorly preserved. The

---

4. S. Schechter and C. Taylor, *The Wisdom of Ben Sira: Portions of the Book of Ecclesiasticus from Hebrew Manuscripts in the Cairo Genizah Collection Presented to the University of Cambridge by the Editors* (Cambridge: Cambridge Univ. Press, 1899).

5. For the details, see Skehan and DiLella, *The Wisdom of Ben Sira*, 51–53.

6. M. Baillet, J. T. Milik, and R. de Vaux, *Les 'Petites Grottes' de Qumrân* (*DJD* 3; Oxford: Clarendon, 1962) 75.

7. J. A. Sanders, *The Psalms Scroll of Qumrân Cave 11* (*DJD* 4; Oxford: Clarendon, 1965) 79–85.

8. Y. Yadin, *The Ben Sira Scroll from Masada* (Jerusalem: Israel Exploration Society, 1965).

9. A. Fuchs, *Textkritische Untersuchungen zum hebräischen Ekklesiastikus* (BibS [F] S 12,5; Freiburg in Breisgau: Herder, 1907).

10. C. Kearns, "The Expanded Text of Ecclesiasticus: Its Teaching on the Future Life as a Clue to Its Origin" (Diss. Pontifical Biblical Institute, Rome, 1951).

edition of the Greek text by J. Ziegler contains more emendations and corrections than any other book of the Septuagint.[11]

Literary Form and Structure

Sirach's primary model was undoubtedly the book of Proverbs. The basic genre of wisdom instruction includes a blend of observational sentences and commands and prohibitions. Sirach 3:1–16 is a typical example: "Those who respect their father will have long life. . . . Honor your father by word and deed." Traditional wisdom forms of speech in Sirach include comparisons (Sir. 20:31: "Better are those who hide their folly than those who hide their wisdom"), beatitudes (26:1: "Happy is the husband of a good wife"), numerical sayings (50:25–26: "Two nations my soul detests and the third is not even a people"), and hymns in praise of wisdom (1:1–10; 24:1–34). But Sirach also incorporates literary forms that are not part of the repertoire of Proverbs. In addition to the use of autobiographical narratives and the critique of the trades, these include hymns of praise to God (39:12–35; 42:15–43:33) and at least one prayer of petition (22:27–23:6; 36:1–22 is probably a later addition). Sirach differs from Proverbs in that its material is not a collection of individual sayings, but consists of several short treatises. Some of these are devoted to traditional practical wisdom (e.g., relations with women, behavior at banquets). Others are theological reflections on wisdom and on the problem of theodicy. Even when the material is largely traditional, Sirach often concludes his reflections by commending the fear of the Lord or observance of the Law (e.g., 9:15–16; 37:15). The most striking formal departure from biblical wisdom is found in the Praise of the Fathers (chapters 44–50), which uses the history of Israel as a source of instructional examples.

One of the hallmarks of the biblical wisdom tradition, as found in Proverbs, Qoheleth, and Job, is the lack of reference to the distinctive traditions of Israel. The concern is with humanity as such, not with the special status of one people. Sirach, in contrast, pays considerable attention to Israel and its scriptures. The grandson, in the preface, says that Sirach "devoted himself especially to the reading of the Law and the Prophets and the other books of our ancestors," and implies that he envisaged his own book as comparable to the ancestral writings. This interest in scriptures cannot be explained simply by the spirit of the times. Qoheleth may be close to Sirach in date, but he makes no mention of the Law and the Prophets. Sirach, however, says that all wisdom is "the book of the

covenant of the Most High God, the law that Moses commanded us" (24:23), and he describes the sage as "one who devotes himself to the study of the law of the Most High . . . and is concerned with prophecies" (39:1–2). Despite Sirach's reverence for the Law, his teaching remains in the form of wisdom instruction. It is neither legal proclamation nor legal interpretation. He subsumes the Law under the rubric of wisdom, as its supreme example. The fact remains, however, that the curriculum of wisdom instruction inherited from Proverbs has been altered profoundly by the inclusion of the Jewish scriptures.

Wisdom instructions, such as Proverbs, are typically loosely structured. Attempts to discern a literary structure in Ben Sira have met with only limited success. In the judgment of A. A. DiLella "the book manifests no particular order of subject matter or obvious coherence."[12] In contrast, an elaborate structure has been proposed by M. H. Segal[13] and W. Roth.[14] These authors distinguish an original book in 1:1–23:27 and chapter 51. This book was made up of four sections: 1:1–4:10; 4:11–6:17; 6:18–14:19; and 14:20–23:27 plus 51:1–30. Each section was introduced by a prologue: 1:1–2:18; 4:11–19; 6:18–37, and 14:20–15:10. Three additional sections were subsequently added: 24:1–32:13; 32:14–38:23; 38:24–50:29. (So Roth; Segal distinguishes the Praise of the Fathers as an additional section.) Each of these sections also has a prologue: 24:1–29; 32:14–33:15; and 38:24–39:11. The key to this structure is provided by five passages on wisdom (1:1–10; 4:11–19; 6:18–37; 14:20–15:10; and 24:1–34). These passages seem to mark stresses in the first part of the book, but they have no discernible effect on the passages that precede or follow them.[15] There are some indications that the book grew by a series of additions. The personal reflection in 24:30–34 looks like the conclusion of a section, rather than the beginning of the second half of the book. A similar autobiographical note is found in 33:16–18. First-person statements at 39:12 and 42:15 may also mark new beginnings, and the Praise of the Fathers in chapters 44–49 is formally distinct. There is a concentration of hymnic material in chapters 39–43. These observations render plausible the hypothesis that the book grew gradually, but they do not amount to proof.[16]

The structure proposed by Segal and Roth may be modified to yield the following division:[17]

12. Skehan and DiLella, *The Wisdom of Ben Sira,* 4.

13. M. H. Segal, *Sēper ben Sîrā haššalēm* (Jerusalem: Bialik, 1958).

14. W. Roth, "The Gnomic-Discursive Wisdom of Jesus Ben Sirach," *Semeia* 17: 35–79.

15. M. Gilbert, "Wisdom Literature," in M. E. Stone, ed., *Jewish Writings of the Second Temple Period* (CRINT 2/2; Philadelphia: Fortress, 1984) 292–93.

16. J. D. Harvey, "Toward a Degree of Order in Ben Sira's Book," *ZAW* 105 (1993) 52–62, suggests that the different sections of the book originated as sets of lecture notes.

17. Harvey, ibid., proposes a similar division, but identifies the fifth, sixth, and seventh units as 24:1–32:13; 32:14–38:23; and 38:24–43:33.

Part I: A: 1:1–4:10; B: 4:11–6:17; C: 6:18–14:19; D: 14:20–23:27; E: 24:1–34.
Part II: A: 25:1–33:18; B: 33:19–39:11; C: 39:12–43:33; D: 44:1–50:29; E: 51:1–30.

It is clear enough that the great poem on wisdom in chapter 24 marks the center of the book. Much, but not all, of the discussion of practical wisdom is found in the early chapters. The most extended discussions of God and theodicy are found later in the book. There are, then, some indications of structure, but nonetheless the book has the character of a collection of instructions rather than a tight, coherent, compositional unity.

Wisdom in Sirach

Ben Sira's understanding of wisdom is thematized in the series of wisdom poems that punctuate the book.[18] The opening poem (Sir. 1:1–10) strikes a note that is characteristic of Sirach: all wisdom is from the Lord. By implication, any wisdom that repudiates the Lord, the God of Israel, is not true wisdom, and so Sirach signals his loyalty to his ancestral tradition. But conversely, whatever is true wisdom is from the Lord, wherever it is found. This passage sets wisdom in the context of creation. It is reminiscent of Job 28 in its insistence on the unfathomable mysteries: the height of heaven, the breadth of the earth, the abyss, and wisdom (1:3). More clearly than the Hebrew text of Proverbs, but in agreement with the Greek, Sirach states that God created wisdom (1:9; this passage is not extant in Hebrew). More positively than Job, Sirach says that God "poured her [wisdom] out upon all his works, upon all the living according to his gift; he lavished her upon those who love him" (1:10). Sirach sets no restriction at the outset on where such people may be found. In principle, at least, wisdom is poured out over all creation.

This passage is followed and qualified by another poem, on the fear of the Lord. This motif recurs over sixty times throughout the book.[19] Sirach repeats the dictum of Proverbs that "to fear the Lord is the beginning of wisdom" (1:14). It is also the fullness of wisdom (1:16), the crown of wisdom (1:18), and the root of wisdom (1:20). While Sirach stops short of an outright equation, it would seem that fear of the Lord is a virtual synonym for wisdom. Like wisdom, it gives "gladness and joy and long life" (1:12). If wisdom is identified so closely with fear of the Lord, it is not only a matter of understanding

---

18. A. A. DiLella, "The Meaning of Wisdom in Ben Sira," in L. Perdue, B. B. Scott, and W. J. Wiseman, eds., *In Search of Wisdom: Essays in Memory of John G. Gammie* (Louisville: Westminster John Knox, 1993) 133–48.

19. J. Haspecker, *Gottesfurcht bei Jesus Sirach* (Rome: Pontifical Biblical Institute, 1967) 48–50.

but also a moral disposition. Fear of the Lord entails patience (1:23), discipline, trust, humility (v. 27), and sincerity (vv. 28–29). It is primarily an attitude of reverence for God and respect for received tradition, and as such it is constitutive of wisdom.

One manifestation of the fear of the Lord is the observance of the commandments: "If you desire wisdom, keep the commandments, and the Lord will lavish her upon you. For the fear of the Lord is wisdom and discipline, fidelity and humility are his delight" (1:26–27). In view of the eventual identification of wisdom with the Torah of Moses, the commandments are presumably those found in that book. In fact, Ben Sira often echoes the injunctions of the Decalogue (e.g., the command to honor parents in 3:1–6) and the social laws of Deuteronomy (compare Sir. 4:1–6, on charity toward the poor, with the spirit of Deut. 15:7–11). He pays scant attention to the ritual commandments of Leviticus. Their observance is arguably taken for granted. We may compare the attitude of Philo of Alexandria, who was far more strongly inclined to spiritualization than Ben Sira, but still faulted those who neglected the literal observance of the laws, and argued that Jews should be "stewards without reproach . . . and let go nothing that is part of the customs fixed by divinely empowered men greater than those of our time" (*De Abr.,* 89–93). Sirach's injunction to "keep the commandments" should probably be understood in a similar spirit, to extend even to matters that were not at the center of his interest. Compare his position on tithes and offerings in 7:31: "Honor the priest, and give him his portion, as you have been commanded." His position on the ritual laws, however, remains uncertain. In his discussion of banquets in 31:16 he urges: "Eat what is set before you, like a man." It has been suggested that this implies a dispensation from insistence on dietary laws, for the sake of good manners and consideration for one's host.[20] But the verse continues with an admonition against chewing greedily, so the point may be that one should eat like a human being rather than like an animal, and the nature of the food itself may not be an issue. Sirach never addresses the issue of dietary laws explicitly. It should be noted in any case that the fear of the Lord is never simply identified with keeping the commandments.[21] It is a disposition that manifests itself in all aspects of a person's life.

The second wisdom poem (4:11–19) concentrates on the rewards of wisdom (vv. 11–16), with a short metaphorical discussion of the process by which wisdom is acquired. As in Proverbs, to love wisdom is to love life (4:12). Some other statements in this passage are novel in the wisdom tradition.

First, the pursuit of wisdom is equated with cultic service in 4:14: those who serve her minister to the Holy One (or to the Sanctuary, if we read *qōdeš* instead

20. J. G. Gammie, "Wisdom in Sirach," in J. G. Gammie and L. Perdue, eds., *The Sage in Israel and the Ancient Near East* (Winona Lake, Ind.: Eisenbrauns, 1990) 361.
21. Haspecker, *Gottesfurcht,* 329.

of *qādōš*). This is hardly the sentiment of a priest, as it gives the pursuit of the sage equal value with the sacrificial cult. There is a similar implication in the discussion of sacrifices in 35:1–2: "The one who keeps the law makes many offerings; one who heeds the commandments makes an offering of well-being," although Sirach is careful to make clear that the righteous should offer the literal sacrifices just the same.

Second, those who obey wisdom are said to judge the nations (4:15). This idea is found in an eschatological context in the Wisdom of Solomon, chapter 3. Since Sirach has no place for an eschatological judgment, the context envisaged here is uncertain. The point may be simply that those trained in wisdom will rise to positions of authority.

The poem concludes with a brief discussion of the process by which wisdom is acquired, emphasizing the necessity of testing: "She will torment them by her discipline until she trusts them." Wisdom is not simply a matter of acquiring knowledge. It is a disciplined way of life that requires the formation of character.

The third poem about wisdom (6:18–37) also discusses the process of acquiring wisdom, but does not speak in wisdom's name. Several analogies and metaphors are used to convey the need for discipline. The student is like a farmer who plows and sows, but who must be patient if he is to reap. (Compare the New Testament parable of the sower in Mark 4 and parallels.) Wisdom is like a stone in the path, and the shortsighted fool casts it aside. Finally, wisdom is compared to various restraining devices — a net, yoke, or bonds. The image of the yoke is used similarly for the teaching of Jesus in Matt. 11:28–30 and the yoke of the law in *m. Aboth* 3:5. Sirach 51:26, a passage found independently at Qumran, also exhorts the disciple to "put your neck under the yoke of wisdom." Another set of images describe the delight of wisdom for one who perseveres: garments of gold or purple, and a crown. A crown is often a symbol of immortality, but here it represents the glory of wisdom.

Sirach 6:32–37 gives more straightforward advice to the pupil. He should frequent the company of the elders and attach himself to a teacher. He should also reflect on the Law of the Most High. It appears then that the student has two sources to study, at least initially: the discourse of the elders and the book of the Torah. Neither is simply equated with wisdom here. Rather, they have the character of a propaideutic. Wisdom is a gift of God, over and above what one can acquire by study. It is a disposition of the mind and character, and as such it cannot be equated with any collection of sayings or laws, although these are indispensable aids in the quest for wisdom.

The fourth wisdom poem (14:20–15:10) also describes the quest for wisdom in poetic images. The poem falls into two halves: 14:20–27 describes the student's quest for wisdom; 15:2–10 describes wisdom's rewards. Chapter 15:1, which associates wisdom with the law, stands as an editorial comment by Ben Sira, repeating a recurring theme in the book.

Sirach 14:20–27 has the form of a beatitude or makarism ("Happy is the person who meditates on wisdom"), a form found about a dozen times in Sirach and almost as frequently in Proverbs.[22] There is a noteworthy parallel in 4Q525 from Qumran, which declares blessed "the man who attains wisdom and walks in the law of the Most High." There is probably an allusion in Sir. 14:20 to Psalm 1, which pronounces blessed those who meditate on the law of the Lord, with the implication that Sirach equates wisdom with the law. Psalm 154, previously known only in Syriac but now found in Hebrew at Qumran, similarly commends those whose meditation is on the law of the Most High. Sirach goes on to compare wisdom to a bride and a mother. The pursuit of wisdom has a mildly erotic connotation in Prov. 4:6–9, while wisdom is cast as the nourishing mother in Prov. 9:1–5. Erotic motifs will appear more prominently in Sir. 51:13–28. Here the imagery of peering in at the window recalls Cant. 2:9. The maternal side of wisdom is expressed through the images of tent and tree, both of which give shelter.

The association of wisdom with the Torah in 15:1 is a favorite theme of Ben Sira and will find its classic expression in chapter 24. Here we must note that it has little impact on the way in which wisdom is described. Rather, the poem continues with the images of bride and mother, but shifts from the agency of the student/suitor to that of wisdom. The imagery of food and drink (15:3) will also be developed in Sirach 24. In the Hebrew Bible, the support of the righteous is usually the Lord (Pss. 18:19; 22:5; 25:2). Here wisdom acts as the surrogate of the Lord. This notion too will be developed in chapter 24. The crown (15:6) is often a symbol of a blessed afterlife. Sirach's hope, however, is for an everlasting name. This is *not* a standard expectation in the wisdom books of the Hebrew Bible. It does not appear at all in Job or Qohelet. According to Prov. 10:4, the memory of the righteous is a blessing but the name of the wicked will rot. The motif is far more prominent in Sirach.[23] This interest reflects the heightened sense of honor and shame in Sirach's Hellenistic milieu. It appears prominently in the Praise of the Fathers in chapters 44–50.

The Praises of Wisdom

The great wisdom hymn in chapter 24 may be regarded as the centerpiece of the book.[24] It differs from other wisdom poems in Sirach insofar as vv. 3–22 constitute a declaration by Wisdom in the first person. As such, it is properly compared to the aretalogies of the Egyptian goddess Isis.[25] There is

22. Rickenbacher, *Weisheitsperikopen*, 83.
23. Ibid., 95–98.
24. On the structure of the poem, see M. Gilbert, "L'éloge de la Sagesse (Siracide 24)," *RTL* 5 (1974) 326–48.
25. J. Marböck, *Weisheit im Wandel: Untersuchungen zur Weisheitstheologie bei Ben Sira* (Bonn: Hanstein, 1971) 47–54.

an obvious biblical precedent in Proverbs 8, which may itself be influenced by Egyptian prototypes.[26] The argument that Sirach drew directly on the aretalogies of Isis has been made especially by Hans Conzelmann.[27] In addition to the formal similarity, there are also thematic parallels. Both Wisdom and Isis are of primeval origin, exercise cosmological functions, and claim dominion over the whole earth. Isis claims to have established law for humanity. Sirach 24:23, which stands outside the first-person aretalogy, equates wisdom with the Law of the Lord. It is quite likely, then, that the concept of Wisdom singing her own praises, in both Sirach and Proverbs, is indebted to the Egyptian Isis hymns. Sirach, however, also draws heavily on biblical phraseology, and so adapts the aretalogy form for his own purpose.[28]

Sirach 24:1–2 gives the setting for Wisdom's speech. Verse 2 clearly locates her in the heavenly council (cf. Ps. 82:1), with the implication that she is imagined as a heavenly, angelic being. It is possible that "her people" in v. 1 refers to this heavenly assembly,[29] but it is more likely to refer to Israel, among whom Wisdom settles in vv. 8–12. She speaks, then, on both earthly and heavenly levels simultaneously.

Sirach 24:3–7 describes the origin and nature of Wisdom. The first-person pronoun (Greek *egō*) is especially characteristic of the Isis aretalogies, but is also used repeatedly in Proverbs 8. Even though the Hebrew text is not extant, the original Hebrew is clearly reflected in the idiom of v. 1, literally, "Wisdom praises her soul." The divine origin of Wisdom is also stressed in Prov. 8:21 and Sir. 1:1. The idea that Wisdom proceeds from the mouth of God may be suggested by Prov. 2:6 ("For the Lord gives wisdom; from his mouth come knowledge and understanding"). This motif lays the foundation for the identification of Wisdom with the *word* of God, which also proceeds from the mouth (cf. Isa. 45:23; 48:3; 25:11). The Greek word *logos,* however, had far-reaching connotations in Greek, especially Stoic, philosophy, where it referred to the rational spirit that pervades the universe. The fusion with Greek philosophical ideas becomes a major issue in the Wisdom of Solomon (cf. Wis. 9:2) and in the Jewish philosopher Philo.[30] The fusion of the Jewish wisdom tradition and Greek philosophy on this point is essential background to the use of the Logos/Word in John 1:1. The notion that Wisdom proceeds from the mouth also invites association with the spirit/breath of God (Greek *pneuma*), which had

26. C. Kayatz, *Studien zu Proverbien 1–9* (Neukirchen-Vluyn: Neukirchener Verlag, 1966) 76–119.

27. H. Conzelmann, "The Mother of Wisdom" in J. M. Robinson, ed., *The Future of Our Religious Past* (New York: Harper, 1971) 230–43.

28. See especially G. T. Sheppard, *Wisdom as a Hermeneutical Construct* (BZAW 151; Berlin: de Gruyter, 1980) 19–71.

29. So R. Smend, *Die Weisheit des Jesus Sirach* (Berlin: Reimer, 1906) 216.

30. B. Mack, *Logos und Sophia* (Göttingen: Vandenhoeck & Ruprecht, 1973).

similar philosophic connotations in Stoic philosophy (cf. the use of *pneuma* in Wis. 1:7). The association with the spirit is suggested here in the statement that Wisdom covered the earth like a mist, a phrase that recalls Gen. 1:2, although the allusion is not precise. The philosophical implications that emerge clearly in the later tradition are present in Sirach only in embryo, if at all, although he does betray a nodding acquaintance with Stoic thought in other passages.

The statement that Wisdom lived "in the heights" is suggested by Prov. 8:2, but here, unlike Proverbs, the heights should be understood as heavenly. What is most striking about the following verses is how language used of God in the Hebrew Bible is now applied to Wisdom. The pillar of cloud of the exodus (Exod. 13–21; 33:9–10) is also identified with the Logos by Philo (*Quis Heres,* 203–6), and Wisdom is given a key role in the exodus in Wisdom of Solomon 10. Here, however, it is removed from the exodus context, and it is associated with the primordial enthronement of Wisdom. While Prov. 8:27 says that Wisdom was there when God established the heavens, Sir. 24:5 has Wisdom circle the vault of heaven *alone,* just as God alone stretched out the heavens in Job 9:8. In Job 38:16 God challenges Job whether he "has walked in the recesses of the deep." Rule over the sea is a divine prerogative in the Hebrew Bible (e.g., Pss. 65:8; 89:10; 93:3–4). Wisdom is never said to be divine, but it appears to be the instrument of God's presence and agency. The quest for a resting place has been compared to the wandering of Israel in the wilderness.[31] Ben Sira, however, shows no interest in the historical process by which Israel settled in its land. Wisdom's quest for a resting place completes the process of creation. There is a sharp contrast here between Ben Sira's theology of wisdom and what we find in the apocalyptic literature. An enigmatic passage in *1 Enoch* 42:1–2 dramatically reverses Sirach's account: Wisdom found no place to dwell and so withdrew to heaven. In Sirach, she finds a home in Israel.

Sirach 24:8–12 describes how Wisdom settles in Israel. The command to settle there may be compared to the command given to Israel to seek out the designated place of worship in Deuteronomy 12.[32] But Sirach implies that Wisdom had settled in Israel before Israel settled in its land. So Wisdom ministered already in the tabernacle, the tent shrine of the wilderness (Exod. 25:8–9). Verse 9 suggests that the association of wisdom with Israel is primordial. The most apt parallel to this passage in Sirach is found in Deut. 32:8–9, which says that when God divided the nations among the "sons of God" he took Israel as is his own portion. Sirach has God exercise the election of Israel through Wisdom. The passage is remarkable for its cultic emphasis. Wisdom finds expression in the cult of the Jerusalem Temple. This idea is exceptional in the wisdom tradition, but it picks up a theme that was introduced briefly in Sir. 4:14,

---

31. Sheppard, *Wisdom as a Hermeneutical Construct,* 39.
32. Ibid., 42.

and it accords with Sirach's high esteem for the priesthood (cf. 44:6–26; 50:1–21). The notion of Wisdom making its dwelling in Israel is picked up, and radically altered, in the New Testament in John 1:14, where the Word becomes flesh and dwells with humankind. In the Christian Gospel, the Word is incarnated in one person. In the older Jewish wisdom text, wisdom is embodied in the book of the Torah and dwells in Israel.

Sirach 24:13–17 compares Wisdom to the luxuriant growth of various trees and plants. Such imagery is not found in Proverbs 8, but is familiar from other parts of the Hebrew Bible, notably Psalm 1, which compares the righteous man to a tree planted by water. The cedar of Lebanon (v. 13) is the most celebrated tree in the Bible (Ps. 92:12; Cant. 5:15). Sirach 24:15 changes the imagery to perfumes, and again evokes the cult by mentioning the incense in the tabernacle. Verses 19–22 complement the images of fertility with the notion of sustenance by comparing Wisdom to food and drink. In the New Testament, John 6:35 rings a change on the same imagery when Jesus says that whoever eats of him will never hunger and whoever drinks of him will never thirst.

Sirach 24:23 introduces a short commentary on the words of Wisdom, drawn in part from Deut. 33:4. The word "inheritance" picks up a motif from 24:8, 12. The fact that the verse has three cola is exceptional in Ben Sira, and has led to the suggestion that the first colon, which refers explicitly to the book and which is not paralleled in Deut. 33:4, is a secondary addition, influenced by Bar. 4:1.[33] Sirach was certainly familiar with the Torah in its written form (cf. 38:34), but this is the only passage that identifies wisdom specifically with the book. We have seen, however, that wisdom is associated with the commandments in several passages, so the assertion that wisdom *is* the book of the law may be regarded as the natural culmination of Sirach's rhetoric. We shall return below to consider how this identification should be understood.

Sirach proceeds to compare Wisdom/Torah to the four rivers associated with Eden in Genesis 2, and also to the Nile and the Jordan. Again, the context is creation. The comparison with foreign rivers may be significant. Wisdom was always an international phenomenon, and its character is not changed in that respect by the identification with the Jewish law. The reason that the first man did not know wisdom fully (v. 28) is not because it was not yet revealed.[34] Sirach 17:7 claims that when God created humanity he filled them with knowledge and understanding and gave them knowledge of good and evil. Besides, Sirach 24:28 insists that the last man is no wiser. No human being can fully comprehend Wisdom. In this respect, Sirach agrees with Job 28, which has a decidedly more negative view of human wisdom.

The chapter closes with a stanza in which Sirach compares himself to an

---

33. Rickenbacher, *Weisheitsperikopen*, 125–27.
34. *Pace* Skehan and DiLella, *The Wisdom of Ben Sira,* 337.

offshoot of the great river of Wisdom. He also compares his teaching to prophecy, without claiming to be a prophet. Sirach views prophecy as part of the textual lore to be studied by the sage (39:1). It is not apparent that he recognized any active prophets in his own time. The specific point of comparison with prophecy here is that it remains for future generations. Sirach concludes with a protestation of altruism. He has not labored for himself alone. The sage is a teacher, first and foremost. There is a similar emphasis on his educational role in the poem that concludes the book in chapter 51.

Sirach 51:13–28

Before we turn to the meaning of Sirach's identification of Wisdom with the book of the Torah, there is one further wisdom poem that requires comment. This is Sir. 51:13–28. We have already touched on some of the problems presented by the poem that concludes the book. Since it is found independently in the Psalms Scroll from Cave 11 at Qumran, it is not certain that it was composed by Ben Sira. Nonetheless, it has several points of contact with the rest of Sirach's book, for which it is in many ways a fitting conclusion. (For example, the reference to travel in v. 13 is paralleled in Sir. 34:9–13; 39:4.) It must at least be regarded as representative of the kind of wisdom circles in which Sirach moved. The poem exists in three recensions, one from Qumran (of which only vv. 11–17 and the last two words of the poem are preserved), one from the Cairo Geniza, and the Greek translation.

The editor of the Qumran text, J. A. Sanders, has argued for a highly erotic interpretation of the poem. According to Sanders, "Our song tells of the experience of a young man who, at the stage in life when he was maturing from childhood into manhood . . . took Wisdom, who had been his nurse and continued to be his teacher, as his mistress. He dedicated his normally developing passions and desires to the pleasures of life with Wisdom, and he did so unstintingly, without pause, without distraction, and without respite." He suggests that this was "a commendable manner of sublimation in celibacy and undoubtedly highly meaningful in every spiritual sense for the celibates at Qumran."[35] This interpretation has been widely criticized,[36] but even Sanders' critics recognize that love imagery is intrinsic to the poem.[37] In v. 14 the Qumran text reads "she came to me in her beauty." The Greek translation eliminated the erotic overtones. This is also true of v. 19, where both Hebrew texts (the Sirach text and the Psalms Scroll) have readings that indicate desire, but the Greek has "my soul grappled with her." Hebrew v. 19e, "my

35. Sanders, *The Psalms Scroll of Qumran Cave 11*, 84.
36. See Skehan and DiLella, *The Wisdom of Ben Sira*, 574–80.
37. T. Muraoka, "Sir 51:13–30: An Erotic Hymn to Wisdom?" *JSJ* 10 (1979) 166–78; C. Deutsch, "The Sirach 51 Acrostic: Confession and Exhortation," *ZAW* 94 (1982) 400–409.

hand opened her gate," may be an allusion to Cant. 5:4, and v. 21 ("my insides were aroused to seek her") recalls the same verse ("my inmost being yearned for him"). The erotic element in these verses is undeniable. There is no reason to suppose that the poem originated in, or was primarily intended for, a celibate community. It is simply a poetic way of describing the love and pursuit of wisdom that absorbed sages like Ben Sira as well as those of Qumran.

The poem ends with an advertisement for the house of instruction, emphasizing that instruction is free, and promising that "through me you will obtain silver and gold" (v. 28). But in order to succeed, one must submit to the yoke of wisdom, the image already found in Sir. 6:30. This image is used for the yoke of the law in the Mishnah (*Aboth* 3:5), but Sirach 51 does not mention the Torah.

Wisdom and the Law

Like Proverbs, Sirach envisages wisdom as more than a matter of instruction and practical advice. It is an ideal that informs one's whole approach to life, but it is also grounded in creation. As such it can be personified and made the object of love and desire. Sirach goes farther than Proverbs in attributing to wisdom roles that are reserved to God in the Hebrew Bible, thereby accenting its association with the divinity. But it is also something that human beings can acquire, and so it forms a bridge between humanity and God. It should be clear, however, that this understanding of wisdom is firmly rooted in the tradition represented by Proverbs, and this tradition provides the primary intellectual context for Sirach's teaching.

It is important to bear this in mind when we consider the identification of wisdom with the law. Sirach was not the first to make such an identification. It is adumbrated in Deut. 4:6, where Moses tells the Israelites that by observing the statutes diligently they will show their wisdom and discernment to the peoples, so that they will say: "Surely this is a wise and discerning people!" It is also implied in the book of Ezra, where the commissioning letter of Artaxerxes refers interchangeably to "the law of your God, which is in your hand" (7:14) and to "the wisdom of your God which is in your hand" (7:25). In these cases, however, the law is the primary category. At least from the time of Ezra onward, there was a tradition of education in the Torah, an activity associated with the Levites in Chronicles. To speak of the Torah as wisdom in this context does not imply that the instruction was at all related to the book of Proverbs or the teaching of the sages. When Sirach identifies wisdom and the law, however, he is in effect introducing the Torah of Moses into the wisdom school, and thereby attempting to combine two educational traditions.

It is often assumed that in doing so "Sirach was intentionally defining the values of the well-established wisdom tradition in terms of the Mosaic

covenant: that wisdom which is universally sought is in fact truly represented by and particularized in the Torah given by God through Moses."[38] This is a fair representation of what is meant by the identification of wisdom and Torah in the rabbinic tradition.[39] It is also supported by the parallel in the apocryphal book of Baruch, 3:9–4:4, which is strongly reminiscent of Job 28 ("Who has found her place, and who has entered her storehouses?").[40] Baruch's hymn begins with an echo of Deuteronomy: "Hear, O Israel, the commandments of life, give ear, and learn wisdom!" and, like Sirach, says that "she [wisdom] is the book of the commandments of God, and the law that endures forever" (Bar. 4:1). The poem ends with the confident assertion: "Happy are we, O Israel, for we know what is pleasing to God" (4:4), leaving no doubt that the identification of wisdom and the law is understood in an ethnocentric, particularist sense.[41] In the case of Sirach, however, it would be more accurate to say that the sage was defining the Mosaic covenant in terms of the well-established wisdom tradition.[42] He does not cite biblical laws directly; he draws on other sources of wisdom besides the Torah, and he grounds all wisdom, including the law, in the order of creation.

While the specific mention of the *book* in 24:23 may be secondary, the association of wisdom with the commandments is pervasive throughout the book.[43] The student who desires wisdom is told to keep the commandments (1:26) and to meditate at all times on the commandments (6:37). We are told that whoever holds to the law will obtain wisdom (15:1). The association is not restricted to the wisdom poems. In 19:20 we read that "all wisdom is fear of the Lord, and in all wisdom there is fulfillment of the law" (the passage is only extant in Greek).[44] The verse is ambiguous in principle. It could mean that the person who acquires wisdom, from whatever source, thereby fulfills the law, or it could mean that the fulfillment of the law constitutes wisdom, even if one draws on no other source. Verse 24 makes clear that Ben Sira intends the latter interpretation. Better a person with little understanding who keeps the law than a learned and clever person who violates it. Ben Sira would probably contend that a truly wise person will keep the law in any case, so there is no

---

38. E. P. Sanders, *Paul and Palestinian Judaism* (Philadelphia: Fortress, 1977) 331.

39. See G. F. Moore, *Judaism* (New York: Schocken, 1971) 1.265–69.

40. See the commentary by C. A. Moore, *Daniel, Esther, and Jeremiah: The Additions* (AB 44; New York: Doubleday, 1977) 295–304.

41. This passage is of uncertain provenance, but is clearly later than Sirach and most probably of Palestinian origin.

42. Cf. D. Winston, "Theodicy in Ben Sira and Stoic Philosophy," in R. Link-Salinger, ed., *Of Scholars, Savants, and Their Texts: Essays in Honor of Arthur Hyman* (New York: Lang, 1989) 240.

43. E. J. Schnabel, *Law and Wisdom from Ben Sira to Paul* (Tübingen: Mohr, 1985), 40–41, lists over fifty references to law or commandments in the Greek text.

44. On this passage see P. C. Beentjes, "'Full Wisdom Is Fear of the Lord.' Ben Sira 19,20–20,31: Context, Composition and Concept," *Estudios Bíblicos* 47 (1989) 27–45.

necessary conflict between the two interpretations. But Sirach recognizes that a person may have many of the attributes of wisdom without the fear of the Lord. Keen but dishonest shrewdness was always a problem in the wisdom tradition. The advice of Jonadab to Amnon in 2 Samuel 13, which leads to the rape of Tamar, is a case in point. Already in Gen. 3:1 the serpent is recognized as crafty. The Hellenistic age offered several models of wisdom to the people of a city like Jerusalem. When Sirach says in 19:23 that there is a resourcefulness that is detestable, it is difficult not to think of the tale of the Tobiads in Josephus, *Antiquities* 12, or of the enterprising ways in which Jason and Menelaus secured the High Priesthood shortly after the time of Ben Sira. The rejection of law and tradition is incompatible with wisdom. The same point is made in 33:2, where the Hebrew reads "One who hates the Torah will not be wise," and the Greek inverts: "A wise man will not hate the law."

But the Torah of Moses cannot be regarded as the only source or manifestation of wisdom in the teaching of Sirach. As Marböck has observed, there is only one passage in the book (32:14–24) in which the law is arguably the primary subject.[45] In all the passages we have considered above, the law is introduced in qualification of a passage that is primarily concerned with wisdom. Ben Sira remains a wisdom teacher, not an exegete or expositor of the Torah.

The relationship between Torah and wisdom in Ben Sira can be considered under two aspects, one practical, concerning the actual sources of wisdom that Ben Sira recommends to the student, and the other theological, concerning the relation of the law to creation.

The Sources of Wisdom

The relation between the Torah and wisdom can be clarified further by two passages in which Sirach comments on the sources from which wisdom is drawn. In Sir. 6:34–37 he recommends two ways to acquire wisdom. First, there is the way of apprenticeship: "Stand in the company of the elders. Who is wise? Attach yourself to such a one. Be ready to listen to every godly discourse, and let no wise proverbs escape you. If you see an intelligent person, rise early to visit him; let your foot wear out his doorstep." The invitation to the house of instruction in chapter 51 is in accordance with this approach. Second, there is the study of the Torah: "Reflect on the statutes of the Lord, and meditate at all times on his commandments." Such meditation is obviously important for Sirach, but it is not the only way to pursue wisdom.

The second passage that discusses the sources of wisdom is the description of the scribe in 38:34–39:5. He devotes himself to the law of the Most High,

---

45. Marböck, *Weisheit im Wandel*, 85. See also his "Gesetz und Weisheit: Zum Verständnis des Gesetzes bei Jesus Sira," *BZ* 20 (1976) 1–21.

but he also seeks out the wisdom of all the ancients. This includes prophecy, but also the sayings of the famous and the subtleties of proverbs and parables. The sage travels in foreign lands, so his wisdom is not restricted to the lore of his own people.

These passages are not necessarily a complete or accurate guide to the sources that Ben Sira himself actually used. We saw at the end of Chapter 2 that his sources probably included the gnomic poetry of the Greek Theognis and the wisdom teaching of the Egyptian Phibis. Wisdom, in principle, can be found anywhere. It is also true, however, that the Hebrew scriptures were a major source for Ben Sira. It has been claimed that he cites or alludes to all the books of the Hebrew Bible except Ruth, Ezra, Esther, and Daniel.[46] This claim is misleading, however. Most of the allusions occur in the Praise of the Fathers. Elsewhere there are frequent allusions to Proverbs, Genesis, and Deuteronomy. But many of the alleged allusions are loose, and may be coincidental. For example, when Sirach writes, "The rich person speaks and all are silent, his wisdom they extol to the clouds" (13:23), an allusion to Job 29:21 is often suggested: "For me they listened and waited; they were silent for my counsel." But the saying is a truism, and the allusion is accordingly doubtful. Sirach's dependence on the scriptures, then, is not as pervasive as is sometimes alleged. He ignores certain sections of the Law, particularly the cultic and dietary laws of Leviticus, and we have seen that there is some question as to whether he would insist on the dietary laws in the context of a banquet (31:16). Not all biblical laws are equally useful as illustrations of wisdom, and there remain other avenues to wisdom besides the Law of Moses. Moreover, when Sirach clearly draws on the scriptures, he does so with considerable freedom. He is not merely transmitting what he found in the Torah, but drawing from it to create his new work of wisdom.

Law and Creation

The question of the relation between the Torah and creation is posed in Sirach 24, where wisdom is identified with the law at the end of a poem that is largely concerned with creation. There are numerous scriptural allusions in this hymn, which might be taken to reflect the progress of Israel's history.[47] The pillar of cloud in 24:4 is an allusion to the exodus, the "holy tent" and Zion in v. 10 recall the story of David. But all of this is subsumed into the process of creation. Wisdom is said to encompass the vault of heaven (v. 5) *after* her throne was in the pillar of cloud. Moreover, the final establishment of wisdom

46. Skehan and DiLella, *The Wisdom of Ben Sira,* 41. See also J. L. Koole, "Die Bibel des Ben-Sira," *OTS* 14 (1965) 374–96.

47. Sheppard, *Wisdom as a Hermeneutical Construct,* 21–71.

in Israel is not associated here with Sinai, but with the transfer of the tabernacle to Zion (v. 10). The giving of the law to Moses is not singled out as a moment in this process. Even though wisdom eventually takes root in Israel, it first
holds sway over every people and nation. The initial revelation of wisdom is
in creation itself.[48]

In this understanding, the law revealed to Moses was implicit in creation
from the beginning, and so it is an actualization (the supreme actualization) of
the natural law.[49] The classic expression of this point of view in ancient Judaism is found two centuries later in Philo of Alexandria: "that the cosmos is
in harmony with the Law, and the Law with the world, and that the man who
observes the law is constituted thereby a loyal citizen of the cosmos, regulating his doings by the purpose and will of Nature, in accordance with which the
entire cosmos itself is also administered."[50] A similar understanding of the law
is implied in Rom. 1:20, although Paul evidently did not regard all details of
the Law as part of the law of creation.[51] It is easier to regard the Decalogue and
the social laws of the Pentateuch as embodiments of natural law than to claim
that the ritual laws of Leviticus are universally valid. In practice, Sirach ignores
most of the Levitical laws, but at no point does he suggest that any of the Torah
is obsolete. He does not consider problems that might arise from his identification of wisdom and the law, nor does he grapple with details of the biblical
stipulations. He is content to affirm in principle the general compatibility between the wisdom embedded in creation and proclaimed in Proverbs and the
wisdom of the book of Moses.

The relation of the law to creation is also an issue in one of the more obviously exegetical passages in Sirach, 16:24–17:20. The theme of creation is
touched on briefly in the preceding section (15:11–16:23), and this is picked
up in 16:26–30: "When the Lord created his works from the beginning, and in
making them, determined their boundaries . . ." Here the emphasis is on the order of nature, in a manner similar to Psalm 104 or, closer to the time of Sirach,
1 Enoch 2–5; 73–82.[52] There are several allusions to Genesis 1–3: from the *beginning* (Sir. 16:26); he filled it with *good* things (16:29); all living creatures
must return to the earth (16:30; 17:1; cf. Gen. 3:19).[53] Then in Sir. 17:1–10 the

48. The understanding of the Torah as *Schöpfungsordnung* is emphasized by E. Zenger, "Die
späte Weisheit und das Gesetz," in J. Maier, ed., *Literatur und Religion des Frühjudentums: Eine
Einführung* (Gütersloh: Mohn, 1973) 43–56.

49. Marböck, *Weisheit im Wandel*, 93–94. For a contrary interpretation see Schnabel, *Law and
Wisdom*, 89–92.

50. Philo, *De Opif.*, 3.

51. J. Barr, *Biblical Faith and Natural Theology* (Oxford: Clarendon, 1993) 51–52.

52. Argall, *1 Enoch and Sirach,* 158; J. D. Martin, "Ben Sira—A Child of His Time," in J. D.
Martin and P. R. Davies, eds., *A Word in Season: Essays in Honour of William McKane* (Sheffield:
JSOT Press, 1986) 148, adduces Jubilees 2 as a comparison here.

53. See further Sheppard, *Wisdom as a Hermeneutical Construct,* 72–82.

focus shifts to the creation of humanity, following the order of the biblical text.[54] Again, there are several echoes of Genesis. Human beings are granted authority and dominion over the other creatures. They are made in God's image, an idea that is explained by juxtaposition with the statement that they are given strength like that of God.[55] Characteristically, Sirach ignores the reference to male and female in Gen. 1:27.

The most surprising aspect of this meditation on Genesis is that it ignores the sin of Adam completely. (Sirach 25:24 ascribes the original sin to Eve: "From a woman sin had its beginning and because of her we all die," but this explanation of the origin of sin and death is anomalous, and unsupported by anything else in Ben Sira.) In chapter 17, death is not considered a punishment for sin. God limited human life from the start (17:2). Similarly in Sir. 40:1: "Hard work was created for everyone, and a heavy yoke is laid on the children of Adam," by the decree of the creator. (In contrast, the sin of Adam is recounted in full in Jubilees 3, a few decades later than Sirach.)[56] Sirach emphasizes that God endowed the first human beings with wisdom and understanding and showed them good and evil (Sir. 17:7; cf. Gen. 2:9). There is no suggestion, however, that they were forbidden to eat from the tree of the knowledge of good and evil. Instead, God "allotted to them the law of life. He established with them an eternal covenant, and revealed to them his decrees. Their eyes saw his glorious majesty, and their ears heard the glory of his voice" (Sir. 17:11–13). There is an unmistakable allusion here to the revelation at Sinai (cf. Exod. 19:16–19). The "law of life" in 17:11 must be identified as the Mosaic law. Sirach 45:5, in the context of the Praise of the Fathers, says that God gave Moses "the law of life and knowledge." The designation "law of life" is derived from Deut. 30:11–20, where Moses tells Israel, "I have set before you life and death, blessings and curses. Choose life." In the context of Sirach 17, the "eternal covenant" of v. 12 would also seem to refer to the Sinai covenant, although Sir. 44:18 uses this phrase for the covenant with Noah. (The Mosaic Torah is called "the law that endures forever" in Bar. 4:1.) It may be, however, that Sirach admits no distinction between the covenant of Noah and that of Moses, since he collapses the interval between the creation and the giving of the Torah. The implication of the passage is that the "law of life," and the attendant choice between life and death, was given to humanity from the

54. The same progression is found in a fragmentary paraphrase of Genesis and Exodus from Qumran, 4Q422.

55. L. Alonso Schökel, S.J., "The Vision of Man in Sirach 16:24–17:14," in J. G. Gammie et al., eds., *Israelite Wisdom: Theological and Literary Essays in Honor of Samuel Terrien* (Missoula, Mont.: Scholars, 1978) 235–60, observes that the creation of humankind is dealt with in the reverse of the biblical order: mortal condition, dominion over the earth, image of God.

56. G. Vermes, "Genesis 1–3 in Post-Biblical Hebrew and Aramaic Literature before the Mishnah," *JJS* 43 (1992) 221–25.

beginning. The same point is made explicitly in 15:14–17: "God made man [Adam] in the beginning and set him in the power of his inclination."[57] The passage continues: "Before each person are life and death, and whichever one chooses will be given." The sin of Adam, which Sirach does not even acknowledge, is no more significant than the sin of anyone else who breaks the law. Conversely, the law set before Adam and Eve was no different from the law given to Moses on Mount Sinai. The law of creation and the law of Sinai are one and the same. We shall find an interesting parallel to Ben Sira in this respect in a fragmentary wisdom text from Qumran, 4Q423.[58]

It is probably significant that the content of that law is summarized here in very general terms: "He said to them: 'Beware of all evil,' and he gave commandment to each of them concerning the neighbor" (17:14; Greek only). Marböck is probably right that we have here a form of the great commandment, to love God and the neighbor, even if the first part of it is expressed weakly.[59] The summation of the law under "two main heads" was typical of the Hellenistic synagogue, according to Philo (*De Spec. Leg.* 2.62–63), and Ben Sira may already show the beginnings of this tendency in Hellenistic Jerusalem.

In view of the cosmic character of wisdom in Ben Sira, Marböck has suggested that the identification with the law was suggested by Stoic philosophy, where the Logos, or cosmic spirit, could also be referred to as *Nomos,* or law.[60] Zeno, the founder of Stoicism, wrote that "the universal law [*nomos*], which is true reason [*logos*] permeating everything, is identical with Zeus, the guide of the arrangement of all things."[61] Cleanthes, in his famous hymn, addresses Zeus as "prime mover of nature, who with your law steer all things," and speaks of "God's universal law."[62] In Cicero's formulation, "Law is the highest reason, implanted in nature, which commands what ought to be done, and forbids the opposite."[63] No Jewish writer would simply identify wisdom with the deity, but we have seen that in Sirach 24 wisdom is described in language hitherto reserved for God. There are clear similarities between the Jewish concept of wisdom and the Stoic Logos, between the Jewish notion of a law given at creation and the Stoic law of

---

57. There is a doublet in the Hebrew text here; a redactor inserted "and set him in the power of his plunderer," presumably with reference to the devil.

58. See Chap. 7 below, and T. Elgvin, "Admonition Texts from Qumran Cave 4," in M. O. Wise et al., eds., *Methods of Investigation of the Dead Sea Scrolls and the Khirbet Qumran Site* (New York: New York Academy of Sciences, 1994) 179–94.

59. Marböck, *Weisheit im Wandel,* 88. Cf. Matt. 11:34–40; Mark 12:28–31; Luke 10:25–28.

60. Marböck, *Weisheit im Wandel,* 93–94. For Hellenistic concepts of *nomos,* see H. Kleinknecht, "Nomos," *TDNT* 4 (1967) 1032–33.

61. Diogenes Laertius 7.88; cf. Cicero, *De re publica* 3.33; *De legibus* 1.16, 18; 2.8.

62. A. A. Long and D. N. Sedley, *The Hellenistic Philosophers* (Cambridge: Cambridge Univ. Press, 1987) 1. 326–27; *SVF* 1.537.

63. Cicero, *De legibus* 1.18.

nature.[64] It is not impossible that the Stoic use of law as a cosmic principle facilitated the identification of the Torah with wisdom, since it provided a precedent for thinking of law in cosmic universal terms. The affinities, however, are far clearer in the Wisdom of Solomon and Philo than they are in Sirach, who still wrote in Hebrew and could scarcely have reproduced the technical terms of Stoicism if he had wished to do so.[65] Sirach does not develop the notion of the law as a cosmic principle. There are no poems describing how Torah came forth from the mouth of God or circled the heavens before creation.[66] The point of the identification is to accredit the Torah as a valid concretization (even as the ultimate concretization) of universal wisdom, not to attribute a cosmic role to the Torah itself.

The importance of *Nomos,* or law, in Stoic thought may have contributed to Sirach's identification of Torah and wisdom, but the analogy is not developed here. The more direct influence on Sirach probably lay in the growing authority of the Torah in the Judaism of his day. The Torah had already been associated with wisdom in Deuteronomy and the Psalms. It had been recognized and confirmed by the Seleucid king Antiochus III, through the mediation of Sirach's hero, the High Priest Simon. Sirach wanted to bring together the wisdom tradition inherited from Proverbs with the Torah-based wisdom of the Levitical teachers. The identification of wisdom and the Law symbolized that merger of educational traditions.

The identification of the wisdom implanted in creation with the law of Moses has important implications for the thinking of later Jewish and Christian tradition on the subject of natural law. In Sirach these notions are embryonic. They emerge full-fledged in Philo of Alexandria, who was thoroughly versed in Greek philosophy. The conceptualization of Wisdom in Greek philosophical categories is also a prominent feature of the other major apocryphal wisdom book, the Wisdom of Solomon, as we shall see in Chapter 11.

---

64. On the Stoic concept of natural law, see G. Watson, "The Natural Law and Stoicism," in A. A. Long, ed., *Problems in Stoicism* (London: Athlone, 1971) 216–38; G. Striker, "Origins of the Concept of Natural Law," in J. J. Cleary, ed., *Proceedings of the Boston Area Colloquium in Ancient Philosophy* (Lanham, Md.: University Press of America, 1987) 79–94; P. Van der Waert, "Zeno's Republic and the Origins of Natural Law," in idem, ed., *The Socratic Movement* (Ithaca, N.Y.: Cornell Univ. Press, 1994) 272–308; P. Mitsis, "Natural Law and Natural Right in Post-Aristotelian Philosophy: The Stoics and Their Critics," *ANRW* 2.36.7 (1994) 4812–50.

65. On the law of nature in Philo, see H. Koester, "Nomos Physeos: The Concept of Natural Law in Greek Thought," in J. Neusner, ed., *Religions in Antiquity: Essays in Memory of E. R. Goodenough* (Leiden: Brill, 1970) 521–41; R. A. Horsley, "The Law of Nature in Philo and Cicero," *HTR* 71 (1978) 35–39.

66. The preexistence of the Torah is later affirmed in rabbinic writings, e.g., *Sifre Deut.* 37; *b. Pesaḥ* 54a, *b. Ned.* 39b; *Bereshith Rabba* 1.1. See M. Küchler, *Frühjüdische Weisheitstraditionen* (OBO 26; Göttingen: Vandenhoeck & Ruprecht, 1979) 55; G. F. Moore, *Judaism* (New York: Schocken, 1971) 1.266–67; G. Boccaccini, "The Preexistence of the Torah: A Commonplace in Second Temple Judaism or a Later Rabbinic Development?" *Henoch* 17 (1995) 329–48.

Chapter 4.
Ben Sira's Ethics

Approximately half of Ben Sira's book is taken up with practical wisdom concerning relations with family members, women, rulers, servants, and friends and other aspects of social behavior. Most of these topics are touched on in Proverbs, but only a few (most notably relations with women) are developed at length. Sirach occasionally recommends that something be done "for the sake of the commandment" (Sir. 35:7, Greek, with reference to cultic offerings), and some of his concerns coincide with those of the Torah (e.g., honoring one's parents). In general, however, the content of Sirach's practical teaching is drawn from traditional wisdom, and much of it is paralleled in the late Egyptian Instruction of Phibis (Papyrus Insinger).

Sirach 7:18–36 touches on many of the relationships that are of greatest concern to Ben Sira. Here the sage gives advice on behavior toward friends, wives, slaves, cattle, sons, daughters, wives (again!), parents, priests, the poor, mourners, and the sick. None of the relationships is discussed in detail here, but several are discussed at greater length elsewhere. All the relationships are viewed in light of the interest of the patriarchal male, with the unfortunate consequence that wives, slaves, cattle, and children are all grouped together. (Compare the Tenth Commandment of the Decalogue, where wife and animals are both classified as possessions, Exod. 20:17; Deut. 5:21.) We shall return to the question of motivation after we have considered what Sirach has to say about the various relationships.

Household Relationships

The proper relations between members of a household was the subject of "unwritten laws" in Greek tradition, which are often reflected in the fifth-century tragedians and later rhetoricians.[1] This was a popular topic of Hellenis-

---

1. See R. Hirzel, *ΑΓΡΑΦΟΣ ΝΟΜΟΣ* (Leipzig: Teubner, 1900; reprint, Hildesheim: Olms, 1979); J.E. Crouch, *The Origin and Intention of the Colossian Haustafel* (Göttingen: Vandenhoeck & Ruprecht, 1972) 37–46.

tic philosophy.[2] It was addressed by Plato and Aristotle (in his *Politics*), and their views influenced Stoics (Ariston, Seneca), neo-Pythagoreans (Bryson, Callicratides), and Hellenistic Jews (Philo, *De Decal.* 165–67; *De Spec. Leg.* 2.225–27; Josephus, *Ag. Ap.* 2.198–210). A virtual manual on social relations can be found in the Jewish-Hellenistic Sayings (or Sentences) of Pseudo-Phocylides, 175–227.[3] The household codes become a feature of the later books of the New Testament.[4] Increased interest in the regulation of these relations can also be seen in the late Egyptian wisdom literature.[5] It is likely, then, that Sirach is reflecting to some degree his Hellenistic context. Relationships that were self-evident to earlier generations could no longer be taken for granted in the new political and social context, and philosophers and wisdom teachers felt the need to be more explicit in their instructions.

Honor of Parents

The command to honor father and mother is found already in the Decalogue. In Lev. 19:2 this commandment follows immediately on the command to be holy, before the injunction to keep the sabbath. It occupies a similarly prominent place in the moral instructions of Hellenistic Judaism. *Pseudo-Phocylides,* v. 8, tells the reader to "honor God first and foremost, and thereafter your parents." Josephus, in his summary of the Jewish law in *Ag. Ap.* 2.206 likewise links honor of God and parents.[6] The "unwritten laws" of Greek tradition likewise demand honor first for the gods and then for parents, and this injunction is ubiquitous in Greek gnomic poetry.[7] According to Diogenes Laertius (7.120) "the Stoics approve also of honouring parents and brothers in the second place, next after the gods." Ben Sira is the first Jewish writer to offer an extended discussion of the subject. In this, as in several other respects, he parallels the late Egyptian wisdom book of Phibis, found in Papyrus Insinger.[8] The primary discussion of honoring parents is found in Sir. 3:1–16.

---

2. D. L. Balch, *Let Wives Be Submissive: The Domestic Code in 1 Peter* (SBLMS 26; Chico, Calif.: Scholars, 1981) 21–59; "Household Codes," in D. E. Aune, ed., *Greco-Roman Literature and the New Testament: Selected Forms and Genres* (SBLSBS; Atlanta: Scholars, 1988) 25–50.

3. See below, Chap. 9.

4. Col. 3:18–4:1; Eph. 5:21–6:9; 1 Pet. 2:11–3:12; 1 Tim. 2:18–15; 5:1–2; 6:1–2; Titus 2:1–10; 3:1. See D. L. Balch, "Household Codes," *ABD* 3 (1992) 318–20.

5. M. Lichtheim, *Late Egyptian Wisdom Literature in the International Context* (Göttingen: Vandenhoeck & Ruprecht, 1983) 158–62.

6. For further references see P. W. van der Horst, *The Sentences of Pseudo-Phocylides* (Leiden: Brill, 1978) 116.

7. R. Bohlen, *Die Ehrung der Eltern bei Ben Sira* (Trier: Paulinus, 1991) 82–117.

8. Bohlen, *Die Ehrung der Eltern,* 138–39; J. T. Sanders, *Ben Sira and Demotic Wisdom* (SBLMS 28; Chico, Calif.: Scholars, 1983) 81.

In Sir. 7:27–28, the motivation for honoring one's parents is gratitude: "Remember that it was of your parents that you were born; how can you repay what they have given you?" The debt to one's parents, and especially to one's mother, is often noted in Egyptian wisdom literature.[9] In chapter 3, however, there is also a factor of self-interest: "Act accordingly, that you may be kept in safety" (3:1; Greek only). In this, Sirach is in accordance with the Decalogue (cf. Exod. 20:12; Deut. 5:16: "Honor your father and your mother, as the Lord your God commanded you, so that your days may be long and that it may go well with you in the land"). The logic of this suggestion is shown by Sir. 3:5: one who honors his parents can expect to be honored by his own children in turn. There is, then, a very practical reason for admonishing the son to be kind to the father who is old and senile (vv. 12–13)—the son may find himself in the same position one day. Sirach does not rely entirely on the reciprocity of human behavior, however. He also offers that one who honors his parents atones for sins (vv. 3, 14). This idea is in accordance with the tendency in Second Temple Judaism to associate atonement for sin with good works (cf. Dan. 4:24).

Throughout Sir. 3:1–16, mothers are honored equally with fathers, although the sage mentions the father more often. This is also true in the wisdom text 4QSapiential Work A from Qumran. The Qumran work also promises "length of days" to one who honors his parents, and exhorts children to honor parents "for the sake of their own honor."[10] Here again the honor of the parent is linked to the self-interest of the son, as his honor too is at stake. The theme of honor and shame will recur frequently as motivating factors in Ben Sira.

Wives

Wives receive considerably more attention than parents in Ben Sira.[11] Since all the instruction is from the male point of view, there is no discussion of husbands at all. The first comments in the book on the subject of wives consist of two verses in chapter 7 (vv. 19, 26), which warn against ill-advised divorce.[12]

---

9. Sanders, *Ben Sira and Demotic Wisdom*, 65.

10. 4Q416, frag. 2 iii 19; D. J. Harrington, "Wisdom at Qumran," in E. Ulrich and J. C. VanderKam, eds., *The Community of the Renewed Covenant* (Notre Dame, Ind.: Univ. of Notre Dame Press, 1994) 148; cf. Sir. 3:11.

11. M. Gilbert, "Ben Sira et la femme," *RTL* 7 (1976) 426–42; W. C. Trenchard, *Ben Sira's View of Women* (Chico, Calif.: Scholars, 1982). See also T. Ilan, *Jewish Women in Greco-Roman Palestine* (Tübingen: Mohr, 1995) passim.

12. See, however, the objections of Trenchard, *Ben Sira's View of Women*, 26–28, who points out that this is not the usual divorce terminology.

Divorce and Polygamy

Divorce appears to have been widespread in Second Temple Judaism. We have several divorce documents from Elephantine in Upper Egypt in the fifth century B.C.E. and from Naḥal Ḥever near the Dead Sea from the early second century C.E. Divorce was the prerogative of the husband. According to the Mishnah, "A woman is divorced irrespective of her will; a man divorces of his own accord" (*m. Yebam.* 14:1). The Jewish community at Elephantine was exceptional in allowing women to initiate divorce. There has been much debate as to whether women could initiate divorce in the Roman era, but the evidence is at best ambiguous.[13] Ben Sira cautions against gratuitous divorce, but he does not challenge the right to divorce as such. On the contrary, he declares emphatically in 25:25–26 that a wife who does not "go as you direct" (literally, "according to your hands") should be "cut off from your flesh" (thereby negating the union of flesh attributed to marriage in Genesis 2). Sirach thereby qualifies the advice not to divorce a good wife in Sir. 7:26. The Hebrew verb *krt*, cut off, gives rise to the standard word for divorce, *krytwt* (Deut. 24:1). Deuteronomy allowed that man could divorce his wife if she did not please him because he found something objectionable (*'erwat dābār*) about her. This text was invoked in a famous debate between the houses of Shammai and Hillel in the first century B.C.E. The Shammaites tried to restrict its application to cases of adultery. Hillel ruled that a man was justified in divorcing "even if she spoiled a dish for him" (*m. Giṭ.* 9:10). Rabbi Akiba went farther, saying that it sufficed if he found another woman who was fairer.[14] The Mishnah also provides that a woman could be sent away without her *ketubah* (the *mohar* or bride-price owed by the husband) if she transgressed the law of Moses or violated Jewish custom, even by going out with her hair unbound, spinning in the street, or speaking with a man (*m. Ketub.* 7:6). R. Tarfon also permitted this in the case of a scolding woman, who spoke inside her house so that a neighbor could hear. Ben Sira does not suggest that the dowry can be retained in this case, and indeed Sir. 25:21 implies that financial considerations should not determine matrimonial decisions. There is criticism of the practice of divorce in Mal. 2:13–16, but the text is difficult and obscure. Such criticism of divorce is exceptional in the Hebrew Bible. Challenges become more frequent after

13. J. J. Collins, "Marriage, Divorce, and Family in Second Temple Judaism," in L. Perdue et al., *Families in Ancient Israel* (Louisville: Westminster John Knox, 1997), 120–21; T. Ilan, "Notes and Observations on a Newly Published Divorce Bill from the Judaean Desert," *HTR* 89 (1996) 195–202. The primary piece of evidence is *Papyrus Se'elim* 13, which appears, prima facie, to refer to a bill of divorce given by the wife to the husband, although the interpretation is disputed.

14. L. J. Archer, *Her Price Is Beyond Rubies: The Jewish Woman in Graeco-Roman Palestine* (Sheffield: JSOT Press, 1990) 219.

Sirach's time, in the Dead Sea Scrolls (CD 4:20–5:2) and then in the New Testament (Mark 10:2).[15]

Sirach 7:26b is ambiguous. The Hebrew literally reads "Do not trust a woman who is hated." Skehan and DiLella render "Where there is ill-feeling, trust her not." The verb "to hate," however, is often used in the sense of "divorce" (e.g., at Elephantine). Ben Sira here is most probably advising against trusting a divorced woman, probably on the realistic ground that "hell hath no fury like a woman scorned." So the advice is: Be slow to divorce, but do not trust a woman you have sent away.

The issue of polygamy arises in connection with Sir. 25:14 ("Any suffering, but not suffering from those who hate! and any vengeance, but not the vengeance of enemies"). Smend suggested that "those who hate" and "enemies" in v. 14 are mistakes by the Greek translator.[16] (The Hebrew is not extant.) The original would have read feminine forms, "hated" (i.e., repudiated, divorced) and "rival," and so the woman's anger would arise from a situation of either polygamy or divorce. The subject of rivalry between women is explicit in 26:6 and 37:11. The jealousy of a wife for her rival raises the question of polygamy. While polygamy is never forbidden by biblical law and is still permitted by the Mishnah (*m. Ketub.* 10:5; *m. Ker.* 3:7), it has often been thought to have died out by the Hellenistic period, except for people in high places like the sons of Herod. This common assumption has been put in doubt, however, by the Babatha archive from the early second century C.E.[17] Babatha was an illiterate woman from the region of the Dead Sea, who was involved after her husband's death in a dispute with another woman who claimed to be his wife, and whose claim is not disputed. While Babatha was not a poor person, she lived in a remote area of Judea, and she was far removed from the social circumstances of the Herodian family. Polygamy may not have been as exceptional in the Hellenistic and Roman periods as was previously thought.

The Bad Wife

Sirach's most sustained treatment of marriage, or rather of the good and bad wife from the husband's point of view, is found in 25:13–26:27. The bad wife receives more than twice as many verses as the good. The first stanza (25:13–15) sets the tone by comparing a woman's anger to a snake's venom. The contentious or nagging wife is a common subject of complaint in folklore,

15. J. A. Fitzmyer, "The Matthean Divorce Texts and Some New Palestinian Evidence," in idem, *To Advance the Gospel: New Testament Studies* (New York: Crossroad, 1981) 79–111.

16. R. Smend, *Die Weisheit des Jesus Sirach erklärt* (Berlin: Reimer, 1906) 229.

17. N. Lewis, *The Documents from the Bar-Kokhba Period in the Cave of the Letters* (Jerusalem: Israel Exploration Society, 1989) 19–22.

and appears also in Proverbs (21:19; 25:24; 27:15). The Egyptian Instruction of Phibis refers to an otherwise unknown book "Faults of Women," so we should assume that passages such as this were a *topos* of Near Eastern wisdom in the Hellenistic period.[18]

Sirach's comparisons are more violent than those we find in Proverbs. Even if we make allowance for Semitic hyperbole, the statement that any iniquity is small compared to that of a woman (Sir. 25:19) is exceptional. This sentiment is developed further in 42:14, which says that the wickedness of a man is better than the goodness of a woman! There is an extreme quality to these sayings that cannot be dismissed as simply part of the culture of the time (Euripides, *Phoenician Women*, 805, refers to women as the wildest evil, but the playwright does not necessarily endorse the view).[19] The wish that a sinner's lot befall her may mean that a sinner should marry her. A similar idea is found in Qoh. 7:26: "I found more bitter than death the woman who is a trap. . . . One who pleases God escapes her, but the sinner is taken in by her." Sirach 25: 21–22 warns against marrying a woman for either her beauty or her wealth. The deceptiveness of beauty was noted in Prov. 31:30. The wealth of a wife might prevent a man from seeking divorce, since the woman could take her own possessions with her. The same sentiment is found in Ps.-Phoc., 199–200, and in Euripides, *Melannipus,* frag. 502.[20]

No verse in Ben Sira is more pregnant with implications or more controversial in a modern context than 25:24: "From a woman sin had its beginning, and because of her we all die." The notion that the "strange woman" can lead a man to sin and death is developed in Proverbs 7 and finds colorful development in 4Q184 ("The Wiles of the Wicked Woman"). The Qumran text has been adduced as a parallel to Sir. 25:24 because it says that "she is the start of all the ways of wickedness" (4Q184:8).[21] Ben Sira, however, is not concerned only with the strange or loose woman. (It is clear from the parallels with Proverbs 7 that this is the figure envisaged in the fragmentary 4Q184.) Sirach speaks not only of the death of the sinner, but why we *all* die. There can be no doubt that Sir. 25:24 represents an interpretation of Genesis 3, and that it is the earliest extant witness to the view that Eve was responsible for the introduction of sin and death.[22] Even the view that Adam was the source of sin and death emerges only in literature of the first century C.E. (Rom. 5:12–21; 1 Cor. 15:22; Wis. 2:23–24; *4 Ezra* 4:30; 7:116–21; *2 Bar.* 17:3; 48:45–46; 54:19; the

---

18. *Phibis* 8:10; Sanders, *Ben Sira and Demotic Wisdom,* 86.

19. Th. Middendorp, *Die Stellung Jesu Ben Siras zwischen Judentum und Hellenismus* (Leiden: Brill, 1973) 21.

20. Ibid.

21. J. Levison, "Is Eve to Blame? A Contextual Analysis of Sirach 25:24," *CBQ* 47 (1985) 622.

22. C. Meyers, *Discovering Eve* (New York: Oxford Univ. Press, 1988) 75. Levison argues that the woman in question is the bad wife.

latter, however, contends that Adam is only responsible for himself).[23] Sirach 17, which clearly reflects Genesis 2–3, contains no mention of an original sin. In the apocalyptic literature roughly contemporary with Sirach the origin of evil was attributed to fallen angels (*1 Enoch* 6–11) or to God's design at creation (1QS 3). Sirach elsewhere insists that death is simply the decree of the Lord, with no implication that it is a punishment (41:3–4). Nonetheless, this verse is extant in Hebrew and there is no reason to doubt its authenticity. Sirach's inconsistency on this matter shows only that his argumentation was influenced by the immediate context in which an issue is raised.

There is no precedent in Hebrew tradition for the view that woman is the source of all evil, but there is a clear Greek precedent in the story of Pandora's box.[24] It would be too simple to ascribe the misogynist aspects of Ben Sira's thought to Hellenistic influence. Pseudo-Phocylides represents a more heavily Hellenized form of Judaism but does not pick up these elements. There is undoubtedly Greek influence here, but Ben Sira's personality also played a part in his selective use of Greek culture.

In Sir. 26:9, Sirach turns to the subject of the adulterous wife: "The haughty stare betrays an unchaste wife; her eyelids give her away." Proverbs 6:25 describes the eyelashes of the adulterous woman as instruments of seduction. The point here is that a woman intent on adultery makes up her eyelids, while the faithful wife has no reason to do so. In *1 Enoch* 8:1 the art of making up the eyes is taught to human beings by the fallen angel Azazel. Sirach 26:12 recalls Ezek. 16:23–25 in its obscene portrayal of the promiscuous woman, but Sirach attributes this behavior not to an exceptional individual but to a daughter who is not held in check. Both Hebrew and Greek traditions had plenty of negative views about women, but Sirach pushes them to new extremes.[25]

There is a further treatise on adultery in 23:16–26. It is introduced by a numerical proverb, which presents the adulterer as the climactic sinner in a series: the person of unrestrained passion, the person guilty of incest, and the adulterer.

Sirach gives equal time to the adulterer and the adulteress. The discussion of the adulterer can be viewed as an extrapolation from Prov. 9:17, which refers

23. See J. R. Levison, *Portraits of Adam in Early Judaism from Sirach to 2 Baruch* (Sheffield: JSOT Press, 1988).

24. Hesiod, *Works and Days,* 42–105; Middendorp, *Die Stellung,* 21.

25. Sirach 26:19–27 is found in the second Greek recension and is not extant in Hebrew. It is usually regarded as secondary, but N. Peters, *Das Buch Jesus Sirach oder Ecclesiasticus* (Münster: Aschendorff, 1913) 218 and Skehan and DiLella, *The Wisdom of Ben Sira,* 351 regard the verses as authentic. They add little to the foregoing discussion. Verse 26c, d repeats 26:1a,b. The advice in vv. 19–22 is closely parallel to Prov. 5:7–14. The concern in sexual activity is to propagate a line of offspring. Relations with a prostitute are wasted. Verse 23 recapitulates 25:19 and 26:3. Some of the analogies in this passage are very crude: a prostitute is like spittle and a headstrong wife is like a dog.

to the sweetness of stolen water and bread eaten in secret. Sirach speaks of sweet bread and dwells at length on the issue of secrecy. (Compare 16:17–23, on the futility of hiding from the Lord.)

Sirach does not specify how the adulterer will be punished. Proverbs implies that the adulterer will be beaten up by the wronged husband and publicly disgraced, and that he will have to pay a heavy fine (Prov. 6:31–35: "sevenfold," "all the goods of his house"). Sirach evidently envisages public disgrace. Neither Proverbs nor Sirach make any mention of the death penalty for the adulterer, prescribed by biblical law (Lev. 20:10; Deut. 22:22).

The treatment of the adulteress differs from that of the adulterer in several respects. Her sin is said to be threefold—the offense against God and against her husband and the fact that she produced children by another man. Sirach implies that the adulterer sins against God (v. 18), although he does not say so directly. There is no implication, however, that the adulterer sins against his wife. The imbalance in this regard reflects the common ancient tendency to group the wife with the possessions of her husband. The sin against the husband is that she has violated his rights and his honor. The production of children by adultery is considered a separate offense. Sirach 23:23 does not imply that the woman's adultery was prompted by the desire to have a child.[26] Neither is there any reason to think that the woman acts out of economic necessity.[27] If an adulterous affair ended in pregnancy, the woman would have little choice but to try to pass the child off as her husband's offspring. One of the main reasons for prohibiting adultery was to guarantee the legitimacy of a man's children. At issue here is the right of inheritance, and so the adultery has economic consequences, which are deemed to constitute a separate, third, offense.

While the adulterer will be punished in the streets of the city, presumably by the cuckolded husband, the adulteress is led to the assembly. Sirach is not explicit as to what action the assembly may take. The story of Susanna, which may be roughly contemporary, comes to mind. Susanna is sentenced to death, in accordance with the biblical punishment for adultery (Lev. 20:10; Deut. 22:22). The death sentence is also proposed for the woman taken in adultery in John 8. Susanna is also ordered to be uncovered, and in the Old Greek version the implication is that she was stripped naked.[28] This was also part of the punishment of an adulterous woman in Hos. 2:3, 10 and Ezek. 16:37–39. The Mishnah stipulated that a priest should lay bare the bosom of the adulteress,

26. *Pace* Trenchard, *Ben Sira's View of Women*, 99.
27. *Pace* C. V. Camp, "Understanding Patriarchy: Women in Second Century Jerusalem through the Eyes of Ben Sira," in A. J. Levine, ed., *"Women like This": New Perspectives on Women in the Greco-Roman World* (Atlanta: Scholars, 1991) 27–28.
28. J. J. Collins, *Daniel* (Minneapolis: Fortress, 1993) 431; the Theodotion version adds a gloss to indicate that she was only unveiled.

but only if it was not comely (*m. Soṭa* 1.5). It is very unlikely, however, that these stories reflect actual practice in the Hellenistic or Roman periods. Already in the Elephantine papyri (5th century B.C.E.), the punishment for adultery is divorce, with loss of some property rights.

The extension of punishment to the children recalls Ezra 10:44, where the foreign wives were sent away with their children. Ben Sira, however, seems to indicate a divine punishment rather than a human one. His contention is that the children of an adulteress will not prosper. A similar idea is found in Wis. 3:16–19. Sirach does not provide any human mechanism to ensure that this punishment will be effected.

Sirach 23:27 brings his discussion of adultery to a conclusion by making the disgrace of the adulteress into a moral lesson that it is better to keep the Law. It is noteworthy that his discussion of the punishment of the adulteress does not call for literal fulfillment of the Law. Sirach's concern is with conformity to the tradition in principle, with the attitude of reverence, rather than with legal details.

The Good Wife

Sirach 26:1–4 turns briefly to the joys of a good wife. She is considered solely in terms of her effect on her husband. The point of this stanza is the converse of 25:19. As the sinner deserves a bad wife, the one who fears the Lord deserves a good one. The good wife here seems to exist to reward the deserving man rather than having a value in her own right. The value of a good wife for a wise man is also noted in the late Egyptian Instruction of Phibis 8:5.[29] Sirach 26:13–18 is more explicit than earlier passages on the attributes of the good wife. Although she puts flesh on her husband's bones, this is not the capable wife of Proverbs 31, who can buy a field and deal with merchants. Sirach's ideal wife is a homebody, characterized by silence, modesty, and chastity, virtues also recommended by Aristotle.[30] In part, the difference in perspective reflects the transition from a rural to an urban culture. The wife of a scribe in Jerusalem has no occasion to buy a field, and her labor is not needed outside the house. Instead she is portrayed as an ornament in his home. This is the only passage where Ben Sira shows an appreciation of physical beauty (contrast 25:21: "Do not be ensnared by a woman's beauty"). It is characteristic of ancient Near Eastern love poetry to single out parts of the body for praise.[31] Examples can be found in Cant. 4:1–7; 1QApGen 20:2–7. The de-

---

29. Sanders, *Ben Sira and Demotic Wisdom*, 86.
30. Aristotle, *Politics* 1260a; Balch, *Let Wives Be Submissive*, 35.
31. This kind of poetry is often referred to by the Arabic term waṣf. See A. Bloch and C. Bloch, *The Song of Songs* (New York: Random House, 1995) 15; M. V. Fox, *The Song of Songs and the Ancient Egyptian Love Songs* (Madison, Wis.: Univ. of Wisconsin Press, 1985).

scription of Sarah in the latter passage comments on the perfection of her legs. Ben Sira differs from the other passages, however, in drawing his analogies from the furnishings of the Temple, and thereby projecting a sense of admiration rather than physical desire.

Things that make a woman attractive are also the subject of 36:27–28: beauty, kindness and humility. The verses that follow digress on the advisability of marriage. Sirach borrows the phrase of Gen. 2:18, 20 to refer to the help a wife can give her husband. Moreover, she can give him a "nest" and prevent him from wandering. Sirach implies that the unattached man cannot be trusted (cf. the language applied to Cain in Gen. 4:12). A wife is necessary for social respectability. Most revealing of Sirach's attitude on marriage, however, is the statement that a wife is a man's best possession (v. 29). Even while Sirach expresses the high value he places on a wife, he still regards her as a possession of her husband. The patriarchal quality of this statement is not negated by the fact that the language recalls Prov. 8:22, which says that the Lord acquired (or created, *qānāh*) wisdom as the beginning of his way.

Daughters

The females whose behavior weighed most heavily on Sirach, however, were daughters:

> A daughter is a secret anxiety to her father, and worry over her robs him of sleep; when she is young, for fear she may not marry, or if married, for fear she may be repudiated; while a virgin, for fear she may be seduced and become pregnant in her father's house; or having a husband, for fear she may go astray, or though married, for fear she may be barren. Keep strict watch over a headstrong daughter, or she may make you a laughingstock to your enemies. . . . See that there is no lattice in her room, no spot that overlooks the approaches to the house. Do not let her parade her beauty before any man or spend her time among married women.
>
> (Sir. 42:9–12)

Ben Sira's anxiety is extreme, and must be seen in the context of the general anxiety about life that pervades his book (cf. Sir. 40:1–2: "A heavy yoke is laid on the children of Adam. . . . Perplexities and fear of heart are theirs, and anxious thought of the day of their death"). Nonetheless, he reflects certain social and economic realities that prevailed throughout the Second Temple period. Fathers had to provide dowries for their daughters, but no longer received any benefit from the *mohar,* or bride-price, in this period. If there were no sons and a daughter should inherit, this resulted in the transference of the inheritance from the father's house to that of her husband. If the woman were divorced, the father had to take her in. The economic considerations, however,

are minor in Ben Sira's view in comparison to the risk of shame. A headstrong daughter can make her father "a byword in the city and the assembly of the people, and put you to shame in public gatherings" (Sir. 42:11). Hence the pre-occupation with virginity before marriage, and the demand that daughters be carefully secluded.

Concern for the virginity of unmarried girls is ubiquitous in the ancient world, but especially in Hellenistic Judaism. The draconian laws of the Pentateuch that required the death penalty for a woman who was found not to be a virgin at marriage were not enforced, but a woman who was not a virgin would be difficult to give in marriage. Pseudo-Phocylides (215–16) advises that virgins be locked up and not seen outside the house until their wedding day.[32] Ben Sira warns against a lattice, lest the young woman even be seen. The warning against her spending time in the company of married women (42:12) probably reflects a fear that the virgin may become aware of her sexuality.[33]

There is abundant evidence that sons were valued more highly than daughters in ancient Judaism. Ben Sira stands at or near the negative extreme of his society's attitude toward women, but his pronouncement that "a daughter is born to his [the father's] loss" (Sir. 22:3) cannot be dismissed as his personal eccentricity. Similar sentiments are found in the rabbinic literature: "Without both male and female children the world could not exist, but blessed is he whose children are male, and woe to him whose children are female" (*B. Bat.* 16b). While daughters are not always viewed so negatively, the preference for sons was commonplace in the ancient Near East. Compare Ahikar 1:4–5: "But I ask of thee, O God, that I may have a male child, so that when I shall die, he may cast dust on my eyes" (cf. Tob. 6:15).

But while some of Ben Sira's concerns reflect the society in which he lived, his anxiety is extreme. The economic and social realities of raising a daughter in Ben Sira's time do not seem greatly different from those of earlier centuries. Yet no earlier Jewish writer displays such deep anxiety on the subject. Daughters are never discussed as an isolated topic in the Hebrew Bible. The metaphorical use of daughter as a term of endearment for Zion or Israel contrasts sharply with Sirach's recommendation "Do not let your face shine upon them" (7:24). Sirach was scarcely typical of the Hellenistic period either. The roughly contemporary book of Tobit paints a much more affectionate picture of family life. Few parents had as much reason for anxiety as Raguel and Edna, parents of Sarah, the eventual bride of Tobias, whose first seven husbands had died on their wedding night! Yet the concern of the parents is simply that "the Lord of heaven grant you joy in place of your sorrow" (Tob. 7:16).

32. See further Philo, *De Spec. Leg.* 3.169; *In Flacc.* 89; 2 Macc. 3:19; 3 Macc. 1:18; 4 Macc. 18:7; Archer, *Her Price Is Beyond Rubies,* 113–15.
33. Trenchard, *Ben Sira's View of Women,* 158.

Sons

Ben Sira has less to say on the subject of sons. His advice is well summed up in 7:23: "Do you have sons? Discipline them, and make them obedient from their youth." The method of discipline seems to have relied heavily on corporal punishment: "Lashes and discipline are at all times wisdom," and "He who loves his son will whip him often, so that he may rejoice at the way he turns out" (Sir. 30:1). Pseudo-Phocylides, writing in the Diaspora, takes a gentler approach: "Be not harsh with your children but be gentle" (v. 207), but Sirach will have none of this: "Do not laugh with him, or you will have sorrow with him, and in the end you will gnash your teeth. Give him no freedom in his youth, and do not ignore his errors. Bow down his neck in his youth and beat his sides while he is young, or else he will become stubborn and disobey you, and you will have sorrow of soul from him" (30:10–12). Here again, considerations of reputation and shame play a part: "It is a disgrace to be the father of an undisciplined son" (22:3).

The patriarchal perspective of Sirach's thought is as painfully obvious in his discussion of sons as it is in his discussion of daughters. The goal is the production of a son in the father's image and likeness: "When the father dies he will not seem to be dead, for he has left behind him one like himself" (30:4). There is little sense that the son is an individual in his own right. There is no cult of the individual in Sirach. Rather, the goal is the conformity of the individual to the tradition, as it is transmitted from father to son, with only subservient roles for women as wives and daughters.

Slaves

The existence of slaves was taken for granted throughout the ancient Mediterranean world.[34] Ben Sira's advice on their treatment vacillates. In 33:25–30, he advocates harsh treatment, comparing the slave to a beast of burden. A slave who is underworked will seek liberty, and idleness creates mischief. This advice is in line with Prov. 29:19, 21 and is also paralleled in Phibis.[35] This advice, however, is severely qualified, if not undercut, by Sir. 33:30c, d, which warns against overbearing behavior toward anyone. Here Sirach is probably influenced by the Torah, which granted slaves limited but important rights (Exod. 21:1–11, 20–21, 26–27; Lev. 25:39–55; Deut. 15:12–18; 23:16–17). Leviticus 25:39, 46 permits the acquisition of Gentiles as slaves but says that Israelites who are forced into debt slavery should be treated as hired

---

34. For a recent overview: J. A. Harrill, *The Manumission of Slaves in Early Christianity* (Tübingen: Mohr, 1995) 11–67.
35. Papyrus Insinger 14:6–11; Sanders, *Ben Sira and Demotic Wisdom*, 95.

servants. The Hellenistic Jewish Ps.-Phoc. 223–26 also advocates humane treatment for slaves, as Sirach does also in 7:20–21 and 33:31. Finally Ben Sira takes his characteristic line of self-interest. A slave who is ill-treated will run away. According to Deut. 23:15–16, it was forbidden to return a runaway slave to the owner. The need to take good care of a slave is especially acute if there is only one. It seems then that Ben Sira is transmitting a traditional hard line on the treatment of slaves, but recognizes that gentler treatment is sometimes more practical.

It has been suggested that 7:21b ("Do not withhold from him his freedom") is an allusion to the biblical law in Exod. 21:2 that Hebrew slaves should be released after six years,[36] but Sirach recommends freedom only for a wise slave. (Compare Paul's plea for Onesimus in the letter to Philemon.)

Friendship

The subject of friendship is one to which Ben Sira returns repeatedly (6:5–17; 9:10–16; 11:29–12:18; 22:19–26; 36:23–37:15; 37:16–31).[37] Friends should be chosen carefully and trusted slowly, but a true friend is invaluable. The theme of true and false friendship is sounded briefly in Prov. 18:24 (cf. Prov. 19:4, 7). Job complains that his friends have failed him (7:14–23; 19:19–22). The closest parallels to Ben Sira, however, are found in the Greek gnomic poet Theognis and in the late Egyptian Instruction of Phibis.[38] Phibis is especially close to Sirach in warning against premature trust. Compare Sirach 6:13 ("Keep away from your enemies and be on guard with your friends") and Theognis 575: "It is my friends that betray me, for I can shun my enemy." Theognis also says that the trusty friend outweighs gold and silver (cf. Sir. 6:15). Sirach strikes his own distinctive note, however, when he says that one who fears the Lord should seek a friend like himself.

The theme of selective friendship is repeated in 9:14–16: "As much as you can, aim to know your neighbors, and consult with the wise. Let your conversation be with intelligent people and let all your discussion be about the law of the Most High. Let the righteous be your dinner companions and let your glory be in the fear of the Lord." This restrictive view of friendship is not sustained throughout the book, however. The advice on behavior at banquets in 32:1–9 is much more worldly in character. But the need for selectivity finds even stronger expression in 11:29–12:18. What is most striking about this passage, however, is the vigorous insistence that one should only do good to the just and give no comfort to the wicked (12:2–3), and even that God hates sinners (12:6). We are reminded of the more extreme view of the Qumran

36. Skehan and DiLella, *The Wisdom of Ben Sira,* 205.
37. See the essays in F. V. Reiterer, ed., *Freundschaft bei Ben Sira* (Berlin: de Gruyter, 1996).
38. Sanders, *Ben Sira and Demotic Wisdom,* 30–31; 64–65; 70–71.

Community Rule, where those who enter the covenant commit themselves to hate all the sons of darkness, with the implication that God detests them (1QS 1:4, 10). A similar proverb is found in the midrash *Qoh. Rab.* 5. 8f. §5 (Soncino edition): "Do no good to an evil person and harm will not come to you; for if you do good to an evil person, you have done wrong." The contrast with the teaching of Jesus in the New Testament is obvious (Matt. 5:43–48; Luke 6:27–28, 32–36). But the idea that God hates sinners is also exceptional in Jewish literature. Contrast Wis. 11:24: "For you love all things that exist, and detest none of the things that you have made, for you would not have made anything if you had hated it." This idea is illustrated in a colorful way in *T. Abr.* 10:14, where God tells the archangel Michael: "Abraham has not sinned and has no mercy on sinners. But I made the world, and I do not want to destroy any one of them." Ben Sira presumably could not claim to be as innocent of sin as Abraham was.

There is also a more positive side to friendship in Sirach. In 22:23 we are told to "gain the trust of your neighbor in his poverty, so that you may rejoice with him in his prosperity. Stand by him in time of distress, so that you may share with him in his inheritance." Even here, there is a strong note of self-interest, but we should remember that an enlightened self-interest also underlies the principle of the Golden Rule, "As you would that men should do to you, do you also to them" (Luke 6:31). The wisdom of loyalty to friends is reiterated in Sirach's last pronouncement on the subject in 37:1–6.

The Basis for Ethics in Sirach

The ethical teaching of Ben Sira has often been judged harshly by modern scholars. Writing in the Victorian era, Alfred Edersheim dismissed it as "a most unpleasant mixture of selfishness and Eastern world-wisdom with religiousness."[39] While this formulation is somewhat extreme, the charge of selfishness, arising from eudaemonism and utilitarianism, runs like a refrain through the modern literature. H. M. Hughes concluded that "the ethical teaching of Sirach is somewhat individualistic and self-centred. . . . He gives many evidences of a humane feeling, but none of a spirit of genuine altruism."[40] D. Michaelis condemns Sirach for hardening faith into ideology, by losing the sense of a personal relationship with God.[41] E. G. Bauckmann claims that Sirach divorces the Law from its relationship to the exodus, and makes it into a mechanism for the human control of life, in the manner of the older wisdom

39. A. Edersheim, "Ecclesiasticus," in H. Wace, ed., *The Holy Bible According to the Authorised Version: Apocrypha* (London: Muray, 1888) 2.17.

40. H. M. Hughes, *The Ethics of Jewish Apocryphal Literature* (London: Culley, 1910) 39.

41. D. Michaelis, "Das Buch Jesus Sirach als typischer Ausdruck für das Gottesverhältnis des nachalttestamentlichen Menschen," *TLZ* 83 (1958) 601–8.

teaching.[42] Only a few authors evaluate Sirach more positively. Otto Kaiser emphasizes the fundamental place of the fear of the Lord.[43] In this perspective, wisdom is the humble submission to the will of God. The Torah provides a discipline by which human beings are brought into conformity with the order of creation, which is itself the expression of the divine will. E. P. Sanders, who also notes the importance of "the fear of the Lord," regards Sirach as an exponent of "covenantal nomism," who "presupposed the biblical view of the election of Israel and wrote within the context of the doctrine of the covenant."[44]

There can be no dispute that Sirach's teaching is eudaemonistic (in the sense that its goal, at least in part, is a good and happy life) and utilitarian. In this respect it stands fully in the tradition of Proverbs, which also has a strong pragmatic emphasis on results rather than on intentions. It should be remembered, however, that the covenantal relationship also appealed strongly to enlightened self-interest. The observance of the Law would result in blessing, while disobedience would bring about a curse.[45] Even the Golden Rule, the centerpiece of New Testament ethics, is not simply an appeal to altruism. Doing to others as you would wish them to do to you is also a pragmatic way to ensure one's own interest.[46] This is essentially the logic of Sirach's advice on honoring parents. The children do not hope for further benefit from the parents in their old age, but set a precedent for their own children, from which they may benefit in due time.

Ben Sira's utilitarianism sometimes leads to enlightened advice, as when he counsels humane treatment of slaves. But Near Eastern wisdom teachers were not moral philosophers, and were not given to original thinking. Sirach too is generally content to pass along the tradition he inherited, modified by the conventions and prejudices of his own time. Established institutions such as divorce and slavery are never called into question, and the differences between rich and poor are accepted as inevitable. Moreover, Sirach's utilitarian thought is limited to the perspective of the patriarchal male. There is virtually no empathy with wives or daughters, slaves, or even sons.

The traditional eudaemonism of Near Eastern wisdom literature is overshadowed in Sirach by his great concern for honor and shame, which goes far

---

42. E. G. Bauckmann, "Die Proverbien und die Sprüche des Jesus Sirach: Eine Untersuchung zum Strukturwandel der israelitischen Weisheitslehre," *ZAW* 72 (1960) 33–63.

43. O. Kaiser, "Die Begründung der Sittlichkeit im Buche Jesus Sirach, *ZTK* 55 (1958) 51–63 = *Der Mensch unter dem Schicksal* (Berlin: de Gruyter, 1985) 63–90; compare J. Haspecker, *Gottesfurcht bei Jesus Sirach* (Rome: Pontifical Biblical Institute, 1967).

44. E. P. Sanders, *Paul and Palestinian Judaism* (Philadelphia: Fortress, 1977) 330–31.

45. J. J. Collins, "The Biblical Vision of the Common Good," in O. F. Williams and J. W. Houck, eds., *The Common Good and U. S. Capitalism* (Lanham, Md.: University Press of America, 1987) 50–69.

46. For the history of interpretation, see H. D. Betz, *The Sermon on the Mount* (Minneapolis: Fortress, 1995) 508–19.

beyond anything that we find in the Hebrew tradition. It finds its most egregious expression in his worry about daughters, lest a daughter "make you a laughingstock to your enemies, a byword in the city and the assembly of the people, and put you to shame in public gatherings" (42:11). But as J. T. Sanders observed, "For Ben Sira shame lurked every where."[47] It determines the relationships of rich and poor, and the need to behave properly at banquets. It is acutely present in anything that touches on sexuality: "Do not give yourself to a woman and let her trample down your strength" (9:2).[48] This concern with honor and shame intensifies the impression of self-centeredness in Sirach's teaching. The sage is too anxious about his own honor to take thought of the way other people may be affected. To a great degree, this anxiety is culturally determined and induced.

Sirach is not entirely a slave to convention, and he makes some attempt to criticize the cultural assumptions of his day. It should be noted that the pursuit of honor was sometimes criticized by Hellenistic philosophers, especially Epicureans and Cynics.[49] Sirach recognizes that "there is a shame that leads to sin, and there is a shame that is glory and favor" (4:21), and he returns to this contrast several times throughout the book (10:19–11:6; 20:21–23) The most elaborate discussion is in 41:14–42:8, a section with the title "Instruction about Shame" in Hebrew MS B. There is no place for false modesty with respect to wisdom (41:14–15, repeated from 20:30–31; cf. Mark 4:21–25; Luke 8:16–19). Not surprisingly, the Torah heads the list of things of which one should not be ashamed. But Sirach also recommends keeping accounts in dealings with a companion, strict discipline for children and slaves, and even locking up an unreliable wife. Sirach here inclines to the practical, hardheaded side of traditional wisdom, which has little place for trust (cf. 6:7; 11:29–12:18). While Sirach diverges from Hellenistic mores in his insistence on the honor of the Torah, he retains a quite conventional code of patriarchal control.

In Hellenistic culture, fear of shame was often cited as a motivation for bold action.[50] In Sirach, however, it serves to reinforce what J. T. Sanders has called his ethics of caution. Sirach 32:19–24 provides a typically cautious piece of advice: "Do nothing without deliberation, but when you have acted, do not regret it. . . . Do not trust the road for bandits, and take care for your future. In all your ways, mind yourself, for whoever does this keeps the commandment. The one who keeps the Law preserves himself, and whoever trusts in the Lord shall not be put to shame." The cautious, defensive tone of a passage like this is closer to the late Egyptian wisdom texts than to the Hellenistic philosophers.

---

47. J. T. Sanders, "Ben Sira's Ethics of Caution," *HUCA* 50 (1979) 99.

48. See Camp, "Understanding Patriarchy," 14–23, who emphasizes the sage's anxiety about control.

49. H. Moxnes, "Honor and Shame," *BTB* 23 (1993) 167–76.

50. E.g., Plato, *Laws,* 647B; J. T. Sanders, "Ben Sira's Ethic of Caution," 97.

More immediately, Sirach's ethic is informed by the ideal of the fear of the Lord, which required a humble submissive attitude toward the tradition. The virtue of humility was quite alien to the Greek sense of honor, but is deeply ingrained in Near Eastern wisdom. In part, this too was a defensive measure, to avoid embarrassment: "Do not be forward, or you may be rebuffed" (Sir. 13:10; cf. Prov. 25:6–7; Luke 14:7–11). It also reflects the dependent social position of the sage, who must look to others for approval. Yet Sirach also warns against false modesty: "My son, honor yourself with humility and give yourself the esteem you deserve. Who will acquit those who condemn themselves? And who will honor those who discredit themselves?" (Sir. 10:28).

The Shadow of Death

There is another factor that plays a significant role in Ben Sira's ethical argumentation. Like his near-contemporary Qoheleth, and unlike the older Hebrew tradition, Sirach is haunted by the shadow of death: "A heavy yoke is laid on the children of Adam. . . . Perplexities and fear of heart are theirs and anxious thought of the day of their death" (40:1–2; cf. 41:1–4). This prospect influences ethical behavior in a number of ways. First, it undermines all human pride: "How can dust and ashes be proud? Even in life the human body decays" (10:9). While this in no way eliminates the fear of shame, it sets a distinct limit to the honor and glory that one may hope to attain. Second, the common lot of humanity engenders sympathy. In 7:36 Sirach concludes an exhortation to charity with the injunction: "In all you do remember the end of your life and then you will never sin." In 28:6 the same remembrance is invoked as a reason to set enmity aside and not bear grudges. Admittedly, Sirach's reasoning here is not simply an appeal to sympathy. He lives not only in the shadow of death but also under the shadow of divine judgment. The person who harbors wrath against another human being cannot expect forgiveness from the Lord. The prospect of divine retribution is also invoked as a reason for charity to the poor in 4:1–6: "If in bitterness of soul some should curse you, their creator will hear their prayer."

The nature of the retribution that Sirach expects is not entirely clear. He has no place for judgment after death, but he apparently thinks of the day of death as a day of judgment: "For it is easy for the Lord on the day of death to reward individuals according to their conduct. An hour's misery makes one forget past delights, and at the close of one's life one's deeds are revealed. Call no one happy before his death; by how he ends, a person becomes known" (11:26–8; cf. 18:24). The sentiment that one should call no one happy before the day of his death is commonplace in Greek tragedy.[51] The point in the tragedies is that anything can go wrong up to that point. Sirach's point is that death itself can be the occasion of divine judgment. The question of judgment bears on the is-

sue of theodicy, which we will consider in the following chapter. For the present it is sufficient to note that the thought of death and the expectation of divine judgment are significant motivating factors in Sirach's ethical system.

While the imminence of death qualifies the pursuit of honor, it by no means eliminates it. Rather, it modifies one's priorities. The most important honor is that of a good name. "The good of life is a limited number of days, but the good of a name is for days without end" (41:13). Wisdom confers not only joy and gladness but also "an everlasting name" (15:6). The fathers who are praised in chapters 44–51 are those who have left a name, "so that people might tell of their inheritance" (44:8). Thought for one's future reputation has an impact on one's behavior: "In great and small matters cause no harm . . . for a bad name incurs shame and reproach" (5:15–16).

The immortality of a good name is noted in earlier wisdom literature. Proverbs 10:7 says that "the memory of the righteous is a blessing, but the name of the wicked will rot," while Job 18:17 says that the memory of the wicked perishes from the earth. This theme receives relatively little prominence in the earlier tradition. In Sirach, it acquires major importance. But this again involves us in the sage's views on theodicy and retribution, which will be taken up in their proper context in the following chapter.

51. Aeschylus, *Agamemnon,* 928; Sophocles, *Oedipus Rex,* 1529; Skehan and DiLella, *The Wisdom of Ben Sira,* 241.

Chapter 5.
The Problem of Evil and the Justice of God

Ben Sira's ethics were highly conventional and tradition-bound. Nonetheless, the sage also made an attempt to construct a context for ethical behavior, by addressing questions of the origin of sin and evil and of retribution and divine justice.[1] In so doing, he draws on the resources of the wisdom tradition and the Hebrew scriptures, but he also ventures his own suggestions and draws on Greek philosophy, although only to a very limited degree. His philosophical competence was very modest, but Sirach was a pioneer in trying to combine Greek philosophy with the Hebrew scriptures at all. The wisdom teachers of the Diaspora, who were better educated in Greek learning, would go much farther in the direction of a philosophical theology.

The Origin of Sin

The story of Adam and Eve, which is usually taken as *the* canonical account of the origin of sin in Jewish and especially Christian tradition, receives no attention outside of Genesis in the Hebrew Bible. With the possible exception of some texts of uncertain date from Qumran, it is Ben Sira who provides the first attempt to grapple with the implications of this story.[2] Even the book of Jubilees, which contains the oldest intact narrative paraphrase of these chapters, has surprisingly little to say about the sin of Adam, although it provides a very full exegesis with respect to the halakic implications of the text.[3]

Ben Sira's most explicit reference to the story of Adam and Eve is singularly unfortunate, as it inaugurates a line of interpretation that can only be described as misogynistic: "From a woman sin had its beginning and because of her we all die" (25:24). But while Sir. 25:24 is indicative of the sage's notori-

---

1. J. J. Collins, "Wisdom, Apocalypticism and the Dead Sea Scrolls," in A. A. Diesel et al., eds., *"Jedes Ding hat seine Zeit . . .": Studien zur israelitischen und altorientalischen Weisheit Diethelm Michel zum 65. Geburtstag* (BZAW 241; Berlin: de Gruyter, 1996) 21–26.

2. See J. R. Levison, *Portraits of Adam in Early Judaism from Sirach to 2 Baruch* (Sheffield: JSOT Press, 1988).

3. G. Vermes, "Genesis 1–3 in Post-Biblical Hebrew and Aramaic Literature before the Mishnah," *JJS* 43 (1992) 221–25.

ously negative view of women, it is not consistent with his other pronouncements on the origin of sin and death.[4] It seems to be an ad hoc comment, made in the context of a lengthy reflection on "the wicked woman," but it has not been integrated into a coherent theological system.

Sirach addresses the origin of sin most directly in 15:11–20. The passage takes the form of a controversy: "Do not say it was the Lord's doing that I fell away, for he does not do what he hates." This literary form had a long history in Egyptian wisdom literature, but is rare in the Hebrew Bible. It occurs eleven times in Sirach.[5] There was in fact a lively debate on the origin of sin in Hellenistic Jerusalem. One current explanation was provided by the Book of the Watchers in *1 Enoch* 1–36, which expanded the story of the sons of God in Genesis 6 and attributed various kind of evil (violence, fornication, astrology) to the fallen angels. This apocalypse refrains from attributing the origin of sin to the creator, but it implies that the problem is not of human origin either. Even within the Enoch literature, this explanation did not go unchallenged. In the Epistle of Enoch, which may be roughly contemporary with Ben Sira, we read: "I swear to you, you sinners, that as a mountain has not, and will not, become a slave, nor a hill a woman's maid, so sin was not sent on the earth, but man of himself created it" (*1 Enoch* 98:4).

The implied opponents of Ben Sira neither appeal to fallen angels nor accept human responsibility, but they actually had good biblical precedents for their position. Compare the "evil spirit from Yahweh" that fell on King Saul in 1 Sam. 19:9. Ben Sira himself seems to entertain a similar position on occasion. In Sir. 33:10–13, a passage that also alludes to the creation of Adam, he proclaims: "Every man is a vessel of clay, and Adam was created out of the dust. In the fullness of his knowledge the Lord distinguished them and appointed their different ways. Some he blessed and exalted, and some he made holy and brought near to himself; but some he cursed and brought low, and turned them out of their place. Like clay in the hand of the potter, to be molded as he pleases, so all are in the hand of their Maker, to be given whatever he decides." The problem is how to balance a monistic belief in a good, omnipotent, creator with the evident presence of evil in the world.

Sirach addresses this problem most directly in 15:14: "God created the human being [*adam*] in the beginning and placed him in the power of his inclination [*běyad yiṣrô*]." The word *yēṣer*, inclination, is related to the word for "potter" in Sirach 33 (*yôṣēr*) and to the verb used in Gen. 2:7 ("The Lord God formed man out of the dust of the ground"; the fact that there are two *yods* in the word *wyyṣr*, "and he formed," was later used to argue that there were two

4. See F. R. Tennant, "The Teaching of Ecclesiasticus and Wisdom on the Introduction of Sin and Death," *JTS* 2 (1900–1901) 207–23.

5. J. L. Crenshaw, "The Problem of Theodicy in Sirach: On Human Bondage," *JBL* 94 (1975) 48–51.

inclinations, one good and one bad).[6] One might infer that the "inclination" is the form given to human beings by the creator. While there is no mention of an inclination in Genesis 1–3, the term appears twice in the Flood story (J source): Gen. 6:5, "Every inclination of the thoughts of their hearts is evil continually," and Gen. 8:21: "The inclination of the human heart is evil from youth." The association of the *yēṣer* with evil is typical of biblical usage.[7] Only two passages use the term in a positive sense: Isa. 26:3 speaks of *yēṣer sāmûk,* a steadfast disposition, and in 1 Chron. 29:18 David asks that God preserve the inclination of the thoughts of the heart of the people. (The word appears to be neutral in 1 Chron. 28:9.) Later, in rabbinic literature, the *yēṣer* acquires a technical sense and is conceived as a force that determines behavior. The Talmud attributes to R. Jose the Galilean the view that "the righteous are ruled by the good inclination . . . ; the wicked are ruled by the evil inclination . . . ; average people are ruled by both."[8] Rabbinic usage attributes a power to the inclinations that is not implied in the biblical usage. Urbach summarizes the situation as follows:

> In Sirach, as in the Bible, the *yēṣer* is the natural inclination of man, and also in the teaching of the Tannaim and Amoraim it sometimes denotes the power of thought, or serves as a synonym for the heart as the source of human desires. However, rabbinic teaching did to some extent personify "the Evil Inclination," to whom were ascribed attributes, aims and forms of activity that direct man, even before he was explicitly identified, as by the Amora Resh Laqish, with Satan and the angel of death.[9]

The potency of the evil inclination (or "evil heart," *cor malignum*) plays a prominent part in the apocalypse of 4 Ezra, written at the end of the first century C.E.: "For the first Adam, burdened with an evil heart, transgressed and was overcome, as were also all who were descended from him. Thus the disease became permanent; the Torah was in the people's heart along with the evil root, but what was good departed, and the evil remained."[10] Fourth Ezra stops short of saying that God created the evil heart, but the sages are explicit on this

---

6. *Gen. Rab.* 14:4; G. F. Moore, *Judaism in the First Centuries of the Christian Era* (New York: Schocken, 1975) 1.484.

7. R. E. Murphy, "*Yēṣer* in the Qumran Literature," *Bib* 39 (1958) 334–44; F. C. Porter, "The Yeçer HaRa: A Study in the Jewish Doctrine of Sin," in *Biblical and Semitic Studies* (New York: Scribners, 1901) 93–156.

8. *B. Ber.* 61b. See Moore, *Judaism,* 1.474–96; E. E. Urbach, *The Sages: Their Concepts and Beliefs* (Jerusalem: Magnes, 1975) 1.471–83; G. H. Cohen Stuart, *The Struggle in Man between Good and Evil: An Inquiry into the Origin of the Rabbinic Concept of Yeser Hara'* (Kampen: Kok, 1984).

9. Urbach, *The Sages,* 1.472.

10. 4 Ezra 3:21–22; 4:20; see M. E. Stone, *Fourth Ezra* (Hermeneia; Minneapolis: Fortress, 1990) 63–67.

point. So *Sifre Deuteronomy* §45: "My children I have created for you the Evil Inclination, (but I have at the same time) created for you the Torah as an antidote."[11]

There is clearly some progression between the Bible and the rabbinic literature. The question is, where does Sirach fit in this process? Recent scholarship has been consistent in emphasizing the neutrality of the inclination in Sirach, and its conformity to the biblical view.[12] It is clear from the following verses that Sirach envisages free choice. The formulation is Deuteronomic: "If you choose, you can keep the commandments. . . . Before each person are life and death, and whichever one chooses will be given" (Sir. 15:15, 17; cf. Deut. 30:15). The inclination is not an external, supernatural force. Yet if Sirach is credited with any coherence at all, this passage must be read in the light of chapter 33, which insists that people are clay in the hand of the potter (*yōṣēr*), to be given whatever God decides. The exercise of human choice is conditioned by the inclination with which a person is fitted at creation, and so the word *yēṣer* in 15:14 cannot be simply equated with "free choice" (as in the NRSV). The emphasis in Sirach's argumentation is influenced by the immediate context of a passage. In chapter 15, he is concerned to defend God from implication in human sin, and so he puts the emphasis on free will, but in chapter 33 his focus is on the omnipotence of God and the symmetrical order of creation. There is an unresolved tension in his thought between divine determination and human free will.[13]

Sirach fills out his understanding of the creation of humanity in 17:1–24, in a passage that we have already discussed in connection with Wisdom and the Law. The clearest references are to Genesis 1 rather than Genesis 2–3, although the notice that God created the human being (*anthrōpon*, Adam) out of the ground shows that Genesis 2 is also in view. There is no reference, however, to a "Fall" or to an original sin of Adam. Death is part of creation from the beginning (17:1–2; cf. 41:4). God filled humanity with knowledge and understanding and showed people good and evil (Sir. 17:7; cf. Gen. 2:9), and gave them the law of life from the start. Sirach appears to be close to the rabbinic position cited above from *Sifre Deuteronomy* §45 that God provided the Torah as an antidote to the human inclination.

11. Urbach, *The Sages,* 1.472.
12. J. Hadot, *Penchant Mauvais et Volonté Libre dans La Sagesse de Ben Sira (L'Ecclésiastique)* (Brussels: University Press, 1970) 209; G. L. Prato, *Il Problema della Teodicea in Ben Sira* (AnBib 65; Rome: Pontifical Biblical Institute, 1975) 240; Skehan and DiLella, *The Wisdom of Ben Sira,* 272. Hadot provides an extensive survey of passages where *yēṣer* might be reconstructed on the basis of the Greek. There is a clear reference to the evil inclination in the Greek text of Sir. 37:3, but it seems to derive from a mistranslation of the Hebrew.
13. G. Maier, *Mensch und Freier Wille* (Tübingen: Mohr, 1971) 98–115. In Maier's view, the deterministic view was traditional, and Ben Sira moves away from it in debate with opponents in chapter 15.

Despite this vigorous endorsement of Deuteronomic theology and human responsibility, Sirach's overall position remains ambiguous. A Hebrew redactor of chapter 15 complemented the statement that God left humanity in the power of its inclination with the phrase "He set him in the power of his spoiler" (*ḥōtpô*). The phrase is not supported by the versions. The original Sirach had no place for a demonic "spoiler" (unlike the Enochic tradition or the Qumran Community Rule). Consequently, the human "inclination" ultimately comes from God. There was, then, in Sirach's own theology a basis for the view that sin also comes from God, even though this inference was unacceptable to the sage.

In fact, the implications of divine responsibility are drawn out in the secondary recensions of Ben Sira. Sirach 11:14 reads: "Good and evil, life and death, poverty and riches, are from the Lord." The Hebrew MS A from the Cairo Geniza adds another line that is not reflected in the Greek: "Sin and righteous ways are from the Lord." The Greek adds two verses, the first affirming that "wisdom and understanding and knowledge of the Law are from the Lord," and the second stating that "error and darkness were formed with sinners from their birth." None of these verses can be accepted as the work of Ben Sira himself.[14] We can see, however, how a scribe might arrive at such statements by reflecting on Ben Sira's text. We find a much clearer acknowledgment of ultimate divine responsibility for evil in the Qumran Community Rule, where the treatise on the Two Spirits begins: "From the God of knowledge stems all there is and all there shall be. . . . He created man to rule the world and placed within him two spirits so that he would walk with them until the moment of his visitation" (1QS 3:15, 18).

Evil and the
Goodness of Creation

The view that evil has its place in the design of creation is implied in several passages in Ben Sira. So in 11:14 we are told that "good and bad, life and death, poverty and wealth are from the Lord," but this passage probably does not have moral evil in mind. There is a fuller discussion in 33:7–15. Here Sirach starts with the question why one day should be different from or more important than another. His answer: "By the Lord's wisdom they were distinguished." He goes on to discuss the differences between human beings, in the passage already cited above. People are different, too, because God appointed their different ways, molding them as a potter molds his clay. The illustration of this principle in v. 12 contrasts the election of Israel with the dispossession of the Canaanites, but both are taken by way of example. The idea that God

14. See Smend, *Die Weisheit des Jesus Sirach,* 106; Skehan and DiLella, *The Wisdom of Ben Sira,* 237.

makes people walk in their different paths seems remarkably close to the deterministic view of the Qumran Community Rule (1QS 3:15–6) and is at odds
with Sirach's vigorous defense of human responsibility in chapters 15 and 17.
Finally, in 33:14–15, Sirach argues that divine election is not random, but is
part of a coherent system: "Good is the opposite of evil, and life is the opposite of death; so the sinner is the opposite of the godly. Look at all the works
of the Most High: they are all in pairs, one opposite the other."[15] The principle
of the duality of all things is repeated in 42:24–25.

The doctrine of opposite pairs is one of the clearer instances of the influence
of Greek philosophy on Ben Sira.[16] The Stoic philosopher Chrysippus (late
third century B.C.E., and therefore close to Ben Sira's time) held that

> there is absolutely nothing more foolish than those who think that there could
> have been goods without the coexistence of evils. For since goods are opposite
> to evils, the two must necessarily exist in opposition to each other and supported
> by a kind of opposed interdependence. And there is no such opposite without its
> matching opposite. For how could there be perception of justice if there were no
> injustices? What else is justice, if not the removal of injustice? . . . For goods and
> evils, fortune and misfortune, pain and pleasure, exist in just the same way: they
> are tied to each other in polar opposition.[17]

The doctrine of complementary opposites is also found in Pythagoras and Heraclitus.[18] For the Stoic philosopher, duality is simply an innate quality of
things. For the Jewish sage, it is the design of a transcendent creator. This idea
of such a systematic division of creation, however, has no precedent in the Hebrew scriptures. (There are some binary opposites in Genesis 1, such as light
and darkness, day and night, but there is no suggestion that all the works of the
Lord are so paired.) The appearance of this idea in the Hellenistic period, and
its resemblance to the Stoic doctrine, can hardly be coincidental.

The order of creation is the subject of two further reflections in Sir. 39:12–35
and 42:15–43:33. Both of these passages are cast in the form of hymns of praise,
but they indirectly address questions of theodicy. The Stoic philosopher Cleanthes also used the form of the hymn (to Zeus) to present a discourse on cosmic
order. The Egyptian Instruction of Phibis includes a section on the works of "the
god" in creation, but does not present it in the form of a hymn.

Sirach 39:14–15 introduces the following passage with a call to praise, and
the imperative to praise is repeated in 39:35. The passage itself is made up of

15. For a full exegesis, see Prato, *Il Problema della Teodicea,* 13–61.
16. Winston, "Theodicy in Ben Sira and Stoic Philosophy," 242.
17. Chrysippus, *On Providence,* Book 4 in Gellius 7.1.1–13; *SVF* 2.1169; cited from A. A. Long
and D. N. Sedley, *The Hellenistic Philosophers* (2 vols.; Cambridge: Cambridge Univ. Press,
1987) 1.329.
18. Th. Middendorp, *Die Stellung Jesu Ben Siras zwischen Judentum und Hellenismus* (Leiden:
Brill, 1973) 29.

declarative sentences. At the outset, we are told that the works of the Lord are all good, in accordance with the judgment of Gen. 1:31, but Sirach is aware of the problem of evil. In this passage he offers two suggestions as to how the evil in the world can be reconciled with the goodness of creation.[19]

First, everything will be clarified at the appointed time (v. 17). This solution is not unlike what we find in apocalyptic literature, especially in 4 Ezra, where Ezra's persistent questioning about the justice of God's dealing with Israel is overcome by a series of eschatological visions that shift the focus from past and present to future. In effect, justice will prevail at the appointed time. Unlike the apocalyptic visionaries, Sirach projects no eschatological scenario to silence the critics. However, the notion of the appointed time is common to sapiential and apocalyptic writings.[20] In the wisdom tradition, it is developed especially by Qoheleth (e.g., Qoh. 3:1–8) but has a long history in Egyptian wisdom.[21] Sirach also shares with the apocalypses the belief that God can see everything from age to age (39:20), but he differs by not attempting to describe history from a revealed perspective. Sirach would probably agree with Qoh. 3:11 that such comprehensive knowledge is not accessible to humanity, but he is content that God knows even if we do not.[22]

Second, everything has been created for a purpose (Sir. 39:21). Here again Sirach reflects the influence of Stoic philosophy.[23] Chrysippus is said to have taught that bedbugs are useful for waking us and that mice encourage us to be tidy.[24] Carneades (mid-second century B.C.E.) taught that everything is benefited when it attains the end for which it was born. So the pig fulfills its purpose when it is slaughtered and eaten.[25] The Stoics also conceded that the usefulness of some plants and animals remains to be discovered.[26] Sirach's elaboration of this notion, however, is somewhat confusing. All God's works are good (39:16, 33) but for sinners good things and bad were created (39:25),

19. Crenshaw, "The Problem of Theodicy," 52–53.

20. G. von Rad, *Wisdom in Israel* (Nashville: Abingdon, 1972) 138–43; 251–56.

21. Crenshaw, "The Problem of Theodicy," 58. See also H. H. Schmid, *Wesen und Geschichte der Weisheit*, 190.

22. On the (limited) analogies between Sirach and early apocalyptic literature, see J. D. Martin, "Ben Sira—A Child of His Time," in J. D. Martin and P. R. Davies, eds., *A Word in Season: Essays in Honor of William McKane* (Sheffield: JSOT Press, 1986) 141–61 and R. A. Argall, *1 Enoch and Sirach* (Atlanta: Scholars, 1995).

23. For the debates about teleology in antiquity, see Long and Sedley, *Hellenistic Philosophers,* 1.58–65; 121–22; 323–33.

24. *SVF* 2.1163; Plutarch, *On Stoic Self-Contradictions,* 1044D; Long and Sedley, *Hellenistic Philosophers,* 1.328–29.

25. *SVF* 2.1152. Porphyry, *On Abstinence,* 3.20.1,3; Long and Sedley, *Hellenistic Philosophers,* 1.329.

26. *SVF* 2.1172; Lactantius, *On the Anger of God,* 13.9–10; Long and Sedley, *Hellenistic Philosophers,* 1.330.

or the same things are good for the righteous but bad for sinners (39:27). In part, the confusion lies in the ambiguity of the term "bad." What is bad for sinners is really good. But there is also a reluctance on the part of Ben Sira to admit that bad things can happen to good people. The idea that nature discriminates between the righteous and the wicked is also found in Wis. 19:6.

The language of Sir. 39:12–35 has occasional biblical overtones: 39:17 alludes to the exodus; 39:23 to the conquest; 39:29–30 to the curses of the covenant (Lev. 26:14–22; Deut. 28:20–24). Here again there is a parallel with the Wisdom of Solomon, insofar as Israelite history is used to illustrate the workings of the cosmos. Sirach's discussion, however, is quite ahistorical. He is concerned with the universal working of nature, not with the history of a particular people.

The hymn to the creator in 42:15–43:33 concludes the book except for the Praise of the Fathers and the concluding materials in chapter 51. Chapter 42:15–20 praises the omniscience of God, 42:21–43:26 lists the works of creation, 43:27–33 concludes the hymn with a call to praise. The praises of nature in chapter 43 recall Job 28; 38–41, but also Psalms 104; 148, and the Song of the Three Young Men in the Greek additions to Daniel. We may also compare the praise of God as creator in the hymns of Qumran (e.g., 1QH 9:10–14, formerly = 1QH 1).

The praise of God's omniscience in Sir. 42:15–20 is replete with biblical echoes. On 42:15a, cf. Ps. 77:11; on 42:15b, cf. Job 15:17. On creation by the word, cf. Ps. 33:6; Wis. 9:1. On God's knowledge of past and future, cf. Isa. 41:22–23; 44:7. God's ability to reveal hidden things is also emphasized in Dan. 2:22. The introduction to God's works in Sir. 42:22–25, however, introduces some nonbiblical concepts: 42:23a expresses the teleological, Stoic view that all things are created to meet a need (cf. 39:21 and the discussion above); 42:24 repeats the idea of complementary opposites, already encountered in 33:14–15, which also has its roots in Stoic philosophy.

The praise of nature in chapter 43 envisages the sun as a charioteer, racing his steeds.[27] The horses and chariots of the sun were familiar in ancient Israel, but were destroyed in Josiah's reform (2 Kings 23:11). The image of the solar charioteer was standard in Greece, and this may have led to its rehabilitation here. In *1 Enoch* 72:5, the wind blows the chariots on which the sun ascends. The permanence of the astral world is also celebrated in *1 Enoch* 75:1, but *1 Enoch* 80 anticipates that the order will be disrupted in "the days of the sinners." The rainbow is praised for its beauty, but no reference is made to its role as a sign of the covenant of Noah (Gen. 9:13–17). The description of lightning and thunder has overtones of the traditional language of theophany (cf. Ps. 18:7–15). Sirach 43:23–26 refers to God's mastery over the deep and its

---

27. Hebrew *abbîrîm*, see Skehan and DiLella, *The Wisdom of Ben Sira,* 488. The Greek translator (followed by NRSV) missed the reference.

monsters (cf. Job 41:1–11). It is possible that the word *rabbah*, great, in the Hebrew of vv. 23, 25 should be emended to Rahab, a traditional name for the sea-monster (Job 26:12; Isa. 51:9).

The most remarkable statement in this hymn, however, comes in 43:27: "He is the all." (There is a remarkable parallel to this expression in a fragment of the Damascus Document found in Qumran Cave 4.)[28] This formulation clearly evokes the pantheism of the Stoics.[29] Chrysippus taught that "divine power resides in reason and in the mind and intellect of universal nature. He says that god is the world itself, and the universal pervasiveness of its mind; also that he is the world's own commanding-faculty, since he is located in intellect and reason; that he is the common nature of things, universal and all-embracing; also the force of fate and the necessity of future events."[30] Because the Stoic deity is the commanding faculty, he can also be called "father of all" and identified with Zeus.[31] Cleanthes's *Hymn to Zeus* portrays him as the one that the whole cosmos obeys, the giver of the universal law. The Stoic deity is immanent, however, and is not a transcendent creator.[32]

It is clear from Ben Sira's book taken as a whole that the author is no pantheist. His use of the phrase "He is all" is exceptional, and therefore probably hyperbolic. It is quickly qualified in the following verse with the reminder that "he is greater than all his works." A better-attested appellation is "God of all," which occurs in 36:1; 45:23c (Hebrew only); and 50:22a (Greek only; Hebrew reads "God of Israel"). The immanence implied in Sir. 43:27 should not be dismissed, however. There was always a tendency in the wisdom tradition to see the chain of act and consequence as self-regulated, and to regard the role of the deity as that of midwife.[33] We have seen that Sirach transfers to Wisdom many roles and characteristics that were reserved for God in the Hebrew Bible, and

28. 4QD[b] frag. 18, col. 5, line 9. See B. Z. Wacholder and M. G. Abegg, *A Preliminary Edition of the Unpublished Dead Sea Scrolls: The Hebrew and Aramaic Texts from Cave Four* (Washington: Biblical Archaeology Society, 1991) 1.21; F. García Martínez, *The Dead Sea Scrolls Translated* (Leiden: Brill, 1994) 57. The parallel between this text and Ben Sira is noted by M. Kister, "On a New Fragment of the Damascus Covenant," *JQR* 84 (1993–94) 249–52.

29. R. Pautrel, "Ben Sira et le stoicisme," *RSR* 51 (1963) 543; M. Hengel, *Judaism and Hellenism* (2 vols.; Philadelphia: Fortress, 1974) 1.148; J. Marböck, *Weisheit im Wandel: Untersuchungen zur Weisheits-theologie bei Ben Sira* (Bonn: Hanstein, 1971) 170; Middendorp, *Die Stellung Jesu Ben Siras,* 29.

30. *SVF* 2.1077. Cicero, *De Natura Deorum* 1.39; Long and Sedley, *Hellenistic Philosophers,* 323.

31. *SVF* 2.1021. Diogenes Laertius 7.147. On the ambiguity of the Stoic usage of the word "God," to refer both to the world as a whole and, more restrictively, to its active principle, see F. H. Sandbach, *The Stoics* (New York: Norton, 1975) 73.

32. See M. Pohlenz, *Die Stoa: Geschichte einer geistigen Bewegung* (2d ed.; Göttingen: Vandenhoeck & Ruprecht, 1959) 95.

33. K. Koch, "Is There a Doctrine of Retribution in the Old Testament?" in J. L. Crenshaw, ed., *Theodicy in the Old Testament* (Philadelphia: Fortress, 1983) 57–87.

Wisdom is certainly immanent in the world. The Stoic view of the immanent God, then, was not entirely alien to the thought-world of Jewish wisdom. Sirach, however, was a quintessentially eclectic thinker, not distinguished for consistency. His most basic views of the deity were incompatible with Stoicism and were rooted in Hebrew tradition. The idea of a transcendent creator was one such idea. Another was the idea of God as judge.

Prayer and Atonement

Despite the pantheistic-sounding "He is all" of Sir. 43:27, Sirach speaks of God in personal terms more often than any previous wisdom writer. He is exceptional in this tradition in addressing a prayer of petition to God (22:27–23:6; the authenticity of the prayer in chapter 36 is disputed). This is a prayer for protection against temptations of the lips and tongue. The most noteworthy feature of the prayer is undoubtedly the fact that God is addressed as "father" in 23:1, 4. God is only rarely called father in the Hebrew Bible, and is never so addressed by an individual. (God is called father of the people of Israel in Isa. 63:16; Mal. 2:10; and possibly 1 Chron. 29:10, where "our father" could refer to either God or Israel.) The Hebrew text of the psalm in Sir. 51:10 reads, "Lord, you are my father," but the Greek has a confused reading, "Lord, father of my Lord."[34] The Hebrew of chapter 23 is not extant. Joachim Jeremias argued that there was no evidence for the use of "my father" as a form of direct address to God in Hebrew before the Christian era and suggested that Sir. 23:1 originally read "God of my father."[35] The direct address, however, is now attested in the Prayer of Joseph (4Q372) from Qumran, which is dated tentatively about 200 B.C.E.[36] The Prayer begins, "My father and my God." In view of this parallel there is no reason to question the authenticity of the Greek text of Sir. 23:1, 4.

We have noted that some Stoic philosophers also spoke of the deity as "father of all," but this is scarcely the model for the personal address to "my father" in Sirach 23 or the Prayer of Joseph. Sirach's understanding of the fatherhood of God is better illuminated by the analogy of human fatherhood in Sir. 4:10: "Be a father to orphans and be like a husband to their mother; you will then be like a son of the Most High, and he will love you more than does your mother." The same analogy is most probably attested in reverse in Sapiential Work A from Qumran (4Q416 frag. 2.iii.16), although the text requires emendation: "For as God [reading *'ēl* rather than *'ab*] is to a man, so is his father."[37]

---

34. A. Strotmann, *"Mein Vater Bist du!"* (*Sir 51:10*) (Frankfurt am Main: Knecht, 1991) 83–92.

35. J. Jeremias, *The Prayers of Jesus* (Philadelphia: Fortress, 1967) 29.

36. E. Schuller, "4Q372 1: A Text about Joseph," *RevQ* 14 (1990) 349–76.

37. D. J. Harrington, "Wisdom at Qumran," in E. Ulrich and J. C. VanderKam, eds., *The Community of the Renewed Covenant* (Notre Dame, Ind.: Univ. of Notre Dame Press, 1994) 148.

Sirach is also exceptional in the wisdom tradition in his attention to cult and sacrifices.[38] He devotes a whole treatise to the subject in 34:21–35:26. The first part of this treatise, 34:21–31, is a critique of the abuse of the cult, in the spirit of the prophets. Especially striking are vv. 24–27, which equate the offerings of the unjust with murder: "Like one slaying a son in his father's presence is whoever offers sacrifice from the possessions of the poor." (A possible parallel can be found in Isa. 65:3, which can be read as equating sacrifice with murder, but the text is ambiguous.) Sirach is quite clear that the problem is not with sacrifice as such but with the abuse of the poor; sacrifice cannot compensate for social injustice. Sirach may be commenting on contemporary abuses here, or he may be simply reflecting the teaching of the prophets (cf. Amos 5:21–27; 8:4–8).

In 35:1–5 Sirach addresses those things that are most pleasing to the Lord and insists that the ethical demands of the Law are more important than sacrifices: "The one who keeps the law makes many offerings; one who heeds the commandments makes an offering of well-being." The point here is not that the Law requires many sacrifices (a point that Sirach would also grant) but that observance is the equivalent of many sacrifices. Sirach displays his familiarity with the different kinds of sacrifice, but the point is that kindness and almsgiving are as effective as sacrifice in pleasing God. This kind of spiritualizing of the cult is found already in the Hebrew Bible (e.g., Ps. 51:17: "The sacrifice acceptable to God is a broken spirit"). In the Qumran Community Rule (1QS 8:1–4) righteousness serves as a substitute for the cult. Hellenistic Jews like Philo also placed their primary stress on the spiritual, symbolic meaning of sacrifice. Ben Sira, however, goes on to say that one should also observe the literal commandments in this respect (cf. Sir. 7:31). This is in accordance with Ben Sira's general insistence on the fulfillment of the Law.

Sirach evidently attaches value to the sacrificial cult insofar as it is required by the fulfillment of the Law. Yet he never mentions a private offering of atonement.[39] There is a probable allusion to the ritual on the Day of Atonement in Sir. 50:5, which refers to the High Priest Simon coming out through the curtain (*pārōket,* the veil at the entrance to the Holy of Holies, Exod. 36:31–35).[40] But here, and throughout the praise of the High Priest in chapter 50, Sirach is concerned with the spectacle of the ritual rather than with its efficacy. There is no reason to doubt that Sirach favored observance of all the prescribed rituals, but he is not an advocate for the sacrificial cult. In the words of E. P. Sanders, "His concern is rather to denounce abuses of the Temple service, to contest any

38. See L. G. Perdue, *Wisdom and Cult* (Missoula, Mont.: Scholars, 1977) 188–260.
39. See A. Büchler, "Ben Sira's Conception of Sin and Atonement," *JQR* 13 (1922/23) 303–35.
40. See, however, F. O'Fearghail, "Sir 50,5–21: Yom Kippur or The Daily Whole Offering?" *Bib* 59 (1978) 301–16, who argues that the reference is to the daily offering.

possible view that it might be efficacious automatically, and to connect the sacrificial system with the moral life."[41]

Whatever misgivings Sirach has about the abuse of the sacrificial cult, it is clear in all this that he allows for the possibility of atonement.[42] Whoever honors his father atones for sin (3:3); also almsgiving atones for sin (3:30). Whoever does not show mercy to others cannot seek pardon for his own sins (28:4), but in principle one can appeal for divine mercy. The point is most vividly made in 35:21–25:

> The prayer of the humble pierces the clouds,
>   and it will not rest until it reaches its goal;
> it will not desist until the Most High responds
>   and does justice for the righteous, and executes judgment.
> Indeed, the Lord will not delay,
>   and like a warrior will not be patient
> until he crushes the loins of the unmerciful
>   and repays vengeance on the nations; . . .
> until he repays mortals according to their deeds,
>   and the works of all according to their thoughts;
> until he judges the case of his people
>   and makes them rejoice in his mercy.

With the exception of the disputed passage in chapter 36, which follows directly on this passage, this is the closest Sirach comes to the typical biblical picture of a God who intervenes in history on behalf of his people. Even here, the concern is primarily with the poor rather than with the people of Israel, despite the biblical idiom of the passage. Leaving aside for the moment the role of Israel in Sirach's thought, it is at least clear that individuals can make atonement, whether by sacrifices or by good works, and can appeal to the mercy of God. (Cf. also 2:7–11; 5:5–7; 18:1–15; 21:1–3.)

Such interventionist language is interspersed in Ben Sira with the more typical sapiential view that wisdom yields its fruit by following its course. So we are told that the fear of the Lord "gives gladness and joy and long life. Those who fear the Lord will have a happy end; on the day of their death they will be blessed" (1:12–13). Again, "God's ways are straight for the faithful but full of pitfalls for the wicked" (39:24). What is remarkable in either case is the apparent naïveté of the sage. The view that wisdom and virtue lead to a long life and happiness was traditional in the Hebrew Bible, especially in Deuteronomy and Proverbs, but by the time of Sirach it had been subjected to devastating critique,

---

41. E. P. Sanders, *Paul and Palestinian Judaism* (Philadelphia: Fortress, 1977) 339. For an argument that Sirach attached greater importance to the sacrificial cult, see H. Stadelmann, *Ben Sira als Schriftgelehrter* (Tübingen: Mohr, 1980) 40–138.

42. Sanders, *Paul and Palestinian Judaism,* 338.

especially by Job and Qoheleth. Consequently, even before Sirach's time, some Jews argued that retribution must come after death. This belief is first attested in the Book of the Watchers, and it gained ground rapidly after the persecution in the time of Antiochus Epiphanes.[43] It is already implied in Qoheleth, who rejects it with the skeptical question: "Who knows whether the human spirit goes upward and the spirit of animals goes downward to the earth?" (3:21).

Sirach's View of Death

Sirach resolutely rejects the belief in retribution after death. Consistently in Sirach (except for 25:24!), death is viewed as the end for which humanity was created rather than as punishment for sin.[44] We have seen this point already in 17:1–2: "The Lord created human beings out of the earth, and makes them return to it again. He gave them a fixed number of days. . . ." The most extended discussion of human mortality is found in 40:1–41:13, a cluster of short poems framed by two reflections on death. Chapter 41:3–4 expresses Sirach's view of death in a nutshell:

> Do not fear death that is decreed for you;
>   remember that those who went before and those who will come after
>   are with you.
> This is the portion of all flesh from God,
>   and why should you reject the decree [tôrāh!] of the Most High?
> Whether [life is for] a thousand, or a hundred, or ten years
>   there is no reproof in Sheol.

This is Sirach's most definitive statement on the finality of death, and leaves no room for resurrection or a blessed afterlife. Sirach's views on this subject are no different than those of Qoheleth, except that he holds them with resignation, whereas Qoheleth chafes against them. Sirach recognizes that death can be bitter for one who is at peace among his possessions (40:1). But he also recognizes that death can be welcome "to one who is needy and failing in strength, worn down by age and anxious about everything" (41:2). The attractiveness of death in certain circumstances received classic expression in the Egyptian *Dispute of a Man with His Ba* (Soul) about 2000 B.C.E.[45] Such sentiments are not common in the Hebrew Bible but occur more than once in Ben Sira. Accord-

---

    43. See J. J. Collins, *Daniel* (Minneapolis: Fortress, 1993) 394–98.
    44. J. J. Collins, "The Root of Immortality: Death in the Context of Jewish Wisdom," *HTR* 71 (1978) 179–85; L. J. Prockter, "95

ing to Sir. 30:17, "Death is better than a futile life, and eternal sleep than chronic sickness." (The repose of the dead is commonly called sleep in Jewish epitaphs of the Hellenistic and Roman periods.)[46] The same sentiment is found in Tob. 3:6, 10, 13 in the prayers of Tobit and Sarah.[47] Sirach, however, does not speak out of personal misery, nor is he a skeptic like Qoheleth. His observation is all the more remarkable for its dispassionate objectivity. A parallel is found in Theognis 181–82: "To the needy, dear Cyrnus, death is better than a life oppressed with grievous penury."

Sirach's argument that one should not fear death because there is no judgment thereafter is in some tension with his earlier assertions regarding the day of death as a day of judgment, when God can reward people according to their conduct (11:26–8; 18:24). His remarks in chapter 41 are closer to the spirit of Epicurus: "A correct understanding that death is nothing to us makes the mortality of life enjoyable, not by adding infinite time, but by ridding us of the desire for immortality. For there is nothing fearful in living for one who genuinely grasps that there is nothing fearful in not living."[48] Sirach's general understanding of the world is remote from that of Epicurus. For the philosopher, death is the absence of sensation. Sirach still retains the traditional belief in Sheol. They converge, however, in the argument that death is not something to be feared. Neither Sirach nor Epicurus inferred that one could live a life of licentiousness with impunity. In this respect, their reasoning is in sharp contrast with the argument attributed to the wicked in Wis. 2:1–20. Sirach occasionally appeals to the finality of death as a reason to enjoy life, and also to be generous and do good: "My son, use freely whatever you have, and enjoy it as best you can; remember that there is no pleasure in Sheol and death does not delay, and the ordinance of death has not been told to you. Before you die do good to your friend, and give him a share in what you possess" (14:11–13). The same kind of eudaemonism is implied in 40:18–27, where the sage's reflections on death are interrupted by a list of ten things that are surpassingly good.[49] Sirach shows his appreciation not only for wealth, wisdom, and a good wife, but also for wine, music, and beauty (40:20–22). Characteristically, Sirach concludes with the superiority of the fear of the Lord. The argument that life should be enjoyed because it is short had a long and distinguished history in the ancient Near East. In the Epic of Gilgamesh the hero, in the course of his vain search for immortality, encounters the ale-wife Siduri, who tells him: "When the gods created

---

46. P. van der Horst, *Ancient Jewish Epitaphs* (Kampen: Kok/Pharos, 1991) 114–17, but see already Job 3:13.

47. Compare also 1 Kings 19:4 (Elijah); Jonah 4:3; Job 3:11, 13, 17; Qoh. 4:2.

48. Epicurus, *Letter to Menoeceus* 124; Long and Sedley, *Hellenistic Philosophers,* 149.

49. In each case, Sirach lists two things that are good and a third that is better. On the form, see G. S. Ogden, "The 'Better'-Proverb (Tôb-Spruch), Rhetorical Criticism, and Qoheleth," *JBL* 96 (1977) 489–505.

mankind / Death for mankind they set aside / Life in their own hands retaining. Thou Gilgamesh, let full be thy belly, / Make thou merry by day and by night."[50] Closer to the time of Sirach, Qoheleth taught: "So I commend enjoyment, for there is nothing better for people under the sun than to eat and drink and enjoy themselves" (Qoh. 8:15). This theme is more prominent in Qoheleth than it is in Sirach, where it is always qualified by the fear of the Lord.

Moreover, Sirach is aware that for most people the anticipation of death is a source of anxiety: "Perplexities and fear of heart are theirs, and anxious thought of the day of their death" (40:2). He goes on to comment on the anxiety of disturbed sleep, a theme also found in Qoh. 2:22–23 and Job 7:4, and also in Sir. 31:1–2. It should be said that Sirach himself feeds this anxiety on occasion, when he portrays the day of death as a day of judgment. The tone in chapter 40 is more sympathetic, and designed to mitigate the fear of death. The only hope for immortality that he entertains, however, is for the person's name and reputation (41:12–13) and the continuity of one's progeny (30:4–6).

Sirach's view of death, admirably realistic though it is, only serves to exacerbate the problem of theodicy, since the sentence of death falls on just and wicked alike and there is no judgment in Sheol. Sirach offers several suggestions on this problem, not all of them fully consistent with one another.[51] We have already noted his claim that God rewards people for their deeds on the day of their death, but this claim can hardly be sustained by experience. Equally unconvincing are the claim that things that are good for the godly turn into evils for sinners (39:27) and the unsupported assertion that lawbreakers will utterly fail (40:17; compare the theology of the friends of Job in Job 8:11–15). Sirach offers one of his more original suggestions in the context of his discussion of human anxiety: "To all creatures, human and animal, *but to sinners seven times more,* come death and bloodshed and strife and sword, calamities and famine and ruin and plague. All these were created for the wicked, and on their account the flood came" (40:8–9, italics added). The context suggests that the wicked also suffer more from anxiety, although this is not explicitly stated. The claim that disasters (including death!) befall the wicked at a greater rate can scarcely be taken seriously. The idea that lawbreakers suffer from anxiety has the advantage that it cannot be verified. Crenshaw is prepared to grant "that there may be some truth in Sirach's conviction that wicked men experience excessive nightmares."[52] It is difficult, however, to avoid the suspicion that all Sirach has to offer here is wishful thinking.

50. *ANET,* 90. See T. Abusch, "Gilgamesh's Request and Siduri's Denial," part 1 in M. E. Cohen et al., eds., *The Tablet and the Scroll: Near Eastern Studies in Honor of W. W. Hallo* (Bethesda, Md.: CDL Press, 1993) 1–14; part 2 in *JANESCU* 22 (193) 3–17.

51. See Crenshaw, "The Problem of Theodicy."

52. Crenshaw, "The Problem of Theodicy," 63; he refers to David Bakan's theory of "telic decentralization," in his *Disease, Pain and Sacrifice* (Chicago: Univ. of Chicago, 1968).

Conclusion

Sirach's most original and substantial contribution to the discussion of theodicy lies in his theory that there is a duality inherent in creation that serves the purposes of God.[53] In the end, one can only bow before the will of the creator and trust that whatever happens is part of a greater design. "No one can say, 'What is this?' or 'Why is that?' for everything has been created for its own purpose" (39:21). "No one can say, 'This is not as good as that,' for everything proves good in its appointed time" (39:34). There may be an implication here that the goodness of whatever happens eventually becomes evident to humanity; if so, it is a questionable assumption. But unlike Qoheleth, Sirach is informed by a basic trust in the goodness of creation, so that occasional demonstration is sufficient to establish the general principle. He does not question the *tôrāh* of the Most High (41:4).

In all this, Sirach bears at least a general similarity to the Stoics, who held that "neither men nor gods have any greater privilege than this: to sing for ever in righteousness of the universal law."[54] But there are also plenty of precedents for submission to the will of the creator in the Hebrew tradition. The great hymns to the creator in Sir. 39:16–35 and 42:15–43:33 have the effect of silencing opposition just as surely as God's speeches from the whirlwind in Job. The difference is that Sirach, unlike Job, has never assumed the role of the critic, and has not addressed the question of theodicy in as direct a manner. Sirach lacked the philosophical sophistication to develop a consistent theory in the manner of the Stoics. He is more concerned with passing on the hodgepodge of tradition than with achieving consistency. Nevertheless, he is not devoid of original thought. By introducing the philosophical concept of complementarity in creation he made a significant contribution to the development of the tradition in the direction of a more philosophical theology.

Appendix: Resurrection in
the Hebrew Text of Sirach?

It is well known that the Greek translator of Sirach introduced a belief in resurrection at several points in the text, e.g., 7:17b and 48:11b, and that the redactor of the Greek text (GII) added further allusions to the afterlife, e.g., at 2:9c; 16:22c; 19:19.[55] Recently, however, Emile Puech has argued that there are allusions to resurrection in

53. O. S. Rankin, *Israel's Wisdom Literature* (Edinburgh: Clark, 1936) 35.
54. Cleanthes, *Hymn to Zeus*.
55. C. Kearns, "The Expanded Text of Ecclesiasticus: Its Teaching on the Future Life as a Clue to its Origin." Diss. Rome (Biblical Commission, 1951); idem, "Ecclesiasticus, or the Wisdom of Jesus the Son of Sirach," in R. C. Fuller, ed., *A New Catholic Commentary on Holy Scripture* (London: Nelson, 1969) 541–62; Skehan and DiLella, *The Wisdom of Ben Sira,* 86.

the original Hebrew text of 48:11, 13.[56] The text of 48:11 is difficult. The Greek reads: "Blessed are those who saw you and have fallen asleep in love, for we also shall certainly live." The Hebrew (MS B) is fragmentary at this point. The first half of the verse reads, "Blessed is he who sees you and dies" (i.e., sees you before he dies). The second half has been restored, plausibly, to read, " . . . for you give life, and he will live."[57] While granting that Sirach did not believe in a general resurrection, Puech thinks he anticipated a limited resurrection at the return of Elijah. The prophet is often associated with the eschatological resurrection in later tradition (*m. Soṭa* 9:15; *Pesiq. Rab. Kah.* 76a). Elijah was also credited with reviving the dead in a noneschatological context in 2 Kings 18. Presumably the resurrection was temporary in these cases, so the life that Elijah is said to confer is not necessarily eternal life. Again, in 48:13 it is said of Elisha that "from his place his flesh was [re]created" (*mitaḥtāw nibra' bǎsārô*). The Greek reads that his flesh *prophesied* in death (reading *nb'* instead of *nbr'*). Puech has made a plausible case for the authenticity of the Hebrew. The resurrection of Elisha, however, would be an exceptional event, like the assumption of Elijah, and would be compatible with Sirach's general denial of resurrection. The expectation of a limited resurrection at the return of Elijah is more difficult. In view of Sirach's emphatic insistence on the finality of death elsewhere (Sir. 14:11–19; 38:21–22; 41:4), such a view cannot be attributed to Sirach himself. We have seen that both the text and the interpretation are uncertain in any case.

56. E. Puech, "Ben Sira 48:11 et la Résurrection," in H. Attridge et al., eds., *Of Scribes and Scrolls: Studies on the Hebrew Bible, Intertestamental Judaism and Christian Origins* (Lanham, Md.: University Press of America, 1990) 81–90; idem, *La Croyance des Esséniens en la Vie Future: Immortalité, Résurrection, Vie Éternelle?* (Paris: Gabalda, 1993) 73–79. F. Saracino, "Risurrezione in Ben Sira?" *Henoch* 4 (1982) 185–203, claims to find further references in 46:12 and 49:10, but he has found no following.

57. Puech, "Ben Sira 48:11," 81–90.

Chapter 6.
The History and Destiny of Israel

The traditional wisdom teaching found in Proverbs, Job, and Qoheleth is notable for its lack of attention to the history of Israel and its claims of special revelation. Ben Sira's attempt to deal with this history marks a significant shift in the tradition. The Mosaic Law could be assimilated to wisdom more easily, since both wisdom and law deal with the regulation of ethical life. There was no precedent in the wisdom tradition for using the history of a particular people as a source of sapiential instruction.

The Genre of the
"Praise of the Fathers"

The last major section of Ben Sira (chapters 44–50) follows the outline of biblical history from the antediluvian patriarchs to Nehemiah, and then concludes with a eulogy of the contemporary High Priest, Simon the Just. Historical reviews are a staple of several genres of Jewish literature, beginning with the covenantal recitations in Deuteronomy 26 ("A wandering Aramean was my father . . .") and Joshua 24.[1] But Sirach's review has no precedent in the biblical writings. He does not attempt to reconstruct history or even to retell the story. His focus is not on revelatory events such as the exodus. The long review in chapters 44–50 singles out individuals as examples to be praised, but presents no continuous historical narrative. This section of the book bears the title "Praise of the Fathers of Old" in the Hebrew and "Hymn of the Fathers" in the Greek. Its stated purpose is to sing "the praises of pious men ['anšēy ḥesed; the Greek reads "famous men"], our fathers in their generations." As Baumgartner noted, this "hymn" is fundamentally different from the hymns of the Psalter, because here praise is directed to men, not to

---

1. On historical reviews in postbiblical Jewish literature, see E. Janssen, *Das Gottesvolk und seine Geschichte: Geschichtsbild und Selbstverständnis im palästinensischen Schrifttum von Jesus Sirach bis Jehuda ha-Nasi* (Neukirchen-Vluyn: Neukirchener Verlag, 1971); R. G. Hall, *Revealed Histories* (Sheffield: JSOT Press, 1991).

God.[2] There is no real parallel for such a catalog of praises in the Hebrew Bible.[3] The closest parallels are found in other books of the Apocrypha, 1 Macc. 2:51–60; 4 Macc. 16:20–23; 18:11–19, and in the New Testament in Hebrews 11. Each of these passages recalls heroes of the past as examples of virtue. In 1 Maccabees 2, Mattathias tells his sons: "Remember the deeds of the ancestors, which they did in their generations; and you will receive an everlasting name," and he proceeds to list examples of faithfulness and other virtues. In 4 Maccabees 16, the mother encourages her sons in the face of persecution by recalling the examples of Isaac and of Daniel and his companions. In chapter 18, she adds Abel and Joseph to the list, and also reminds them of the zeal of Phinehas. The Letter to the Hebrews assembles "a cloud of witnesses" to the efficacy of faith. Each of these passages, however, has a hortatory purpose, and appeals directly for imitation on the part of the reader. Similarly, the Damascus Document from Qumran provides a list of people who did and who did not walk in the stubbornness of their hearts, with obvious hortatory implications (CD 2:17–3:12). In Ben Sira, the context is laudatory rather than hortatory, and it may not be possible to emulate the exalted deeds of the heroes in question, especially since their glory is associated with the offices they held.

Hellenistic literature offers a more promising background for this section of the book. There are ample Hellenistic precedents for the listing of examples, especially for hortatory purposes.[4] The homiletical practice of Diaspora Judaism, insofar as it can be reconstructed from the writings of Philo and from such texts as the Testaments of the Twelve Patriarchs, also made extensive use of examples to illustrate virtues and vices.[5] Sirach must surely have encountered Hellenistic rhetoric in his travels, or even in Jerusalem. One can hardly infer from the Praise of the Fathers that he had any technical training in the subject, but the very fact that he devotes the concluding section of his book to the praise of human beings betrays the influence of Hellenistic culture on a fairly deep level.

A more specific generic analogy for Sirach's Praise of the Fathers was proposed by Thierry Maertens, who pointed to the genre *De Viris Illustribus* in Latin literature, from a somewhat later period.[6] (Noted practitioners included Cornelius Nepos in the first century B.C.E. and Suetonius in the late first and early second centuries C.E.) This genre was a development of the kind of biography

2. W. Baumgartner, "Die literarischen Gattungen in der Weisheit des Jesus Sirach," *ZAW* 34 (1914) 173.

3. E. Jacob, "L'Histoire d'Israel vue par Ben Sira," in *Mélanges bibliques rédigés en l'honneur de André Robert* (Paris: Bloud et Guy, 1957) 288–94; R. T. Siebeneck, "May Their Bones Return to Life! Sirach's Praise of the Fathers," *CBQ* 21 (1959) 411–28.

4. A. Lumpe, "Exemplum," *RAC* 6 (1966) 1229–57.

5. See H. Thyen, *Der Stil der Jüdisch-Hellenistischen Homilie* (Göttingen: Vandenhoeck & Ruprecht, 1955).

6. T. Maertens, *L'Éloge des pères (Ecclésiastique XLIV–L)* (Bruges: Abbaye de Saint-André, 1956).

practiced in the Peripatetic school in the Hellenistic period, which is believed to have been developed initially by the fourth-century B.C.E. writer Aristoxenus.[7] Both the Hellenistic and Roman biographies, however, were largely anecdotal and often made use of gossip. They do not in fact bear much analogy to the brief eulogies of the fathers in Ben Sira. The best Hellenistic analogy proposed to date is the encomium, a genre originally developed by Isocrates (436–338 B.C.E.).[8] Here at least we have a common purpose: to praise the subject of the speech or poem. T. R. Lee has argued that Sirach 44–50 should be understood specifically as an encomium of the High Priest Simon II. In his analysis, the structure of the composition is as follows: *Prooemium* (44:1–15); *genos* (enumerating the ancestors of the subject and their merits; 44:16–49:16); *praxeis* (the achievements of the main subject; 50:1–21); and epilogue (50:22–24). The praise of Simon in chapter 50 is certainly the climax of this section, but the fathers are praised in their own right, and not merely as a buildup for Simon. The explicit purpose of the poem, stated at the beginning (44:1) is to praise pious men, "our fathers in their generations." The poem, then, must be viewed as an encomium of all the heroes of Israelite history, and not just as an encomium of Simon.

Two other suggestions about the genre of the Praise of the Fathers require a brief comment.

Martin Hengel has noted that the theme of succession appears several times (Sir. 44:17; 46:1, 12; 47:12; 48:8, 12).[9] The Peripatetic philosopher Sotion of Alexandria, who was a contemporary of Sirach, wrote a work on *The Succession of the Philosophers* in thirteen books, in which he treated each philosopher as the definitive successor of another. Further Jewish examples of the interest in establishing a line of succession can be found in the historian Eupolemus, who wrote of the succession of kings and prophets, in the Maccabean period, and Josephus, who refers to "the exact succession of the prophets" (*Ag. Ap.* 1.41). The classic expression of the principle of succession in Judaism is found in the Mishnaic tractate *Pirke Aboth,* which begins by declaring that "Moses received Torah from Sinai and delivered it to Joshua, and Joshua to the Elders, and the Elders to the Prophets, and the Prophets delivered it to the men of the Great Synagogue." It goes on to link the rabbinic authorities down to the second century C.E. (the Tannaim) in a chain of succession.[10] Lee objects to this analogy, on the ground that Sirach does not develop a single line of succession but refers variously to the succession of judges, kings, and prophets.[11] Nonetheless, the fact that the theme of succession is noted so

7. T. R. Lee, *Studies in the Form of Sirach 44–50* (SBLDS 75; Atlanta: Scholars, 1986) 54–73.

8. Lee, *Studies,* 83–245.

9. Hengel, *Judaism and Hellenism* (Philadelphia: Fortress, 1974) 1.136.

10. R. Travers Herford, *The Ethics of the Talmud: Sayings of the Fathers* (New York: Schocken, 1962).

11. Lee, *Studies,* 79.

frequently at all testifies to a new interest on Ben Sira's part, which arises from his Hellenistic cultural context rather than from Hebrew tradition.

Finally, Burton Mack has argued that while the Praise of the Fathers is "a poem with decidedly encomiastic traits," it "should not be called an encomium, any more than a chronicle or epic historiography. It is an epic poem that cannot be reduced to fit any of the genres thus far noted as precursor literatures."[12] It may be true enough that this passage does not fit any genre exactly, but it is surely not an "epic poem," if that expression bears any relation to the paradigmatic epics of Homer. The trademark of the epic is narrative continuity, and this is precisely what is lacking in Ben Sira's review of Israelite history. "Encomium" remains the most satisfactory genre label for the Praise of the Fathers.

The Fathers in Sequence

The Praise of the Fathers begins with an introductory section in Sir. 44:1–15. Sirach lists the kind of people he is about to praise. These reflect the major categories of the Hebrew scriptures: kings and rulers, prophets, and sages. Those who composed musical tunes (v. 5) may be the psalmists. In v. 6, the Hebrew "stalwart men" (*'anšēy ḥayil*) is rendered somewhat tendentiously as "wealthy men" in the Greek. The priesthood is noticeably absent here, but figures prominently in the subsequent chapters. The praise extends to all who were famous in their generations. Of necessity, only those who have left behind a lasting name can be listed. Sirach recognizes another form of qualified immortality, however, in the continuity and loyalty of descendants, even when the names of the ancestors have been forgotten. In the end, the honor of all the forefathers is ratified by the approval of the congregation.

From Noah to Phinehas

The review follows the order of the Hebrew scriptures. Sirach 44:16–45:26 draws on the Pentateuchal narratives. The initial mention of Enoch is textually suspect. It is not found in the Masada manuscript or in the Syriac, although it is in the Greek and Hebrew MS B. Enoch is said to walk with the Lord, rather than with *'ĕlohîm,* God (or angels) as in Genesis. In the Hebrew he is a sign of knowledge, because of his knowledge of the heavenly world. The Greek makes him a symbol of repentance, probably under the influence of Philo.[13] It is noteworthy that Sirach shows no awareness of the story of Enoch as amplified in *1 Enoch.*

---

12. B. L. Mack, *Wisdom and the Hebrew Epic: Ben Sira's Hymn in Praise of the Fathers* (Chicago: Univ. of Chicago Press, 1986) 136.

13. *De Abrahamo* 17.

Most probably, Sirach's list began with Noah, as the recipient of the first covenant. Abraham's covenant is also emphasized. Abraham is said to have kept the law of the Most High, even though it was not yet revealed to Moses. This is in accordance with Sirach's tendency to associate the Law with creation (cf. 17:11; 24:1–7), and also with the tendency in some other texts from the Hellenistic period (notably *Jubilees*) to retroject the observance of the Law back to the beginnings of human history. There is a passing reference to the sacrifice of Isaac, seen purely as a test of Abraham. As we should expect in view of the encomiastic character of the composition, no mention is made of Jacob's trickery. Isaac and Jacob are of interest primarily as links between Abraham and Moses in the transmission of the divine blessings.

Moses, predictably, is praised as the recipient of the Torah. In contrast to some Hellenistic Jewish writers, such as Philo, Sirach does not call Moses a lawgiver, nor does he attribute any creativity to him. He makes him equal in glory to the angels (holy ones), whereas Philo, following Exod. 7:1, makes him a god (*De Vita Mos.* 1.155–58). The "law of life and knowledge" (45:5) echoes the "law of life" given by the creator in 17:11. The most striking thing about the praise of Moses, however, is that it is less than half as long as the praise of Aaron.

Although biblical tradition ranked both Moses and Aaron as priests (Ps. 99:6), Sirach does not acknowledge the priesthood of Moses. He follows the Priestly source in emphasizing the eternal covenant of priesthood with Aaron, but he ignores Zadok, and does not refer to the sons of Zadok, who are prominent in the Dead Sea Scrolls.[14] We can scarcely infer, however, that he was polemicizing against the restriction of the priesthood to the Zadokites. He may equally well have regarded them as the only legitimate Aaronids, and so found it unnecessary to single them out. The only individual who receives treatment of length comparable to that of Aaron is the Zadokite High Priest, Simon II, in chapter 50. The covenant with Aaron, however, extends to all the priesthood, not just the office of High Priest.

Sirach touches only briefly on Aaron's role in offering sacrifices, and gives equal time to his teaching authority. The basis of that authority was stated in the blessing of Moses, in Deut. 33:10: "They teach Jacob your ordinances, and Israel your law."[15] (The teaching role of the eschatological priest is illustrated powerfully in 4Q541 [4QAaron A] from Qumran.) Sirach's interest in sacrifices does not match his interest in the priesthood. In the Hellenistic period, the High Priest also wielded political power in Jerusalem and could be a powerful patron for a scribe like Sirach. Sirach notes how rebellion against Aaron was put down by God. The implications for his own day were obvious.

14. See S. Olyan, "Ben Sira's Relationship to the Priesthood," *HTR* 80 (1987) 261–86.

15. Compare the emphasis on the teaching role of the eschatological High Priest in the Aramaic 4Q541 (4QAaron A) from Qumran. See J. J. Collins, *The Scepter and the Star: The Messiahs of the Dead Sea Scrolls and Other Ancient Literature* (New York: Doubleday, 1995) 88–89.

Phinehas is third in the priestly line, after Aaron and Eleazar (45:23; cf. Num. 25:7–13). In 1 Macc. 2:26, Phinehas is cited as the model for the violent action of Mattathias. Ben Sira ignores the militancy of Phinehas. His interest is in the covenant he receives. It is clear from v. 25 that this is not conceived as a separate covenant but is part of the heritage of Aaron. This covenant is contrasted with the Davidic covenant in a way that implies its superiority, because of its inclusiveness: "The inheritance of a man is for his son alone, but the heritage of Aaron is for all his descendants" (45:25).[16] There is no implication, however, that the priesthood has inherited the promise to David.[17] The offices of kingship and priesthood are clearly distinct.

This section of the Praise of the Fathers ends with a benediction addressed to the priesthood:

> And now bless the Lord who has crowned you with glory. May the Lord grant you wisdom of mind to judge his people with justice, so that their prosperity may not vanish and that their glory may endure through all their generations.
>
> (45:26)

This is the only time that the Praise of the Fathers is interrupted by a benediction, but there is another benediction at the end of the praise of Simon II in 50:22–24. It is no coincidence that both benedictions follow the praises of priestly figures.

Judges, Kings, and Prophets

After Phinehas, Sirach turns to Joshua, son of Nun, whose praise extends to ten verses. (Moses received five.) This extensive praise of Joshua is initially surprising, since there is little militancy in Sirach apart from the disputed prayer in chapter 36. Even more surprising is the statement that he was an aide (Hebrew; Greek: successor) to Moses in the *prophetic* office, despite the fact that neither Moses nor Joshua is said to have delivered oracles. Of primary importance to Sirach is the glory enjoyed by Joshua. In this respect he resembles the High Priest Simon (compare 46:2 with 50:5). He also resembles the priesthood in his role as intercessor (46:5), although this role might also be deemed prophetic (Josh. 10:6; cf. Moses in Num. 14:13–19). Finally, Joshua and Caleb are praised for loyalty, a virtue already commended by Sirach (6:14–17; 26:19–26).

---

16. The Hebrew text must be corrected in the light of the Greek. See Skehan and DiLella, *The Wisdom of Ben Sira*, 510; K. E. Pomykala, *The Davidic Dynasty Tradition in Early Judaism: Its History and Significance for Messianism* (Atlanta: Scholars, 1995) 132–44.

17. This was suggested by H. Stadelmann, *Ben Sira als Schriftgelehrter* (Tübingen: Mohr, 1980) 157. Stadelmann follows the Hebrew text of Sir. 45:25, reading "the inheritance of a man is in accordance with his glory" (rather than "for his son alone"), and reads this as a reference to the priesthood.

The prayer for the judges in 46:11–12, that their bones sprout from their place, is not found in the Hebrew at this point in the text, but appears apropos of the minor prophets in 49:10. The new life envisaged by Sirach is the immortality of their names in their children.

Samuel is characterized primarily as a prophet, by anointing rulers, judging in light of the Law, and being a trustworthy seer. He is also admired for offering sacrifice (without consideration of his priestly rank), and for his profession of innocence. His apparition to Saul (46:20; cf. 1 Sam. 28:19) adds to his glory, with no hint of disapproval of Saul for consulting the witch of Endor. Rather the incident redounds to the glory of Samuel by showing how he transcended his death.

After a brief mention of Nathan, chapter 47 deals with the early kings. Saul is passed over in silence, but David is glorified for his early exploits, with some elaboration. Where 1 Sam. 17:34–35 has David rescue animals from lions and bears, Sirach has him play with lions and bears as if they were lambs and kids.[18] There may be overtones here of the idyllic scene in Isa. 11:6–9, where wolves and leopards and lions are said to be pacified in the time of the messianic shoot of David. Sirach 47:8 reflects David's reputation as author of the psalms.[19] Verses 9–10 reflect the portrayal of David in 1 Chronicles 15–26, emphasizing his role as organizer of the temple cult and liturgy. The most controversial statement about David is found in 47:11, which says that God exalted his "horn" or strength forever. Some scholars see here an expression of messianic hope,[20] while others disagree.[21] Sirach does not cite Nathan's oracle, and expresses no hope or expectation for the restoration of the Davidic line. He does, however, acknowledge the biblical record that everlasting kingship was promised to David. While the word translated "covenant" in 47:11c is *ḥōq* (statute) rather than the usual word for covenant (*běrît*), the latter word is used in 45:25, and so there can be no doubt that Sirach affirmed a Davidic covenant. The perpetuity of the line is also affirmed in 47:22. In short, Sirach acknowledged the promise, but it was far from the center of his own devotion. He attached far greater importance to the High Priesthood, the actual seat of authority in his time. We shall comment further on the issue of messianic expectation below, with reference to the psalm found in Sirach 51, between vv. 12 and 13 in the Hebrew text.

18. Contrast the more subdued portrayal of David's youth in Psalm 151 (= 11Q5, col. 28).
19. Compare the list of David's compositions in 11QPsalms (11Q5, col. 27).
20. Smend, *Die Weisheit des Jesus Sirach,* 452; J. D. Martin, "Ben Sira's Hymn to the Fathers: A Messianic Perspective," in A. S. van der Woude, ed., *Crises and Perspectives* (Leiden: Brill, 1986 = *OTS* 24) 107–23; Skehan and DiLella, *The Wisdom of Ben Sira,* 526; Olyan, "Ben Sira's Relationship to the Priesthood," 282–83.
21. A. Caquot, "Ben Sira et le Messianisme," *Semitica* 16 (1966) 43–68; Stadelmann, *Ben Sira als Schriftgelehrter,* 157; Mack, *Wisdom and the Hebrew Epic,* 35–36; Pomykala, *The Davidic Dynasty Tradition,* 145.

The success and prosperity of Solomon are accounted to the credit of David (47:12). Solomon is praised as the one who built the Temple and, inevitably, for his wisdom. He is said to overflow like the Nile, as Wisdom or the Torah does in 24:27. But Solomon also illustrates a favorite theme of Sirach, the danger of women. The Hebrew of 47:19b reads "and you let them rule over your body," which recalls Sir. 9:2, and the fear that a woman can trample a man's strength. Sirach makes Solomon's sexual transgressions rather than idolatry responsible for the division of the kingship.[22] He nonetheless affirms the enduring validity of the promise to David. While Solomon's record is mixed, Rehoboam and Jeroboam are the only figures in the review who are entirely negative. Sirach follows the standard Deuteronomic line in making the sin of Jeroboam responsible for the exile of northern Israel.

The treatment of Elijah (48:1–11) dwells on the miraculous and therefore glorious aspects of his career. His ascent in a chariot of fire (v. 9) fits this theme and is already found in 2 Kings 3:11. Sirach 48:10, however, is exceptional in Ben Sira in citing a prophecy as eschatological prediction: "At the appointed time, it is written, you are destined to calm the wrath of God before it breaks out in fury, to turn the hearts of parents to their children, and to restore the tribes of Jacob." The prophecy in question is Mal. 3:23–24, supplemented by Isa. 49:10. Because there is so little eschatological interest in Sirach, some scholars argue that this verse must be secondary.[23] But Sirach here is only affirming what he found in the older scripture. There is no implication of imminent expectation. Like the promise to David, Elijah's return was part of the tradition, even if it had little importance for Sirach's overall theology. The idea of an appointed time is reminiscent of Dan. 10:14; 11:29, 40, and so on, but it is also quite compatible with the wisdom tradition. Sirach himself argued that God's commands would be accomplished and the goodness of God's works would become clear each in its (proper) time (39:16–17), and that the Lord had made one day more important than another (33:7–9).[24]

The praise of Elisha is in a similar vein to that of Elijah. Sirach notes that "even when he was dead, his body prophesied" (48:13–14; cf. 2 Kings 13:21). As in the case of Samuel, Sirach is interested in the continuing power of the prophet after death, but there is no implication of a lasting resurrection.[25]

The kings of Judah are judged by the Deuteronomic criterion of observance of the Torah (49:4, cf. 2 Kings 18:3; 23:25). Sirach emphasizes the miraculous in the accounts of Hezekiah and Isaiah (cf. 2 Kings 20:8–11; Isa. 38:7–8). The Hebrew text of 48:21 attributes the destruction of the Assyrians to a plague.

22. Contrast the biblical account in 1 Kings 11:11–13, 33.
23. Th. Middendorp, *Die Stellung Jesus Ben Siras zwischen Judentum und Hellenismus* (Leiden: Brill, 1973) 134; Mack, *Wisdom and the Hebrew Epic,* 200.
24. Cf. Qoh. 3:1–8; G. von Rad, *Wisdom in Israel* (Nashville: Abingdon, 1972) 263–83.
25. See the discussion of Sir. 48:11 in the preceding chapter.

The Greek substitutes the angel of the Lord, in conformity to the biblical text (2 Kings 19:35; Isa. 37:36). It is clear from Sir. 48:24–25 that Sirach attributed the whole book of Isaiah to the eighth-century prophet, who is credited with foretelling the future return from the exile.

Jeremiah is credited with foretelling the destruction of Jerusalem and the Temple. Ezekiel is remembered only for his vision, which was influential in apocalyptic circles (e.g., Daniel 10) and was also elaborated in 4QPseudo-Ezekiel (4Q385) at Qumran. Job is mentioned between Ezekiel and the Minor Prophets. It is possible that Josephus also included Job among the prophets when he said that they wrote the history from Moses to Artaxerxes in thirteen books (*Ag. Ap.* 1.40). The order of the biblical books was not set in the time of Sirach. The Minor Prophets are treated as one book (Sir. 49:10), and are understood to convey a message of hope rather than doom. There is no reference to Daniel. The book of Daniel was presumably not yet composed when Sirach wrote.

Sirach's review of the major personalities in the Hebrew scriptures is selective and not exhaustive. The book of Esther, like Daniel, may not have been known in Jerusalem at this time, since it is also absent from the Dead Sea Scrolls. But Sirach also ignores Ruth and fails to select a single woman for praise. He passes over Joseph, an oddity that may be explained by his antipathy to the Samaritans (if indeed the reference to "the foolish people who live in Shechem" in 50:26 is to be attributed to Ben Sira himself).[26] Joseph, however, is mentioned in the retrospective stanza in 49:14–16. Saul may be omitted as insufficiently glorious or inspiring. Most striking, however, is the omission of Ezra, especially in view of the inclusion of Nehemiah (49:13). It would be rash to conclude that the book of Ezra was not yet written, or that it was unknown to Ben Sira.[27] Several explanations have been proposed, for example, a rejection of Ezra's policies on mixed marriages,[28] or the view that Ezra was too narrowly concerned with the Mosaic law,[29] or that Sirach's priestly sympathies were offended by the prominence of the Levites in Ezra.[30] But these suggestions are hardly convincing. In view of Sirach's own enthusiasm for the Law, he should have found it possible to say something positive about Ezra, just as he did about Solomon. All we can safely conclude is that the story of Ezra had not yet

26. J. D. Purvis, "Ben Sira and the Foolish People of Shechem," *The Samaritan Pentateuch and the Origin of the Samaritan Sect* (Cambridge, Mass.: Harvard Univ. Press, 1968) 119–29.

27. K. F. Pohlmann, *Studien zum Dritten Esra* (Göttingen: Vandenhoeck & Ruprecht, 1970) 72–73, argues that Sirach did not know the book of Ezra, and the argument is occasionally repeated. See J. Blenkinsopp, *Ezra-Nehemiah* (Philadelphia: Westminster, 1988) 55.

28. Smend, *Die Weisheit des Jesus Sirach,* 474.

29. G. H. Box and W. O. E. Oesterley, "Sirach," in R. H. Charles, ed., *The Apocrypha and Pseudepigrapha of the Old Testament* (Oxford: Clarendon, 1913) 1.506.

30. P. Höffken, "Warum schwieg Ben Sira über Ezra," *ZAW* 87 (1975) 184–202. See the critique of this suggestion by C. R. Begg, "Ben Sirach's Non-Mention of Ezra," *BN* 42 (1988) 14–18.

acquired the kind of "canonical" status enjoyed by Solomon, and consequently that Sirach felt no obligation to include him. It may be, as Joseph Blenkinsopp has suggested, that "Ezra's single-minded theocratic ideal was uncongenial to the author,"[31] but in fact the omission remains an enigma. The inclusion of Nehemiah is readily intelligible, because his building activity offered a precedent to that of Simon II.[32] Sirach places similar emphasis on the building activities of Hezekiah, Zerubbabel, and Joshua the High Priest (49:12).

Sirach 49:14–16 concludes the review of the ancient past, by commenting on the glory of Enoch, Joseph, Shem, Seth, Enosh, and Adam. Except for the questionable reference to Enoch in 44:16, none of these figures has been mentioned in the Praise of the Fathers. Only Adam has figured in the rest of Sirach's book. All except Joseph are antediluvian (Shem is son of Noah; Gen. 6:10). The authenticity of this passage has been questioned, as it does not fit any pattern of characterization in Sirach,[33] but this is not necessarily a decisive objection to a concluding stanza. If the passage goes back to Sirach, it represents the earliest reference to the splendor of Adam.[34]

The High Priest Simon
(50:1–28)

Even though Sir. 49:14–16 seems to conclude the praise of the ancestors, the passage on Simon is the culmination of all that has gone before.[35] Simon II was High Priest in the years 219–196 B.C.E. He was presumably dead when Ben Sira wrote. (Sirach 50:1 refers to what he did "in his generation" and "in his days.") Under his leadership, Jerusalem welcomed Antiochus III of Syria, and assisted him in besieging the garrison of the Egyptian general Scopas.[36] Antiochus, in return, assisted in the restoration of the Temple. Sirach does not mention the support of the foreign king, but he takes evident pride in the renewed splendor of the Temple. Sirach had already noted building projects under Solomon, Hezekiah, Zerubbabel and Joshua, and Nehemiah. Verses 5–21 describe the splendor of the High Priest performing his functions, recalling the splendor of Aaron in Sir. 45:6–13. A comparable account of the splendor of the High Priest is found in the *Letter of Aristeas*, 96–99. All the sons of Aaron

31. Blenkinsopp, *Ezra-Nehemiah*, 55.
32. Begg, "Ben Sirach's Non-Mention of Ezra."
33. Mack, *Wisdom and the Hebrew Epic*, 201.
34. Another early reference to the glory of Adam is found in CD 3:20. This motif was later elaborated, notably by Philo, *De Opif.*, 136–41.
35. See the discussion of this issue in Lee, *Studies*, 10–21. Scholars who view chap. 50 as an appendix that is not integral to the foregoing poem include Smend, *Die Weisheit des Jesus Sirach*, 412; Box and Oesterley, "Sirach," 479; Maertens, *L'Éloge des pères*, 195–96; and Jacob, "L'Histoire d'Israel," 290.
36. Josephus, *Ant.* 12.129–53.

share in the splendor. The recollection of the blessing pronounced by Simon (vv. 20–21) leads into the benediction in vv. 22–24. The Hebrew (MS B) includes in v. 23 a prayer for Simon, that God might fulfill for him the covenant with Phinehas forever. In fact, Simon's line came to an end in the next generation, in the reign of Antiochus IV. Simon's son Onias III was murdered in 172 B.C.E. (2 Macc. 4:34), while another son, Jason, became a protagonist in the so-called "Hellenistic Reform." His grandson, Onias IV, fled to Egypt and founded a temple at Leontopolis. We cannot know whether Ben Sira had an inkling of impending problems when he prayed for the preservation of the line. The Greek translator dropped the prayer for Simon and substituted a prayer that God might redeem Israel "in our days." If Sirach wrote during the High Priesthood of Onias III, the praise of Simon would redound to the glory of his son, but would also serve as a reminder to the son of the standards set by the father.

It is quite possible that the benediction in 50:22–24 was the conclusion of Sirach's book, except for the subscription in vv. 27–28. The numerical proverb in vv. 25–26 ("two nations my soul detests, and the third is not even a people") has no relation to the context, and could easily have been added by a scribe. The Edomites of Seir and the Philistines were old enemies of Israel. The thrust of the proverb is to express dislike for the Samaritans. There was conflict between Samaritans and Jews in the time of Ezra. The books of Maccabees imply that the Samaritans were sympathetic to Antiochus Epiphanes in his suppression of Judaism (1 Macc. 3:10; 2 Macc. 4:2). At the end of the second century B.C.E., Shechem was sacked and the temple on Mount Gerizim razed by John Hyrcanus. We have no evidence for Jewish-Samaritan relations in Sirach's time. The fact that open hostility developed in the Hasmonean era leads to the suspicion that the epilogue to Ben Sira was added by a scribe in that period or later, rather than by the sage himself.

A Pattern of Characterization

Burton Mack has claimed to find a consistent pattern of characterization in the Praise of the Fathers, which has seven components: designation of office, mention of divine approbation or election, reference to a covenant, mention of the person's character or piety, an account of the deeds, reference to the historical situation, and mention of rewards.[37] Obviously, this pattern is abbreviated in some of the shorter characterizations, and even the longer accounts do not necessarily have all seven components. There are no covenants with judges or with prophets. Mack further maintains that "it is the concept of office that determines the pattern as a whole." "The assignment of a figure to an office is so consistently emphasized that one must ask whether it is not the office that

---

37. Mack, *Wisdom and the Hebrew Epic,* 18.

makes the man for Ben Sira. . . . The greatness of these heroes is directly related to the great significance of these offices."[38] All the figures in question are
public figures, who play significant roles in the interest of the people. Consequently, "the congregation proclaims their praise" (44:15). Their glory is attained through their discharge of their official functions. Glory is not individualistic, but is derived from contributing to the well-being of the people. The
emphasis on human glory is surely a reflection of Ben Sira's Hellenistic culture. Yet the things that are considered glorious, such as priesthood and
prophecy, are not especially Hellenistic, and are rooted in traditional Jewish
values.

Sirach's review of the glorious figures of Israel's history attains a point of
fulfillment in the description of the High Priest Simon. There is no admission
of any lack in Simon's glory. The fact that he was subject to the Seleucids de-
tracts nothing from him, because he used that circumstance to improve the situation of his people. In view of Sirach's evident contentment with the glory of
Simon, there would seem to be very little room for any eschatological expectation in his book.

Messianism in Sirach?

Nonetheless, scholars intermittently claim to find evidence of eschatology,
or more specifically of messianic expectation, in Sirach's book. R. T. Siebeneck suggested "that Sirach went to the past not only to enlighten the present
but also the future, specifically the future messianic kingdom."[39] The characterization of the fathers, then, would carry implications for a new Abraham, a
new Moses, and so on. Siebeneck admitted, however, that the only explicitly
eschatological passage in the poem was the reference to the second coming of
Elijah in 48:10. There is no reason whatever to suspect eschatological implications in the rest of the poem.

We have already considered the reference to the horn of David in 47:11,
which serves as the mainstay for the argument that Sirach entertained messianic expectations. It is true that "horn" sometimes has a messianic nuance,[40]
but this is not necessarily so. In Sir. 49:4–5 we read that the "horn" of the Davidic kings was given to others because all but three were sinful. The same passage refers to the end of the Judean royal line without any hint of a future
restoration.[41]

---

38. Ibid., 19.
39. Siebeneck, "May Their Bones Return to Life," 425, following Maertens, *L'Éloge des pères,*
195–96.
40. Olyan, "Ben Sira's Relationship to the Priesthood," 283, citing Ezek. 29:21; Pss. 132:17;
148:14.
41. Pomykala, *The Davidic Dynasty Tradition,* 147.

There is a messianic reference in the Hebrew text B from the Cairo Geniza, chapter 51, but it is generally admitted that the psalm in which it is found was not composed by Sirach. This Hebrew psalm is inserted between vv. 12 and 13 (according to the numbering of the Greek version). It is modeled on Psalm 136, insofar as it has the refrain "for his mercy endures forever." Lines 8 and 9 read:

> Give thanks to him who makes a horn to sprout for the house of David,
> for his mercy endures forever.
> Give thanks to him who chose the sons of Zadok to be priests,
> for his mercy endures forever.

Line 8 must be understood as expressing hope for a Davidic messiah. Compare 1QSb 5:26, where the blessing for the prince of the congregation, that he may establish the kingdom of his people forever, includes the prayer "May he place upon you horns of iron." While Sir. 47:11 affirmed the covenant with David, it showed no such messianic hope. The following line affirms the priesthood of the sons of Zadok. Since messianic expectation was conspicuously lacking even in the Maccabean period,[42] it is unlikely that this combination of Davidic hope and Zadokite priesthood dates from pre-Hasmonean times. It is more likely that this psalm originated in the Qumran community, which was staunchly pro-Zadokite and had lively messianic expectations.[43] DiLella suggests that the Hebrew MS B from the Cairo Geniza was one of the documents found by the Karaites in a cave near Jericho about 800 C.E., and had originated at Qumran.[44] This would explain how the messianic ideology of the Dead Sea sect could have found its way into a manuscript of Sirach's book.

The Prayer for
Deliverance in Chapter 36

There is one passage in Ben Sira that burns with eschatological fervor. This is the prayer for deliverance in chapter 36, which asks God to hasten the day, remember the appointed time, crush the heads of the hostile rulers, gather all the tribes of Jacob, and have pity on the city of the sanctuary.[45] The prayer begins with an appeal for mercy to the "God of all" (36:1). The phrase recurs in 45:23c (Hebrew only) and 50:22a (Greek only; Hebrew reads "God of Israel"). The prayer then asks God to put all the nations in fear, as had been the case during the original conquest of Canaan (cf. Exod. 15:15–16). The nations should be brought

---

42. See Collins, *The Scepter and the Star,* 31–41.
43. Ibid., 74–101.
44. Skehan and DiLella, *The Wisdom of Ben Sira,* 569.
45. J. Marböck, "Das Gebet um die Rettung Zions Sir 36,1–22 (G:33,1–13a; 36,16b–22) im Zusammenhang der Geschichtsschau Ben Siras," in J. B. Bauer, ed., *Memoria Jerusalem* (Jerusalem/Graz: Akademische Druck- und Verlagsanstalt, 1977) 93–116.

low just as Israel has been; as God humiliated Israel to show the nations his holiness, so now he should bring down the nations to show his glory. The prayer asks for new signs and wonders in the manner of the exodus (Exod. 7:3). This is the only passage in the book where the exodus is evoked as an event of liberation.

The notion that God determines the times has been encountered already in Sir. 33:7–9. In Sir. 36:10, Hebrew "end" (*qēṣ*) is rendered in the Greek as *kairos,* time. There is some tension in 36:10 between the belief that God can hasten the day of vengeance and the belief that the time is appointed and God need only remember it. The linking of the terms "end" and "appointed time" derives from Hab. 2:3, and is reflected several times in Daniel (10:14; 11:27, 35), where it invariably implies that the time is fixed. The idea that God can hasten the end arises from the urgency of prayer. Sirach 36:11 calls for complete destruction of the enemy, leaving no survivors. The crushing of the heads of the enemy is an allusion to Balaam's oracle in Num. 24:18 (cf. also Ps. 110:6). Especially noteworthy is the emphasis on the fulfillment of prophecy in Sir. 36:20–21. While Sirach's sage studies prophecies (39:1), we do not get the sense that he expects them to be fulfilled. The fulfillment of prophecy is of urgent concern in Daniel (cf. Daniel 9) and in the Dead Sea Scrolls (e.g., the Pesher on Habakkuk). The Apostrophe to Zion from Qumran (11QPs 22:5–6, 13–14) also recalls the visions of the prophets for the restoration of Zion.

This prayer is exceptional both in the context of the biblical psalms and in the context of Ben Sira. In the canonical psalter, communal prayers for deliverance are usually embedded in psalms of complaint, which include some description of the abject state of the community.[46] Comparable prayers from the Second Temple period also typically include a confession of sin. Examples can be found in Ezra 9:6–15; Neh. 9:6–37; Dan. 9:4–19; Prayer of Azariah; Bar. 2:11–26; 4QWords of the Luminaries. There is no confession of sin in Sirach 36, and the distress of Jerusalem is only hinted at. Instead we find a direct appeal for divine intervention.

This prayer is the main passage in Sirach whose authenticity is disputed.[47] Nowhere else in the book does Sirach express antagonism toward foreign nations. If this prayer was composed by Ben Sira, the hostile rulers would have to be the Seleucids, who ruled Palestine from 198 B.C.E. But Josephus reports that Seleucid rule was initially welcomed by the Jews, and that Antiochus III (the Great) helped restore the city and supported the temple cult (*Ant.* 12.129–53). The High Priest of the day was Simon II (the Just), who is eulogized in Sir. 50:1–21. The restoration of Temple and city are listed as his outstanding achievements. It is scarcely conceivable, then, that Sirach would have

---

46. Pss. 44; 74; 79–80; 83; E. Gerstenberger, *Psalms: with an Introduction to Cultic Poetry* (Grand Rapids: Eerdmans, 1988) 14.

47. Middendorp, *Die Stellung Jesus Ben Siras,* 125–32.

viewed Antiochus III as a hostile ruler, or asked God to crush his head.[48] In fact, such sentiments make sense only in or after the time of Antiochus IV Epiphanes, and there is no other reflection of that reign in Sirach's book. The possibility that the poem was composed before the Syrian takeover, and regards the Ptolemies as the enemy, is unsatisfactory because of the generic denunciation of foreign nations, which does not discriminate between friend and foe. Ben Sira's book was certainly compiled after the Seleucid conquest. The likelihood that this prayer is a secondary addition to the book is overwhelming. It is true that 35:21–26 provides a lead into the prayer.[49] This explains why the prayer was inserted at this particular point. But the passage in chapter 35 is concerned with the universal judgment of God on the unrighteous, whereby "he repays mortals according to their deeds" (35:24). The prayer in chapter 36 calls for a highly particular judgment on the enemies of Israel.

In fact, this prayer in chapter 36 is remote in spirit from the rest of the teaching of Sirach, and was most probably inserted into the book at the time of the Maccabean crisis. Sirach's own view of history has no eschatological urgency. Rather, he takes a synchronic view, where the goal of history lies in the establishment of certain institutions and offices. When a High Priest like Simon II is in office in Jerusalem, there is no need to crush the heads of foreign rulers; they can be manipulated for the greater glory of the Jewish people. Zion is already filled with the divine majesty.

Sirach's lack of eschatological concern is typical of the biblical wisdom tradition. Eschatology is equally absent from Proverbs, Job, and Qoheleth. We should not necessarily conclude that eschatology is incompatible with wisdom literature as such. Sirach modified the tradition boldly in some respects. Later wisdom writers would modify it in others. Some of the sapiential texts from Qumran, at most a century after Sirach, combined their traditional wisdom teaching with an eschatological perspective, which entailed a cosmic judgment. We shall find elaborate eschatological expectations in the Wisdom of Solomon, but these are more concerned with the immortality of the soul than with the restoration of Israel. Neither the wisdom texts from the Dead Sea nor the Wisdom of Solomon exhibit the kind of eschatological urgency reflected in the prayer in Sirach 36 or in some apocalyptic literature. Nonetheless, wisdom literature was a flexible macro-genre that could incorporate a wide and changing array of concerns. Ben Sira's lack of eschatology is a result not of the genre he uses but of his social location, which led him to eulogize the status quo, and of the relative peace and prosperity of the time at which he wrote. It would be much more difficult to view the institutions of Israel, and especially the High Priesthood, with such uncritical contentment after the upheavals of the Maccabean era.

48. *Pace* Skehan and DiLella, *The Wisdom of Ben Sira,* 422, who argue that Antiochus III was arrogant enough to say, "There is no other beside me" (36:12b).

49. Skehan and DiLella, *The Wisdom of Ben Sira,* 420.

Chapter 7.
Wisdom in the Dead Sea Scrolls

The corpus of Hebrew wisdom literature from the Hellenistic period has been greatly increased by the Dead Sea Scrolls.[1] There are fragments of the biblical books of Proverbs (4Q102, 103), Qoheleth (4Q109, 110), and Job (2Q15; 4Q99, 100, 101).[2] There are also two Aramaic Targums of Job (4Q157, 11Q10). Ben Sira is represented by two small fragments from Cave 2 (2Q18), but Sir. 51:13–19a is found in the Psalms Scroll, and extensive fragments of the book were found at Masada.

The Psalms Scroll from Qumran Cave 11 also contains the Hebrew text of a wisdom psalm that was previously known only in Syriac (Psalm 154 = 11QPsª 18:1–16).[3] This psalm locates the voice of wisdom in "the assembly of the pious" (*qĕhal ḥăsîdîm*): "When they eat in fullness, she is mentioned; and when they drink in community together, their meditation is on the Law of the Most High." It also contends that praise is as acceptable to the Most High as sacrifice. Inevitably, one thinks of the Qumran Community Rule, which pre-scribes Torah study every night of the year (1QS 6) and speaks of atonement by righteous action (1QS 8). The psalm, however, is not necessarily a product of the Qumran community, since there may have been other assemblies of the pious who studied the Torah. In the words of the editor: "Although Psalm 154 may have been proto-Essenian and may have originated in early circles which later became part of the Qumran group, the psalm itself lacks any characteristic that should be called exclusively Essenian. It is biblical in vocabulary and tone, not Essenian or Qumranian."[4] The psalm is closer in spirit to the Torah

---

1. The most comprehensive review available is that of D. J. Harrington, *Wisdom Texts from Qumran* (London: Routledge, 1996). See also L. H. Schiffman, *Reclaiming the Dead Sea Scrolls* (New York: Jewish Publication Society, 1994) 197–210. An older survey before the unpublished scrolls became available was included in M. Küchler, *Frühjüdische Weisheitstraditionen* (OBO 26; Göttingen: Vandenhoeck & Ruprecht, 1979) 88–109.

2. E. Ulrich, "An Index of the Passages in the Biblical Manuscripts from the Judean Desert (part 2: Isaiah-Chronicles)," *Dead Sea Discoveries* 2 (1995) 86–107.

3. The "Hymn to the Creator" (11Q5 26:9–15), a previously unknown composition also found in the Psalms Scroll, resembles some of the material in Sir. 39–43, but it is an independent hymn and not part of a wisdom book.

4. J. A. Sanders, *The Dead Sea Psalms Scroll* (Ithaca, N.Y.: Cornell Univ. Press, 1967) 109.

psalms of the Psalter than to Ben Sira, as it does not deal with practical wisdom and it is not clear that it envisages any other sources of wisdom apart from the Torah and the worship of the Lord.

Even this brief comment on Psalm 154 raises one of the most persistent problems in the study of the sapiential materials in the Dead Sea Scrolls: Should they be regarded as products of the community, or communities, responsible for hiding them in the caves, or should they be viewed as part of the general heritage of Judaism around the turn of the era?[5] There are plenty of examples of wisdom language and motifs in texts that are clearly sectarian, such as the Community Rule, the Damascus Document, and the Hodayot.[6] Wisdom traditions were a significant source for the thinking of the Dead Sea sect. Our concern here, however, is with works that are formally sapiential instructions, not rule books or hymns (although some passages in both the Community Rule and the Damascus Document can reasonably be regarded as wisdom instructions). Such texts typically give little indication of their provenance. On the one hand, they do not refer to community structures or organization, but deal rather with family relationships and individual piety. Nevertheless, a text that deals with family issues, and presupposes married life, could be a product of the Dead Sea sect or a branch thereof. (The Damascus Document clearly envisages married members.) On the other hand, some of these texts, in varying degrees, contain language and motifs that link them with sectarian compositions such as the Community Rule. This linkage does not prove sectarian origin, but at least it shows that the texts in question belong to a stream of tradition that was congenial to the sectarians and not necessarily common to all parties in Judaism at the time.

Traditional Wisdom in the Scrolls

The more traditional end of the spectrum of wisdom instructions at Qumran is represented by several fragmentary works.[7] 4Q420–21 describes the characteristics of a wise and righteous person. 4Q424 describes persons to be avoided and others to be cultivated as friends. Even though 4Q413 is introduced as a psalm, its subject is the way of wisdom. 4Q525 is known as 4QBeatitudes because it contains a series of five macarisms that invite comparison

---

5. On the methodological problem, see C. Newsom, " 'Sectually explicit' Literature from Qumran," in W. Propp et al., eds., *The Hebrew Bible and Its Interpreters* (Winona Lake, Ind.: Eisenbrauns, 1990) 167–87.

6. A. Lange, *Weisheit und Prädestination: Weisheitliche Urordnung und Prädestination in der Textfunden von Qumran* (Leiden: Brill, 1995) 195–295; A.-M. Denis, *Les thèmes de connaissance dans le Document de Damas* (Studia Hellenistica 15; Louvain: Leuven Univ. Press, 1967); S. J. Tanzer, "The Sages at Qumran: Wisdom in the *Hodayot*" (Ph.D. Diss. Harvard, 1987).

7. Harrington, *Wisdom Texts from Qumran*, 60–74.

with the Beatitudes in the Gospels.[8] The most notable of these is found in vv. 3–4: "Happy is the man [who] has attained wisdom, and walks by the Law of the Most High," a theme familiar from Psalm 1 and Psalm 154. The wisdom expounded in these texts, however, is unexceptional, and gives no hint of sectarian provenance.

Two texts published in the 1960s also resemble traditional wisdom, but their interpretation is more controversial. One of these, 4Q184, was dubbed "The Wiles of the Wicked Woman" by its editor, John Allegro.[9] Allegro reconstructed "the harlot" (*hazzōnāh*) in the opening line to read "the harlot utters folly," but this reconstruction is not possible.[10] He also exaggerated the sexual explicitness of the poem (e.g., interpreting references to "the pit" as "the pit of her legs" rather than the netherworld). But while his characterization of the poem is exaggerated, the general tenor has been maintained in subsequent translations.[11]

There can be no doubt that the poem is modeled on the portrayal of the "strange woman" of Proverbs 2, 5, 7, and 9. Already in Proverbs, this figure is ambiguous. She is portrayed realistically as a streetwalker, who seduces the unsuspecting youth, in Proverbs. But in Proverbs 9 "the foolish woman" (or "Lady Folly") is clearly the antitype to Lady Wisdom, an allegorical representation of foolishness rather than a mere prostitute.[12] Since the paths of this woman are repeatedly said to lead to the netherworld (Prov. 2:18–19; 5:5; 7:27; 9:18), some scholars have suspected an allusion to a goddess.[13] It is not surprising, then, that the Qumran text has also given rise to a wide range of interpretations. These range from the fanciful (a rival sect, Simon Maccabee)[14] to the intriguing (the

---

8. E. Puech, "4Q525 et les péricopes des béatitudes en Ben Sira et Matthieu," *RB* 98 (1991) 80–106.

9. J. M. Allegro, "The Wiles of the Wicked Woman: A Sapiential Work from Qumran's Fourth Cave," *PEQ* 96 (1964) 53–55; idem, *Qumrân Cave 4: I (4Q158–4Q186) (DJD* 5; Oxford: Clarendon, 1968) 82–85. Also indispensable is the review by J. Strugnell, "Notes en marge du volume V des 'Discoveries in the Judaean Desert of Jordan,'" *RevQ* 7 (1970) 163–276 (pp. 263–68 deal with this text).

10. Strugnell, "Notes en marge," 264. Only the final *he* is preserved. If the preceding letter were *nun,* the ligature should be visible.

11. G. Vermes, *The Dead Sea Scrolls in English* (4th ed.; London: Penguin, 1995) 273, entitles the poem "The Seductress." F. García Martínez, *The Dead Sea Scrolls Translated* (Leiden: Brill, 1994) 379, retains "Wiles of the Wicked Woman."

12. On the symbolism of these passages, see C. Newsom, "Woman and the Discourse of Patriarchal Wisdom: A Study of Proverbs 1–9," in P. L. Day, ed., *Gender and Difference in Ancient Israel* (Minneapolis: Fortress, 1989) 142–60.

13. R. J. Clifford, "Proverbs IX: A Suggested Ugaritic Parallel," *VT* 25 (1975) 298–306.

14. J. Carmignac, "Poème allégorique sur la secte rivale," *RevQ* 5 (1965) 361–74, argues that the woman represents a rival sect. Cf. A. M. Gazov-Ginzberg, "Double-Meaning in a Qumran Work: The Wiles of the Wicked Woman," *RevQ* 6 (1967) 279–85. Even more fanciful is H. Burgmann, "The Wicked Woman: Der Makkabäer Simon?" *RevQ* 8 (1974) 323–59.

demoness Lilith).[15] It is probably safe to say that something more is intended than a warning against adultery. The statement that "she is the beginning of all the ways of iniquity" (v. 8) invites a contrast with the figure of wisdom in Prov. 8:22, and suggests that a way of life is at stake. She looks at

> the righteous man to overtake him, and at the important man to trip him up, at upright men to pervert their way, and at the righteous elect to keep them from the commandment, at the firmly established to bring them down wantonly, and those who walk in uprightness to change the statute, to cause the humble to transgress from God, and to turn their steps from the ways of righteousness . . . to lead people astray in the ways of the pit, and to seduce with flatteries the sons of men.[16]

What is at issue here is not just sexual transgression but a whole way of life, of which sexual transgression is only a representative instance. The word translated "flatteries" (*ḥălāqôt*) is the same word that is often used to characterize the teachings of the opponents of the Dead Sea sect as "seekers after smooth things."[17] Nevertheless, it is too narrow to say that the text warns against "the dangers and attraction of false doctrine."[18] The woman in the poem represents the way of folly, and this is not only a matter of false doctrine.[19]

On the one hand, 4Q184 lacks the realism of Proverbs 7 in portraying the harlot, and relies on more abstract formulations. On the other hand, the association of the foolish woman with death and the netherworld, which was already prominent in Proverbs, becomes more pronounced. The relatively short poem contains no fewer than eleven allusions to the netherworld.[20] Most significant is the statement in v. 7: "Amid everlasting fire is her inheritance, not among all those who shine brightly." Neither Proverbs nor Sirach entertained the prospect of everlasting fire for the wicked. In Jewish tradition, this was an innovation of the apocalyptic literature (cf. *1 Enoch* 10:6, 13; 18:15). It is also the punishment of those who walk in the spirit of darkness in 1QS 4:13. The older wisdom of Proverbs, Qoheleth, and Sirach was resolutely this-worldly in its worldview. In the Dead Sea Scrolls we find that wisdom instruction could also envisage the prospect of judgment after death.

---

15. J. Baumgarten, "On the Nature of the Seductress in 4Q184," *RevQ* 57 (1991) 133–43, identifies her as the malevolent female spirit Lilith.

16. Lines 13–17, trans. Harrington.

17. This is usually taken as a reference to the Pharisees, because of its use in the pesher on Nahum with reference to the opponents of King Alexander Jannaeus. The word *ḥălāqôt* may be a play on the *halakah* of the Pharisees.

18. Vermes, *The Dead Sea Scrolls in English*, 273.

19. Compare R. D. Moore, "Personification of the Seduction of Evil: The Wiles of the Wicked Woman," *RevQ* 10 (1981) 505–19.

20. Baumgarten, "On the Nature of the Seductress," 139.

The threat of everlasting fire is not the only motif that 4Q184 has in common with the treatise on the Two Spirits in the Community Rule. The "wicked woman" is associated with "foundations of darkness" (v. 4); "her lodgings are beds of darkness. In the deep of night are her tents; in the foundations of gloom she sets up her dwelling"(vv. 5–6). She could easily be taken to symbolize the way of darkness, and the text was probably read this way at Qumran. This interpretation does not require that the text was composed as a sectarian allegory, but it is closer in spirit to the sectarian texts (such as 1QS) than to the practical, this-worldly wisdom of Ben Sira.

The use of a female figure to symbolize the way of folly and wickedness undoubtedly has negative implications for the author's view of women. Nonetheless, it does not warrant the conclusion that either the author or the people who hid the scrolls were misogynists. The semierotic poem in praise of wisdom as a feminine figure in Sirach 51 is also preserved in the Psalms Scroll. Neither poem was necessarily composed for a sectarian context. All we can say is that 4Q184 continues an old tradition of using the sexually promiscuous woman as a symbol for the way of folly. It differs from the older texts primarily by introducing an eschatological perspective, and by heightening the dualistic implications of the symbolism through the imagery of darkness.

Another relatively traditional piece of wisdom teaching is found in 4Q185.[21] The addressees of this text are called not only "you simple" and "my sons," but also "sons of men" and "my people." The last appellation led Strugnell to compare the text to "sapiential meditations in the style of Psalm 78" rather than to the standard wisdom books.[22] (Psalm 78 begins, "Give ear, O my people, to my teaching," and proceeds to reflect on the history of Israel.) The occasional address to "you, sons of men," however, shows that the horizon of the text is not limited to Israel. The text uses the familiar sapiential mixture of commands and prohibitions. The extant fragments conclude with beatitudes, congratulating "the man to whom she has been given." The "she" is presumably wisdom.[23]

Three features of this fragmentary text are noteworthy in light of the earlier wisdom tradition.

First, the fragmentary beginning of the text speaks of an impending judgment by the angels. We shall find that the most extensive wisdom text found at Qumran (4QSapiential Work A) also begins with a passage about divine judgment. The role of angels in judgment is noted prominently both in the Community Rule (1QS 4:11–13) and the Damascus Document (CD 2:5–6), both of which speak

21. H. Lichtenberger, "Eine weisheitliche Mahnrede in den Qumranfunde (4Q185)," in M. Delcor, ed., *Qumrân: Sa piété, sa theologie et son milieu* (BETL 46; Louvain: Leuven Univ. Press, 1978) 151–62; T. H. Tobin, "4Q185 and Jewish Wisdom Literature," in H. W. Attridge et al., eds., *Of Scribes and Scrolls* (Lanham, Md.: University Press of America, 1990) 145–52.

22. Strugnell, "Notes en marge," 269.

23. Harrington, *Wisdom Texts from Qumran*, 38, allows that it may be either wisdom or the Torah.

of "the angels of destruction." Angels also play a part in judgment in the books of Daniel and *Enoch,* both of which are older than the Qumran sect.[24] Here again we see the influence of apocalyptic traditions on a wisdom instruction. Since the following passage compares the "sons of men" to grass that sprouts and dies, the judgment envisaged is probably the judgment of the individual dead.

Second, the speaker calls on "my people" to reflect on the might of God[25] and remember the marvels he did in Egypt (1:14–15). The use of Israel's history as a source of wisdom and teaching was pioneered by Ben Sira, but also in a different way by the psalmists (e.g., Psalm 78). It would be developed further, in a different context, in the Wisdom of Solomon. Despite the avoidance of Israel's history in Proverbs and Qoheleth, its inclusion in a wisdom book no longer occasions surprise in the second century B.C.E.

Third, the text admonishes its readers not to rebel against the words of the Lord (2:3). This insistence on the Commandments in a wisdom text is also unsurprising in a text from the second century B.C.E., and follows from Sirach's identification of wisdom with the Torah.

This text, too, warns against holding fast to wisdom with flatteries (*ḥălāqôt*), but there is no reason to posit a sectarian setting. The use of the divine name in 2:3 would be exceptional in a sectarian context. This text reflects a stage in the wisdom tradition when appeal to the specific traditions of Israel and apocalyptic notions of eschatological judgment had become part of sapiential instruction. It is unlikely that this was the case before the second century B.C.E.[26]

4QSapiential Work A

The most extensive wisdom instruction found at Qumran is the text known as 4QSapiential Work A.[27] Fragments of this work are preserved in 1Q26, 4Q415, 416, 417, 418, and 423.[28] The fact that six (or seven)[29] copies have

24. E.g., Dan. 12:1–4; *1 Enoch* 1:9; 10:9–10; 20:1–4; 88:1–3, etc. See Tobin, "4Q185," 151.

25. The might of God is often associated with wisdom at Qumran, e.g., 1QS 4:3; 10:16; 1QH 12:13. See Tobin, "4Q185," 150.

26. The text to which 4Q185 is most closely related is 4Q370, "An Admonition Based on the Flood." See C. Newsom, "4Q370: An Admonition Based on the Flood," *RevQ* 13 (1988) 23–43. Newsom argues that there must be some interdependence between the two texts, since they have two *topoi* in common, the ephemeral nature of human existence and the need to pay attention to the wonders of God. It is not possible to determine which text is prior.

27. This is distinguished from 4QSapiential Work B (4Q419) and 4QSapiential Work C (4Q424).

28. Harrington, *Wisdom Texts from Qumran,* 40–59. See also Harrington, "Wisdom at Qumran," in E. Ulrich and J. VanderKam, eds., *The Community of the Renewed Covenant* (Notre Dame, Ind.: Univ. of Notre Dame Press, 1994) 137–52; Lange, *Weisheit und Prädestination,* 45–92.

29. T. Elgvin counts seven copies rather than six, distinguishing between 4Q418a and 4Q418b. See Elgvin, "Wisdom, Revelation and Eschatology in an Early Essene Writing," in E. H. Lovering, ed., *SBL Seminar Papers* (Atlanta: Scholars, 1995) 440; "The Mystery to Come: Early Essene Theology of Revelation," in T. L. Thompson and N. P. Lemche, eds., *Qumran between the Old and the New Testament* (Sheffield: Sheffield Academic Press: forthcoming).

survived is an indication of the importance of the work at Qumran, and the fact that a copy was hidden in Cave 1, with several major sectarian scrolls, may also be significant. Although substantial parts of the text have survived, it is extremely fragmentary, and therefore it is impossible to get a clear picture of its literary structure. The available evidence suggests that, like the book of Ben Sira, it was loosely structured at best. Like Sirach (and late Egyptian wisdom texts) it combines passages of a practical nature with theoretical, theological reflections.[30] Unlike Sirach, the extant passages have no poems on wisdom itself, either personified or not. This work has, however, a frame of reference that distinguishes it from Sirach and biblical wisdom. The addressee is told repeatedly to "gaze on the mystery that is to be" (*raz nihyeh*). While the exact understanding of this mystery is, appropriately enough, mysterious, it appears to involve a cosmological and eschatological frame that is quite different from the this-worldly perspective of Sirach.

The practical instruction of this text is found mainly in 4Q416 and 417. These texts are punctuated by reminders that "you are poor." They are not explicit as to whether the poverty is material or spiritual, but the context indicates that material poverty is involved. In 4Q416, the comments on poverty follow a section that deals with credit and responsibility in financial matters: "As much as a man's creditor will lend him in money, hastily pay him back and you will be on an equal footing with him. If your treasure purse [lit. "cup"] you have entrusted to your creditor on account of your friends, you have given away all your life for its price. Hasten and give what is his, and take back your purse" (4Q416 frag. 2, col. ii. 4–5 [=4Q417 frag. 1, col. ii. 6–8]; cf. 4Q416 2. iii. 5–7).[31] This advice is in accordance with age-old wisdom (cf. Prov. 22:26–27). But the Qumran text has no precedent in Jewish wisdom literature for its insistence on the poverty of the addressee.

This poverty is not at all an ideal. The addressee is warned, "Do not esteem yourself highly for poverty when you are a pauper, lest you bring into contempt your own life" (4Q416 2. ii. 20–21). One should not refuse prosperity if the opportunity offers: "If they cause you to dwell in splendor, walk in it. . . . To Him who glorifies you give honor, and praise His name always. For out of poverty He has lifted up your head and with nobles He has seated you" (4Q416 2. iii. 9–12). The author realizes that people want more than they can afford, but warns against

---

30. Harrington, *Wisdom Texts from Qumran*, 40–41.

31. Translations follow those of Harrington, with minor modifications. A provisional transcription of the Hebrew text can be found in B. Z. Wacholder and M. G. Abegg, *A Preliminary Edition of the Unpublished Dead Sea Scrolls* (Washington: Biblical Archaeology Society, 1992) Fascicle 2. 44–154; 166–71. Translations can also be found in García Martínez, *The Dead Sea Scrolls Translated*, 383–93; and in R. H. Eisenman and M. Wise, *The Dead Sea Scrolls Uncovered* (Rockport, Mass.: Element, 1992) 241–54 (of 4Q416 and 418). On the Eisenman and Wise translation, see D. J. Harrington and J. Strugnell, "Qumran Cave 4 Texts: A New Publication," *JBL* 112 (1993) 491–99.

it: "You are poor. Do not desire something beyond your share and do not be confused by it, lest you displace your boundary" (4Q416 2. iii. 8). Also, poverty should not be made into an excuse for not studying (4Q416 2. iii. 12–13). In all of this it would seem that the text has material poverty in mind.[32] The ideal seems to be one of moderation and self-sufficiency: "Do not sate yourself with food when there is no clothing, and do not drink wine when there is no food; do not seek after luxury when you lack bread" (4Q416 2. ii. 18–20); or again: "That which He gives you for food eat, and do not [eat] any more lest [you sh]orten your life" (4Q417 1. i. 20–21). Similar advice on moderation and self-sufficiency can be found in Proverbs and Ben Sira, but there is no assumption in the earlier tradition that the addressee is poor. On the contrary, it is assumed that Ben Sira's instruction, and that of the sages in general, is primarily directed toward the well-to-do. The social setting of the Sapiential Work from Qumran would seem to be significantly different from that of the earlier wisdom books.

The poverty of the addressees is implied in one other text from the early second century B.C.E., the Epistle of Enoch (*1 Enoch* 92–105). But the Enochic text has a very different tone, as it repeatedly pronounces woes against the rich and promises the poor redress in the life to come.[33] The Sapiential Work from Qumran expresses no anger against the rich. It does, however, share with the Enochic text an eschatological perspective to which we shall return below.

The Qumran Sapiential Work also advocates humility, but the advice seems to be bound up with the low estate of the addressee. A very fragmentary and obscure passage at the beginning of 4Q417, on the subject of reproof, cautions, "Do not overlook your own sins." Underlying this advice is the reminder: "For what is more insignificant than a poor man?" (4Q417 1. i. 10). Honor and shame play some role in these relationships. 4Q416 2. ii. 15–16 counsels: "Do not abase your soul before one who is not equal to you. . . . Do not smite one who does not have your strength lest you make him stumble, and your own shame you increase greatly." These concerns, however, are not nearly as prominent in the Qumran text as they were in Ben Sira.

The poverty of the addressees does not appreciably alter their familial relations, except perhaps that it underlines the need for respectful and proper behavior. The Sapiential Work agrees with Sirach, and all of Hellenistic Jewish ethics, in demanding honor for both father and mother,[34] but it adds some

---

32. A further indication of the addressee's low estate can be seen in 4Q417 1. i. 25, which gives advice for a person subjected to flogging.

33. E.g., *1 Enoch* 94:8: "Woe to you, you rich, for you have trusted in your riches, but from your riches you will depart for you did not remember the Most High in the days of your riches." See G. W. Nickelsburg, "The Apocalyptic Message of 1 Enoch 92–105," *CBQ* 39 (1977) 309–28; "Riches, the Rich, and God's Judgment in 1 Enoch 92–105 and the Gospel according to Luke," *NTS* 25 (1979) 324–44.

34. Sir. 4:1–17; 7:27–28. See the discussion in Chapter 4 above.

interesting motivational phrases: "for as God is to a man, so is his father, and as a master [or: the Lord? *ădōnîm*] is to a fellow, so is his mother" (4Q416 2. iii. 16).[35] Several reasons are given for this exalted status. First, "They are the smelting-pot that was pregnant with you" (cf. Sir. 7:27–28). Second, "God set them in authority over you." Third, "They uncovered your ear to the mystery that is to be." Finally, one should revere one's parents "for the sake of your honor . . . for the sake of your life and the length of your days" (cf. Sir. 3:11: "His father's glory is a person's own glory").

There are two distinctive notes here. Family relations are not egalitarian. They are based on an order, which is believed to be God-given. The concern for hierarchical authority is also typical of sectarian texts such as the Community Rule. This text may be unique in making gratitude for religious education a reason for honoring one's parents. (Incidentally, it also shows that the primary locus for religious education was the home.) The importance attached to this education is entailed by the importance of "the mystery that is to be." It also suggests that this document is not addressed to Jewish society at large, but to those who share an understanding of this mystery and therefore have been initiated into some kind of movement, whatever its relationship to the settlement at Qumran.

Relations between man and wife are characterized by respect, but also by hierarchical authority. The implied addressee of the document is male.[36] He is admonished not to "dishonor the vessel of your bosom" (4Q416 2. ii. 21), although we are not told what that might entail.[37] The main discussion of marriage in 4Q416 frag. 2, col. iv emphasizes that it is "you He has set in authority over her. . . . Her father He has not set in authority over her; from her mother He has separated her." The passage frequently alludes to Genesis. The wife is called "the helpmeet of your flesh" (Gen. 2:20; an allusion also found in Sir. 36:29). The unity of flesh, however, is interpreted primarily in terms of authority. The chief example of this authority that is preserved concerns the making and fulfilling of vows: "Let her not make numerous vows and votive offerings. . . . Every oath binding on her, to vow a vow, annul it according to an utterance of your mouth." This passage addresses an old problem, where the piety of the wife incurred expense for the husband.[38] The biblical basis for the advice given here is found in Num. 30:6–15. The subject is also addressed in CD 16:10–12, but there the advice is more cautious: no one should annul a vow without checking as to whether it should be kept; it should be annulled only if it violates the covenant.

35. The manuscript actually reads "for as a father [*ab*] is to a man, so is his father," but this is obviously a mistake. Read *'ēl*, with Harrington. See Harrington, "Wisdom at Qumran," 148.

36. There is an exception to this in 4Q415. See below.

37. For the wife as "vessel," cf. 1 Thess. 4:4. Ps.-Phocylides 189 admonishes against outraging one's wife for shameful ways of intercourse, but the context in 4Q416 is not sexual. The addressee is also told not to bring his own life into contempt.

38. K. van der Toorn, *From Her Cradle to Her Grave: The Role of Religion in the Life of the Israelite and the Babylonian Woman* (Sheffield: JSOT Press, 1994) 97–99.

In the Sapiential Work, however, the annulment of vows is only an instance of a broader principle: "He has set you in authority so that she should walk in your good pleasure" (4Q416 2. iv. 8). Ben Sira exploited that principle and used it as a justification for divorce: "If she does not conform to your authority, cut her off from your flesh" (Sir. 25:26). It may be significant that there is no mention of divorce in the Sapiential Work. Since the work is so fragmentary we cannot be sure that the subject was not addressed, but divorce (or at least remarriage) was prohibited by the Damascus Document (CD 4:20–21), and the Sapiential Work may have had a similar position.

One other feature on the subject of women should be noted. One fragment of the manuscript 4Q415 (frag. 2, col. ii) includes imperatives and prohibitions in the feminine form and so seems to be addressed to women, at least in part. (Other fragments of the manuscript contain masculine verbs, and also contain some of the characteristic phrases of Sapiential Work A, such as "the mystery that is to be" and "you are poor.")[39] The actual advice given is quite conventional. The addressees are told to beware of violating the "holy covenant" and to be a subject of praise for all men. But the very fact that a wisdom instruction is addressed to women is highly unusual.

The Mystery That Is to Be

The ethics advocated in this Qumran wisdom text are not merely ad hoc. They are grounded in a comprehensive view of the purpose of creation, summed up in the enigmatic phrase *raz nihyeh*, which is variously translated as "the mystery that is to come,"[40] "the mystery of existence,"[41] or, here, "the mystery that is to be." The phrase occurs more than twenty times in Sapiential Work A. The word *raz*, mystery, appears in Hebrew and Aramaic as a loanword of Persian origin. It appears nine times in the Aramaic chapters of Daniel. It occurs repeatedly in the Qumran Community Rule and Hodayot, and nine times in the Book of Mysteries.[42] The phrase *raz nihyeh* also occurs in the Book of Mysteries and in the Community Rule (1QS 11:3–4). The word *nihyeh* is a niphal participle of the verb to be. It also occurs, without the word *raz*, in 1QS 3:15 and CD 2:10 (plural: *nihyot*). It is usually taken to have a

---

39. García Martínez, *The Dead Sea Scrolls Translated,* 500, regards this manuscript as only "possibly" part of Sapiential Work A. Wacholder and Abegg, *A Preliminary Edition,* 44, list it as part of a separate work.

40. So Harrington. Cf. J. T. Milik in *DJD* 1.102–104: "le mystère future."

41. So Eisenman and Wise, *The Dead Sea Scrolls Uncovered,* 241–55; cf. Lange, *Weisheit und Prädestination,* 52, "das Geheimnis des Werdens."

42. Elgvin, "The Mystery to Come."

future sense ("that which is to be"), but that sense does not appear to do full justice to its use in Sapiential Work A.

In the Sapiential Work, this mystery is repeatedly mentioned as an object of study. It is taught by parents to their children (4Q416 2. iii. 18). People should study it despite their poverty (4Q416 2. iii. 14). People should meditate on it by day and by night (4Q417 2. i. 6). Only a few passages, however, betray the content of this mystery. One important text is found in 4Q417 1. i. 10–12: "Gaze on the *raz nihyeh* and understand the birth-time of salvation, and know who is to inherit glory and evil." The passage goes on to promise "eternal joy for their sorrow." From this we may gather that the mystery concerns eschatological salvation and judgment. This datum supports the view that the phrase should be translated as "the mystery to come." Another passage, however, is more comprehensive. 4Q417 2. i. 8–9 is a difficult text, and the correct reading and translation is disputed. Elgvin translates literally: "The God of knowledge is the secret of truth. With the mystery to come, he separated the woman. . . ."[43] Harrington, by slight emendation, produces a more satisfactory text: "The God of knowledge is the foundation of truth and by the mystery that is to be/come He has laid out its foundation and its deeds."[44] In either case, the passage associates the *raz nihyeh* with creation. It also speaks of "truth and iniquity; wisdom and foolishness you will . . . in all their ways together with their punishment(s) in all ages everlasting and eternal punishment" (lines 8 and 9). There is an obvious parallel here to the discourse on the Two Spirits in 1QS 3–4, which uses the same Hebrew phrase for the God of knowledge, and also uses the niphal participle *nhyh* for that which is to be. The Sapiential text does not speak of two spirits of light and of darkness, but it does distinguish between "a people of spirit" and "a spirit of flesh" (17.2. i. 16–17) and outlines two ways, truth and iniquity or wisdom and folly, which lead to eternal reward and punishment. The *raz nihyeh* seems to encompass the entire divine plan, from creation to eschatological judgment.[45] If it has an eschatological thrust, this is because the marvelous mysteries become clear only in the end. The person who studies the mystery, however, can know "the glory of His might together with His marvelous mysteries and His mighty acts" (line 13). The mystery encompasses "the coming of the years and the going of the periods" (4Q418 123. ii. 2–8). Study of the mystery can also explain anything else that happens in life. So, if one rises from poverty to dwell in splendor, one should study the source of this good fortune by the *raz nihyeh* (4Q416 2. iii. 9).

---

43. Ibid.

44. Harrington, 53, reading *yswd*, foundation, instead of *swd*, council, for the first "foundation" and *'wšh*, foundation, rather than *'išh*, woman, for the second.

45. Lange, *Weisheit und Prädestination*, 60, understands the phrase to refer to the preexistent order of creation. J. Licht, *The Rule Scroll: A Scroll from the Wilderness of Judaea: 1QS. 1QSa. 1QSb. Text, Introduction and Commentary* (Hebrew; Jerusalem: Bialik, 1965) 90, 228, takes it as the mystery of the universe, including the future.

Harrington has suggested that the mystery is "a body of teaching" distinct from the Torah.[46] Possible candidates include the Instruction on the Two Spirits in 1QS 3–4; the Book of Meditation (the Book of Hagu or Hagi), by which youths are to be educated for ten years according to 1QSa 1:6–8 and which judges are supposed to study, according to CD 10:6 and 13:2; or the Book of Mysteries (1Q27, 4Q299–301). It is not apparent that the mystery must be identified simply with the contents of one writing. It may be the subject matter to which each of these writings refers. The Book of Meditation is especially intriguing, as it is discussed in a passage in 4Q417 2. i. 14–18:

> Engraved is the ordinance, and ordained is all the punishment. For engraved is that which is ordained by God against all the iniquities of the children of Seth. And written in His presence is a book of remembrance of those who keep His word, and it is the Vision of Meditation (Hagu/i) and a Book of Remembrance. He gave it as an inheritance to *ĕnôš* (Man), together with a spiritual people, for his inclination (*yiṣrô*) is (or: He fashioned him, *yāṣārô*) after the likeness of the Holy Ones. But the Meditation is no longer given to the spirit of flesh, for it did not distinguish between good and evil, according to the judgment of its spirit. And now, O understanding son, gaze on the mystery that is to be and know the inheritance of all the living.[47]

The "Book of Remembrance" is an allusion to Mal. 3:16: "A book of remembrance was written before Him of those who revered the Lord and thought on His name." In the Qumran context, this book has strongly apocalyptic overtones. Heavenly tablets and books figure prominently in the books of *Enoch, Daniel,* and *Jubilees.*[48] The reference to engraving also recalls 1QH 9:24 (formerly 1:24): "All things are graven before Thee with the stylus of remembrance for everlasting ages." In some of these cases the emphasis is on the record of rewards and punishments,[49] but in others the whole divine plan is implied.[50] This book may not be the only formulation of the mystery of that which is made to be, but it is surely one formulation of it.

The knowledge contained in the Book of Hagu is angelic. (Compare *1 Enoch* 93:1–2: "Enoch began to speak from the books . . . according to that which appeared to me in the heavenly vision, and which I know from the words of the holy angels and understand from the tablets of heaven.") It is given to *ĕnôš* (Man)

46. Cf. Wacholder and Abegg, *A Preliminary Edition*, xiii, who also consider the possibility that the reference is to specific writings.

47. This passage is the subject of an extensive analysis by Lange, *Weisheit und Prädestination*, 66–90.

48. *1 Enoch* 47:3; 93:1–2; 108:3; Dan. 7:10; 10:21; 12:1; *Jub.* 30:20–22. On the Babylonian background of this motif, see S. Paul, "Heavenly Tablets and the Book of Life," *JANESCU* 5 (1973) 345–53. See the extensive excursus in Lange, *Weisheit und Prädestination*, 69–79.

49. E.g., Dan. 12:1; 4QDibHam.

50. E.g., *1 Enoch* 93:1–2.

because his inclination is after the likeness of the Holy Ones.[51] The reference to *'ĕnôš* here has puzzled commentators. The Hebrew word *'ĕnôš* may be either the proper name of the son of Seth (Gen. 4:26; 5:6–7, 9–11) or a general designation for a human being. Harrington takes it in the latter sense. Lange objects that since *'ĕnôš* here is distinguished from "the spirit of flesh" the reference cannot be to humanity in general and must be to the antediluvian patriarch.[52] There is no parallel, however, for the revelation of a heavenly book to Enosh. *'ĕnôš* in the sense of human being occurs repeatedly in the Hodayot, Community Rule, and other scrolls. Many of these references emphasize the sinful state of the human being.[53] In the Sapiential text, we are told that his *yēṣer* (inclination, nature) is after the likeness of the Holy Ones. Here again the interpretation is disputed, but Lange is on the right track when he takes the point to be the affinity of *'ĕnôš* with the Holy Ones, or angels. The "spiritual people" linked with *'ĕnôš* is contrasted with "the spirit of flesh," which failed to distinguish between good and evil.

This latter phrase holds the key to the correct interpretation of the passage. The context is supplied not by Genesis 4–5 (Enosh) but by the creation of humanity in Genesis 1–3. As we shall see below, the author holds that the knowledge of good and evil is set before humanity from the beginning. The story of Adam in Genesis 3, which is understood as a "Fall" in later tradition, is taken here as a failure to distinguish between good and evil. But this is not the only depiction of Adam in Genesis 1–3. According to Gen. 1:27 he was created "in the image of God" (*bĕṣelem 'ĕlōhîm*). I suggest that the *'ĕnôš* of the Sapiential text is none other than the Adam of Gen. 1:27. In fact, the word *'ĕnôš* is used in precisely this context in 1QS 3:17 in the Instruction on the Two Spirits: "He created *'ĕnôš* to rule the world." The likeness of the Holy Ones, in which his *yēṣer* is fashioned, represents an interpretation of the image of God. (The word *'ĕlōhîm* is often used in the sense of angels in the Scrolls.)

It is well known that Philo of Alexandria understood Genesis to refer to a double creation of man, and that he derived this understanding from an exegetical tradition. In the words of T. H. Tobin: "The double creation of man is an interpretation which tries to explain why the description of the creation of man occurs twice in Genesis. In such an interpretation this is taken to mean that two different "men" were created, the one heavenly and part of the intelligible world, the other earthly and part of the sensible world."[54] Philo understands the two Adams in his own philosophical framework. The Qumran Sapi-

51. Elgvin, "The Mystery to Come," understands this as "a model for the holy ones," taking the holy ones as the members of the community. Lange correctly takes the holy ones as angels.

52. Lange, *Weisheit und Prädestination,* 88.

53. E.g., 1QH 9:25 (= 1:25); 19:10 (= 11:10).

54. T. H. Tobin, *The Creation of Man: Philo and the History of Interpretation* (CBQMS 14; Washington, D. C.: The Catholic Biblical Association, 1983) 108. The clearest example of Philo's interpretation is in *De Opif.* 134–35. Philo's reliance on earlier tradition is apparent in the Questions on Genesis, (*Quaest. Gen.* 1.8a).

ential text understands them as two types of humanity, a spiritual people in the likeness of the Holy Ones and a "spirit of flesh." The duality of human existence is formulated differently in the Instruction on the Two Spirits in the Community Rule: God created *ĕnôš* to rule the world and appointed for him two spirits. The two formulations, however, are attempting to express the same conviction, that humanity is divided dualistically right from creation.

The addressees of the Sapiential text are offered the opportunity to share in the knowledge of the Holy Ones that is withheld from mere flesh. This idea fits well with the "realized eschatology" of such sectarian texts as the Hodayot and Community Rule. This book of remembrance is also called "the Vision of Meditation" (*ḥāzôn hehāgî*).[55] The designation "vision" is unusual, but should probably be related to the repeated exhortations to "gaze upon the mystery that is to be." It also suggests an absorption of a prophetic form, the vision, in the genre of wisdom instruction.

The Origin of Sin

The understanding of the origin of sin and of Genesis 2–3 in the Qumran Sapiential Work can be understood as a development of the understanding that we already found in Sirach. We have noted that Sir. 17:7 ignores the prohibition of eating from the tree of the knowledge of good and evil, but insists that from the beginning God "filled them with knowledge and understanding." Sapiential Work A suggests the kind of exegesis that may underlie this position, by combining Gen. 2:9 and 3:6 so that "every good fruit and every pleasant tree is desirable to give knowledge" (4Q423 2) and any tree in the garden can serve as the tree of the knowledge of good and evil. The garden is a metaphor for life, and the situation of the addressee of the text is the same as that of Adam: "Is [it] not a n[ice] garden. . . . He set you in charge of it to till it and guard it. . . . Thorns and thistles will it cause to sprout for you, and its strength it will not yield to you . . . in your being unfaithful. . . . She who gives birth, and every womb that bears . . . in all your business, for everything it will produce for you."[56] The passage goes on to mention "an eternal planting" and how someone rejects (?) the bad and knows the good.

The passage implies that Adam was not forbidden to eat from the tree of the knowledge of good and evil, but that good and evil were set before him and he

---

55. With Elgvin and Lange. Harrington takes *ḥāzôn* here as "the appearing [of] the meditating on the book of memorial." See further Elgvin, "Wisdom, Revelation and Eschatology in an Early Essene Writing," *SBL Seminar Papers* (1995) 456. Elgvin suggests that the Book of Hagi provided the right interpretation of scripture, but there is no clear evidence for this.

56. T. Elgvin, "4Q423," *DJD* 20 (forthcoming). See also Elgvin, "Admonition Texts from Qumran Cave 4," in M. O. Wise et al., eds., *Methods of Investigation of the Dead Sea Scrolls and the Khirbet Qumran Site: Present Realities and Future Prospects* (New York: New York Academy of Arts and Sciences, 1994) 188; "Wisdom, Revelation and Eschatology," 452–53.

had to choose, as in Sirach 17. In view of the passage we have seen above from 4Q417 2 we should expect two different choices, depending on whether one's inclination is after the likeness of the angels or belongs to the spirit of flesh. For one who chooses the good, the garden of life is pleasant. For one who transgresses, it yields thorns and briars. From the mention of the "eternal planting" Elgvin infers that the one who rejects the bad and knows the good is a member of an elect community, and that "the enlightened members of the community already have a share in the glory of Adam" (cf. CD 3:20; 1QS 4:23; 1QH[a] 17:15). It appears, however, that the text does not describe a permanent, eschatological state, but still envisages the possibility of transgression.

The danger of transgression is related to the effect of the evil inclination. The author cautions his readers: "Do not be deluded with the thought of the evil inclination [. . . .] Investigate the truth" (4Q417 2. ii. 12–13).[57] The term *yēṣer* is used in a positive sense in 4Q417 2. i. 11, "to walk in the inclination of his understanding," and also in 4Q417 2. i. 17, where the inclination of *ʾĕnôš* is after the likeness of the angels. It appears, then, that the "inclination" in 4Q Sapiential Work A can be either good or bad. People can resist the evil inclination, and exercise at least a measure of free choice. The context for human choice in this Sapiential Work is significantly different from that of Sirach, since it is made in view of an impending eschatological judgment.[58]

The Eschatology
of the Sapiential Work

The Sapiential Work differs most radically from the older wisdom teaching of Ben Sira and Qoheleth by its strong eschatological perspective. 4Q416 frag. 1 appears to preserve the beginning of the work. (There is an extensive margin on the righthand side before the writing begins.)[59] While this fragment is badly damaged, so that no complete line survives, it is clear that it provided a cosmological and eschatological framework for the document.[60] (Cf. *1 Enoch* 1.) The cosmic aspect is indicated by phrases such as "Season by season . . . the host of the heavens He has established . . . and luminaries for their portents and signs for their festivals." The eschatological element is clearly preserved: "In

---

57. A reference to *yēṣer bāśār* in 4Q416 1. i. 15–16 is translated by Elgvin as "a creature of flesh" rather than "inclination of the flesh" ("Early Essene Eschatology").

58. On the role of the *yēṣer* in other Qumran texts, see J. J. Collins, "Wisdom, Apocalypticism and the Dead Sea Scrolls," in A. A. Diesel et al., eds., *"Jedes Ding hat seine Zeit . . .": Studien zur israelitischen und altorientalischen Weisheit. Diethelm Michel zum 65 Geburtstag* (Berlin: de Gruyter, 1996) 26–30.

59. Harrington, *Wisdom Texts from Qumran*, 41.

60. For a reconstruction, see T. Elgvin, "Early Essene Eschatology: Judgment and Salvation According to Sapiential Work A," in N. Reynolds and D. Parry, eds., *Proceedings of the Judaean Desert Scrolls Conference at Brigham Young University, 1995* (Leiden: Brill, forthcoming). Elgvin notes several overlapping phrases in 4Q418.

heaven He shall pronounce judgment upon the work of wickedness, but all the sons of truth will be accepted with favor . . . and all iniquity shall come to an end until the epoch of destruction will be finished."

The division of history into ages or periods is typical of apocalyptic literature and also of the major sectarian documents. Here we find a contrast between the *qēṣ rišʿāh*, the epoch of wickedness, and the *qēṣ hāʾemet*, the era of truth. God will put an end to the era of wickedness at the appointed time. The nature of the judgment is spelled out in 4Q418 69. 4–15.[61] The foolish are told: "[For Sheo]l you were formed, and your return will be eternal damnation. . . . All the foolish of heart will be destroyed and the sons of iniquity will not be found any more, and all those who support evil will be asham[ed] at your judgment." In contrast, the righteous are those "whose inheritance is eternal life." Their destiny is "eternal light," glory, and honor. The manner in which this passage addresses the wicked and the righteous in turn is reminiscent of the Epistle of Enoch. The extant description of the judgment, however, has its closest parallel in the Instruction on the Two Spirits, where the wicked are destined for "shameful extinction in the fire of the dark regions," while the righteous anticipate "eternal joy in life without end, a crown of glory and a garment of majesty in unending light." There is an element of realized eschatology in the Sapiential Work, insofar as the elect are granted in this life to share the knowledge of the angels and gaze at the mystery that is hidden from most of humanity. The Sapiential Work says nothing of national restoration, messianism, or an eschatological war, but these themes are also missing in the Instruction on the Two Spirits.[62] It does, however, speak of the punishment ordained by God against the children of Seth (4Q417 2. i. 15). If this is a reference to Balaam's oracle (Num. 24:17), as Harrington suggests, then it may presuppose militant messianic expectations after all.[63]

The Book of Mysteries

The mystery that is to be is also the subject of an instruction known as "The Book of Mysteries" (1Q27 1. i. 1–12; 4Q299 1. 1–4; 4Q300 3. 1–6).[64] Like the Sapiential Work, this text envisages a time when "the begotten of

61. Elgvin, "Early Essene Eschatology."

62. See further Elgvin, "Wisdom, Revelation and Eschatology," 458; idem, "Early Essene Eschatology."

63. On the messianic interpretation of Balaam's Oracle at Qumran, see J. J. Collins, *The Scepter and the Star* (New York: Doubleday, 1995) 49–73.

64. L. H. Schiffman, "4QMysteries b, A Preliminary Edition," *RevQ* 16 (1993) 203–23; "4QMysteries a: A Preliminary Edition and Translation," in Z. Zevit et al., eds., *Solving Riddles and Untying Knots: Biblical, Epigraphic, and Semitic Studies in Honor of Jonas C. Greenfield* (Winona Lake, Ind.: Eisenbrauns, 1995) 207–60; *Reclaiming the Dead Sea Scrolls*, 206–10. See also Lange, *Weisheit und Prädestination*, 93–120.

unrighteousness are delivered up, and wickedness is removed from before righteousness, as darkness is removed from before light. . . . Wickedness will cease forever and righteousness will be revealed as the sun throughout the measure of the world."[65] Another passage denounces magicians who teach transgression.[66] In language reminiscent of Daniel the author insists: "Sealed is the vision, and on the eternal mysteries you have not looked, and you have not come to understand knowledge" (4Q300 1a. ii. 1–5; cf. Dan. 12:9). The vision, traditionally the medium of the prophet, is here appropriated as the vehicle of wisdom. The mysteries of God are revealed in creation, but the author's wisdom rests on a further, special revelation: "With an abundance of insight He opened our ears so that we might hear" (4Q299 8. 6).

The appeal to special revelation suggests strongly that the Book of Mysteries originated in a sectarian milieu. It also poses a question about the nature of sapiential instructions at Qumran. One of the trademarks of the sapiential tradition in the Hebrew Bible was the avoidance of claims to special revelation. The authority of the sage rested to a great degree on tradition, but his teachings were in principle accessible to anyone. In the Qumran texts we find a style of instruction that is based on a mystery, but borrows forms and vocabulary from the traditional wisdom instruction: imperatives and prohibitions, beatitudes, and a range of terms for wisdom and understanding. Wisdom terminology no longer necessarily indicates an empirically based worldview. It can also be used in the service of apocalyptic revelation.

Sectarian Instructions

The combination of wisdom forms with an apocalyptic worldview can be seen most clearly in a series of specifically sectarian instructions. The "Words of the Maskil to the sons of dawn" (4Q298), which is written in cryptic script, is apparently a manual of instruction for novices or postulants.[67] Much of the content is unexceptional: "You who pursue righteousness, understand my words . . ." Only at the end of the extant fragments do we find an apocalyptic note: "You may understand the end of the ages."

Another wisdom instruction intended for a sectarian context is found in CD 2, in a passage that begins: "God loves knowledge. Wisdom and understand-

---

65. Both Schiffman, *Reclaiming the Dead Sea Scrolls,* 207, and Harrington read in the next line, "and all the adherents of the mysteries of Belial will be no more," but the word Belial is not legible in the photographs (Schiffman puts it in brackets). For the light imagery, cf. the Aramaic text 4Q541 (4QAaron A).

66. Lange, *Weisheit und Prädestination,* 93–120, argues that these magicians are associated with the false wisdom spread on earth by the Watchers or fallen angels.

67. S. Pfann, "4Q298: The Maskil's Address to All Sons of Dawn," *JQR* 85 (1994) 203–35.

ing He has set before him, and prudence and knowledge serve Him."[68] The passage goes on to speak of the destruction of those who depart from the way by the hand of all the angels of destruction, and the election of a remnant. God, we are told, "knew the years of their coming and the length and exact duration of their times for all ages to come throughout all eternity."

The most developed, and best preserved, sectarian instruction is the Instruction on the Two Spirits in the Community Rule. Because of its striking dualistic and apocalyptic content, this passage has seldom been considered as a wisdom instruction.[69] Yet it is specifically an instruction: "The Master shall instruct all the sons of light and shall teach them the nature of all the children of men according to the kind of spirit which they possess, the signs identifying their works during their lifetime, their visitation for chastisement, and the time of their reward." We have already noted several points of similarity between the eschatology of this instruction and that of the Sapiential Work. The account of origins goes beyond the Sapiential Work by developing an explicit dualism of two spirits, of light and darkness, but it nonetheless continues a debate about the origin of sin, and the interpretation of Genesis 1–3, that we have already encountered in Ben Sira and the Sapiential Work.

The Instruction on the Two Spirits (1QS 3–4) says that God "created man to rule the world and placed within him two spirits so that he would walk with them until the moment of his visitation." The phrase "to rule the world" (*lĕmemšelet tebel*) reflects the sovereignty given to Adam in Genesis 1. (While the verb in Genesis is *rādāh,* the verb *himšîl* is used in several texts from Cave 4 with reference to the role of Adam [4Q381, 4Q422, the Words of the Heavenly Luminaries, and 4QSapiential Work A].) No exegetical justification is given for the introduction of two spirits, although one may be presupposed. It is possible that the author read the *nišmat ḥayyîm* (breath of life) and the *nepeš ḥayyāh* (living being) of Gen. 2:7 as two spirits.[70] But neither the later midrash nor any source outside of Qumran understood the Genesis text to refer to opposing spirits. Here, then, we have a clear break with the interpretation of Genesis that we have found in Ben Sira and in various texts from Cave 4.

P. Wernberg-Møller has argued that the Instruction on the Two Spirits should be understood in terms of the good and evil inclinations, and that it does not represent a radical break with earlier interpretations:

68. On the sapiential terminology of this passage, see A.-M. Denis, *Les thèmes de connaissance dans le Document de Damas.* On the parallels with the Instruction on the Two Spirits, see Lange, *Weisheit und Prädestination,* 242.

69. See, however, C. Newsom, "The Sage in the Literature of Qumran: The Functions of the Maskil," in J. G. Gammie and L. G. Perdue, eds., *The Sage in Israel and the Ancient Near East* (Winona Lake, Ind.: Eisenbrauns, 1990) 373–82.

70. Compare *Gen. Rab.* 14:10: "Here the *neshamah* (soul) is identified with *nefesh,* whereas in another text [Gen. 17:22] the *neshamah* is equated with *ruah* (spirit) . . . because 'life' (*ḥayyîm*) is written in both texts, proving that they are analogous."

It is significant that our author regards the two "spirits" as created by God, and that according to IV, 23 and our passage both "spirits" dwell in man as created by God. We are therefore not dealing here with a kind of metaphysical, cosmic dualism represented by the two "spirits," but with the idea that man was created by God with two "spirits"—the Old Testament term for "mood" or "disposition." That RWḤWT is used here as a psychological term seems clear; and the implication is that the failure of man to "rule the world" is due to man himself because he allows his "spirit of perversion," that is to say his perverse and sinful propensities, to determine his behaviour. We have thus arrived at the rabbinic distinction between the evil and the good *YEṢER*.[71]

It is certainly true that the two spirits have a psychological dimension. They struggle in the heart of human beings (1QS 4:23). It is also true that the entire passage is based, however loosely, on Genesis 2–3. The Instruction concludes with a statement that God "has given a legacy to the sons of men for knowledge of good [and evil]," a statement that suggests that this document, like Sirach and 4QSapiential Work A, may not have regarded the tree of knowledge as off-limits. Significantly, the Community Rule, like CD, promises the elect that "the glory of Adam" will be theirs (1QS 4:23). But Wernberg-Møller's inference that "we are therefore not dealing here with a kind of metaphysical, cosmic dualism" is a non sequitur. The Instruction clearly identifies the two spirits with the Prince of Lights and the Angel of Darkness (3:20–21). The dualism is simultaneously psychological, moral, and cosmic. There is a synergism between the psychological realm and the agency of the supernatural angels or demons. The cosmic dimension of this dualism unmistakably shows the influence of Zoroastrianism. The passage is also exegetical, but the hermeneutical lens is provided by the Zoroastrian dualism of light and darkness.[72]

The teaching on the two spirits provides a nice focal point for comparison of Ben Sira and Qumran wisdom. Despite the startling novelty of the Community Rule, we can now see its formulation in the context of an ongoing debate in the wisdom schools of Judea in the second century B.C.E. Ben Sira, the Sapiential Work, and the Community Rule all try to understand the problem of sinful behavior in the context of the Genesis account of creation. None of them has a doctrine of original sin, in the sense that Adam is responsible for the sin of his descendants. All of them take some liberties with the biblical text in the process, Ben Sira no less than the Community Rule. We noted the

---

71. P. Wernberg-Møller, "A Reconsideration of the Two Spirits in the Rule of the Community 1Q Serek III,13—IV, 26," *RevQ* 3 (1961) 413–41. The citation is from p. 422.

72. See further J. J. Collins, "The Origin of Evil in Apocalyptic Literature and the Dead Sea Scrolls," in J. A. Emerton, ed., *Congress Volume: Paris* (Leiden: Brill, 1995) 25–38; M. Philonenko, "Mythe et histoire qoumrânienne des deux Esprits: ses origines iraniennes et ses prolongements dans le judaïsme essénien et le christianisme antique," in G. Widengren et al., eds., *Apocalyptique Iranienne et Dualisme Qoumrânien* (Paris: Maisonneuve, 1995) 163–211.

tension in Ben Sira between the Deuteronomic theology with its emphasis on free choice and the recognition that the Lord appointed the different ways of humanity (Sir. 33:11). Sirach lays the foundation for a dualistic view of the world with his assertion that all the works of the Lord come in pairs, one the opposite of the other (33:15). His dualism, which may be influenced by Stoic philosophy, is primarily ethical and psychological. It is not metaphysical. Human beings have both a good and a bad inclination, but they are not bereft of the power of choice. This is also the case in the Sapiential Work from Qumran. Despite its deterministic language, the Community Rule also presupposes the power to choose. The opening columns of the Scroll describe a Deuteronomic covenant renewal in which the covenanters freely choose to submit to the commandments. Insofar as the two spirits are placed within human beings, and "feud in the heart of man" (1QS 4:23), they function in a way similar to the two inclinations. The dualism of Qumran is ethical and psychological. But it is more, for the two spirits are also metaphysical powers, the Prince of Light and the Prince of Darkness, or Belial. Moreover, the Community Rule presupposes a mythic structure, whereby history is divided between these conflicting powers, but in the end God will intervene with a decisive judgment. The appeal to supernatural forces as an explanation of the origin of sin clearly separates the sectarian scrolls such as the Community Rule from the traditional wisdom of Ben Sira.

This appeal to supernatural forces is not, however, necessarily incompatible with all wisdom literature. The Instruction on the Two Spirits is not an apocalypse; it is not presented as a revelation. Its literary genre is, in fact, a typical wisdom genre. 4QSapiential Text A, which does not have the doctrine of the Two Spirits, has an eschatological perspective which we associate with apocalypticism rather than with traditional Hebrew wisdom. The Wisdom of Solomon is also informed by apocalyptic traditions about the judgment of the dead. "Wisdom" cannot be identified with any one worldview. The apocalyptic mindset of the Scrolls can furnish the content of a wisdom instruction just as well as the empirical, this-worldly mindset of Proverbs and Qoheleth.[73]

---

73. See J. J. Collins, "Wisdom, Apocalypticism, and Generic Compatibility," in L. G. Perdue, B. B. Scott, and W. J. Wiseman, eds., *In Search of Wisdom: Essays in Memory of John G. Gammie* (Louisville: Westminster John Knox, 1993) 165–85.

PART TWO.
WISDOM IN THE
HELLENISTIC DIASPORA

Chapter 8.
The Diaspora Setting

The second great wisdom book of the Apocrypha, the Wisdom of Solomon, was almost certainly composed in Alexandria in the early Roman period.[1] In this case the cultural context was very different from that of Sirach. The Wisdom of Solomon was written in Greek. This was undoubtedly the primary, and probably the only, language of the author, who exhibits a far greater familiarity with and mastery of Hellenistic thought than the Hebrew sage had. The social location of a Jewish sage in Alexandria was also very different from that of his counterpart in Jerusalem. In Egypt, Judaism was a minority culture, and relations with the Gentile world assumed a far greater importance than was the case in the Jewish homeland. Consequently, the wisdom literature of the Diaspora takes on an apologetic character. Even if we assume that it was written for the internal instruction and edification of the Jewish community, there is always an element of apologetics in the attempt to explain and extol the Jewish religion in the categories of the Hellenistic world.

The history and literature of Alexandrian Judaism present numerous complex problems that cannot be addressed here.[2] We will focus on three issues that have a bearing on the discussion of the wisdom literature: first, the legal status of the Jewish community and its ancestral laws in Alexandria; second, the related issue of the access of Jews to the gymnasium and to Greek education; and finally the question of a Jewish mission, or the degree to which Jews attempted to win Gentile converts, or even sympathizers, to their faith.

---

1. See David Winston, *The Wisdom of Solomon* (AB 43; New York: Doubleday, 1979) 20–25 and the discussion in Chap. 10 below.

2. On the history, see V. Tcherikover, *Hellenistic Civilization and the Jews* (New York: Jewish Publication Society, 1959); V. Tcherikover and A. Fuks, *Corpus Papyrorum Judaicarum* (Cambridge, Mass.: Harvard Univ. Press, 1957) 1.1–93; A. Kasher, *The Jews in Hellenistic and Roman Egypt* (Tübingen: Mohr, 1985); E. Schürer, *The History of the Jewish People in the Age of Jesus Christ, vol. 3, part 1,* (rev. and ed. G. Vermes, F. Millar, and M. Goodman (Edinburgh: T. & T. Clark, 1986) 87–137; J. M. Modrzejewski, *The Jews of Egypt: From Rameses II to Emperor Hadrian* (Philadelphia: Jewish Publication Society, 1995); J.M.G. Barclay, *Jews in the Mediterranean Diaspora, from Alexander to Trajan (323 BCE–117 CE)* (Edinburgh: T. & T. Clark, 1996) 19–81. On the literature, J. J. Collins, *Between Athens and Jerusalem: Jewish Identity in the Hellenistic Diaspora* (New York: Crossroad, 1983); Schürer, *The History,* 3.470–704.

The Jewish Community
in Alexandria

The Alexandrian Jewish community had its origin in the period after Alexander's conquests. There had always been traffic between Palestine and Egypt. Many Jews sought refuge by the Nile in the wake of the Babylonian conquest (see Jeremiah 41–44). Jewish mercenaries had served at Elephantine in the fifth century, having come to Egypt before the Persian invasion under Cambyses (525).[3] The coming of the Greeks, however, marked a new era. While Jews settled in many parts of Egypt, they were especially drawn to the newly founded Greek city on the delta. Josephus claimed that Jews came to Egypt under Alexander.[4] This claim is unsupported, and therefore suspect.[5] There is much better evidence for Jewish settlement under the first two Ptolemies. Hecataeus of Abdera reports the willing migration of a group of Jews led by the priest Hezekiah after the battle of Gaza in 312 B.C.E.,[6] while the *Letter of Aristeas* (12–14) claims that Ptolemy I transported 100,000 Jewish captives to his country, drafted the men into the army, and sold the rest as slaves. According to the *Letter,* the slaves were later redeemed by Ptolemy II Philadelphus. While the numbers are probably exaggerated, the report is generally thought to have a historical basis.[7] The earliest Jewish inscriptions in Egypt date from the third century B.C.E.[8] Another migration is known from the Maccabean period, when Onias IV, son of the murdered High Priest Onias III, sought refuge in Egypt and was eventually allowed to found a colony, complete with a temple, at Leontopolis.[9] Josephus boasts that Ptolemy VI Philometor entrusted his whole army to Onias and his friend Dositheus (*Ag. Ap.* 2.49). Again, allowing for exaggeration, we may accept that they were generals in his army. In the next generation, we again encounter Jewish generals, Helkias and

3. B. Porten, *Archives from Elephantine: The Life of an Ancient Jewish Military Colony* (Berkeley: Univ. of California Press, 1968). This settlement seems to have been wiped out at the end of the fifth century. On the presence of Jews in Egypt before the Hellenistic period, see Modrzejewski, *The Jews of Egypt,* 5–44.

4. Josephus, *J. W.* 2.487; *Ag. Ap.* 2.35.

5. Tcherikover, *Hellenistic Civilization,* 272; Tcherikover and Fuks, *Corpus Papyrorum Judaicarum,* 1.3. Kasher, *The Jews in Hellenistic and Roman Egypt* 2, finds it "quite credible."

6. Hecataeus, in Josephus, *Ag. Ap.* 1.186–89. See M. Stern, *Greek and Latin Authors on Jews and Judaism* (Jerusalem: The Israel Academy of Sciences and Humanities, 1976) 1.35–43.

7. Tcherikover, *Hellenistic Civilization,* 273; Schürer, *The History,* 3.46; Modrzejewski, *The Jews in Egypt,* 73.

8. W. Horbury and D. Noy, *Jewish Inscriptions of Graeco-Roman Egypt* (Cambridge: Cambridge Univ. Press, 1992).

9. Tcherikover, *Hellenistic Civilization,* 276–81; Schürer, *The History,* 3.47–49; D. Noy, "The Jewish Communities of Leontopolis and Venosa," in J. W. van Henten and P. W. van der Horst, eds., *Studies in Early Jewish Epigraphy* (Leiden: Brill, 1994) 162–82; Modrzejewski, *The Jews in Egypt,* 121–33.

Hananiah (*Ant.* 13.349). There was some tension in the reign of Ptolemy VIII Euergetes, the brother and rival of Philometor, due to Jewish support for Philometor in the civil war that raged between the brothers in the second century B.C.E. (*Ant.* 13.349). Nonetheless, Jewish communities continued to grow and flourish throughout the Ptolemaic period.

By the early first century, Philo claims that they occupied two of the five quarters of Alexandria and that "there were no less than a million Jews resident in Alexandria and the country from the slope into Libya to the boundaries of Ethiopia" (*In Flacc.* 43). Philo's tally is unreliable: there was no census of Jews in the Diaspora until 71–72 C.E., when the Jewish tax was imposed by Rome in the wake of the great Revolt.[10] Nonetheless, it is clear that there was a large Jewish population in Egypt, with a high concentration in Alexandria. Even a modern estimate that puts the Jewish population of Alexandria at 180,000 still allows that they may have made up as much as one third of the population of the city.[11]

The Jews as a group were never citizens of Alexandria, but the Jewish community had its own internal organization and enjoyed certain rights that were recognized by the ruling authorities.[12] Strabo of Amaseia, in the reign of Augustus, wrote (apropos of Sulla's suppression of a revolt in Cyrene):

> Cyrene, which had the same rulers as Egypt, has imitated it in many respects, particularly in notably encouraging and aiding the expansion of the organized groups of Jews, which observe the national Jewish laws. In Egypt, for example, territory has been set apart for a Jewish settlement, and in Alexandria a great part of the city has been allocated to this nation. And an ethnarch of their own has been installed, who governs the people and adjudicates suits and supervises contracts and ordinances, just as if he were the head of a sovereign state.[13]

The office of ethnarch was apparently discontinued by Augustus in 11–12 C.E., but the organization of the Jewish community was not seriously altered. The ethnarch was replaced by a *gerousia,* or council of elders. Philo tells us

---

10. Tcherikover and Fuks, *Corpus Papyrorum Judaicarum* 1.4; S.J.D. Cohen, "'Those Who Say They Are Jews and Are Not': How Do You Know a Jew in Antiquity When You See One?" in S.J.D. Cohen and E. S. Frerichs, eds., *Diasporas in Antiquity* (Atlanta: Scholars, 1993) 22–23. Philo's estimate is accepted by L. H. Feldman, *Jew and Gentile in the Ancient World* (Princeton, N.J.: Princeton Univ. Press, 1993) 65–66, who wishes to argue that the size of the community would militate against assimilation.

11. Modrzejewski, *The Jews in Egypt,* 73.

12. P. M. Fraser, *Ptolemaic Alexandria* (Oxford: Clarendon, 1972) 1.38–92, and especially pp. 54–55; Schürer, *The History,* 3.87–125; S. Applebaum, "The Organization of the Jewish Communities in the Diaspora," in S. Safrai and M. Stern, eds., *The Jewish People in the First Century* (CRINT 1/1; Assen: Van Gorcum/Philadelphia: Fortress, 1974) 464–503.

13. Strabo, in Josephus, *Ant.* 14.114–18; M. Stern, *Greek and Latin Authors on Jews and Judaism* (Jerusalem: The Israel Academy of Sciences and Humanities, 1976) 1.277–82.

that "our senate [*gerousia*] was appointed to take charge of Jewish affairs by our saviour and benefactor Augustus, after the death of the *genarch*."[14] From Strabo's account, it would seem that the Jewish community had a measure of autonomy in running its own affairs. The analogy with a sovereign state, however, would seem to entail some exaggeration.

Other ethnic minorities in Ptolemaic Egypt also enjoyed a measure of self-regulation. Dorothy Thompson describes the Idumaean community in Memphis as follows:

> The Idumaean mercenaries act here as a corporate group in a religious context. The unit of organization is the *politeuma*, . . . which holds meetings, *synagogai*, in the temple of Qos which may result in decrees, *psephismata*. The community, however, is broader than just the troops, and the Idumaeans from the city join in many of its activities; in Hermoupolis and elsewhere these supporting members are called "those sharing in the politeuma," the *sympoliteuomenoi*.[15]

Similar ethnic community organizations, or *politeumata*, are also found elsewhere in Egypt and in other parts of the Hellenistic world.[16] Other ethnic groups have representatives variously known as *timouchoi*, or *prostatai*.[17] The Jewish communities in Alexandria and Cyrene were exceptionally large, and the Jews were exceptional in their adherence to their ancestral laws. It is doubtful, however, whether the Jewish communities enjoyed any greater autonomy than other ethnic organizations.

The prototypical charter of Jewish rights in the Hellenistic world was that issued by Antiochus III of Syria when he captured Jerusalem in 198 B.C.E. In a letter to an official named Ptolemy, who had apparently been appointed to govern Coele-Syria, Antiochus provided a subsidy for the temple cult and remission of certain taxes for the council of elders (*gerousia*) and Temple personnel. He also provided that the Jews should conduct their political affairs in accordance with their ancestral laws.[18] The principle of allowing people to live

---

14. *In Flacc.* 74. It is generally assumed that *genarch* and *ethnarch* are equivalent terms for the same office. Philo dates this transition to the time when Magius Maximus was about to take office for the second time as governor of Alexandria, that is, 11–12 C.E. Josephus claims that "on the death of the ethnarch of the Jews, Augustus did not prevent the continued appointment of ethnarchs" (*Ant.* 19.283), but Philo's account is more credible.

15. D. J. Thompson, *Memphis under the Ptolemies* (Princeton, N.J.: Princeton Univ. Press, 1988) 101–2. See also her essay, D. J. Thompson-Crawford, "The Idumaeans of Memphis and the Ptolemaic Politeumata," in M. Gigante, ed., *Atti del XVII Congresso Internazionale di Papirologia* (Naples: Centro Internazionale per lo Studio dei Papiri Ercolanesi 1984) 3.1069–75.

16. Compare the ethnic organizations called *koina*, listed in Schürer, *The History*, 3.108–12. See also Kasher, *The Jews in Hellenistic and Roman Egypt*, 179–80.

17. Thompson, *Memphis*, 97.

18. *Ant.* 12.138–44. On the authenticity of this document, see E. J. Bickerman, "La Charte séleucide de Jérusalem," in *Studies in Jewish and Christian History* (Leiden: Brill, 1980) 2.44–85.

according to their ancestral laws seems also to have been honored by the Ptolemies and the Romans, and to have been extended to Jewish communities in the Diaspora, although there is little documentary evidence. Josephus preserves a letter of Antiochus providing for the transfer of two thousand Jewish families from Babylonia to Mesopotamia to serve as a military colony, and stipulating that they should be allowed "to use their own laws" (*Ant.* 12.150). A similar general formula is often repeated in documents from the Roman period. Julius Caesar affirmed the right of Jews on Paros and Delos "to live in accordance with their customs and to contribute money to common meals and sacred rites, for this they are not forbidden to do even in Rome."[19] When the Jews of Asia and Libya appealed to Augustus that the Greeks were confiscating their sacred funds, the emperor responded by issuing a decree, affirming that "the Jews may follow their own customs in accordance with the law of their fathers." He specifically affirmed their right to collect money for the Jerusalem Temple and their exemption from appearing in court on the sabbath (*Ant.* 16.162–65). Decrees such as these, however, were issued in response to specific complaints. While the general principle of respecting ancestral laws was widely acknowledged, it does not appear that there was any formal Jewish charter or bill of rights either in Alexandria or elsewhere.[20]

Despite the strong tradition that Jews could live according to their ancestral laws, the evidence of the papyri shows Jews in litigation only before Greek courts.[21] One of these documents shows that contracts could indeed be made in accordance with the law of the Jews, but that a plaintiff could appeal beyond that law to the king. The papyrus in question (*CPJ* 128) dates from 218 B.C.E. A woman named Helladote, daughter of Philonides, complained that a Jew named "Jonathas" had married her in accordance with Jewish law, but now wanted to repudiate her and cast her out of the house. There seems to be some cross-cultural misunderstanding here. In Jewish tradition, the husband was allowed to divorce his wife "if he found something objectionable in her" (Deut.

19. *Ant.* 14.214. The manuscripts read Parium (which was on the coast of the Troad), but the mention of Delos suggests that the reference was to Paros. The proconsul L. Valerius Flaccus, who was tried for maladministration in 59 B.C.E. (and defended by Cicero), was accused inter alia of confiscating the money collected by Jews in Asia for the Jerusalem Temple. The charge implies that the Jewish right in this matter was acknowledged.

20. So T. Rajak, "Was There a Roman Charter for the Jews?" *Journal of Roman Studies* 74 (1984) 107–203. See further J. Juster, *Les Juifs dans l'empire romain* (2 vols.; Paris: Geuthner, 1914) 2.1–18; E. J. Bickerman, "Une Question d'authenticité: les privilèges Juifs," in *Studies in Jewish and Christian History* 2.24–43; S. Applebaum, "The Legal Status of the Jewish Communities in the Diaspora," in S. Safrai and M. Stern, eds., *The Jewish People in the First Century* (CRINT 1/1; Assen: Van Gorcum, 1974) 420–63. Consequently, attempts to date the origin of such a supposed charter are moot (Fraser, *Ptolemaic Alexandria*, 1.56, dates it to the time of Philometor).

21. The Tosefta claims that Jewish courts in Egypt had independent jurisdiction. *t. Ketub.* 3:1; *t. Pe'ah* 4:6. *CPJ* 143 says that a certain Theodorus deposited his will in "the Jewish archive," but this is the only reference to an autonomous Jewish legal institution in the papyri.

24:1). Greek law recognized the equality of husband and wife in divorce proceedings.[22] Helladote, who presumably was not Jewish, took her case to the king. Another papyrus gives some indication as to how the conflict between different laws might be resolved. In 226 B.C.E., one Dositheus, an Egyptian Jew, sued Herakleia, daughter of Diosdotos, who was also Jewish, before a panel of Greek judges in Crocodilopolis, for insulting him and ripping his coat. Even though Dositheus failed to appear in court and forfeited his case, Herakleia submitted documents in her defense. One of these was an extract from a royal regulation on judicial procedure. The judges were instructed "on all points that any person knows or shows us to have been dealt with in the regulations of king Ptolemy, [to give judgments] in accordance with the regulations; and on all points not dealt with in the regulations, but in the civic laws [*politikoi nomoi*], in accordance with these laws; and on all other points to follow the most equitable view."[23] The civic laws were presumably the Greek common law. It has been suggested that in disputes between Jews the law of Moses could serve as the relevant civic law. (It was apparently the operative law in the marriage of Jonathas in *CPJ* 128.) It was never the highest court of appeal. In Ptolemaic Egypt, the king was always the ultimate authority. But where the king had not issued a relevant regulation, the judges could abide by whatever local law, Greek or Jewish, was acceptable to the litigants.

There is plenty of evidence in the papyri of the observance of Jewish laws (e.g., regarding the sabbath), but there are also exceptions. The biblical prohibition of loans with interest among Jews was not observed, although the notion of a "free loan" was well established in Greek tradition. In the Roman period we find a Jewish couple dissolving their marriage by mutual consent, after the Greek rather than the Jewish custom.[24] Inevitably, the Jewish observance of their ancestral laws was modified by the influence of the law of the land.

The Politeuma

Modern scholarship has commonly characterized the legal status of the Jewish community in Alexandria as that of a *politeuma*, a term that is also encountered with reference to other ethnic groups, such as the Idumaeans of Memphis. In the context of discussions of Jewish rights, the *politeuma* is usually understood as "a formally constituted corporation of aliens enjoying the right of domicile in a foreign city and forming a separate, semi-autonomous civic body, a city within a city; it had its own constitution and administered its internal affairs as an ethnic unit through officials distinct from and independent

---

22. Modrzejewski, *The Jews in Egypt,* 112.
23. *CPJ* 19; Modrzejewski, *The Jews in Egypt,* 108.
24. *CPJ* 144; Modrzejewski, *The Jews in Egypt,* 112–13.

of the host city."[25] In fact, however, the term has a rather wide range of meanings. It could refer to the governing class of a *polis* as a sovereign body, or it could be applied to various other associations, including "festival associations of women, a cult society, a club of soldiers, associations of citizens from the same city living abroad, and ethnic communities."[26] The clear definition as "a semiautonomous civic body" is an unwarranted generalization, at best. It is unsafe, then, to draw inferences about the civic status of the Jewish community in Alexandria from the supposed implications of the term *politeuma*.

In fact, the term *politeuma* is attested only once with reference to the Jews of Alexandria, and twice with reference to another Diaspora community, that of Berenice in the Cyrenaica.[27] (Some new evidence may be forthcoming from the archive of the Jewish *politeuma* at Heracleopolis, which is reportedly being edited by James Cowey for his dissertation at the University of Heidelberg, but this material is not available at the time of writing.)[28] The inscriptions from Berenice are honorary decrees from the first century B.C.E. to the first century C.E. They show that the community had leaders and funds and could pass decrees, but they show nothing about its status vis-à-vis the city of Berenice.[29] The usage in the *Letter of Aristeas* is more problematic. There we are told that the translation of the Torah into Greek was acclaimed by "the priests and the elders from among the translators and from among the people of the *politeuma* and the leaders of the congregation [*tou plēthous*]" (*Ep. Arist.* 310). It seems reasonable to assume that the *politeuma* in question pertains to the Alexandrian Jewish community.[30] It is less clear whether it is identical with the *plēthos,* or congregation,[31] or a separate body "distinguishable somehow from the other Jews of Alexandria—for example persons with some property, who had organized themselves in a *politeuma* and were mentioned here separately because

25. So E. Mary Smallwood, *The Jews under Roman Rule* (Leiden: Brill, 1976) 225, cited with approval by Kasher, *The Jews in Hellenistic and Roman Egypt,* 30. Cf. also Kasher, "The Civic Status of the Jews in Ptolemaic Egypt," in P. Bilde et al., eds., *Ethnicity in Hellenistic Egypt* (Aarhus: Aarhus Univ. Press, 1992) 100–121.

26. G. Lüderitz, "What Is the Politeuma?" in Jan Willem van Henten and Pieter Willem van der Horst, eds., *Studies in Early Jewish Epigraphy* (Leiden: Brill, 1994) 183–225. (The quotation is from p. 189.) Compare C. Zuckerman, "Hellenistic Politeumata and the Jews: A Reconsideration," *Scripta Classica Israelica* 8–10 (1985–88) 171–85.

27. Schuerer, *The History,* 3.88.

28. J. Cowey, "Zwei Archive aus dem zweite Jahrhundert vor Christus," a paper presented to the Twenty-first International Congress of Papyrology in Berlin in August 1995. (I owe this information to Gideon Bohak.)

29. *CIG* 5361, 5362. See the discussion by Lüderitz, "What Is the Politeuma?" 210–22.

30. Contra Zuckerman, "Hellenistic Politeumata," 182–84, who argues that it refers to the *polis* of Jerusalem, and Lüderitz, "What Is the Politeuma?" 206–8, who suggests that it is the *politeuma* of the city of Alexandria.

31. Schürer, *The History,* 3.88; Tcherikover and Fuks, *Corpus Papyrorum Judaicarum* 1.9, n. 24.

of their importance."[32] If the *politeuma* were such an elite group, however, it would surely have included the leaders of the *plēthos*, and so the two terms should probably be identified. The reference remains obscure. In view of the parallels with Berenice and Heracleopolis, it is not unreasonable to suppose that the Jewish community in Alexandria could also be called a *politeuma*, but the usage is poorly attested.[33]

Citizenship and the Jews

The term *politeuma* has been so prominent in the discussion because it has seemed to some scholars to have a bearing on the question of Jewish citizenship in Alexandria. Josephus claims explicitly that "Julius Caesar made a bronze tablet for the Jews in Alexandria, declaring that they were citizens [*politai*] of Alexandria."[34] This claim was decisively denied by the *Letter* of Claudius in 41 C.E., in which he states clearly that the Jews "live in a city not their own."[35] It has been argued that the discrepancy between the claim of Josephus and the ruling of Claudius can be attributed to an ambiguity in the word "citizens" (*politai*): "the term *politai* was used in an ambiguous and rather imprecise way for citizens of both the *polis* and the Jewish *politeuma*."[36] As we have seen, there is very little evidence for the use of the term *politeuma* with reference to the Jewish community in Alexandria, and in any case *politeuma* and *polis* were not comparable entities. It is true, however, that the word *politai,* citizens, is sometimes used in an imprecise, nontechnical sense. An epitaph found near Leontopolis with some definitely Jewish inscriptions praises the deceased as "a friend to all the citizens." As Horbury and Noy aptly remark, such a conventional phrase cannot be pressed as evidence of community organization, even assuming that the epitaph is in fact Jewish.[37] Again, when Philo expresses the fear "that people everywhere might take their cue from Alexandria, and outrage their Jewish fellow-citizens [*tois politais autōn Ioudaiois*] by rioting against their synagogues and ancestral customs" (*In Flacc.* 47), he must be

---

32. Lüderitz, "What Is the Politeuma?" 205, allows this as a secondary possibility. See also Kasher, *The Jews in Hellenistic and Roman Egypt,* 208–11.

33. See further Modrzejewski, *The Jews in Egypt,* 82; S. Honigmann, "The Birth of a Diaspora: The Emergence of a Jewish Self-Definition in Ptolemaic Egypt in the Light of Onomastics," in Cohen and Frerichs, eds., *Diasporas in Antiquity,* 95.

34. *Ant.* 14.188; cf. *Ag. Ap.* 2.37. Tcherikover regards this as an obvious error, since Julius Caesar was never official ruler of Alexandria, but he supposes that Josephus is referring to an actual edict by Augustus (Tcherikover and Fuks, *Corpus Papyrorum Judaicarum* 1.56).

35. Tcherikover and Fuks, *Corpus Papyrorum Judaicarum,* 2.43 (*CPJ* 153).

36. So Kasher, *The Jews in Hellenistic and Roman Egypt,* 278.

37. *CIJ* 1489; Horbury and Noy, *Jewish Inscriptions of Graeco-Roman Egypt,* no. 114, pp. 193–96. The same is true of the use of the words *polis* and *politarchēs* in *CPJ* 1530a, Horbury and Noy, no. 39.

assumed to be using the term in a nontechnical sense. It is possible that Josephus was either trying to exploit this ambiguity or was genuinely confused in his claim that the Jews as a group were citizens of Alexandria.

The term "Alexandrian" was also ambiguous, insofar as it might refer either to a person from Alexandria or, in the strict sense, to an Alexandrian citizen. The contrast is nicely noted in a papyrus (*CPJ* 151) in which the petitioner, one Helenos son of Tryphon, described himself initially as "an Alexandrian," but then crossed that out and wrote "a Jew from Alexandria." Both Josephus and Philo exploit the ambiguity,[38] but there is no evidence that Jews as a class were ever Alexandrians in the legal sense of the term.

The claim of Josephus that Jews, as a group, were citizens of Alexandria had no legal basis.[39] Julius Caesar, or Augustus, may well have granted citizenship to some individual Jews (including the family of Philo)[40] and recorded them on the tablet to which Josephus refers, but the privilege cannot have extended to the entire Jewish community. That some Jews, at least, claimed to be citizens, may also be inferred from the challenge of Apion: "Why then, if they are citizens (*cives*), do they not worship the same gods as the Alexandrians?"[41] It is likely, however, that citizenship was an issue only for the upper-class stratum of Alexandrian Jews.[42]

The precise status of the Jewish community in Alexandria became a subject of conflict only after the Roman conquest of Egypt. Lack of citizenship in the Greek cities (Alexandria, Naucratis, and Ptolemais) does not appear to have caused any serious problems for Jews in the Ptolemaic period. Like other foreign ethnics, they found a way to advancement in the military. Some Jews jettisoned their traditional religion in pursuit of their careers. One Dositheus son of Drimylus, who makes a cameo appearance in 3 Maccabees, rose to become eponymous priest of the cult of Alexander and the deified Ptolemies, one of the highest honors in the service of the king, in 222 B.C.E.[43] Others found a way to combine Jewish religion and royal service. We have already noted the success of the Jewish priest Onias and his colony at Leontopolis. The situation changed, however, with the coming of the Romans.

At the root of the conflict was a poll tax (*laographia*) imposed by the Romans in 24/23 B.C.E. The Greek citizens of Alexandria (and the other *poleis*, Ptolemais and Naucratis) were exempt from this tax. Native Egyptians were

---

38. Philo, *De Leg.,* 183, 350; Josephus, *Ant.* 19.281; *Ag. Ap.* 2.38. Tcherikover, *Hellenistic Civilization,* 315.

39. This conclusion does not preclude the possibility that the situation may have been different in Asia Minor. For the claim that Jews were citizens of Sardis see Josephus, *Ant.* 14.235, 259.

40. Modrzejewski, *The Jews in Egypt,* 185.

41. *Ag. Ap.* 2.65. The Greek text of this passage is not preserved. For further evidence of Jewish citizens in Alexandria see Barclay, *Jews in the Mediterranean Diaspora,* 67–69.

42. Barclay, *Jews in the Mediterranean Diaspora,* 66–67.

43. *CPJ* 127. Modrzejewski, *The Jews in Egypt,* 60.

not. In 4/5 C.E. a third class was created, to take account of Greeks outside the *poleis*.[44] Since there had been considerable mixing of Greek and Egyptian elements in Egypt, the criteria in this case were primarily cultural. Those who had a gymnasium education (*hoi apo tou gymnasiou*) and the hellenized inhabitants of the larger towns (*metropolitai*) were acknowledged as an intermediate class. They still paid the *laographia*, but at a reduced rate. The Alexandrian Jews, however, received no benefit from this concession.[45]

The line between citizen and noncitizen was now more sharply drawn than ever before. The issue not only had financial implications, but also put in question the self-understanding of hellenized Jews, who thought of themselves as culturally akin to the Greeks and despised the native Egyptians. Their dilemma is reflected in the petition of Helenos, the son of Tryphon, who began by calling himself an Alexandrian, but corrected this to "a Jew from Alexandria" (*CPJ* 151). While the papyrus is fragmentary, the gist of the petition is clear enough. Helenos argues that his father was "an Alexandrian," and that he himself had received "the appropriate education, as far as my father's means allowed." Hence his petition for exemption from the *laographia*. The petition had little hope of success.

The Alexandrian Greeks, in contrast, welcomed the poll tax and the clear distinction between citizens and noncitizens that it entailed. A papyrus from 21–19 B.C.E. (*CPJ* 150) preserves an appeal to Rome for the restoration of the Alexandrian city council, or boulē. In return, the Alexandrians promised to "take care that the citizen-body of Alexandria is not corrupted by men who are uncultured and uneducated." The pretensions of Jews like Helenos led to conflict with the Alexandrian Greeks. Matters came to a head in the reign of Caligula (37 C.E.). The prefect Flaccus had previously shown no ill will toward the Jews, but when Caligula came to power he acquiesced in the demand of the Alexandrians that statues of the emperor be erected in Jewish synagogues. He then proclaimed that the Jews were "foreigners and aliens."[46] What ensued has been aptly called "the first pogrom in history."[47] Members of the Jewish *gerousia* were flogged with whips in the theater. The outrage was aggravated by the fact that they were beaten with the whips usually used for Egyptians,

44. Tcherikover and Fuks, *Corpus Papyrorum Judaicarum*, 1.59; Modrzejewski, *The Jews in Egypt*, 163; Kasher, *The Jews in Hellenistic and Roman Egypt*, 76.
45. Modrzejewski, *The Jews in Egypt*, 163: "Not a single Jewish name can be found among the numerous documents dealing with the processing of qualification [*epikrisis*] for the fourteen-year-old sons of notables, to warrant their eligibility for the reduced tax rate." Some individual Jews may have qualified for the reduction as the descendants of military settlers (Kasher, *The Jews in Hellenistic and Roman Egypt*, 88–93), but the evidence is very limited.
46. Philo, *In Flacc.* 54.
47. Tcherikover and Fuks, *Corpus Papyrorum Judaicarum* 1. 66.

whereas hitherto Jews who were flogged were beaten with flat blades, like the Alexandrians.[48] Jewish houses were plundered. The philosopher Philo headed a mission to plead their case before Caligula.[49] They had to wait for months for an audience, and then they met with contempt and ridicule. At this very time Caligula provoked a crisis in Judea by ordering that his statue be installed in the Temple, but the crisis was forestalled by his assassination. The Jews of Alexandria seized the opportunity to take vengeance on the Greeks. Riots broke out which were suppressed by Roman soldiers.

Claudius, who succeeded Caligula, settled the question of Jewish rights in 41 C.E. His *Letter to the Alexandrians,* fortuitously preserved in papyrus and first published in 1924, sheds some invaluable light on the events of the time.[50] He refused to make an exact inquiry into the responsibility for "the disturbances and rioting, or rather, to speak the truth, the war, against the Jews," and demanded that both sides desist from their mutual enmity. He urged the Alexandrians

> to behave gently and kindly towards the Jews who have inhabited the same city for many years, and not to dishonour any of their customs in their worship of their god, but to allow them to keep their own ways, as they did in the time of the god Augustus and as I too having heard both sides have confirmed. The Jews, on the other hand, I order not to aim at more than they have previously had and not in future to send two embassies as if they lived in two cities, a thing which has never been done before, and not to intrude themselves into the games presided over by the *gymnasiarchoi* and the *kosmetai,* since they enjoy what is their own, and in a city which is not their own they possess an abundance of all good things. Nor are they to bring in or invite Jews coming from Syria or Egypt. . . . If they disobey, I shall proceed against them in every way as fomenting a common plague for the whole world.[51]

Several points in this letter require comment.[52] The statement that Claudius had confirmed the right of the Jews to keep their own ways, having heard both sides, has been taken to imply that he had already issued an edict on the subject. Josephus, in fact, presents an alleged edict of Claudius in *Ant.* 19.280–85, that is much more favorable to the Jews than the *Letter* preserved in the papyrus. The edict in Josephus, however, shows clear signs

---

48. *In Flacc.* 78. It may be that only members of the Jewish *gerousia* enjoyed this modest privilege (Barclay, *Jews in the Mediterranean Diaspora,* 69).

49. The mission is recorded in his treatise *De Legatione ad Gaium.*

50. *Corpus Papyrorum Judaicarum* 2.36–55 (no. 153).

51. Tcherikover and Fuks, *Corpus Papyrorum Judaicarum,* 2.43.

52. The reference to two embassies is puzzling. Tcherikover has suggested that the delegation to Caligula, led by Philo, was still in Rome when a second delegation arrived. The second delegation may have been more radical, because of the worsened situation in Alexandria. This suggestion is speculative, but the reference should probably be taken to imply some division within the Jewish community.

of Jewish propaganda, and little confidence can be placed in it. Some scholars regard it as entirely spurious; others think it may contain an authentic
core embellished by interpolations.[53] According to Josephus, Claudius acknowledged that "the Jews in Alexandria, called Alexandrians, were fellow
colonizers from the very earliest times jointly with the Alexandrians and received equal civic rights [isēs politeias] from the kings."[54] In contrast, the
indisputably authentic Letter says that the Jews live in a city not their own,
in effect denying them the title Alexandrians, and makes quite clear that
they did not have "equal civic rights."[55] The Letter reaffirms the traditional
right of the Jews to live according to their ancestral laws, but the overall
tone is not sympathetic. It ends by suggesting that the Jews foment a plague
for the whole world. They have no claim to citizenship. Most significantly
of all, they are told not to intrude themselves into the games organized by
the officials of the gymnasium, with the obvious implication that they had
done so in the past.[56]

Claudius ordered the Jews "not to aim at more than they have previously
had." The actual goal of the Jewish agitation has been a matter of dispute in
modern scholarship. Victor Tcherikover found that "the fundamental idea of
Philo's politics is quite clear: Jewish claims for full citizenship are quite justified because Jews differ but little from the Greeks."[57] Aryeh Kasher, in contrast, argues that Jews could not aspire to full citizenship, as it would have entailed some form of homage to pagan deities. Hence he envisages a status that
is separate but equal: "Their true aim was a separate, independent life."[58]
Kasher's argument, which has a transparent apologetic quality, depends heavily on his understanding of the politeuma as a quasi-independent political
entity that could afford a status equal to that of citizen. As we have seen, this

53. See the discussion in Tcherikover and Fuks, Corpus Papyrorum Judaicarum, 1.70–71. A
much more positive assessment of the edict in Josephus can be found in Kasher, The Jews in Hellenistic and Roman Egypt, 262–89.

54. Ant. 19.281.

55. The edict in Josephus also claims that Augustus did not prevent the appointment of ethnarchs, a claim that is contradicted by the evidence of Philo, In Flacc. 74.

56. Kasher, The Jews in Hellenistic and Roman Egypt, 314–21, argues that Claudius did not
warn the Jews against infiltrating the gymnasium, but rather sought to dissuade them from ha-
rassing public performances (reading epispairein, "harass," rather than Tcherikover's reading epi-
spaiein). This reading is rejected by Tcherikover in CPJ 2.53. The context, which is warning the
Jews not to seek more than they have, favors Tcherikover's interpretation.

57. Tcherikover and Fuks, CPJ 1.63.

58. Kasher, The Jews in Hellenistic and Roman Egypt, 230. Kasher makes extensive use of 3
Maccabees, which he dates implausibly to the early Ptolemaic era. In that book, some Jews are offered equal rights with the citizens of Alexandria on condition that they participate in Greek rites,
but they refuse (3 Macc. 2:28–30). In fact, the book is likely to reflect one Jewish reaction to the
crisis of the Roman era. See Collins, Between Athens and Jerusalem, 104–11.

understanding is unfounded. *Isopoliteia* in the strict sense is a reciprocal arrangement between Greek cities, and no such agreements are known between a Greek and a non-Greek community.[59] Josephus does not use the term in an accurate technical sense, but only loosely, to imply that Jews had equal status with Greeks.

In fact, different Jews may have had different aspirations. Some Jews abandoned their religion to embrace Greek citizenship. We have noted the case of Dositheus, son of Drimylos, in the Ptolemaic period. The most celebrated case in the Roman period was Philo's nephew, Tiberius Julius Alexander, who went on to become prefect of Egypt and to participate in the Roman siege of Jerusalem.[60] Others may have found a way to finesse the religious demands of the *polis* and continue in the Jewish faith. There is reason to suspect that Philo's whole family may have enjoyed Roman citizenship, since his brother Alexander held the position of *arabarch* in Alexandria and several members of the family had the middle name Julius, in tribute to Julius Caesar. The question of Apion, "Why then, if they are citizens, do they not worship the same gods as the Alexandrians?" (*Ag. Ap.* 2.65), implies that some Jews claimed citizenship and still refrained from apostasy.

Philo's viewpoint is reflected in a famous passage in his *Life of Moses,* where he is ostensibly speaking of the ancient Israelites in Egypt: "For strangers, in my judgment, must be regarded as suppliants of those who receive them, and not only suppliants but settlers and friends, who are anxious to obtain equal rights [*isotimia*] with the burgesses and are near to being citizens because they differ little from the original inhabitants."[61] If we may assume, as seems likely, that Philo is making a veiled reference to the situation in Alexandria, the passage clearly acknowledges that Jews were not in fact citizens. His concern is for equal rights. Exemption from the *laographia* would surely have ranked high among these rights. Access to the gymnasium was probably also at issue. In Roman Alexandria, these rights would probably have required citizenship in the *polis,* but if they could be obtained otherwise, the issue of citizenship might well be moot, as it was in the Ptolemaic period. The view of Kasher, that Jews would not have sought Alexandrian citizenship in principle, imposes a falsely rigid orthodoxy on the ancient community. But the goal of Jewish agitation was not citizenship in itself; rather, it was the restoration of the rights and status that had been lost in the Roman era.

---

59. Applebaum, "The Legal Status," 436, 438; Kasher, *The Jews in Hellenistic and Roman Egypt,* 279.

60. Modrzejewski, *The Jews in Egypt,* 185–90.

61. *De Vita Mos.* 1.34–36; H. A. Wolfson, *Philo* (Cambridge, Mass.: Harvard Univ. Press, 1948) 399–401.

The Jews and the Gymnasium

Participation in the gymnasium involved more than a love of athletics. It may have been a stepping-stone to citizenship, it had some implications for access to Greek education, and it had enormous significance for social status in the Hellenistic world.

The love of sport and athletics was one of the primary characteristics that distinguished Greek from barbarian in the ancient world. Consequently, wherever Greeks went, they built gymnasia.[62] Any barbarian community that aspired to the status of a Greek *polis* also required a gymnasium; the so-called Hellenistic Reform that preceded the Maccabean revolt in Jerusalem is a case in point.[63] Beginning in the fifth century, the Sophists frequented the gymnasia in search of students. Socrates did likewise. Plato set up his school in the Academy, a gymnasium on the outskirts of Athens. Other philosophers, including Antisthenes and Aristotle, also taught in gymnasia.[64] In the Hellenistic period, a gymnasium usually had an auditorium or lecture hall. Some, such as the Ptolemaeum at Athens, also had libraries. The degree of intellectual activity varied, and should not be exaggerated. The primary functions of the gymnasium remained athletic, social, and to some degree religious.[65] Nonetheless, the institution played a significant part in Hellenistic education.

The importance of the gymnasium both for citizenship and for education is bound up with another Greek institution, the *ephebeia*. This was originally conceived at Athens as a period of military service for young men, beginning at age eighteen and lasting for two years, of which the first was devoted to training. By the Hellenistic period, the period of service was limited to one year, and its military character was greatly reduced. Instead, it became a finishing school for young citizens. In Egypt, it served to initiate the youth into the Greek way of life, and it began when they were fourteen, on the threshold of adolescence. The curriculum consisted of athletic training and studies in the liberal arts. During the year, ephebes participated in athletic and rhetori-

---

62. On the diffusion of gymnasia in the Hellenistic world, see Jean Delorme, *Gymnasion* (Paris: Boccard, 1960).

63. A.H.M. Jones, *The Greek City from Alexander to Justinian* (Oxford: Clarendon, 1940); R. Doran, "Jason's Gymnasion," in H. W. Attridge et al., eds., *Of Scribes and Scrolls* (Lanham, Md.: University Press of America, 1990) 99–109.

64. M. L. Clarke, *Higher Education in the Ancient World* (London: Routledge, 1971) 59.

65. See the comments of U. Wilcken, *Grundzüge und Chrestomathie der Papyruskunde I.1* (Leipzig and Berlin: Teubner, 1912) 138–45; Diana Delia, *Alexandrian Citizenship during the Roman Principate* (Atlanta: Scholars, 1991) 84–85, and William V. Harris, *Ancient Literacy* (Cambridge, Mass.: Harvard Univ. Press, 1989) 134–35. Harris stresses the lack of evidence for intellectual instruction in the Egyptian gymnasia.

cal contests, and there were annual ephebic games at the end of the year.[66] These are presumably the games from which Claudius barred the Jews of Alexandria.

In his *Letter to the Alexandrians*, Claudius confirmed the Alexandrian citizenship of "all those who have been registered as *epheboi* up to the time of my principate . . . with the exception of any who, though born of slave-parents, have made their way into your ephebate."[67] This would seem to imply that those who completed the *ephebeia* were normally regarded as citizens. The same implication appears in the *Boule* papyrus (*CPJ* 150), in which the Alexandrian Greeks petitioned Augustus for the restoration of their city council. In the course of the petition they promise "that the Council will see to it that none of those who are liable to enrollment for the poll tax [*laographia*] diminish the revenue by being listed in the public records along with the epheboi for each year; and it will take care that the pure(?) citizen body [*politeuma*] of Alexandria is not corrupted by men who are uncultured and uneducated."[68] This passage shows that people could evade the poll tax by being registered among the ephebes. Even if enrollment in the *ephebeia* was not formally either a prerequisite or a guarantee of citizenship, it is clear that the two were closely associated.[69] At the same time, it is apparent that some people who were not entitled to citizenship managed on occasion to get themselves enrolled among the ephebes, and so to gain entry into an elite social class. Those who attained this status might then claim privileges normally enjoyed by members of the class, such as exemption from the poll tax.

The case of Helenos son of Tryphon, the "Jew of Alexandria" who was not allowed to call himself an Alexandrian (*CPJ* 151) is once more pertinent here. Helenos begins his petition by pointing out that his father was "Alexandrian" and that he had received "the appropriate education, as far as my father's means allowed."[70] Most scholars assume that "the appropriate education" was obtained in the gymnasium.[71] The *Letter* of Claudius probably made it more difficult for Jews to obtain "the appropriate education" thereafter, even if their means allowed.

---

66. H. I. Marrou, *A History of Education in Antiquity* (London: Sheed & Ward, 1956; reprint: Madison: Univ. of Wisconsin Press, n.d.) 107–12; Delia, *Alexandrian Citizenship,* 71–88.

67. Tcherikover and Fuks, *Corpus Papyrorum Judaicarum,* 2.43.

68. Ibid., 2.28.

69. Delia, *Alexandrian Citizenship,* 71–88, denies that there was any formal connection between the ephebate and citizenship, but she grants that this education was a cultural and social requirement for those who claimed to be Greek, and that the exercise of citizen rights was postponed until the ephebate was completed.

70. Tcherikover and Fuks, *Corpus Papyrorum Judaicarum,* 2.31.

71. Despite the objections of Kasher, *The Jews in Hellenistic and Roman Egypt,* 204.

Jews and Greek Education

The primary argument in favor of the view that some Egyptian Jews received a Greek education, at least to the level of the ephebate training and sometimes beyond it, lies in the considerable literary output of Egyptian Judaism. The situation in Alexandria was very different from that in Jerusalem. While Palestinian Judaism, even in Ben Sira's time, was by no means devoid of Hellenistic influence, the Jews of the Diaspora were far more profoundly imbued with Greek culture. To begin with, Greek was never the primary language in Judea. In Egypt, it was the lingua franca from the time of Alexander. Even though Jews typically lived close together in communities, there seems to have been little attempt to maintain the Hebrew language, or Aramaic either. The Jewish inscriptions of Greco-Roman Egypt include 114 epitaphs, which are all in Greek except for five in Hebrew or Aramaic.[72] The Torah was translated into Greek in the third century B.C.E. Even recent compositions, such as Ben Sira's book, were translated within a generation or two.

By the time of Ben Sira, there was already a flourishing Jewish literature being composed in Greek in Alexandria.[73] The oldest composition was that of Demetrius the Chronographer, who retold the biblical history in Greek and attempted to resolve some of its chronological problems. He is also our earliest witness to the existence of the Greek translation of the Bible. But the Greco-Jewish writers did not confine themselves to resolving problems in the biblical text. They explored the full range of Hellenistic genres. The history of Artapanus was indebted to Hecataeus and Manetho at least as much as to the Pentateuch. Ezekiel recast the story of the exodus in the form of a Greek tragedy. Philo the Elder composed an epic on the history of Israel. Other Diaspora Jews produced prophetic verses in epic hexameters in the name of the Sibyl, or imitated the style of the Orphic verses. Aristobulus practiced philosophy by developing an allegorical interpretation of the Torah, a technique learned from Hellenistic philosophers and their critiques of religion. This remarkable literary output shows that Alexandrian Jews in the Ptolemaic era must have had access to Greek education in whatever form was available to them.

H. A. Wolfson argued vigorously that all Jewish education in the Diaspora took place in Jewish institutions, but his arguments have been rejected by most recent scholars.[74] Wolfson argued that the gymnasium was religious in nature,

---

72. W. Horbury, "Jewish Inscriptions and Jewish Literature in Egypt, with Special Reference to Ecclesiasticus," in J. W. van Henten and P. W. van der Horst, *Studies in Early Jewish Epigraphy* (Leiden: Brill, 1994) 11.

73. On this literature see Collins, *Between Athens and Jerusalem;* Schürer, *A History of the Jewish People*, 470–704. For the texts see Carl R. Holladay, *Fragments from Hellenistic Jewish Authors* (4 vols., Atlanta: Scholars, 1983, 1989, 1996).

74. Alan Mendelson, *Secular Education in Philo of Alexandria* (Cincinnati: Hebrew Union College Press, 1982) 29.

and so would have required the apostasy of any Jew who attended it. He further argues that Egyptians were excluded from these institutions, "and so undoubtedly were the Jews."[75] The latter assertion is questionable for the period before Claudius. In the Ptolemaic period, anyone who could afford a gymnasium education could acquire one. According to A.H.M. Jones, membership of the gymnasium at the end of the Ptolemaic period was "socially uniform, consisting of the well-to-do Hellenized class, but racially very mixed, including besides such families as had preserved their Greek blood unmixed a large number of half-caste and Hellenized Egyptian families."[76] The Romans adopted a more restrictive policy of excluding non-Greeks, but it is apparent from the *Boule* papyrus and the *Letter* of Claudius that this policy was not always successful.

The view that observant Jews would have rejected the gymnasium founders on the evidence of Philo, who, as Feldman remarks, has all the appearance of an observant Jew but nonetheless speaks only positively about the gymnasium and liberal education.[77] In commenting on the beneficence of parents to children he writes that they have not only given them life but education of body and soul,

> so that they may have not only life, but a good life. They have benefited the body by means of the gymnasium and the training there given, through which it gains muscular vigour and good condition and the power to bear itself and move with an ease marked by gracefulness and elegance. They have done the same for the soul by means of letters and arithmetic and geometry and music and philosophy as a whole which lifts on high the mind lodged within the mortal body and escorts it to the very heaven.
>
> (*De Spec. Leg.* 2.230)

He displays intimate knowledge of the methods of reproach and punishment used by the gymnasium officials, the *sophronistai* (*De Mig. Abr.* 116), and draws numerous examples from athletic contests.[78] He describes his pursuit of philosophy in terms reminiscent of Ben Sira's erotic hymn to wisdom:

> When first I was incited by the goads of philosophy to desire her I consorted in early youth with one of her handmaids, Grammar, and all that I begat by her, writing, reading and study of the writings of the poets, I dedicated to her mistress. And again I kept company with another, namely Geometry, and was charmed with her beauty, for she showed symmetry and proportion in every part. Yet I took none of her children for my private use, but brought them as a gift to the lawful wife. Again my ardour moved me to keep company with a third; rich

---

75. Wolfson, *Philo,* 1.79.

76. A.H.M. Jones, *The Cities of the Eastern Roman Provinces,* 2d ed. (Oxford: Clarendon Press, 1971) 308–9.

77. Feldman, *Jew and Gentile,* 57–59.

78. Ibid., 60.

in rhythm, harmony and melody was she, and her name was Music, and from her I begat diatonics, chromatics and harmonics, conjunct and disjunct melodies, conforming with the consonance of the fourth, fifth or octave intervals. And again of none of these did I make a secret hoard, wishing to see the lawful wife a lady of wealth with a host of servants ministering to her.

(De Cong. 74–76)

Alan Mendelson has argued persuasively that such passages should be taken to reflect Philo's own education.[79] The ephebate year (at age fourteen) would only have been the introduction to the liberal or encyclical studies, which would then have continued, in the gymnasium, until about the age of twenty.[80] Philo never mentions the *ephebeia,* but he could scarcely have proceeded to his liberal studies without completing it. The possibility that he received his education from a tutor, at home, should be discounted in view of his frequent references to the gymnasium and athletic contests. It is true that the gymnasium had religious associations, and was usually adorned with statues of Hermes and Heracles, but Philo does not seem to have found therein any significant impediment to his education. He also remarks that he has often been to the theater *(De Ebr.* 177). Jewish familiarity with theatrical productions could already be inferred from the tragedy of Ezekiel. An inscription from Asia Minor shows that a special place was reserved for Jews in the theater at Miletus.[81]

In contrast, the only Jewish schools that Philo describes are connected with the sabbath synagogue service: "Each seventh day there stand wide open in every city thousands of schools of good sense, temperance, courage, justice and the other virtues" *(De Spec. Leg.* 2.62). Again, in *De Vita Mos.* 2.16:

> The Jews every seventh day occupy themselves with the philosophy of their fathers, dedicating that time to the acquiring of knowledge and the study of the truths of nature. For what are our places of prayer throughout the cities but schools of prudence and courage and temperance and justice and also of piety, holiness and every virtue by which duties to God and men are discerned and rightly performed?

Sabbaths, according to Philo, should be devoted to philosophy *(De Opif.* 128). This, of course, is a philosopher's understanding of his religion. The signifi-

---

79. Mendelson, *Secular Education,* 25–26.

80. On the stages of Hellenistic education, see M. Hengel, *Judaism and Hellenism* (2 vols. Philadelphia: Fortress, 1974) 1.66, and, with specific reference to Philo, Mendelson, *Secular Education,* 40–42, 99. Where the ephebate began at 18, some liberal studies would have preceded it, and in any case the line between elementary and secondary education was sometimes blurred. Marrou, *A History of Education in Antiquity,* 160–75, warns, with reference to secondary education, that "it is impossible to say definitely when it began or how long it lasted" (p. 161).

81. Feldman, *Jew and Gentile,* 62. The inscription is *CIJ* 748.

cant point for our present purpose is that these sabbath schools are obviously not the setting for secular education. Jews who became versed in Greek literature and philosophy must have acquired that competence elsewhere.

We should not conclude that all Jews, or a majority of them, had the benefit of a gymnasium education. This education was the prerogative of the well-to-do. Philo was exceptional not only for his philosophical ability, but also for his family background. His brother was a banker, and his nephew rose to become prefect of Egypt. There were class distinctions within Alexandrian Judaism, as appears from the treatise *In Flaccum*, where Philo complains that the Jewish magistrates who were flogged with whips "fared worse than their inferiors," the commoners among the Alexandrian Jews. When sums of money are mentioned in the Jewish papyri, they are "always small, whether given as dowries or bequeathed as legacies or loaned."[82] The number of those whose means allowed a gymnasium education was probably quite limited.[83]

The authors of wisdom literature were by definition an educated class. The author of the Wisdom of Solomon, probably a contemporary of Philo, is likely to have had a similar education, but he does not display the same grasp of philosophy and cannot have persevered as long in his studies. His work shows an acquaintance with rhetoric and some familiarity with philosophy, although he had not thoroughly mastered either. Nonetheless, the Jewish wisdom teacher of the first century C.E. in Alexandria had a much better opportunity really to understand Hellenistic ideas than was possible for Ben Sira two centuries earlier in Jerusalem.

Education in the Hellenistic cities at the beginning of the Roman era was more developed, systematic, and sophisticated than can possibly have been the case in Ben Sira's *bêt midraš*. The wisdom literature of the Greek-speaking Diaspora was likewise more complex. The closest parallel to traditional Hebrew wisdom is found in Greek gnomic poetry, which is represented in Jewish literature by the poem of Pseudo-Phocylides. At the other end of the spectrum is the work of Philo. Here wisdom is properly philosophy, distinguished from its traditional forebear by its systematic and critical nature. The sustained character of Philo's thought goes far beyond anything found in the wisdom books of the Bible or the Apocrypha, and also goes beyond the scope of this book. The Wisdom of Solomon occupies an intermediate place. It contains little gnomic wisdom, and is informed by philosophy, but it also bears a resemblance to the longer reflective poems of Sirach on the subject of wisdom, and it follows the Hebrew sage in bringing the history of Israel into the purview of the sage.

82. Tcherikover and Fuks, *Corpus Papyrorum Judaicarum* 1.51–52.
83. Mendelson, *Secular Education,* 27.

Propaganda and God-fearers

The Wisdom of Solomon speaks of the Israelites as those "through whom the imperishable light of the law was to be given to the world" (Wis. 18:4). For a long time modern scholarship assumed that the Jewish literature written in Greek was missionary literature, intended to promote Judaism in the Hellenistic world.[84] Closely bound up with this idea was the notion of a Jewish mission to the Gentiles, which succeeded not only in making converts to Judaism but also in creating a class of God-fearers and sympathizers who stopped short of full acceptance of the Jewish Law. All these assumptions have been sharply disputed in recent years.

The propagandistic character of Greco-Jewish literature was called into question by Tcherikover in a famous article in 1956.[85] Tcherikover argued that this literature was primarily intended for the edification of Jews rather than for the conversion of Gentiles. There is very little evidence that Gentiles paid any attention to this literature, although much of it was collected by the polymath Alexander Polyhistor in Rome in the first century B.C.E., and the opening verse of Genesis is cited in the first-century-C.E. rhetorical treatise *On the Sublime,* which is attributed to Longinus.[86] The high esteem for Judaism in works (falsely) attributed to the Sibyl and Orpheus would have the effect of bolstering the self-respect of the Jewish community.[87] The alternatives on this issue are not mutually exclusive, however. Much of this literature attempts to develop a view of Judaism that would be both intelligible and congenial to a cultivated Greek. In so doing, it shapes the self-perception and self-understanding of the Jewish community, but by no means excludes a Gentile readership, if such could be found.[88]

Recent scholarship is sharply divided on the question of a Jewish mission. Louis Feldman defends the traditional view and argues that extensive proselytism must be posited to explain the supposed growth of Judaism in this period.[89] The estimates of the numbers of Jews in antiquity are unreliable, however, and so this argument is not compelling. At the other end of the spectrum, Martin Goodman has examined the texts that are usually adduced as evidence for a Jewish mission and found them wanting. Rather, he finds striking "the

---

84. E.g., M. Friedländer, *Geschichte der jüdischen Apologetik* (Zurich: Schmidt, 1900); P. Dalbert, *Die Theologie der Hellenistisch-Jüdischen Missionsliteratur unter Ausschluss von Philo und Josephus* (Hamburg: Reich, 1954).

85. V. Tcherikover, "Jewish Apologetic Literature Reconsidered," *Eos* 48 (1956) 169–93.

86. Stern, *Greek and Latin Authors,* 1.361–65.

87. Cf. M. Goodman, *Mission and Conversion* (Oxford: Clarendon, 1994) 80.

88. See further Collins, *Between Athens and Jerusalem,* 8–10.

89. Feldman, *Jew and Gentile,* 293. So also D. Georgi, *The Opponents of Paul in Second Corinthians* (Philadelphia: Fortress, 1986) 83–84.

lack of proselytizing attitudes in first-century Judaism."[90] So, for example, the famous dictum in Matt. 23:15 about scribes and Pharisees crossing land and sea to make one proselyte may refer to the eagerness of Pharisees to convert other Jews to their *halakah* rather than to the conversion of Gentiles. Goodman is surely right that there was no systematic or organized attempt to win converts to Judaism in this period in the manner of Christian missionary activity.[91] He acknowledges, however, that there was "an apologetic mission," to win the approval and esteem of Gentiles for Judaism.[92] To some degree, this was accomplished through the synagogue service. Philo says that "each seventh day there stand wide open in every city thousands of schools of good sense, temperance, courage, justice and the other virtues . . ." (*De Spec. Leg.* 2.282), and Josephus claims that the Jews of Antioch "were constantly attracting to their religious ceremonies multitudes of Greeks, and these they had in some measure incorporated with themselves" (*J.W.* 7.45). To some degree it was accomplished by Jews in the course of their regular work. The royal house of Adiabene was converted to Judaism by a salesman, Hananias, who nonetheless advised the heir to the throne, Izates, against undergoing circumcision (*Ant.* 20.34–38). At least some of the Greco-Jewish literature could also have contributed to this "apologetic mission" by presenting Judaism in an attractive light.

Gentiles who were attracted to Judaism but stopped short of full conversion are often called "God-fearers" in modern scholarship, following the terminology of the Acts of the Apostles. Here again modern scholarship is sharply divided, and presents extreme views that cannot be maintained.[93] On the one hand, there can be no doubt that many Gentiles sympathized with Judaism to varying degrees. Josephus boasts that "the masses have long since shown a keen desire to adopt our religious observances; and there is not one city, Greek or barbarian, nor a single nation, to which our custom of abstaining from work on the seventh day has not spread, and where fasts and the lighting of lamps and many of our prohibitions in the matter of food are not observed" (*Ag. Ap.* 2.282). This testimony is corroborated by the Roman satirist Juvenal, a younger contemporary of Josephus:

---

90. Goodman, *Mission and Conversion,* 89. Cf. S. McKnight, *A Light among the Gentiles: Jewish Missionary Activity in the Second Temple Period* (Minneapolis: Fortress, 1991).

91. Even Georgi, *The Opponents,* 88, who regards the Jewish mission as widespread, acknowledges that it was not directed by any central authority.

92. Goodman, *Mission and Conversion,* 86.

93. One extreme is presented by A. T. Kraabel, "The Disappearance of the 'God-Fearers,'" in J. A. Overman and R. S. MacLennan, eds., *Diaspora Jews and Judaism* (Atlanta: Scholars, 1992) 119–30, and R. S. MacLennan and A. T. Kraabel, "The God-Fearers—A Literary and Theological Invention," ibid., 131–43. The other extreme can be found in L. H. Feldman, "The Omnipresence of the G-d Fearers," *BAR* 12 (1986) 58–69; *Jew and Gentile,* 342–82.

Some chance to have a father who fears the sabbaths,
They adore nothing beside the clouds and the deity of heaven
Nor do they think swine's flesh to be different from human,
From which the father abstained, and soon they lay aside their foreskins;
But used to despise the Roman laws
They learn, and keep, and fear the Jewish law,
Whatsoever Moses delivered in the secret volume:
Not to show the ways, unless to one observing the same rites,
To lead the circumcised only to a sought-for fountain;
But the father is in fault, to whom every seventh day was
Idle, and he did not meddle with any part of life.

(*Satires* 14.96–106)[94]

Juvenal's account does not imply any proselytizing activity on the part of Jews; the conversion comes about because of the curiosity of the Romans about foreign ways. Gentile respect for the sabbath was already reported by Philo, half a century or so earlier. The Jewish laws, he claimed, "attract and win the attention of all, of barbarians, of Greeks, of dwellers on the mainland and islands, of nations of the east and the west, of Europe and Asia, of the whole inhabited world from end to end. For who has not shown his high respect for that sacred seventh day, by giving rest and relaxation from labor to himself and his neighbors, freemen and slaves alike, and beyond these to the beasts" (*De Vita Mos.* 2.20–21). The Roman philosopher Seneca also noted the widespread observance of the sabbath, and complained that "the vanquished have given their laws to the victors."[95] While the references to the God-fearers in the Acts of the Apostles may be stylized for theological purposes, and the phrases used to refer to them, *phoboumenos ton theon* and *sebomenos ton theon,* do not occur in inscriptions,[96] the existence of Gentiles who partially observed Jewish laws cannot seriously be questioned.

Much of modern scholarship, however, has assumed a much more distinct profile of these "God-fearers" than is warranted by the evidence. According to one standard reference article: "They frequent the services of the synagogue, they are monotheists in the biblical sense, and they participate in some of the ceremonial requirements of the Law, but they have not moved to full conversion to Judaism through circumcision. They are called . . . *sebomenoi* or *phoboumenoi ton theon.*"[97] Their numbers have been estimated as "perhaps millions by the first century."[98] In fact, we have no evidence of their number,

94. Stern, *Greek and Latin Authors,* 2.102–7.
95. Seneca, in Augustine, *De Civitate Dei,* 6.11; Stern, *Greek and Latin Authors,* 1.431.
96. Kraabel, "The Disappearance of the 'God-Fearers.'"
97. K. G. Kuhn and H. Stegemann, "Proselyten," *Pauly-Wissowa, Real-Encyclopädie* Supp. 9 (1962) 1260.
98. *Enc. Jud.* (1971) 10.55.

and it does not appear that they constituted a defined class with specific requirements for membership. There were many ways in which a Gentile might express sympathy for Judaism.[99] These could range from a quite vague admiration of the Jewish laws, or from financial contributions to the construction of a synagogue, to the practice of some Jewish rituals or the veneration of the God of Israel. This situation is not at all altered by the much-discussed inscription from Aphrodisias in Asia Minor (third century C.E.), which was discovered in 1976 and published in 1986.[100] This inscription contains the names of 125 individuals, of whom the first 71 were Jews (including three proselytes). The second part of the list is distinguished by a slight gap on the stone and a heading that reads: "as many as are God-fearers" (*kai hosoi theosebeis*). None of the names that follow are distinctively Jewish. Some of the individuals are indicated as "councillors." If they were councillors of the city of Aphrodisias, their duties would presumably have entailed idolatry.[101] The inscription has rightly been hailed as conclusive evidence for the existence of "God-fearers,"[102] but it throws no light at all on the beliefs and practices of these people. They may have qualified as "God-fearers" by financial or political support for the Jewish community, and need not have endorsed any Jewish beliefs or rituals at all. Not all sympathizers frequented the synagogue or were practical monotheists.

The existence of Gentile "God-fearers," however defined, is relevant to the wisdom literature of the Hellenistic Diaspora. This literature presents Jewish traditions in Greek dress, drawing heavily on Greek philosophy and ethical teaching. Pseudo-Phocylides makes no overt reference whatever to Judaism. This literature may still have been addressed primarily to Jews, but it would also seem to be very congenial to interested Gentiles. To a great degree, it explores common ground between Jews and Gentiles. The common ground that it explores, however, is on a fairly high intellectual and moral level. The sabbath-observers described by Josephus and Juvenal may have been merely superstitious, attracted by curiosity about Jewish practices. Other Jewish writers, such as Artapanus, sought a rapprochement with popular Greco-Egyptian culture, even going so far as to attribute the founding of the Egyptian animal cults to Moses. The appeal of the wisdom writers is to educated, cultured Hellenes, who were philosophically sophisticated. Whether or not they hoped to attract such Greeks to Judaism, they sought to understand their religion in such a way that they themselves could be both faithful Jews and cultured Hellenes.

99. J. J. Collins, "A Symbol of Otherness: Circumcision and Salvation in the First Century," in J. Neusner and E. S. Frerichs, eds., *To See Ourselves as Others See Us: Christians, Jews, "Others" in Late Antiquity* (Chico, Calif.: Scholars, 1985) 179–85; S.J.D. Cohen, "Crossing the Boundary and Becoming a Jew," *HTR* 82 (1989) 13–33.

100. J. Reynolds and R. Tannenbaum, *Jews and God-Fearers at Aphrodisias* (Supp. 12; Cambridge: Cambridge Philological Society, 1987).

101. Goodman, *Mission and Conversion,* 118.

102. Feldman, *Jew and Gentile,* 362–69.

Chapter 9.
Jewish Ethics in Hellenistic Dress:
The Sentences of Pseudo-Phocylides

The principal formulation of practical wisdom from the Hellenistic Diaspora is found in a didactic poem of 230 verses attributed to the Greek gnomic poet Phocylides, who lived in Miletus in Ionia in the middle of the sixth century B.C.E. This poem achieved wide popularity in the Middle Ages, on the assumption that it was an authentic work of Phocylides. The fact that it contained several reminiscences of the Old Testament was taken as independent corroboration of the universal validity of biblical norms. Its authenticity was first seriously challenged by Joseph Scaliger in 1606.[1] Scaliger inclined to Christian rather than Jewish authorship, but he made a valuable contribution in showing the dependence of the poem on the LXX. After Scaliger's critique, interest in Pseudo-Phocylides declined, until it was revived by Jacob Bernays in 1856.[2] Bernays accepted the dependence on the LXX as an established fact, but showed that the poem betrays no knowledge of Christianity. The Jewish authorship of Pseudo-Phocylides was still disputed by a few scholars early in the twentieth century,[3] but it is now universally accepted as an established fact.[4] A date around the turn of the era seems most likely. The poem uses some words that are not attested before the first century B.C.E.[5] The universalist tone, which betrays no hint of conflict between Jew and Gentile, makes a date after the reign of Caligula (37–41 C.E.) unlikely.[6] With the possible exception of v. 39

1. J. Scaliger, "Animadversiones in Chronologica Eusebii," in idem, *Thesaurus Temporum* (London, 1606). An excellent history of research is provided by P. W. van der Horst, *The Sentences of Pseudo-Phocylides* (Leiden: Brill, 1978) 3–54.
2. J. Bernays, *Über das phokylideische Gedicht: Ein Beitrag zur hellenistischen Literatur* (Berlin, 1856); reprinted in Bernays' *Gesammelte Abhandlungen I* (Berlin: Hertz, 1885) 192–261.
3. See van der Horst, *The Sentences,* 19–22, on the theories of K.F.A. Lincke (1903) and A. Ludwich (1904), and pp. 39–42 on F. Dornseiff (1939).
4. M. Goodman, in E. Schürer, *The History of the Jewish People in the Age of Jesus Christ, vol. 3, part 1* (rev. and ed. G. Vermes, et al.; Edinburgh: T. & T. Clark, 1986) 688, favors Jewish authorship but grants that "it is nonetheless not entirely clear whether the author was Jewish."
5. Van der Horst, *The Sentences,* 81, claims that there are about 15 such words.
6. P. W. van der Horst, "Pseudo-Phocylides Revisited," *Journal for the Study of the Pseudepigrapha* 3 (1988) 15. This essay is reprinted in P. W. van der Horst, *Essays on the Jewish World of Early Christianity* (Göttingen: Vandenhoeck & Ruprecht, 1990) 35–62. In his earlier work, van der Horst dated the composition between 30 B.C.E. and 40 C.E., but he now extends the period to include the whole first century B.C.E.

("Strangers should be held in equal honor with citizens"), which may reflect the agitation concerning the rights of Jews in Alexandria in the time of Philo, there is little in the book to indicate a specific date, and even the place of origin is uncertain.[7]

The Pseudonym

An initial clue as to the nature of this work is provided by the attribution to Phocylides. We have several examples of Jewish writings from the Hellenistic Diaspora that are falsely attributed to famous pagan authorities, including the Sibyl, Orpheus, and the great tragedians.[8] We have noted the long-standing dispute as to whether this literature was primarily addressed to the Gentile world for missionary or propagandistic purposes, or was rather intended to bolster the self-confidence of the Jewish community. We shall return later to the purpose of this particular pseudepigraphon. If a pseudonym was to be credible, however, there had to be some affinity between the kind of literature usually attributed to the famous authority and the Jewish pseudepigraphon.

Phocylides was cited as an authority in ethical matters by Plato (*Republic* 407a7), Aristotle (*Politics* IV.11.1295b34), and Isocrates (*Ad Nicoclem* 42–43), and by a host of later authors.[9] Isocrates groups him with Hesiod and Theognis as the best counselors for human life. Only fragments of his poems have survived.[10] Like the poems of Theognis, they belong to the category of gnomic poetry, which is the closest Greek analogue to the proverbial wisdom found in Proverbs and Sirach. A *gnōmē* is "a short sentence giving a rule for conduct in daily life."[11] Gnomic poetry is distinguished by the juxtaposition of single-line sayings (monostichs), which lend themselves to citation in other contexts. It deals with traditional moral themes, and was widely used for educational purposes, for preliminary exercises in philosophical and rhetorical training.[12] Gnomic poems may be the work of individual authors, or they may

7. While Alexandrian provenance is not certain, it remains the most likely option. There is no evidence whatever to suggest any other location (*pace* J.M.G. Barclay, *Jews in the Mediterranean Diaspora*, 336, who categorizes it as "outside Egypt").

8. For a survey of this literature see Goodman, in Schürer, *The History*, vol. 3, 617–700. For the texts in translation, see J. H. Charlesworth, ed., *The Old Testament Pseudepigrapha* (New York: Doubleday, 1985) 2. 775–919.

9. The testimonia are collected by van der Horst, *The Sentences*, 60–62.

10. B. Gentili and C. Prato, *Poetarum Elegiacorum testimonia et fragmenta*, vol. 1(Leipzig: Teubner, 1979) xii, xxxviii, 130–40.

11. Van der Horst, *The Sentences*, 79.

12. P. Derron, *Pseudo-Phocylide: Sentences* (Paris: Société d'Édition "Les Belles Lettres," 1986) xxii; A. J. Malherbe, *Moral Exhortation: A Greco-Roman Sourcebook* (Philadelphia: Westminster, 1986) 109. For an overview of Greek gnomic poetry see Derron, *Pseudo-Phocylide*, VII–XXVI; M. Küchler, *Frühjüdische Weisheitstraditionen* (Göttingen: Vandenhoeck & Ruprecht, 1979) 237–61.

be constituted by anthologies of sayings (*gnomologia*) from different sources. Such verses were sometimes attributed to famous ancient figures in Greek circles, quite apart from Jewish pseudepigraphy. (The "Golden Verses" attributed to Pythagoras provide an instance of the phenomenon.) Like wisdom instructions, they exhibit varying degrees of thematic organization, but are often loosely structured. Gnomic sayings were widely used in philosophical instruction in the Hellenistic period, especially by the Cynics, but also by philosophers of virtually every school.[13]

Literary Structure

Most scholars have seen little structure in Pseudo-Phocylides. Van der Horst argues that what is true of Prov. 10:1–22:16 is also true of Pseudo-Phocylides: "Mostly no ordering principle can be discerned and each single line has to be looked at on its own."[14] Like most scholars, he contents himself with a list of topics that occupy the body of the book ("exhortations to justice, admonitions to mercy, etc.").[15] Recently, however, Walter Wilson has argued that "the poem has been designed in a fairly sophisticated and systematic manner according to certain literary and argumentative strategies familiar from contemporary gnomic, paraenetic, and philosophical sources."[16] In his view, vv. 3–8 function as a type of *prothesis* or *propositio*, setting forth the basic principles and presuppositions of the work. The body of the poem, vv. 9–227, constitutes the *pistis* or *probatio*, which expands on the introduction in concrete terms. This in turn is divided into two major sections. Verses 9–131 are structured according to the cardinal virtues: justice (9–54), moderation (55–96), fortitude (97–121), and wisdom (122–31). Verses 132–227 are organized according to the different social relationships in the life of an individual. Finally, the poem is framed by a prologue and epilogue that identify the author and indicate the nature of the poem.

This attempt to identify a literary structure in Pseudo-Phocylides is at least partially successful. It is quite clear that the second half of the poem deals with social relationships. The organization of the first half in accordance with the cardinal virtues is not immediately obvious, as it is not indicated explicitly in the

13. See further W. T. Wilson, *The Mysteries of Righteousness: The Literary Composition and Genre of the Sentences of Pseudo-Phocylides* (Tübingen: Mohr, 1994) 18–33.

14. Van der Horst, *The Sentences*, 78.

15. J. Thomas, *Der Jüdische Phokylides* (Göttingen: Vandenhoeck & Ruprecht, 1992) 320, provides a convenient tabulation of the lists of contents identified by van der Horst, Derron, and Thomas himself. The most detailed list is provided by N. Walter, *Poetische Schriften* (JSHRZ 4.3; Gütersloh: Mohn, 1983) 197–216, but the sheer detail of the list obscures rather than clarifies the structure of the work.

16. Wilson, *The Mysteries of Righteousness*, 178.

text. Wilson's interpretation requires, for example, that the reflections on death
and afterlife in vv. 97–121 be related to the virtue of fortitude. The theme of fortitude is present in this passage: v. 118 urges the reader not to be dismayed by
evils, and v. 121 advises accommodation to the vicissitudes of life. But the passage also recommends moderation in grief and respect for the dead, and it argues against covetousness in vv. 109–10. A warning against "love of money"
in v. 42 is classified under "justice" in Wilson's schema. Again, the classification is somewhat forced. Derron favors a looser structure, with short sequences
on several topics, several of which are virtues (justice, vv. 9–21; *philanthropia,*
22–41; wealth, 42–47; prudence, 48–58; moderation, 59–69; envy, 70–75; temperance, 76–96; death and afterlife, 97–115; fortune, 116–21; wisdom, 122–
31).[17] This part of the poem does deal with virtues, however, and justice, moderation, and wisdom are all highlighted in turn. At the least, Wilson's proposal
is helpful in clarifying the major emphases in the different parts of the poem. If
we dispense with his insistence on the four cardinal virtues as an organizing
principle, we may still accept his division of the body of the poem: vv. 9–131
provide instruction that is largely, though not entirely, concerned with various
virtues, while vv. 132–227 provide instruction on social relationships.

The Introductory Summary
(vv. 3–8)

The body of the work is introduced by a short poem of six verses that briefly
states several moral principles in apodictic form:

> Do not commit adultery nor rouse homosexual passion,
> Do not stitch wiles together nor stain your hands with blood.
> Do not become unjustly rich, but live from honourable means.
> Be content with what you have and abstain from what is another's.
> Do not tell lies, but always speak the truth.
> Honour God first and foremost, and thereafter your parents.

Many of these topics are taken up later at greater length, although they are not
examined in systematic fashion.

Bernays was the first to identify these verses as "a selection from the decalogue," and to recognize in the juxtaposition of God and parents an allusion to
Leviticus 19.[18] The passage reflects the commandments against adultery, murder (staining hands with blood), theft, and telling lies—all the commandments
about social relations except for the commandments against covetousness. The
injunctions to honor God and parents represent the first half of the Decalogue.

---

17. Derron, *Pseudo-Phocylide,* xxvi–xxvii.
18. See Thomas, *Der jüdische Phokylides,* 89; van der Horst, *The Sentences,* 66.

Yet the departures from the biblical precedents are noteworthy. There is no prohibition of idolatry and no mention of the sabbath, although both topics appear prominently in Leviticus 19. Moreover, Pseudo-Phocylides inserts a prohibition of homosexuality that is not part of either the Decalogue or Leviticus 19 but has a biblical basis in Leviticus 18 and 20. We shall return to the issue of homosexuality below, in the context of sexual relationships. Although the denunciation of homosexuality would be relatively unusual in the Greek world, it is not without parallel.[19] Despite the real dependence of this opening summary on the Decalogue, there is nothing in it that could not conceivably have been written by a Greek moralist.[20]

The Virtues

The pursuit of virtues has a time-honored place in Near Eastern wisdom. The book of Proverbs is dedicated to "learning about wisdom and instruction . . . righteousness, justice and equity" (Prov. 1:2–3). The concept of virtue, however, is far more developed in Greek tradition. The Greek word *aretē* originally referred to any form of human excellence for which a person might be admired. In Homer, it was associated with the small upper class. The sixth-century gnomic poet Theognis broke with tradition when he declared that "the whole of *aretē* is summed up in justice, every man is good [*agathos*] if he is just."[21] Long after Theognis, however, *aretē* remained a matter of competitive success, closely bound up with the pursuit of honor.[22] Only with the rise of philosophy did the word take on the moral sense of "virtue."

The notion of four cardinal virtues was defined primarily by Plato in Book 4 of the *Republic,* where they are identified as wisdom, justice, temperance (*sōphrosynē*), and courage, and was popularized especially by the Stoics. The identity, and even the number, of the primary virtues remained fluid, however.[23] Not only may different names be used for the same virtue (e.g., *egkrateia* for *sōphrosynē*) but the list could be expanded. Piety was frequently added. One text, falsely attributed to Aristotle, lists eight virtues with corresponding vices.[24] Aristotle discusses courage, temperance, and justice at

---

19. Van der Horst, *The Sentences,* 111.

20. An analogous moral poem attributed to Philemon is also recognized as Jewish because of its dependence on the Decalogue, although it makes no explicit reference to Judaism. See Wilson, *The Mysteries of Righteousness,* 67.

21. Theognis 145–46. See A.W.H. Adkins, *Moral Values and Political Behavior in Ancient Greece* (London: Chatto & Windus, 1972) 42.

22. K. J. Dover, *Greek Popular Morality* (Indianapolis: Hackett, 1994; first published 1974) 226–34.

23. Wilson, *The Mysteries of Righteousness,* 42–59.

24. H. Rackman, *Aristotle: The Athenian Constitution, The Eudemian Ethics, On Virtues and Vices* (LCL; Cambridge, Mass.: Harvard Univ. Press, 1961) 484–503.

length as moral virtues in the *Nicomachean Ethics* Book 3, and several varieties of wisdom as intellectual virtues in Book 5, but he also discusses assorted virtues concerned with money, honor, and social intercourse in Book 4. The norm of four virtues is found in Jewish writings from the Hellenistic Diaspora.[25] Wisdom of Solomon 8:7 lists temperance, prudence, justice, and courage (*phronēsis,* prudence or wisdom, was a widely accepted alternative for *sophia*). The same virtues are singled out in 4 Macc. 1:1–4. Philo also contends that each of the ten commandments "incite and exhort us to wisdom and justice and godliness and the rest of the company of virtues. . . . Of the queen of the virtues, piety or holiness, we have spoken earlier, and also of wisdom and temperance. Our theme must now be she whose ways are close akin to them, that is justice."[26] We should not, then, be surprised to find an interest in these virtues on the part of Pseudo-Phocylides, although the gnomic poet does not appear to attach any importance to a specific number of cardinal virtues.

The theme of justice is quite explicit in vv. 9–21. This passage has biblical overtones at several points.[27] Verse 10b, literally "Do not judge a face," uses a Hebrew idiom (*nāśā' pānîm*) to forbid partiality. False witness is, of course, forbidden in the Decalogue. There are biblical laws about deposits (v. 13; cf. Lev. 5:20–26; Exod. 22:6–12; Josephus *Ant.* 18.7) and just measures (Deut. 25:14–15; Lev. 19:35–36; and numerous passages in the prophets and wisdom books).[28] Pseudo-Phocylides adds an interesting motivating clause in v. 11: "If you judge wickedly, God will judge you thereafter." The idea that there is retribution for wrongdoing is endemic in the Wisdom literature, and indeed in most of the Bible. In view of the discussion of afterlife in Ps.-Phoc. 97–115, however, it is reasonable to assume that "thereafter" refers to a judgment after death. As we shall see in the Wisdom of Solomon, this was an issue on which the wisdom teachers of the Hellenistic Diaspora departed from the tradition of Proverbs and Ben Sira.

Justice in Pseudo-Phocylides is tempered with mercy and kindness. Verses 22–41 address the duty of charity, in the sense of almsgiving, and ground this duty in the common lot of human beings. Again, there are biblical overtones. Verse 38 ("Do not damage fruits that are growing on the land") recalls the Deuteronomic law of war, which forbids the army to cut down trees in the

25. Some scholars find the four cardinal virtues already in Sir. 36:23–38:23, where the instructions deal in turn with justice (36:23–37:15), wisdom (37:16–26), moderation (37:27–31), and courage (38:1–23). See Wilson, *The Mysteries of Righteousness,* 56.

26. Philo, *De Spec. Leg.* 4.134–35 (trans. F. H. Colson, *Philo VIII,* LCL; Cambridge, Mass.: Harvard Univ. Press, 1968) 93.

27. Thomas, *Der jüdische Phokylides,* 161–70, following Bernays, argues that this section is a paraenesis based on Leviticus 19 in conjunction with the Decalogue. There are several parallels to Leviticus 19 in this section, but there are also influences from other sources, both Greek and Jewish. See K.-W. Niebuhr, *Gesetz und Paränese* (Tübingen: Mohr, 1987) 20–26.

28. Van der Horst, *The Sentences,* 122.

course of a siege, and specifically trees that bear fruit.[29] The most striking parallels in this passage, however, are Greek. Verse 27: "Suffering is common to all; life is a wheel; prosperity is unstable," is a commonplace of Greek tragedy and of classical literature in general.[30] It is not, however, paralleled in the Hebrew Bible. The obligation to be kind to strangers is grounded in enlightened self-interest "for we all experience the poverty that makes one wander; and the land has nothing constant for men" (vv. 40–41). The anthropocentric character of Pseudo-Phocylides's ethic here is typical of Greek thought, but it is also in line with the general orientation of Hebrew wisdom. Both Pseudo-Phocylides and Ben Sira make some appeal to divine retribution, and both take cognizance of the common fate of humanity and its leveling effect. Ben Sira, however, is somewhat more theocentric. He promises that one who is like a father to orphans will be like a son to the Most High (Sir. 4:10), and that kindness to a father will be credited against one's sins (Sir. 3:14). Pseudo-Phocylides, conversely, has a stronger sense of human sympathy and solidarity, and in this he shows the influence of Greek tradition.

One sentence in this passage, however, may reflect a distinctively Jewish interest. Verse 39 urges that "strangers should be held in equal honor with citizens." This formulation recalls the argument of Philo that "strangers, in my judgment, must be regarded as suppliants of those who receive them, and not only suppliants but settlers and friends who are anxious to obtain equal rights with the burgesses, and are near to being citizens because they differ little from the original inhabitants."[31] Philo's argument must be seen in the light of the proclamation of the Roman prefect Flaccus, that Alexandrian Jews were "strangers and foreigners."[32] Pseudo-Phocylides, too, may reflect the struggle for Jewish rights in Alexandria in this period. The further argument in vv. 40–41 that "we all experience the poverty that makes one wander" is a plea for sympathy for exiles, but it may also be an *apologia* for the Jews as foreign settlers in Alexandria.

The sayings on moderation and temperance are Hellenistic commonplaces to a great extent. The statement that money is the mother of all evil (v. 42) parallels 1 Tim. 6:10 ("love of money is the root of all evil").[33] The sentiment is found already in Sir. 8:2; 31:5. The ideal of controlling the emotions has a philosophical basis both in Plato and in the Stoics, and the sayings on moderation recall the Delphic maxim, "Nothing too much." Pseudo-Phocylides 69, "Moderation is the best of all," echoes Theognis 335: "Moderation in all things

---

29. Deut. 20:19–20. Cf. also a partial parallel in Deut. 23:25.
30. See the parallels cited by van der Horst, *The Sentences,* 132–33.
31. Philo, *De Vita Mos.* 1.35.
32. Philo, *In Flacc.* 54. See Tcherikover and Fuks, *CPJ* 1. 48–74.
33. For Greek and Roman parallels, see van der Horst, *The Sentences,* 142–46. One of the most powerful condemnations of greed is found in *Sib. Or.* 8:17–36.

is best." But ancient Near Eastern wisdom also counseled moderation. Sirach counsels on moderation in food and drink (31:12–31), and the same advice is found in the Egyptian Papyrus Insinger (Phibis) 12–18.

There is little theological reflection in these sentences, but one statement is noteworthy: "The one God is wise and mighty" (v. 54). This sentence may mean simply "Only God is wise," but the expression *heis theos* inevitably recalls the Shema (Deut. 6:4) and entails an affirmation of the singularity of God. Such affirmations constitute a theme of Hellenistic Judaism (Philo, *De Opif.* 171; *Ep. Arist.* 132; *Sib. Or.* 3:11–12; frag. 1:7–8, 32; frag. 3:3).[34] The epithet *heis* (one, only) is applied to God already in Sir. 1:8. The singularity of God was also proclaimed by some Greek philosophers, such as Xenophanes,[35] and is often found in inscriptions and magical texts, where it reflects popular syncretism.[36] The monotheism implied in this verse is all the more significant because Pseudo-Phocylides does not polemicize against idolatry.

Another quasi-doctrinal passage is found in the reflections on death and afterlife in vv. 97–115. Pseudo-Phocylides clearly posits an afterlife; the form that afterlife is to take is less clear, since the sentences present a jumble of Hebrew and Greek anthropology. On the one hand, vv. 106–8 reflect Genesis 1–3: "For the spirit is a loan from God to mortals, and his image. For we have a body out of earth, and when afterwards we are resolved again into earth we are but dust; but the air has received our spirit." The idea that the spirit survives the body does not necessarily reflect the Greek idea of the immortality of the soul; it is found in thoroughly Semitic contexts in *1 Enoch* 22 and *Jub.* 23.[37] It is also compatible with the resurrection of the body, which is clearly envisioned in v. 103: one should not disturb the graves of the deceased "for in fact we hope that the remains of the departed will soon come to the light again out of the earth." The idea of physical resurrection is exceptional in the Jewish literature that is written in Greek, but there are notable parallels in 2 Maccabees 7 and *Sib. Or.* 4. After the resurrection, we are told, "they become gods" (v. 104). "Gods" in the Greek world were simply immortals. In Jewish apocalyptic literature, however, the righteous dead are often said to become angels (e.g., *1 Enoch* 104:4–6), and angels can be called *'ēlîm,* or *'elōhîm,* "gods."[38] Pseudo-Phocylides is not outside the bounds of Jewish tradition on this point. The

---

34. Cf. the Pseudo-Orphic frags., v. 10, and Pseudo-Sophocles in Eusebius, *Praeparatio evangelica* 13.13.40.

35. Xenophanes, frag. 23: "one God, the greatest among gods and men." Van der Horst, *The Sentences,* 151.

36. E. Peterson, *Heis Theos* (Göttingen: Vandenhoeck & Ruprecht, 1926).

37. See G. W. Nickelsburg, *Resurrection, Immortality and Eternal Life in Intertestamental Judaism* (Cambridge, Mass.: Harvard Univ. Press, 1972) 31–33, 134–37.

38. Y. Yadin, *The Scroll of the War of the Sons of Light against the Sons of Darkness* (Oxford: Oxford Univ. Press, 1962) 230; C. A. Newsom, *Songs of the Sabbath Sacrifice: A Critical Edition* (Atlanta: Scholars, 1985) 23–24.

immortality of the soul (v. 115) is the more typically Greek notion and is logically quite independent of any idea of resurrection. The statement that "Hades is our common eternal home" is a common expression throughout the ancient world, and is echoed on numerous ancient epitaphs, both Greek and Jewish.[39] Normally it does not imply any meaningful afterlife whatever. Pseudo-Phocylides here seems to juxtapose several distinct understandings of death, all of which were traditional, but which were not strictly compatible with one another. He clearly expects some form of afterlife. Unlike the Wisdom of Solomon, however, Pseudo-Phocylides's understanding of life and wisdom is not transformed by this belief. He appeals to judgment after death only in v. 11, and even there it is not certain that postmortem judgment is entailed. Instead, his ethic is based on the inherent value of the virtues and on his sense of human solidarity in face of the uncertainties of life (cf. vv. 116–21).

The discussion of the virtues in Pseudo-Phocylides concludes with an affirmation of the value of wisdom: "Better is a wise man than a strong one. Wisdom directs the course of lands and cities and ships" (vv. 130–31). Such statements can also be found in traditional Hebrew wisdom. Distinctively Greek, however, is the statement that when God allotted every creature a weapon he gave reason to man as his protection (vv. 125–28). Like much of Pseudo-Phocylides, the theme of these verses is commonplace in Greek literature.[40] The notion that reason is God's finest gift to humanity is also found in Philo (*De Somn.* 1.103).

Social Relationships

The affinities of Pseudo-Phocylides with the kind of practical wisdom taught by Ben Sira are most clearly in evidence in vv. 132–227. Here again Wilson's analysis is helpful. He divides this section into three paragraphs or subsections. The first (vv. 132–52) "discusses what we might call social 'outsiders', that is, assorted referents on the periphery of moral life and conduct, with an emphasis on how one ought to deal with evil persons."[41] The second (vv. 153–74) addresses how a person ought to earn a living. Finally, the third subsection discusses obligations within the household (vv. 175–227).

The first of these subsections begins with advice to "turn away an evil-doer forcibly," because "those who are with the bad often die together with them" (133–34), and concludes by urging the reader to "flee dissension and

---

39. P. W. van der Horst, *Ancient Jewish Epitaphs* (Kampen: Kok Pharos, 1991) 42. Cf. Qoh. 12:5: "Man goes to his eternal home."

40. Van der Horst, *The Sentences,* 200–201, gives the references.

41. Wilson, *The Mysteries of Righteousness,* 119.

strife" and "do no good to a bad man, it is like sowing in the sea" (151–52).[42] The need for selectivity in friendship is a commonplace in ancient Near Eastern wisdom.[43] The notion that one should not even do good to a bad person is more extreme than this, and it picks up a theme found explicitly in Sir. 11:29–12:18, which specifically warns against giving alms to the wicked (Sir. 12:7). Sirach goes farther and claims that even God hates sinners (Sir. 12:6). No such statement is found in Pseudo-Phocylides. (The other major wisdom book from the Diaspora, the Wisdom of Solomon, declares emphatically that God loves all things that exist and hates "none of the things that you have made, for you would not have made anything if you had hated it" (Wis. 11:24.) Moreover, *Ps.-Phoc.* 140 repeats the biblical injunction: "If a beast of your enemy falls on the way, help it to rise" (cf. Deut. 22:4). In this case, the kindness is primarily directed to the innocent beast rather than to the enemy, but in general Pseudo-Phocylides is more humane and less severe than Ben Sira. His gentler disposition is evidenced at two other points in this section. Verses 141–42 caution: "Never blame an errant man or a transgressor. It is better to make a gracious friend instead of an enemy." This advice significantly modifies the injunction to do no good to an evil man; at least not all sinners are dismissed as evil. Verse 150 enjoins, "Do not apply your hand violently to tender children" (cf. v. 207). Since ancient education, especially as reflected in Near Eastern wisdom literature, was based on corporal punishment (cf. Sir. 30:1, 12), this injunction is a noteworthy break with tradition.

In addition to the theme of humane behavior, this section of Pseudo-Phocylides also warns against "unnatural" practices. Verses 147–48 ("Eat no meat that is torn by wild animals, but leave the remains to the swift dogs. Animals eat from animals") are drawn from the Bible (Exod. 22:30).[44] Pseudo-Phocylides, however, does not appeal to biblical authority. His appeal is to the law of nature: "Animals eat from animals." This is followed by an admonition to avoid potions and magical books (v. 149). Sorcery of various kinds is outlawed in the Bible (e.g., Deut. 13:1–2), and such prohibitions become more common in the Hellenistic period. Charms and spells are among the illegitimate revelations of the Watchers in *1 Enoch* 6:1–2. The prohibition of magic

42. Wilson, 129f., finds a chiastic structure throughout this passage, but some of the correspondences are questionable. Verses 137 and 150 are paired as sayings on the treatment of children, but the correspondence depends on reading v. 137 as "pay due respect to children [*paisin*]" with N. Walter, rather than "render to all [*pasin*] their due" (so van der Horst, Derron). Both readings have manuscript support. The admonition against magic in v. 149 is classified as a "specific command on moderation," to correspond to v. 138 ("use all things sparingly").

43. Cf. Papyrus Insinger 11:22–15:6. Cf. also Num. 16:26: "Turn away from the tents of these wicked men."

44. On the biblical sources of *Ps.-Phoc.* 132–52, see Thomas, *Der jüdische Phokylides,* 174–79, who points to Exodus 22–23, Deuteronomy 13 and 22.

was sometimes reckoned among the Noachide laws.[45] Despite the prohibitions there was much Jewish magic in antiquity.[46] Pseudo-Phocylides does not give a reason for the injunction. Since the previous sentences were based on the law of nature, we may surmise that magic was deemed to be unnatural. Some objections to such practices can also be found in Greek literature. Plato associates magic with unjust behavior (*Republic* 364; *Laws* 933). In general, those who condemned these practices saw them as ways to injure people.

The second subsection on social relations (vv. 153–74) is a coherent block of verses on the importance and nature of labor. The opening verses (153–57) deal with the theme of self-sufficiency. Ben Sira likewise says that it is better to die than to beg (Sir. 40:28). The underlying issue is one of honor and shame. Pseudo-Phocylides differs from Ben Sira, however, in his evaluation of manual labor. Ben Sira acknowledges that no city could be inhabited without craftsmen (38:32), but he is at pains to emphasize the superiority of the vocation of the scribe. There is no such polemic in Pseudo-Phocylides, who seems to recommend all kinds of work wholeheartedly. The concluding analogies with ants and bees are *topoi* derived from LXX Proverbs (cf. Prov. 6:6–8; 30:24–25 on the ant; LXX Prov. 6:8a–c on bees).[47]

The section of Pseudo-Phocylides that most closely parallels Ben Sira concerns relationships within the household (175–227). This section of the poem also has close parallels in Josephus, *Ag. Ap.* 2.199–206, and Philo, *Hyp.* 7.1–9. Verses 175–94 deal with various sexual relations and sexual acts, while vv. 195–227 deal with relations with wives, children, the elderly, and slaves.

There are some parallels between Pseudo-Phocylides and Ben Sira on the subject of women. Both texts have an explicitly male point of view. Both regard marriage as desirable (*Ps.-Phoc.* 175–76; Sir. 36:29–30) and both are aware of the advantages of a lasting and happy marriage (*Ps.-Phoc.* 195–97; Sir. 8:19; 26:1–4). *Pseudo-Phocylides* in vv. 199–200 warns against marrying "a bad and wealthy woman," lest one become a slave to her dowry. (The husband would be inhibited from divorcing her, because he would have to return the dowry.) The same warning is found in Sir. 25:21–22, where the shame involved in such a marriage is more explicit. Pseudo-Phocylides also advises fathers to "guard a virgin in firmly locked rooms, and let her not be seen outside the house until her wedding-day" (215–16), recalling Ben Sira's anxiety on the same subject (Sir. 7:24; 42:9–14). The tone of the two sages, however, is very different. Pseudo-Phocylides has no polemic against "evil" women and barely alludes to adultery, not even addressing the subject of divorce. While the chastity of daughters is still a concern, the subject does not exercise the gnomic

---

45. L. Ginzberg, *Legends of the Jews* (Philadelphia: Jewish Publication Society, 1925) 5.93.

46. See P. S. Alexander, "Incantations and Books of Magic," in Schürer, *The History,* 342–79.

47. Philo, *De Prov.* 1.25, and Origen, *Contra Celsum* 4:81, also mention the bee and the ant in combination. See van der Horst, *The Sentences,* 224–25.

poet as it did Ben Sira. While the Hebrew sage is open to the charge of misogyny, there is no sign of such prejudice in Pseudo-Phocylides. The contrast between the two teachers in this respect shows that it is simplistic to attribute the misogyny of Ben Sira to Hellenistic influence.

Much of what Pseudo-Phocylides has to say on the subject of marriage is not paralleled in Ben Sira at all, and is concerned with behavior in accordance with the natural law. The reason to marry is to "give nature her due, beget in turn as you were begotten" (v. 176). This is in accordance with Stoic teaching that marriage is "according to nature" (*kata physin*).[48] (Unlike the rabbinic tradition, Pseudo-Phocylides does not speak of a divine command to marry.) The choice of a spouse is also guided by an analogy from nature: "We seek noble horses and strong-necked bulls, . . . yet we fools do not strive to marry a good wife" (201–4).[49] Pseudo-Phocylides does not elaborate the criteria for a good wife, but the analogy with the animal world is typical of his appeal to natural law.[50]

The passage proceeds to list people with whom one should not have sexual relations: stepmother, one's father's concubines, sisters, and sisters-in-law. These prohibitions are in accordance with Leviticus 18 and 20 ("None of you shall approach anyone near of kin to uncover nakedness, says the Lord," Lev. 18:6; cf. also the behavior cursed in Deut. 27:20–23).[51] The prohibition of intercourse with one's stepmother is frequently noted in Jewish literature of the Hellenistic period.[52] Saint Paul, in 1 Cor. 5:1, claims that this is a kind of immorality that is not found even among the Gentiles. Such unions were explicitly forbidden in Roman law,[53] and Cicero denounces the union of a woman with her son-in-law as "an incredible crime."[54] The warning against relations with the concubines of one's father presupposes that a man may keep concubines. Concubines were not forbidden in the Hebrew Bible, and the practice

---

48. See the parallels cited by van der Horst, *The Sentences,* 226. Seneca, frag. 58, also parallels Pseudo-Phocylides in his concern that one's name not die out. On the Stoic idea of living according to nature, see H. Koester, "physis etc." *TDNT* 9 (1974) 264–66; G. Striker, "Following Nature: A Study in Stoic Ethics," *Oxford Society for Ancient Philosophy* 9 (1991) 1–73.

49. This passage is dependent on Theognis 183–90. See van der Horst, *The Sentences,* 245; Adkins, *Moral Values and Political Behavior,* 38.

50. On the role of such analogies in Greek thought, see Dover, *Greek Popular Morality,* 74–75. Aristophanes, *Clouds* 1420–1433, caricatures the attempt to establish what is natural by analogies with birds and animals.

51. Niebuhr, *Gesetz und Paränese,* 26–31.

52. *Jub.* 33:10; Philo, *De Spec. Leg.* 3.20–21; Josephus, *Ag. Ap.* 2.200; *Ant.* 3. 274–75; *m. Sanh.* 7:4. Van der Horst, *The Sentences,* 230.

53. The *Institutes* of Gaius 1.63: "Neither can I marry her who has aforetime been my mother-in-law or step-mother, or daughter-in-law or step-daughter. I say 'aforetime,' for if the marriage which has created the affinity still subsist, I cannot take her to wife for this other reason,—that neither can the same woman have two husbands, nor can the same man have two wives." (Cited by H. Conzelmann, *1 Corinthians* (Hermeneia; Philadelphia: Fortress, 1975) 96.

54. Cicero, *Pro Cluentio* 6 (15).

was also accepted in pagan antiquity. Reuben's intercourse with Bilhah, the concubine of his father, is reported as a scandal in Gen. 35:22 ("and Israel heard of it"), but without any extended commentary. In the Hellenistic period, this became a paradigmatic sin (*Jub.* 33:1–9; *T. Reub.* 3:11–15). The prohibition of incest was deeply rooted in Jewish tradition—cf. the story of Amnon and Tamar in 2 Samuel 13.[55] Incest was also abhorred in Greek tradition. Plato refers to the prohibition as an *agraphos nomos,* or unwritten law (*Laws* 838a–b). Egyptian custom was exceptional in the ancient world in this regard. Pharaohs and Ptolemies had routinely married their sisters, and the custom was not confined to the royal families.[56] Bestiality was also condemned in the Bible (Exod. 22:18; Lev. 18:23; 20:15–16; Deut. 27:21) and in Hellenistic Judaism (Philo, *De Spec. Leg.* 3:43–50; *Sib. Or.* 5:393), although it receives little attention from pagan moralists.[57]

Pseudo-Phocylides also urges restraint in the manner of lawful intercourse with one's wife: "Do not outrage your wife for shameful ways of intercourse" (v. 189).[58] This counsel stands in sharp contrast to the rabbinic teaching that "a man may do whatever he pleases with his wife" (*Ned.* 20b). In the context of Pseudo-Phocylides, the issue is partly one of consideration for the wife but also of self-control and moderation: "Do not deliver yourself wholly unto unbridled *eros* for your wife" (v. 193).[59] Verse 194 adds a remarkable comment: "For 'eros' is not a god, but a passion destructive to all." The divinity of Eros is often asserted in classical Greek literature (e.g., Hesiod, *Theogony* 120; Euripides, frag. 269). We do, however, find polemics against the divinization of Eros in Stoic and Cynic philosophy. So Antisthenes is said to have called *eros* "an evil of nature" and a "disease," which is regarded as a god by inferior people.[60] Pseudo-Phocylides also cautions: "Lay not your hand upon your wife when she is pregnant." This verse may be a prohibition of intercourse during pregnancy, a position that Josephus attributes to the Essenes (*J. W.* 2.61). It may, however, simply require that a husband not strike his pregnant wife, lest he cause a miscarriage.[61]

Two issues in this section of Pseudo-Phocylides stand out as trademarks of Jewish ethical teaching in the Hellenistic world. These are the prohibitions of homosexuality and of abortion and infanticide.

Like many of the injunctions in this section, the prohibition of homosexu-

55. Cf. also Lev. 18:9; 20:17; Deut. 27:22.

56. R. Taubenschlag, *The Law of Greco-Roman Egypt in the Light of the Papyri* (New York: Herald Square, 1944) vol. 1, 83.

57. But see Plutarch, *Brut. anim. rat.* 7. 990F; van der Horst, *The Sentences,* 236.

58. The interpretation of this verse is disputed. See van der Horst, *The Sentences,* 237.

59. Or, simply, "for a woman." See van der Horst, "Pseudo-Phocylides Revisited," 27.

60. Clement of Alexandria, *Stromata* 2.107.3. See further C. Schneider, "Eros," *RAC* 6.309.

61. Van der Horst, *The Sentences,* 235.

ality has a biblical basis, in Lev. 18:22; 20:13. The precise meaning of the biblical phrase "and with a male you shall not lie the lying down of a woman" is disputed, but it seems safe to conclude that all couplings between males are prohibited.[62] Prohibition of male homosexuality is a leitmotiv of Greco-Jewish literature (Philo, *De Abr.* 135; *De Spec. Leg.* 2.50; *Sib. Or.* 3:185, 596, 764; *Sib. Or.* 4:34; 5:387, 430; Josephus, *Ag. Ap.* 2.199, 215, 273). This was an issue on which there was a clear contrast between Greek and Jewish ethics, since homosexuality was widely accepted in the Greek world.[63] The argument of Pseudo-Phocylides, however, does not appeal to a revealed law, but to the law of nature: "Do not transgress the sexual order of nature for illicit sex, for even animals are not pleased by intercourse of male with male" (vv. 190–91). Such an argument would have found some sympathy among Greek philosophers. Despite a positive attitude toward homosexuality in the *Symposium,* Plato declared unequivocally in the *Laws* that "the intercourse of men with men, or of women with women, is contrary to nature" (*Laws* 636). He adds, however, that "if anyone following nature should lay down the law . . . and denounce these lusts as contrary to nature, adducing the animals as a proof that such unions were monstrous, he might prove his point, but he would be wholly at variance with the custom of your states" (*Laws* 836). Occasional denunciations of homosexuality as contrary to nature are found in the Hellenistic philosophers,[64] but the Jewish insistence on this issue remains distinctive in the Hellenistic world. The denunciation extends also to lesbianism: "Let not women imitate the sexual role of men" (*Ps.-Phoc.* 192). The laws do not envisage lesbianism, but it is condemned in the Talmud, *Yebam.* 76a, and the condemnation is implied already in the New Testament, Rom. 1:26.[65]

The prohibition of abortion and infanticide was also distinctive: "A woman should not destroy an unborn babe in the womb, nor after bearing it should she cast it out as prey for dogs and vultures" (vv. 184–85). Abortion and exposure of infants were widespread in the ancient world, and only rarely condemned. Neither was addressed in the Hebrew Bible, but Exod. 21:22–23, which envisages the case where a man strikes a pregnant woman and she miscarries,

---

62. S. M. Olyan, "'And with a Male You Shall Not Lie the Lying Down of a Woman': On the Meaning and Significance of Leviticus 18:22 and 20:13," *Journal of the History of Sexuality* 5 (1994) 179–206. Olyan argues that only the insertive partner is addressed in these laws, and suggests that at an earlier stage only the penetrator was punished. The final form of the laws, however, prescribes death for both parties.

63. K. J. Dover, *Greek Popular Morality,* 213–16; idem, *Greek Homosexuality* (2d ed.; Cambridge: Cambridge Univ. Press, 1989).

64. E.g., Musonius Rufus 12; Plutarch, *Brut. anim. rat.* 7. 990E–F.

65. See J. A. Fitzmyer, *Romans* (AB 33; New York: Doubleday,1993) 285; R. Hays, "Relations Natural and Unnatural: A Response to John Boswell's Exegesis of Romans 1," *JRE* 14 (1986) 184–215. B. J. Brooten, *Love between Women: Early Christian Responses to Homoeroticism* (Chicago: University of Chicago Press, 1996) 239–53.

came to be interpreted with reference to abortion.[66] According to the Hebrew text of Exodus, if there is a miscarriage "but no further harm follows," the perpetrator is only fined, but if the mother suffers harm, "then you shall give life for life, eye for eye, tooth for tooth. . . ." The word for "harm" (*'āsôn*) is translated in the LXX as "form," with far-reaching consequences for the issue of abortion. Philo expounded the passage as follows:

> If a man comes to blows with a pregnant woman and strikes her on the belly and she miscarries, then, if the result of the miscarriage is unshaped and undeveloped, he must be fined both for the outrage and for obstructing the artist Nature in her creative work of bringing into life the fairest of living creatures, man. But, if the offspring is already shaped and all the limbs have their proper qualities and places in the system, he must die, for that which answers to this description is a human being.[67]

The concern here is for harm to the formed fetus rather than to the mother. In rabbinic tradition, however, abortion remained a noncapital crime. The Jewish law that all children be reared was noted with approval by Hecataeus.[68] Occasional protests against abortion and exposure were raised by philosophers, especially the Stoics (e.g., Musonius Rufus 15), and the Roman satirist Juvenal refers scathingly to the practices (*Satire* 6.596), but these were minority voices in the Greco-Roman world.

The recommendations of Pseudo-Phocylides on the rearing of children are also remarkably mild: "Be not harsh with your children, but be gentle" (v. 207). The most remarkable item in the advice on children concerns the warning against effeminate hairstyles for boys, and the need to "guard the youthful beauty of a comely boy" (v. 213). Pederasty was not unknown in Palestinian Judaism. The Qumran War Scroll guards against it by barring young boys as well as women from the military camp (1QM 7:3). But the need to guard the beauty of a boy in normal circumstances was evidently unknown to Ben Sira, and reflects the more Hellenized environment of Alexandria.

The humane attitude of Pseudo-Phocylides extends to slaves.[69] Ben Sira

---

66. D. M. Feldman, *Birth Control in Jewish Law* (New York: New York Univ. Press, 1968) 254–62. See also R. Freund, "The Ethics of Abortion in Hellenistic Judaism," *Helios* 10 (1983) 125–37.

67. *Spec. Leg.* 3.108–9.

68. Diodorus Siculus 40.3. M. Stern, *Greek and Latin Authors on Jews and Judaism* (Jerusalem: The Israel Academy of Sciences and Humanities, 1976) 1.27, 29, 33.

69. On the development of humane attitudes to slaves in the Roman period, see A. Dihle, "Ethik," *RAC* 6 (1966) 667–68. For a recent overview of slavery in the ancient world, see J. A. Harrill, *The Manumission of Slaves in Early Christianity* (Tübingen: Mohr, 1995) 11–67. D. B. Martin, "Slavery and the Ancient Jewish Family," in S.J.D. Cohen, ed., *The Jewish Family in Antiquity* (Atlanta: Scholars, 1993) 113–29, argues that "slavery among Jews seems to have looked like those slave structures prominent in the time and place of the particular Jews under investigation" (p. 129).

vacillated on this subject, between counseling harsher (33:25–30) and gentler treatment (7:20–21; 33:31). Even his gentler advice is given from self-interest: a slave who is treated badly will run away. Pseudo-Phocylides has no place for harsh treatment, and even recommends consulting a well-disposed slave for advice (v. 227). The prohibition against branding a slave (v. 225) must be explained by humane motives. Although Pseudo-Phocylides draws heavily on Leviticus 18–20, there is no reason to see here an allusion to the prohibition of making gashes or tattoos in Lev. 19:28.

Pseudo-Phocylides
and the Torah

Pseudo-Phocylides also has significant overlap with the summaries of the Torah in Josephus, *Ag. Ap.* 2.190–219, and Philo, *Hyp.* 7.1–9, especially, but not exclusively in matters pertaining to social relations.[70] All three texts forbid adultery, homosexuality, and the rape of a virgin, and prohibit abortion and the exposure of infants. Philo and Pseudo-Phocylides forbid emasculation and warn against marrying a woman for her dowry. Both Josephus and Pseudo-Phocylides liken honor of parents to honor of God and emphasize the respect of elders and the rights of aliens. Other parallels outside of the section on social relations include the duty to bury the dead, the need for justice in weights and measures, and the commandment that a mother bird should not be taken with her young (*Ps.-Phoc.* 84–85; cf. Deut. 22:6–7). Josephus backs his ethical code with an affirmation of reward after death (*Ag. Ap.* 2. 218–19). It is highly unlikely that all these parallels are coincidental. All three presumably draw on a tradition of Jewish teaching that combined a selection of the Pentateuchal laws with other requirements that had become established as essential to Judaism, such as the prohibition of abortion.

This teaching is not adequately described as a summary of the Jewish law. It also included elements of Greek origin. Philo identified the source of at least some of these laws when he asked, "What need in heaven's name have we of your Buzyges and his precepts?" (*Hyp.* 7.8). Buzyges was a legendary Attic hero, whose descendants held an annual commemoration at which curses were pronounced against those who refused to bury the dead, share fire and water, and so on. These laws appear to be the source of the "unwritten customs and institutions" listed in the preceding paragraphs of the *Hypothetica* (7.6–7), where the obligation to share fire and water and to bury the dead is noted. This passage also contains a formulation of the Golden Rule: "What a man would hate to suffer he must not do himself to others" (7.6). This formulation reflects

---

70. J. E. Crouch, *The Origin and Intention of the Colossian Haustafel,* 84–87; Niebuhr, *Gesetz und Paränese,* 42–44.

Semitic idiom, and so can scarcely be taken from Buzyges, but a form of the Golden Rule is attributed to Buzyges by Clement of Alexandria.[71] Josephus also reflects the laws of Buzyges relating to fire, water, and burial, although he does not mention Buzyges by name (*Ag. Ap.* 2.211). Pseudo-Phocylides warns in v. 99 against leaving the dead unburied.

The correspondence of Pseudo-Phocylides with Philo and Josephus is by no means complete. Both these authors present their material explicitly as summaries of the Jewish law, and Josephus emphasizes that children must be taught the laws.[72] Josephus has several paragraphs on cult and sacrifice. Pseudo-Phocylides, in contrast, conceals his Jewish identity throughout.

Both Philo and Josephus emphasize the frequency of the death penalty in Jewish law and regard the leniency of the Greeks as a defect. In the case of Josephus, this is somewhat incongruous, since the discussion of penalties (*Ag. Ap.* 2.215) follows directly on a section praising the gentleness and humanity of the Law (*Ag. Ap.* 2.213–14). Both authors extend the applicability of the death penalty beyond what is found in the biblical laws. They deem all extramarital sexual relations punishable by death, and Philo extends the death penalty to all forms of theft. Since both authors appear more severe in these passages than in the rest of their work, it has been plausibly suggested that they drew on a source that was concerned to emphasize the severity of Jewish law.[73] Pseudo-Phocylides makes no argument for the death penalty.

There is also a notable difference in the area of family relationships. Philo insists that "wives must be in servitude to their husbands, a servitude not imposed by violent ill-treatment but promoting obedience in all things" (*Hyp.* 7.3). Josephus echoes Aristotle's view that the woman is in all things inferior to the man, but he attributes this position to the Law (*Ag. Ap.* 2.200).[74] He continues: "Let her accordingly be submissive, not for her humiliation, but that she may be directed; for the authority has been given by God to the man." The parallel with the New Testament has often been noted (cf. Eph. 5:22).[75] Pseudo-Phocylides agrees that the wife should not be humiliated, but never makes an issue of her submission. Josephus goes beyond the Jewish law in forbidding a man to have relations with anyone other than his wife, whereas Pseudo-Phocylides implicitly allows concubines.

---

71. *Stromata* 2.23.139. See Crouch, *The Origin and Intention*, 87–88. On the Golden Rule, see more broadly H. D. Betz, *The Sermon on the Mount* (Hermeneia; Minneapolis: Fortress, 1995) 508–16.

72. On the character of Josephus's summary in its own right, see G. Vermes, "A Summary of the Law by Flavius Josephus," *NovT* 24 (1982) 289–303.

73. Crouch, *The Origin and Intention*, 88.

74. For Aristotle's view of women, see D. L. Balch, *Let Wives Be Submissive* (Chico, Calif.: Scholars, 1981) 33–38.

75. Because of the NT parallel, the authenticity of this passage in Josephus is suspect. Cf. LCL 372.

Despite these differences, it is likely that Pseudo-Phocylides drew on a source that was also shared by Philo and Josephus, but he used it selectively for his purposes. He omitted any overt reference to the Law, and recast the material in the form of paraenesis rather than law. He is consistently less severe in tone than the other authors, and emphasizes the humane dimensions of the material.

The Purpose of
Pseudo-Phocylides

The purposes for which Pseudo-Phocylides wrote remain uncertain. In his 1978 commentary, van der Horst distinguished four theoretical possibilities: (1) the author had no agenda, but wrote purely for the pleasure of writing; (2) the author wrote for his fellow Jews, to reassure them that Greek ethics essentially agreed with the Torah, and that they did not need to look beyond their own tradition; (3) the author wrote for a pagan public, not in order to convert them to Judaism but only to make them sympathetic to Judaism; or alternatively to humanize the pagan world by giving them the benefit of Jewish ethical teaching; (4) the author was a "God-fearer" who accepted certain aspects of Judaism but not the full ritual law; he wrote to win converts to his own way of life. Van der Horst discounted the first possibility, but found it impossible to choose between the latter three. He also canvassed the idea that the book was written for schoolchildren, as was often the case with gnomologies. Ten years later, he revisited the problem and declared that the third and fourth options were no longer viable. Rather, he now favored

> the assumption that the author wrote a kind of compendium of *miṣvot* for daily life which could help Jews in a thoroughly Hellenistic environment to live as Jews without having to abandon their interest in Greek culture. If our author intended to write a school-book (and we have seen how often gnomologies served educational purposes), one could imagine that, as a Jewish writer, he tried to provide a "pagan" text that could be used safely in Jewish schools to satisfy Jewish parents who wanted their children to be trained in the classical pagan authors. However that may be, the hypothesis that Ps.-Phoc addressed himself to a pagan audience in order to win them over to a kind of "ethical monotheism" (and this was the function of his pseudonym) is a theory that has now definitively to be laid *ad acta*.[76]

The notion that Pseudo-Phocylides wrote to prevent the defection of Jews from their tradition because of the attractions of Hellenistic culture had been proposed by the Israeli scholar G. Alon in 1957.[77] In this view, the fact that the

76. Van der Horst, "Pseudo-Phocylides Revisited," 16. Cf. Niebuhr, *Gesetz und Paränese*, 67.
77. G. Alon, "The Halakah in the Teaching of the Twelve Apostles," in idem, *Studies in Jewish History in the Times of the Second Temple, the Mishnah and the Talmud* (Jerusalem: Hakibbutz Hameuchad, 1957) 1.274–94 (in Hebrew).

poem does not condemn idolatry is explained by supposing that the Jewish audience did not need such a prohibition. But then we must wonder, to what were they being tempted by the supposed blandishments of Hellenistic culture? Or conversely, what would it mean "to live as Jews" in van der Horst's phrase? Traditionally, fidelity to Judaism entailed avoiding idolatry, attending synagogue, having one's children circumcised, not marrying Gentiles, and so on — precisely the issues that Pseudo-Phocylides studiously avoids. His failure to condemn idolatry is especially striking, since it is a commonplace in other Hellenistic Jewish writings, although these too may have been intended primarily for Jewish readers.[78] It is difficult to believe that Pseudo-Phocylides wrote for the purpose of confirming adherence to Judaism *when he avoids mention of anything that is distinctively Jewish.* There is, in fact, no trace of apologetics anywhere in this book.

Van der Horst was certainly right to reject the old theory that Pseudo-Phocylides, and most of Greco-Jewish literature, had a missionary purpose. There was no organized or unified Jewish mission to the Gentiles.[79] Pseudo-Phocylides could not possibly have hoped to convert people to Judaism when he told them nothing explicit about the religion to which they were supposed to convert. The same objection holds against the view that he wanted to make "sympathizers" or "God-fearers" of his audience, insofar as these (vaguely defined) groups required some recognition of Judaism. This book cannot be read as an attempt to promote Judaism in any way, although it promotes ethical teachings that are largely derived from Judaism. Contrary to van der Horst's position, the teaching of the book is not inappropriately described as "ethical monotheism."

In view of the educational purposes usually served by gnomologies, the suggestion that Pseudo-Phocylides sentences were intended for schoolroom instruction is almost certainly right.[80] The book was certainly used for this purpose in later times. There is nothing to indicate that the pupils for whom it was intended were exclusively Jewish; neither, of course, were Jews in any way excluded. But in advertising his teachings under the name of Phocylides, the author surely hoped to attract pupils regardless of their adherence to Judaism. The teachings presumably reflect the author's own ethical convictions. Observances peculiar to Judaism play no part in these teachings. They cannot be said to put forward a view of Jewish identity, although the author most probably was Jewish. Judaism was not his subject. His subject was morality, as this

---

78. *Pace* Barclay, *Jews in the Mediterranean World,* 342–43, Pseudo-Phocylides would not have destroyed his pseudonymity if he had included a critique of idolatry, since such critiques can be found in Hellenistic philosophers. See Attridge, *First-Century Cynicism,* 13–23.

79. See the discussion in the preceding chapter.

80. Derron, *Pseudo-Phocylide,* xlix.

might have been the subject of any Greek philosopher who set up a school. The fact that his understanding of morality, or his philosophy, was shaped by the Jewish scriptures was incidental. He did not even inform his readers that these scriptures existed, any more than he lectured them on Plato or Stoicism. His purpose, the only purpose we can safely impute to him, was to impart to his readers, whether Jews or Gentiles, his understanding of the moral life.

At the conclusion of his book Pseudo-Phocylides provides a seal (*sphragis*) which says something about the character of his book:[81] "Purifications are for the purity of the soul, not of the body. These are the mysteries of righteousness; living thus may you live out a good life, right up to the threshold of old age." The first sentence in this conclusion is the only comment on ritual in Pseudo-Phocylides. In effect, it discounts the value of actual rituals, and favors a spiritualizing or allegorizing interpretation. The "mysteries" with which this author is concerned are not very mystical. They are primarily concerned with the mysteries of ethical conduct, which enable one to live a good life. These mysteries do not require that one belong to a specific religious group or observe specific cultic practices. What is important is that one practice righteousness and the other virtues.

The attitude of Pseudo-Phocylides to the Jewish law, then, is rather different from that of Ben Sira, although he too paid relatively little attention to the ritual laws. Pseudo-Phocylides is closer to Proverbs and Qoheleth, neither of whom paid much attention to the cultic side of Yahwism. In the case of the older wisdom literature, this situation is unremarkable, since we assume that there were no rival cults in the immediate environment. Pseudo-Phocylides must have been aware of the multiplicity of cults in Hellenistic Egypt. If we may judge by his sentences, however, these cults were not very important in his eyes, since the mysteries of righteousness were concerned with morality, not with cult. In this respect Pseudo-Phocylides was of one mind with many Hellenistic philosophers, but he could also have found support in the prophets and sages of Hebrew tradition.

---

81. On the notion of a *sphragis,* see Wilson, *The Mysteries of Righteousness,* 64.

Chapter 10.
Wisdom and Immortality

The most important wisdom writing from the Hellenistic Diaspora is undoubt-edly the Wisdom of Solomon (henceforth Wis. Sol.). Like the book of Sirach, this work attained the status of scripture in the Catholic Church, but was rele-gated to the Apocrypha by the Reformers. In antiquity, it was more widely ac-cepted as canonical than any of the other "deuterocanonical" books. It was quoted as authoritative from the end of the second century C.E., and it was re-garded as scripture by Clement of Alexandria, although Origen, in the third century, admitted that it "is not held by all to have authority."[1] Oddly enough, it was listed with the books of the New Testament in the Muratorian Canon, which originated in Rome about 200 C.E.[2]

Provenance and Date

It is usually assumed that the book was written in Alexandria. This is due in part to the resemblances to the thought of Philo that occur frequently in the book, but also to the prominence of Egypt and Egyptians. While chapters 10–19 are inspired by the biblical story of the exodus, the extended emphasis on the Egyptians, in contrast to the brief treatment of the Canaanites, most readily suggests an Egyptian setting. The polemic against idolatry and the worship of animals also fits the Egyptian context very well. While none of these arguments is conclusive, there is no evidence at all in favor of any other location.[3]

---

1. Origen, *On First Principles* 4.4.6.

2. See W. Horbury, "The Christian Use and the Jewish Origins of the Wisdom of Solomon," in J. Day, ed., *Wisdom in Ancient Israel: Essays in Honour of J. A. Emerton* (Cambridge: Cambridge Univ. Press, 1995) 182–96. Various efforts have been made to explain this oddity. The passage in question in the Muratorian Canon refers to the book as "the Wisdom written by friends of Solomon in his honor." It has been suggested that the Latin is a mistranslation, and that the Greek should read "by Philo" instead of "by his friends." The association with the NT might then have resulted from a tradition that Philo had converted to Christianity. See D. Winston, *The Wisdom of Solomon* (AB 43; Garden City, N.Y.: Doubleday, 1979) 68.

3. *Pace* D. Georgi, *Weisheit Salomos* (JSHRZ III/4; Gütersloh: Mohn, 1980) 395–96, who lo-cates the book in Syria because of the author's indebtedness to apocalyptic traditions in chaps. 1–5. But these traditions could be as easily available in Egypt as in Syria.

The date of composition is somewhat more controversial. Some commentators set the date as early as the second century B.C.E.[4] Others favor the first century B.C.E., because of the lack of clear allusions to Philo,[5] but then the fact that Philo shows no acquaintance with Wis. Sol. becomes problematic. By far the most probable date is the early Roman period. David Winston has pointed to some thirty-five words and usages that do not appear in Greek literature before the first century C.E.[6] Several other aspects of the work also fit the early Roman period, notably the contention that idolatry arises from the desire of subjects to flatter a distant ruler (Wis. 14:17). The term *kratēsis,* "dominion" (Wis. 6:3), is elsewhere used specifically for the Roman conquest of Egypt.[7]

The account of the persecution of the righteous and the subsequent divine judgment in chaps. 2–5 figure prominently in attempts to date the book. In Winston's view, this section of the book "could only be called forth by a desperate historical situation."[8] He suggests the reign of the Roman emperor Caligula (37–41 C.E.), when there were riots in Alexandria and the Jews were proclaimed "aliens and foreigners." Whether the book can be tied to such specific events remains questionable, since it never alludes to them explicitly. Moreover, we shall argue that the account of the persecution of the righteous has the character of a quasi-philosophical argument about the profitability of justice, rather than of a veiled historical commentary, and the apocalyptic scene that it evokes was traditional by the Roman period. It cannot be taken as a reliable guide to the circumstances in which the book was composed. The book could have been written at any time in the century from 30 B.C.E. to 70 C.E.

Structure and Genre

The book is usually divided into three main parts: the "book of eschatology" in 1:1–6:21, the "book of wisdom" in 6:22–10:21, and the "book of history" in chapters 11–19, but there are numerous variations in the exact definition of these units.[9] Some scholars define the "book of eschatology" as chapters

---

4. So Georgi, ibid., on the basis of parallels with *1 Enoch.*

5. D. Dimant, "Pseudonymity in the Wisdom of Solomon," in N. Fernández Marcos, ed., *La Septuaginta en la Investigación Contemporánea* (V Congreso de la IOSCS; Madrid: Instituto "Arias Montano" C.S.I.C., 1985) 243–55.

6. Winston, *The Wisdom of Solomon,* 22–23.

7. Ibid., 153. The word is found in *m. Abodah Zārāh* 1.3 and frequently in Greek papyri.

8. Winston, *The Wisdom of Solomon,* 23.

9. For a survey of the history of scholarship on this question, see M. Kolarcik, *The Ambiguity of Death in the Book of Wisdom 1–6* (AnBib 127; Rome: Pontifical Biblical Institute, 1991) 1–28; Winston, *The Wisdom of Solomon,* 10–12; Georgi, *Weisheit Salomos,* 393; J. M. Reese, "Plan and Structure in the Book of Wisdom," *CBQ* 27 (1965) 391–99; A. G. Wright, "The Structure of the Book of Wisdom," *Bib* 48 (1967) 165–84; H. Engel, " 'Was Weisheit ist und wie sie entstand, will ich verkünden.' Weish 7,22–8,1 innerhalb des *egkōmion tēs sophias* (6,22–11,1) als Stärkung der Plausibilität des Judentums angesichts hellenistischer Philosophie und Religiosität," in G. Hentschel and E. Zenger, eds., *Lehrerin der Gerechtigkeit* (Leipzig: Benno, 1991) 67–102.

1–5,[10] or 1–6,[11] or associate chapter 10 with the final section of the book.[12] The definition of the third section as chapters 10–19 has much to commend it, since chapter 10 initiates the biblical paraphrase that is continued in chapters 11–19, but it is also true that Wisdom is the primary subject in chapter 10 (and in 11:1), as it was in 6:22–9:18. After 11:1, the narrative of the saving deed of Wisdom gives way to direct address to God.

In the late eighteenth and early nineteenth centuries, it was customary to ascribe the different parts of the book to different authors.[13] The commentary of Carl Grimm in 1860 went far toward establishing the unity of the book on the basis of language and style.[14] Theories of multiple authorship were revived in the early twentieth century. The most influential arguments were those of Friedrich Focke, who held that chapters 1–5 were originally composed in Hebrew, and that the translator of these chapters added chapters 6–19.[15] His main arguments concerned the supposed lack of Greek philosophy and the relative absence of the personified figure of wisdom in chapters 1–5, and the increased tone of nationalism in chapters 11–19. These arguments have not withstood criticism, however. There is no lack of philosophical terminology in chapters 1–5. The "spirit of the Lord" that holds all things together in 1:7 is indebted to Stoic philosophy and cannot be distinguished from the spirit of wisdom that is eulogized in 6:22–9:18. The doctrine of immortality in these chapters is also indebted to Greek philosophy. Several Greek expressions in chapters 1–5 have no clear equivalent in Hebrew (e.g., *to synechon ta panta,* that which holds all things together, in 1:7; *aphtharsia,* incorruption, in 2:23). Winston concludes that "the strongest argument for the unity of Wisd may be drawn from its language and style," which despite occasional Hebrew features (chiefly the use of parallelism) reflects an excellent command of Greek.[16]

It is now generally agreed that the Wisdom of Solomon is a unified, artful composition, which uses the techniques of Greek rhetoric in a sophisticated

---

10. Georgi, *Weisheit Salomos,* 393.

11. M. Gilbert, "Wisdom Literature," in M. E. Stone, ed., *Jewish Writings of the Second Temple Period* (CRINT 2/2; Philadelphia: Fortress, 1984) 301–2.

12. J. Fichtner, *Weisheit Salomos* (HAT 2/6; Tübingen: Mohr, 1938) 7; J. Reider, *The Book of Wisdom* (Dropsie College Series; New York: Harper, 1957) 2; M. Goodman in Schürer, *The History,* 3.1. 569.

13. Winston, *The Wisdom of Solomon,* 12–13, makes an apt comparison with the history of Homeric scholarship.

14. C. L. Grimm, *Das Buch der Weisheit* (Leipzig, 1860).

15. F. Focke, *Die Entstehung der Weisheit Salomos* (Göttingen: Vandenhoeck & Ruprecht, 1913).

16. Winston, *The Wisdom of Solomon,* 14–15. Cf. A. Schmitt, *Das Buch der Weisheit* (Würzburg: Echter, 1986) 12.

way.[17] Unlike the loosely structured book of Ben Sira, or gnomologion-like Sayings of Pseudo-Phocylides, Wis. Sol. presents a coherent argument to advocate a course of action and show that it is expedient and good. The subject of the exhortation is love of righteousness (1:1) and wisdom (6:9). The "book of eschatology" shows what is at stake by presenting the arguments of the opponents and showing their inadequacy. It also presents the author's most basic argument for the value of righteousness: it leads to vindication in a judgment after death. The "book of wisdom" describes the origin and nature of wisdom and the manner in which it is attained. This part of the book has a (pseudo) autobiographical component, which strengthens the argument by the testimony of personal experience. Finally, the "book of history" elaborates the theme by well-known examples. Biblical history, especially the exodus story, is expounded to show that the efficacy of righteousness is guaranteed by the universe itself. The author makes plentiful use of *synkrisis,* comparison and contrast, to show the superiority of righteousness over its opposite.

The genre of the book as a whole has been identified as *logos protreptikos,* a didactic exhortation, by J. M. Reese and David Winston.[18] Protreptic was a blend of philosophy and rhetoric developed by the Sophists. The earliest example of the genre is found in Plato's *Euthydemus* (278E–282D). The *Protrepticus* of Aristotle, known only in reconstructed form, exhorts its readers to "exercise moral virtue for the sake of wisdom, for wisdom is the supreme end."[19] Another lost protreptic discourse is attributed to Posidonius, the Stoic philosopher of the early first century B.C.E. who numbered Cicero among his pupils, and who has sometimes been suspected as a source for the book of Wisdom.[20] A protreptic discourse was not a formal philosophical lecture, but an appeal to follow a philosophical way of life, or, in other terms, the pursuit of wisdom.

Other scholars have objected, however, that the protreptic genre is poorly attested, since neither the *Protrepticus* of Aristotle nor that of Posidonius has

17. Winston, *The Wisdom of Solomon,* 15–16: "He employs *chiasmus* (1:1, 4, 8; 3:15), *hyperbaton,* the *Sorites* (6:17–20), antithesis, accumulation of epithets (*accumulatio; synathroismos*) (7:22–23), alliteration, assonance, *homoioteleuton,* paronomasia, *isokolia* (balance of clauses), litotes, anaphora (c. 10), and Greek philosophical terminology." See further J. M. Reese, *Hellenistic Influence on the Book of Wisdom and Its Consequences* (AnBib 41; Rome: Pontifical Biblical Institute, 1971) 25–31 (Hellenistic influence on style), and Wright, "The Structure of the Book of Wisdom," who emphasizes the role of concentric composition and *inclusio.*

18. Reese, *Hellenistic Influence,* 119–21; Winston, *The Wisdom of Solomon,* 18. This designation was already applied to Wisdom 1–5 by Focke, *Die Entstehung,* 85.

19. *Protrepticus* B 21; cited by Winston, *The Wisdom of Solomon,* 18.

20. The influence of Posidonius on Wisdom was advocated especially by I. Heinemann, "Die griechische Quelle der Weisheit Salomos," in idem, *Poseidonios' Metaphysische Schriften* (reprint; Hildesheim: Olms, 1968) 136–53. See C. Larcher, *Études sur le Livre de la Sagesse* (Paris: Gabalda, 1969) 224–31.

actually been preserved.[21] Moreover, Wisdom 11–19 fits the genre only with difficulty. Accordingly they propose that Wisdom be viewed as an encomium, which is a genre of epideictic rhetoric, demonstrative rather than didactic. The book, then, would be read as a praise of wisdom rather than as an exhortation to pursue it, although no one disputes that an encomium entails implicit (and some explicit) exhortation. Winston summarizes the situation as follows: "It is thus extremely difficult to determine whether Wis is an epideictic composition with an admixture of protreptic, or essentially a protreptic with a considerable element of epideictic."[22] The distinction is not crucial for our purposes. In fact, the different parts of the book have different characters. The hortatory aspect is most clearly in evidence in the "Book of Eschatology"; the middle part of the book (6:22–9:18) best fits the genre "encomium"; while the "Book of History" is epideictic in character, consisting of a demonstration of the workings of the Wisdom that was praised in the preceding section. Moreover, the author draws on sources of different kinds in each section. He utilizes apocalyptic traditions in the Book of Eschatology, draws heavily on philosophical terminology in the praise of Wisdom, and develops a homiletical exposition of biblical history in chapters 10–19. These units, however, are bound together by transitional passages in chapters 6 and 10, which are variously assigned to the preceding or the following sections. Moreover, there is an underlying coherence to the book as a whole. It proposes an understanding of Wisdom and its role in the cosmos and in history, and draws inferences from this for human conduct.

The Book of Eschatology

Recent studies of the structure of Wis. 1:1–6:21 have emphasized the concentric nature of the composition, which is outlined as follows by Michael Kolarcik:[23]

A. 1:1–15: exhortation to justice
B. 1:16–2:24: speech of the wicked, explaining their reasoning
C. 3:1–4:20: four diptychs contrasting the just with the wicked
B[1] 5:1–23: speech of the wicked in a judgment scene
A[1] 6:1–21: exhortation to wisdom

These sections are woven together by verbal links between one passage and the next. So, for example, the theme of death is raised in 1:12–13 and picked up in 2:24; the righteous are introduced as subjects in 3:1 and again in 5:1, 15; the

21. Gilbert, "Wisdom Literature," 307; idem, "Sagesse," *DBSup* 11 (1986) 77–87; P. Bizzetti, *Il Libro della Sapienza* (Brescia: Paideia, 1984) 157.

22. Review of Bizzetti, *Il Libro della Sapienza, CBQ* 48 (1986) 525–27.

23. Kolarcik, *The Ambiguity of Death*, 62.

word "incorruption" (*aphtharsia*) links 2:23 with 6:18–19; the appeal to the rulers of the earth in 1:1 is resumed in 6:1. The section constitutes a tightly structured and coherent argument.

The argument may be summarized as follows. The reader is invited to love justice and seek the Lord. Injustice is incompatible with Wisdom. But, in good sapiential tradition, this proposal is not based on purely altruistic reasons, but is supported by considerations of ultimate self-interest. The ultimate catalyst of human values is death. Those who pursue unrighteousness "reasoned unsoundly" that death is the end of human existence, after which "we shall be as though we had never been." Consequently, they seize the day, and even afflict the righteous man because his presence is inconvenient. But they fail to understand the mysteries of God. While the righteous seem to die, in fact they enjoy immortality. This prospect calls for a radical reevaluation of usual human values. It is not length of life that should be desired, but wisdom and righteousness. This is eventually made clear in an eschatological trial scene in chapter 5, where the wicked belatedly learn the error of their ways. The section concludes by reaffirming the importance of pursuing Wisdom "so that you may reign forever."

In some respects this argument is firmly grounded in traditional Jewish wisdom. It is couched in terms of the human good, not of divine command. Moreover, the book of Proverbs already taught that Wisdom "is the tree of life to those who lay hold of her" (Prov. 3:18), and had her proclaim: "He who finds me finds life and obtains favor from the Lord; but he who misses me injures himself; all who hate me love death" (Prov. 8:35–36). Life and death often have a qualitative sense in Proverbs.[24] Those who "hate life" and "love death" are not suicidal but are attracted by a life that the sages equated with death. However, Proverbs also promises "length of days and years of life and abundant welfare" (3:2), and says that Wisdom has "long life in her right hand, in her left riches and honor" (3:16). While "life" is measured by the favor of the Lord rather than by duration, it must be experienced on this side of death. There is no suggestion that anyone can enjoy life in the hereafter. Ben Sira is brutally direct on this topic: "Whether life is for ten years or a hundred or a thousand, there are no questions asked in Hades" (Sir. 41:4). This resolutely this-worldly orientation is typical of traditional Jewish wisdom. Only in the Dead Sea Scrolls do we find a hope for eternal life in a Hebrew sapiential text (4Q218).

Apocalyptic Influence

In the Wisdom of Solomon, this perspective is changed utterly. Here, the hope of the righteous is full of immortality. Several factors contribute to this new perspective. First, two centuries had elapsed since the time of Sirach. Belief in retribution after death had become much more widespread in Judaism

---

24. G. von Rad, "Life and Death in the OT," *TDNT* 2.843–49.

in the interim. This belief was initially formulated in the apocalyptic writings attributed to Enoch and Daniel.[25] The judgment scene in Wis. Sol. chapter 5 is couched in apocalyptic idiom.[26] When the wicked see that the righteous are vindicated, they ask "How was he reckoned among the sons of God, and how is his portion among the holy ones?" (5:5). The "sons of God" and "holy ones" refer to the angelic hosts, and the conception parallels *1 Enoch* 104:2–6, which promises the righteous that "you will have great joy as the angels in heaven . . . for you will be companions to the host of heaven."[27] The parallel with this section of *1 Enoch* (the "Epistle of Enoch") is especially striking in view of a passage in *1 Enoch* 102:6–11:

> But when you die, the sinners say about you, As we die, the righteous have died, and of what use to them were their deeds? Behold, like us they have died in sadness and in darkness, and what advantage do they have over us? From now on we are equal. . . . I say to you, you sinners, You are content to eat and drink, and strip men naked and steal and sin, and acquire possessions and see good days. But you saw the righteous, how their end was peace, for no wrong was found in them until the day of their death.

Here, as in Wis. Sol. chapter 2, the wicked ask whether righteousness is ultimately profitable, and mistakenly conclude that it is not. Lothar Ruppert has argued that Wis. 2:12–20; 5:1–7 originated as an apocalyptic composition in a Semitic language in Palestine, and had presumably been brought to Egypt and translated into Greek before it was incorporated in Wis. Sol.[28] It is unlikely that the source document can be simply retrieved from its present context, where it is well integrated, but it is likely that the author had an apocalyptic source here. The passage in question is modeled on the Servant Song in Isa. 52:13–53:12,

25. See J. J. Collins, *Apocalypticism in the Dead Sea Scrolls* (London: Routledge, 1997) 110–29. A comprehensive but maximalist overview of Jewish belief in life after death can be found in E. Puech, *La Croyance des Esséniens en la Vie Future: Immortalité, Résurrection, Vie Éternelle?* (Paris: Gabalda, 1993) 1–324.

26. P. Grelot, "L'eschatologie de la Sagesse et les apocalypses juives," *À la Rencontre de Dieu: Mémorial Albert Gelin* (Le Puy: Mappus, 1961) 165–78.

27. Compare also Daniel 12:1–3, where the wise teachers shine like the stars after the resurrection. The stars are the host of heaven, and symbolize the angels. See J. J. Collins, *Daniel* (Hermeneia; Minneapolis: Fortress, 1993) 393–94. There is a possible reference to astral immortality in Wis. 3:7, where the righteous are compared to sparks in the stubble. See Winston, *The Wisdom of Solomon,* 128.

28. L. Ruppert, *Der leidende Gerechte* (Würzburg: Katholisches Bibelwerk, 1972) 70–105; cf. idem, "Gerechte und Frevler (Gottlose) in Sap 1,1–6,21: Zum Neuverständnis und zur Aktualisierung alttestamentlicher Traditionen in der Sapientia Salomonis," in Hübner, ed., *Die Weisheit Salomos,* 15–19, where he highlights the differences in vocabulary between these passages and the rest of Wis. Sol. Ruppert is overly specific, however, when he dates the Semitic composition to the persecution of the Pharisees by Alexander Jannaeus about 86 B.C.E. (*Der leidende Gerechte,* 103–4).

a passage that also influenced the formulation of hope for an afterlife in Dan. 11:33–35; 12:1–3 and the Similitudes of Enoch (*1 Enoch* 46, 62).[29] Like the Enochic passages, but unlike Daniel, Wis. Sol. does not speak of a resurrection. Rather it envisages exaltation to the heavenly realm. It is noteworthy that the dominant expectation of afterlife in the Dead Sea Scrolls, as found especially in the Hodayot, also avoids resurrection language but speaks instead of exaltation and fellowship with the angels.[30]

The Immortality of the Soul

There was, however, another tradition available to the author of Wis. Sol., of which Sirach betrays no knowledge. This was the Greek idea of the immortality of the soul. As formulated by Plato, this doctrine was closely bound up with the theory of Ideas, and entailed the preexistence of souls. In his dialogue the *Phaedrus*, he depicted the incarnation of the soul as a fall from a higher state, but in the *Timaeus* the soul is meant to be incarnate, as part of the completion of the universe.[31] Wisdom of Solomon certainly does not espouse the full Platonic doctrine, but it does betray acquaintance with the idea of preexistence at one point. In Wis. 8:19–20, (pseudo) Solomon recounts: "I was indeed a child well-endowed, having had a noble soul fall to my lot, or rather being noble I entered an undefiled body." The formulation recalls the myth of Er in Plato's *Republic* Book 10, where Lachesis, daughter of Necessity, addresses assembled souls before they return to earth: "Now is the beginning of another cycle of mortal generation. . . . Let him to whom falls the first lot first select a life to which he shall cleave of necessity" (*Republic* 617E). Pseudo-Solomon gives no hint that he has lived a prior life,[32] but it should be noted that Philo held that souls were preexistent but incarnated only once.[33] The vacillation between two formulations suggests that the author of Wis. Sol. had not taken a firm position on the preexistence of the soul. Preexistence played no significant part in his thought, but his self-correction in 8:20 must be taken as a favorable nod to the Platonic tradition. A more flagrantly Platonic, or Pythagorean, statement is found in 9:15: "For a perishable body weighs down the soul and this tent of clay encumbers a mind full of cares." According to Plato's *Phaedo* 66B, "So long as

29. G.W.E. Nickelsburg, *Resurrection, Immortality and Eternal Life in Intertestamental Judaism* (Cambridge, Mass.: Harvard Univ. Press, 1972) 68–92; Ruppert, "Gerechte und Frevler," 22–32.

30. Nickelsburg, *Resurrection,* 144–69; Collins, *Apocalypticism in the Dead Sea Scrolls,* 110–29. See further M. Delcor, "L'immortalité de l'âme dans le Livre de la Sagesse et dans les documents de Qumrân," *NRT* 77 (1955) 614–30.

31. See Winston, *The Wisdom of Solomon,* 26–27.

32. Larcher, *Études,* 274.

33. *De Somn.* 1.133–43; *Gig.* 6–9; *De Plant.* 11–14. Cicero also presents a doctrine of immortality without metempsychosis in the *Tusculan Disputations* I and the *Dream of Scipio.*

we have the body, and the soul is contaminated by such an evil, we shall never attain completely what we desire."[34] Again, this idea is paralleled in Philo: "But those who bear the burden of the flesh, oppressed by the grievous load, cannot look up to the heavens as they revolve."[35] It should not, then, be dismissed as anomalous in a Hellenistic Jewish author.

The Wisdom of Solomon presents its understanding of the soul only parenthetically in these passages. Elsewhere it seems to regard both soul and body as equally constitutive of the person. (In 1:4 both soul and body are potential dwelling places for Wisdom.) There can be little doubt, however, that the immortality envisaged is immortality of the soul, as in Philo. There is never any suggestion of resurrection of the body, nor indeed of resurrection of the spirit, such as we find in the early Enoch apocalypses.[36] The author does not, however, speak of immortality as a natural property of the soul. Rather it is the fruit of righteousness and wisdom.

The noun "immortality" (*athanasia*) occurs five times in Wis. Sol. (3:4; 4:1; 8:13, 17; 15:3) and adjective *athanatos* once (1:15). In 4:1 and 8:13 it is associated with memory, and presumably refers to an undying reputation. In 3:4 it is the hope of the righteous. In 8:17 it is associated with Wisdom, and in 15:3 the root of immortality is paralleled to righteousness and associated with the knowledge of God. In these contexts, immortality is not just the natural endowment of the soul, but is specifically associated with righteousness and wisdom. In contrast, the fate of the wicked is unclear. In chapter 5 they are present at a postmortem judgment, and according to Wis. 3:10 they will receive punishment in accordance with their reasoning. This may mean, however, that they experience death as final, just as they thought it would be. In this case, the judgment scene in chapter 5 is only a literary fiction to dramatize their miscalculation. Wisdom of Solomon 5:14 emphasizes the transitory character of their hopes and contrasts them with the just, who live forever. The author never describes everlasting punishments of the damned. The immortality that interests him is the blessed afterlife of the righteous.

Another related term, "incorruption" (*aphtharsia*) appears three times, in Wis. 2:23; 6:18, and 6:19, and the corresponding adjective twice, in Wis. 12:1 and 18:4. This word had a technical sense in Epicurean philosophy. The Epicureans held that the gods had material existence, and they explained their unending life by saying that they were incorruptible.[37] According to Wis. 2:23,

---

34. For further references see Winston, *The Wisdom of Solomon*, 207. Cf. Seneca, *Epistles* 65.16: "For this body of ours is a weight upon the soul . . ."

35. *Gig.* 31; *Leg. All.* 3.152; *Quod Det.* 16.

36. P. Beauchamp, "Le salut corporel dans le livre de la Sagesse," *Bib* 45 (1964) 491–526, argues that an interest in the physical restoration of the universe runs through the second half of the book and infers that bodily resurrection is implicit, but this is an unnecessary inference.

37. Reese, *Hellenistic Influence*, 65–66; Winston, *The Wisdom of Solomon*, 121.

humanity was created "for incorruptibility." In 6:18–19 it is ensured by keeping the laws, and it makes one be near to God. In 12:1, God's *pneuma* is imperishable, and in 18:4 the light of the law is similarly described. There is no practical difference between immortality and incorruptibility in Wis. Sol. Similarly, for Philo "incorruption is akin to eternality" (*De Abr.* 55). The passages that speak of incorruption envisage more than everlasting duration. The word also carries a positive evaluation. Again, it is not clear whether the wicked simply perish. Wisdom of Solomon 5:8–14 states that the things on which the wicked based their hopes, such as wealth and posturing, leave no trace. The implication seems to be that since they have no immortal qualities, such as righteousness, they are simply consumed.

The Denial of Death

Wisdom of Solomon attempts to ground its doctrine of immortality in the exegesis of the creation stories in Genesis. So we are told in 2:23–24: "But God created man for incorruptibility, and made him an image of his own proper being [or: his own immortality];[38] but by the devil's envy death entered the world and those who are of his lot experience it." The word "image" points to Gen. 1:27, where Adam is created in the image of God. Philo argued that "it is in respect of the Mind, the sovereign element of the soul, that the word 'image' is used; for after the pattern of a single Mind, even the Mind of the Universe as an archetype, the mind in each of those who successively came into being was moulded." Wisdom of Solomon does not insert a role for the Mind of the Universe, or Logos, here, but makes incorruption or immortality the point of resemblance between deity and creature.[39] Moreover, we are told in 1:14 that God created all things that they might exist (*eis to einai*), and the generative processes of the world preserve life[40] and have no destructive poison in them. Philo similarly argued that "nature in each case strives to maintain and conserve the thing of which it is the nature, and if it were possible to render it immortal" (*De Aet.* 35) and that "God willed that nature should run a course that brings it back to its starting-point, endowing the species with immortality [*aidiotētos*) and making them sharers of eternal existence" (*De Opif.* 44).

The divine plan for creation was disrupted, however, by the introduction of death. Wisdom of Solomon breaks with the entire biblical tradition by stating categorically that "God did not make death" (1:13). The contrast with Ben Sira

38. Some manuscripts read *aidiotētos*, immortality, instead of *idiotētos*, proper being.

39. Philo also differs from Wisdom in positing a double creation of the heavenly and earthly Man. See T. H. Tobin, *The Creation of Man: Philo and the History of Interpretation* (Washington: Catholic Biblical Association, 1983) 102–34.

40. *sōtērioi hai geneseis tou kosmou. Geneseis* may also mean "created things" or "all that has come into existence."

could not be more stark. As Sirach reads Genesis, "The Lord created human beings out of the earth and makes them return to it again" (Sir. 17:1). Death is "the
decree of the Lord for all flesh" and represents the pleasure of the Most High
(Sir. 41:4).[41] Even the dualistic Instruction on the Two Spirits from Qumran attributes to God the creation of both spirits and the destinies that attach to them.

The idea that God did not make death is such a shocking novelty in Jewish
tradition that many scholars have refused to accept it at face value.[42] Since the
author associates death only with the wicked, who are of the lot of the devil, it
is assumed that he must be speaking of spiritual, not physical death. Philo makes
a clear distinction between two kinds of death, "one that of the man in general,
the other that of the soul in particular. The death of the man is the separation of
the soul from the body, but the death of the soul is the decay of virtue and the
bringing in of wickedness."[43] Wisdom of Solomon, however, does not make
this distinction. The implicit allusions to Genesis in 1:13–14 and 2:23–24 favor
the view that physical as well as spiritual death is in view.[44] There is, however,
considerable ambiguity attached to the concept of death in Wis. Sol.[45]

It is clear enough that physical death can serve as a punishment for those
who belong to the lot of the devil. In this case, no distinction is necessary between physical and spiritual death, except insofar as spiritual death may be
thought to occur even before the demise of the body. The case of the righteous
is more complicated. The author is well aware that "in the eyes of the foolish
they seem to die" (3:2). Moreover, the author acknowledges that he is "a mortal [*thnētos*] man, on a par with all" and that all share the same way of enter-
ing and leaving life (7:1, 6; cf. 9:5). Nonetheless, the author denies that the
physical demise of the righteous constitutes "death." They only seem to die, in
the eyes of the foolish, but they are really immortal.[46] The cessation of physical life has different meanings for the righteous and the unrighteous, and herein
lies its ambiguity. Only in the case of the unrighteous is it called "death."

Because of this ambiguity of death, it is not certain how the author envisaged
the original state for which humanity was created. The use of the word *aphtharsia,* incorruptibility, in Wis. 6:18–19, suggests that this state, for which humanity was originally made (2:23) can still be attained by those who keep the

41. See further J. J. Collins, "The Root of Immortality: Death in the Context of Jewish Wisdom," *HTR* 71 (1978) 177–92.

42. See R. J. Taylor, "The Eschatological Meaning of Life and Death in the Book of Wisdom
I–V," *ETL* 42 (1966) 102–13; Kolarcik, *The Ambiguity of Death,* 148–51.

43. *Leg. All.* 1.105–8.

44. So M. Gilbert, "Gn 1–3 dans le livre de la Sagesse," *Lectio Divina* 127 (1987) 323–44.

45. Kolarcik, *The Ambiguity of Death,* 159–90. See also Y. Amir, "The Figure of Death in the
'Book of Wisdom,'" *JJS* 30 (1979) 154–78.

46. Cf. B. R. Gaventa, "The Rhetoric of Death in the Wisdom of Solomon and the Letters of
Paul," in K. G. Hoglund, ed., *The Listening Heart: Essays in Honor of R. E. Murphy* (Sheffield:
Almond, 1987) 127–45.

laws. It may be understood, then, as immortality of the soul. In this case, the disruption of the original divine plan is simply the intrusion of sin, which has disastrous consequences for the wicked but does not ultimately alter the destiny of the righteous. It is also possible, however, that even physical existence was originally supposed to be incorruptible, since *aphtharsia* was a mode of material existence in Epicurean philosophy. In either case, the author's understanding of life and death is very different from that of Ben Sira. Consequently, it is somewhat misleading to speak of "an original, harmonious mortal state."[47] For Wis. Sol., the original state was one of harmonious *immortality,* and the duration of bodily existence was simply not a matter of great importance.

The Origin of Death

Wisdom offers two explanations of how death entered the world. According to Wis. 1:16, "Impious people invited him with hands and words; thinking him a friend, they pined for him and made a covenant with him, because they are worthy to be of his lot." The antecedent of "him" is found in 1:14: "There is no kingdom of Hades on earth." Hades, the Greek counterpart of Sheol, stands metonymically for Death. The notion of a kingdom of Death derives from ancient Near Eastern mythology. In the Canaanite myths from Ugarit, Death (*Mot*) is the god of the netherworld who at one time swallows up Baal, the god of fertility and life. There are occasional references to *Mot* as a supernatural power in the Bible. In Isa. 28:15 the rulers of Jerusalem say, "We have made a covenant with Death, and with Sheol we have an agreement," whence the allusion in Wis. 1:16. Death is the eschatological adversary of God in Isa. 25:7 and Rev. 20:14. In this tradition, which influenced apocalyptic literature much more than wisdom, Death was originally a deity in his own right, and in the monotheistic context of Judaism he still represents a mythical power whose relationship to God's creation is not clarified. The "kingdom of Hades" also brings to mind the figure of Belial, the Satanic figure of the Dead Sea Scrolls, whose name should probably be understood as an allusion to the netherworld.[48] The Scrolls refer both to "the lot of Belial" (1QM 1:5; 1QS 2:5) and "the kingdom/dominion of Belial" (1QM 14:9; 1QS 1:23–24; 2:19). The War Scroll states explicitly, however, that God "made Belial to corrupt" (1QM 13:11). But while Wis. 1:14–16 envisages Death or Hades as a primordial, mythical power, the responsibility for introducing him into the world is placed on impious humanity. This was also the position of Ben Sira, who in turn drew on the

---

47. *Pace* Kolarcik, *The Ambiguity of Death,* 169.

48. *běly ya'al* [the place from which] one does not go up. See Collins, *Apocalypticism in the Dead Sea Scrolls,* 101. The parallels between Death in Wis. Sol. and Belial in the Scrolls are also noted by Y. Amir, "The Figure of Death in the 'Book of Wisdom,'" *JJS* 30 (1979) 154–78.

Deuteronomic tradition: "Before each person are life and death, and whichever one chooses will be given" (Sir. 15:17).

Wisdom of Solomon 2:24, however, introduces a new idea: "By the envy of the devil death entered the world, and they who are of his lot experience it."[49] The Greek word for devil, *diabolos,* is the translation equivalent of satan, *adversary.* In Rev. 12:9, the devil or Satan is identified with "the ancient serpent," presumably the snake of Genesis 3. This passage in Wisdom may be the earliest attestation of that identification. The notion that the devil was motivated by envy is likewise not attested before the first century C.E., at the earliest, when it appears in *The Life of Adam and Eve* 12–17 (cf. *2 Enoch* 31).[50] The agency of a devil or Satan plays no further role in Wis. Sol., but this passage shows that a sapiential author could appeal to supernatural powers on occasion. (Cf. Sir. 15:14, where the secondary Hebrew recension inserts a reference to a demonic "snatcher" in explaining the relation between creation and the origin of sin.)

The primary point that Wis. Sol. makes about the origin of death is that it was not from God. The same presumably holds true of sin. The author expends little effort in clarifying whence these evils arose. The apparent metaphysical dualism of Wis. 2:24 seems inconsistent with the dominance of God and wisdom in the rest of the book. In a world pervaded by the spirit of wisdom, evil is anomalous, and it engages the attention of the author only as a foil for the righteousness that he advocates.

The Ethics of Immortality

Unlike Ben Sira and Pseudo-Phocylides, Pseudo-Solomon provides no instructions on social relations. His attitude to the concerns of everyday life is aptly summed up in the statement that "a perishable body weighs down the soul, and this tent of clay encumbers a mind full of cares" (Wis. 9:15). Most of what the book has to say about sexual relations and family life is found in 3:11–4:20. Much of it has to do with the futility of earthly success and relationships if one lacks wisdom and righteousness. For those who despise wisdom, "their deeds are futile, the wives are frantic, their children worthless, their lineage under a curse" (3:11–12). The traditional values attached to children and wealth are not important in this perspective. Barrenness was traditionally a disgrace, and in *1 Enoch* 98:5 it is even said to be punishment for sin. Wisdom insists that no disgrace should attach to it, so long as the woman "has not gone to bed in sin" (3:13). The eunuch, already rehabilitated in Isa. 56:3–5, is

---

49. In light of this passage we cannot agree with Amir, "The Figure of Death," 158, that "in the *Book of Wisdom* 'Death' (*Thanatos*) and Satan (*Diabolos*) must designate the same figure."

50. J.A.F. Gregg, *The Wisdom of Solomon* (Cambridge: Cambridge Univ. Press, 1909) argued that the reference here was to the sin of Cain rather than to the Garden of Eden.

also affirmed here if he avoids transgression. The children of adulterers are doomed, and even if they do not die young they never attain honor. In all this, nothing is said of the children of faithful married couples. The statement in Wis. 4:1, "It is better to be childless, provided one is virtuous," should probably not be taken absolutely, but in contrast to the fertility of adulterers. Nonetheless, no positive value is attached to children and families, and the author certainly does not acknowledge a commandment to increase and multiply. It is not difficult to see how such a perspective on life could encourage asceticism or even celibacy.[51] Again, the author is explicit that "it is not length of life that makes for an honorable old age, nor is it measured by number of years" (4:8). Rather, he eulogizes the one who, like Enoch, "while yet living among sinful men was translated. He was snatched away lest evil alter his intelligence or wile deceive his mind" (4:11). An early death is not only preferable to a long life of wickedness; it is inherently advantageous, as it lessens the danger of corruption. There is some similarity here to the perspective of apocalyptic texts such as Daniel 11–12, which embrace martyrdom in time of persecution because of the promise of resurrection.[52] But Wisdom's detachment from this life is more radical. If the perishable body weighs down the soul, the attraction of a shortened life is not contingent on persecution. In this respect, Wisdom is primarily informed by the Platonic tradition, and is in accordance with the thought of Philo and even of Middle Stoicism. Winston aptly cites Seneca's *De Consolatione ad Marciam* 22–23: "Those who are treated most kindly by Nature are those whom she removes early to a place of safety. . . . The brighter a fire glows, the more quickly it dies. . . . So with men — the brighter their spirits, the briefer their day."[53]

The goal of immortality, then, leads to a transformation of traditional values in Wis. Sol. The book also has a place, however, for more conventional ethical teachings. These basically conform to the "common ethic" of Hellenistic Judaism, which focused on idolatry and sex-related offenses, especially homosexuality and the exposure of infants. The basic sin is idolatry, which is denounced repeatedly throughout the book.[54] The consequences that result from it are described in 14:22–28: "All is confusion — bloody murder, deceitful theft, corruption, treachery, tumult, perjury, agitation of decent men, ingratitude, soul defilement, interchange of sex roles, irregular marriages, adultery and debauchery." Adultery incurs frequent condemnation throughout

---

51. See D. Georgi, "Der vorpaulinische Hymnus Phil 2, 6–11," in E. Dinkler, ed., *Zeit und Geschichte: Dankesgabe am R. Bultmann* (Tübingen: Mohr, 1964) 273.

52. J. J. Collins, "Apocalyptic Eschatology as the Transcendence of Death," *CBQ* 36 (1974) 21–43.

53. Winston, *The Wisdom of Solomon*, 141–42.

54. See especially M. Gilbert, *La Critique des Dieux dans le livre de la Sagesse* (AnBib 53; Rome: Pontifical Biblical Institute, 1973).

the book. Infanticide is singled out in the account of the oppression of the Hebrews in Egypt (18:5). "Interchange of sex roles" presumably involves homosexuality, but there is less polemic against homosexuality here than is usual in
writings of the Hellenistic Diaspora. There is a reference to "secret mysteries
or frenzied revels connected with strange laws" (14:23), which were also condemned by classical authors.[55] Otherwise the ethical concerns of the author can
be inferred from the speech of the wicked in chap. 2, when they resolve to tyr-
annize the poor and the feeble and let might be their norm of righteousness.
Such action would be condemned in any culture.

The Wisdom of Solomon refers on several occasions to law or laws. In 2:12
the wicked complain that the righteous man accuses them of sins against the
law. In 6:4 the "kings" to whom the book is addressed are reproached because,
although they were stewards of God's kingdom, they did not keep the law. In
the same chapter, in the course of the famous *sorites* on Wisdom in 6:17–20, we
are told that love of instruction entails the keeping of her laws, and keeping of
laws is a guarantee of incorruptibility. Finally, 18:4 refers to "the imperishable
light of the Law" that is given to the world. The last reference is clearly to the
Law of Moses. The references to the laws of Wisdom in 6:17–20, and the law
with which the impious are reproached in chapter 2, may also be identified with
this Law, since the identification of Wisdom with the Torah was already established by Ben Sira. At the same time, since the kings of the earth are account-
able for keeping the law, it must have a universal aspect. As is well known, Philo
held that "the world is in harmony with the Law and the Law with the world and
that the man who observes the Law is constituted thereby a loyal citizen of the
world, regulating his doings by the purpose and will of Nature, in accordance
with which the entire world itself also is administered."[56] It is likely that Wis.
Sol. also saw the Law of Moses as the embodiment of a universal law.

We have seen, however, in the preceding chapter that the Law of Moses was
often interpreted in a highly selective way in Hellenistic Judaism. There is no
reference in Wis. Sol. to such specifically Jewish observances as circumcision,
sabbath observance, or dietary laws. This is true even when the text is alluding
to a biblical passage where such observances were mentioned. Wisdom of
Solomon 3:14 provides a nice illustration: "And the eunuch who has not acted
unlawfully or meditated wickedness against the Lord will receive the exquis-
ite gift of grace in return for his steadfastness and a portion in the temple of the
Lord to delight his heart the more." This is clearly an allusion to Isa. 56:4–5:
"For thus says the Lord: To the eunuchs who keep my sabbaths, who choose

55. E.g., Livy, *History* 39.8–18.
56. *De Opificio Mundi* 3. On the relation between the Torah and natural law in Philo, see H.
Koester, "Nomos Physeos: The Concept of Natural Law in Greek Thought," in J. Neusner, ed.,
Religions in Antiquity: Essays in Memory of E. R. Goodenough (Leiden: Brill, 1970) 533–36.
Koester's thesis that it was Philo who first developed the idea of natural law cannot be maintained.
See R. A. Horsley, "The Law of Nature in Philo and Cicero," *HTR* 71 (1978) 35–59.

the things that please me and hold fast my covenant, I will give, in my house and within my walls, a monument and a name better than sons and daughters; I will give them an everlasting name that shall not be cut off." The reference to sabbath observance in Isaiah is replaced by a more general reference to not acting unlawfully in Wis. Sol. The relation of the law of Moses to the laws of Wisdom is an instance of the problem of particularism and universalism, to which we shall return when we discuss chapters 10–19.

The Identity of the Unrighteous

The ethical teaching of Wis. Sol. is sharpened by antithesis with the views of the unrighteous, in a speech placed on their lips in chap 2. Action follows from reasoning. The problem with the unrighteous is that they do not reason correctly. The crucial argument turns on the understanding of death. In the view of the wicked, "we were born by mere chance [*autoschediōs*], and hereafter we shall be as though we had never been, for the breath in our nostrils is smoke, and reason is a spark kindled by the beating of our hearts; when it is extinguished, the body will turn to ashes, and the spirit will dissolve like empty air" (Wis. 2:2–3). From this premise, they infer how they should behave: "Let us enjoy the good things that exist, and make use of the creation to the full as in youth. . . . Let us crown ourselves with rosebuds before they wither. Let none of us fail to share in our revelry . . . because this is our portion, and this our lot" (2:6–9). Not only this, but they also decide to oppress the righteous man, "because he is inconvenient to us and opposes our actions; he reproaches us for sins against the law, and accuses us of sins against our training" (2:12). So they resolve to condemn the righteous to a shameful death to "test what will happen at the end of his life" and see whether God will in fact deliver him.

The initial part of this argument can be paralleled from many sources in the ancient world. Within the Bible, Isaiah denounced those who say, "Let us eat and drink, for tomorrow we die" (Isa. 22:13; cf. 1 Cor. 15:32). But Sheol was nothing to look forward to in the biblical tradition, and moderate enjoyment of life was generally approved. Qoheleth argued that the same fate comes to the righteous and the wicked, and concluded that one should "go, eat your bread with enjoyment, and drink your wine with a merry heart" (Qoh. 9:7). Even Ben Sira counseled: "Do not deprive yourself of a happy day; let not your share of desired good pass you by" (Sir. 14:14). The speech of the wicked in Wis. Sol., however, is tinged with Greek philosophy. The word *autoschediōs,* "by chance," is first attested here or in Philo,[57] but the idea is typical of Epicurean philosophy.[58] Lucretius writes: "And the seeds of things themselves of their

---

57. Philo, *De Somn.* 2.50. See Winston, *The Wisdom of Solomon*, 116.

58. The view that the wicked in Wis. Sol. are Epicureans was proposed by A. Dupont-Sommer, "Les 'impies' du Livre de la Sagesse ne sont-ils pas des Épicuriens?" *RHR* 111 (1935) 9–109. See the critique of this position by Larcher, *Études,* 213–6.

own accord, jostling from time to time by chance, were driven together in many ways, rashly, idly, and in vain; at last those united, which suddenly cast together, might become ever and anon the beginnings of great things, of earth and sea and sky, and the race of living creatures" (2:1–58). The same idea is found in the philosophy of Atomism, expounded by Leucippus and Democritus. The idea that reason is a spark is reminiscent rather of Stoicism. Seneca, for example, considers the theory "that man is part of the divine spirit, that some part, sparks, as it were, of the stars fell down to earth and lingered here in a place that is not their own."[59] The reference to crowning with rosebuds is a more general allusion to Greek and Roman popular culture. Compare Horace, *Odes* 2.3.13–16: "Hither bid slaves bring wines and perfumes and the too brief blossoms of the lovely rose, while Fortune and youth allow, and the dark threads of the Sisters Three," or Lucretius 3.912–15: "This, too, men often do, when they are lying at the board, and hold their cups in their hands, and shade their brows with garlands: they say from the heart, 'Brief is this enjoyment for us puny men: soon it will be past, nor ever thereafter will it be ours to call it back.'" Epicurus argued that pleasure was the goal of life, but he advocated a frugal and simple life, and the pleasure of sober reasoning. His views, however, were relaxed by some of his later followers, and Epicureanism was easily distorted by rival polemicists.[60] Nonetheless, there is no reason to suppose that the unrighteous of Wis. Sol. were specifically Epicurean. The philosophy of "Eat, drink, and be merry" is too widespread to be identified with a single philosophical school.[61]

The major difficulty with identifying the unrighteous with a philosophical school, however, lies in the turn to violence in Wis. 2:10. The wicked not only enjoy themselves; they must also oppress the poor and the weak, and specifically the righteous. Since they complain that the righteous man rebukes them for sins against the law (2:12) it is reasonable to suppose that they are Jewish, presumably Jewish apostates.[62] There was a well-known precedent for inner-Jewish persecution on the part of Hellenizing apostates in the Maccabean period, and we read of another attempt to suppress Jewish observance in Antioch in 67 C.E., on the part of one Antiochus, whose father was a Jewish magistrate.[63] There is no evidence for such aggressive action by apostates in Alexandria, unless we count the professional role of Tiberius Julius Alexander in

---

59. Seneca, *On Leisure* 5.5. See further Winston, *The Wisdom of Solomon,* 117.

60. Larcher, *Études,* 215.

61. Winston, *The Wisdom of Solomon,* 118, aptly cites a graffito from the tomb of a certain Jason from the time of Alexander Jannaeus in Jerusalem: "Enjoy yourselves, you who remain living . . . eat and drink alike."

62. P. Heinisch, *Das Buch der Weisheit* (Münster: Aschendorff, 1912) 41. *Pace* Barclay, *Jews in the Mediterranean World,* 186, there is no good reason to see a reflection of conflict between Jews and non-Jews here.

63. Josephus, *J. W.* 7.46–53. See Barclay, *Jews in the Mediterranean World,* 256.

putting down disturbances in 66 C.E.[64] It is unlikely, however, that the author of Wis. Sol. is referring to actual occurrences here. Rather he is developing an idealized argument about the consequences of belief in, or denial of, the immortality of the soul.[65]

An illuminating parallel to Wis. Sol. on this point can be found in the second book of Plato's *Republic*. Here Glaucon takes up the argument that injustice is more profitable than justice. He begins by recalling the story of Gyges's ring, which allowed him to become invisible when he so desired. Given such a ring, argues Glaucon, "no man can be imagined to be of such an iron nature that he would stand fast in justice." (This argument is anticipated in Wis. 1:6–11, which insists that no one can escape the vigilance of the spirit of the Lord.) Glaucon proceeds to argue that in order to choose between the just and the unjust we must imagine them in their pure states. The unjust must be deemed just though he is not, and the just must be the best of men and thought to be the worst. Further, "The just man who is thought unjust will be scourged, racked, bound— will have his eyes burnt out; and at last, after suffering every kind of evil, he will be impaled" (*Republic*, 361). We have a similar separation of ideal types in Wis. Sol. In the Jewish text, the picture is also colored by biblical allusions. The suffering righteous figure recalls the suffering servant of Isaiah 53. The purpose of the chapter, however, is simply to establish which way of life is truly profitable. This issue cannot be decided merely on appearances. One must also know "the mysteries of God," which guarantee the immortality of the righteous. The chapter, then, is not a coded reflection of social history in Alexandria or elsewhere, but a quasi-philosophical argument about the best way to live.

The argument is quasi-philosophical because it appeals to "the mysteries of God" and assumes rather than argues that the Jewish law is representative of righteousness. It is simultaneously an attempt to formulate a coherent and rational view of the world and an apologia for a certain understanding of Judaism. The understanding of Judaism in question, however, is strikingly novel if it is viewed in light of the Hebrew Bible and of older wisdom books such as that of Ben Sira. Belief in reward or punishment after death was a late arrival in Jewish tradition, and was vigorously repudiated by Qoheleth and Ben Sira. The idea of immortality, as formulated here, was scarcely possible before the Hellenistic period. Yet Wis. Sol. makes the immortality of the righteous the linchpin of his argument for fidelity to the law. While the way of life that is repudiated is characteristically Greco-Roman, that which is endorsed is no less a product of the Hellenistic age, and indebted to Greek philosophy.

---

64. M. Gilbert, "Il giusto sofferente di Sap 2:12–20," in G. de Gennaro, ed., *L'antico testamento interpretato dal nuovo: il messia* (Naples, 1985) 193–218, concludes that if the people in question are Jewish renegades, they cannot be further identified.

65. Kolarcik, *The Ambiguity of Death*, 123.

Chapter 11.
Wisdom and the Cosmos

According to Wis. 6:17–20 it is the desire for wisdom that leads to immortality and ultimately to a "kingdom." In Wis. Sol., however, wisdom is not only an intellectual virtue. It is a cosmic principle that "holds all things together" and is the connecting link between God and the universe. As such, it clearly stands in a tradition with Proverbs 8 and Sirach 24, but the portrayal of Wisdom here is far more developed and makes extensive use of Greek philosophical terminology. While reference is made to the "laws" of Wisdom (6:18), Wis. Sol. does not endorse the claim of Ben Sira that Wisdom is identical with the Law of Moses.

Wisdom, Pneuma, and Logos

The concept of Wisdom is introduced in Wis. Sol. 1 in the context of an exhortation to seek the Lord. Perverse thoughts separate from God, and when his power is tested it exposes the foolish. The reason, we are told, is that "Wisdom will not enter a fraudulent mind, nor dwell in a body that is mortgaged to sin" (1:4). The language of "dwelling" here immediately brings to mind Sirach 24, where Wisdom is said to be established on Mount Zion and make its dwelling in Israel. Wisdom of Solomon speaks of a more personal indwelling in the individual. Wisdom, we are further told, is a holy spirit (*pneuma* 1:5), benevolent (*philanthropon*), and evidently identical with "the spirit of the Lord" (1:7). The equation of wisdom and spirit was not made in the Hebrew wisdom literature, although we encounter the "spirit of wisdom" in Isa. 11:2 (cf. *1 Enoch* 49:3). The word "spirit" (*pneuma*), however, had its own resonance in a Greek context, especially in the context of Stoic philosophy.

The word *pneuma* basically means "wind" or "breath." Aristotle developed the idea of an inborn *pneuma,* which was the source of growth and generation but was distinct from the soul. Zeno, the founder of Stoicism, as a thoroughgoing materialist identified the two. The *pneuma* was spread throughout the body, but it also had a "command center" (*hēgemonikon*). It was probably Chrysippus who developed the theory of a cosmic *pneuma.*[1] The *pneuma,* then,

---

1. *SVF* 2.1091. See M. Lapidge, "Stoic Cosmology," in J. M. Rist, ed., *The Stoics* (Berkeley: Univ. of California Press, 1978) 170.

was the soul of the universe (which was conceived as a living organism). It was a fine, fiery substance which permeated and vivified all reality, "a breath pervading the whole world."[2] Sometimes this intelligent and fiery spirit was identified as God.[3] It is the physical aspect of the Logos, the rational, active principle in the universe.[4] Reason is a portion of this cosmic spirit, inserted into the human body.[5] The influence of this Stoic *pneuma* on Wis. Sol. is evident in *Wis.* 1:7, where "the spirit of the Lord" is described as "*to synechon ta panta*," that which holds all things together. The Stoics contrasted pneumatic being, which holds things together (*to synechon*) with material being, which is held together (*to synechomenon*),[6] and claimed that one thing, the divine *pneuma*, held the whole cosmos together.[7] In Wis. Sol., likewise, the spirit of the Lord is "that which holds all things together" (*to synechon ta panta*, 1:7).

The Stoic overtones of Wisdom/Pneuma are clearly in evidence in the central section of the book, especially in Wis. 6:22–8:1.[8] Here the author undertakes to expound "what Wisdom is and how she came into being." Solomon, we are told, was enabled to understand this because of his prayer (1 Kings 3:6–15). The understanding is granted by God (7:15) but taught by "Wisdom, the artificer of all" (7:22a). This designation of Wisdom is an allusion to Prov. 8:30, where the LXX reads, "I was with him as a joiner,"[9] but it also brings to mind the Stoic definition of nature as "an artistically working fire [*pyr technikon*] going on its way to create."[10] There is no distinction between the work of Wisdom and the work of God, since God is "the guide of Wisdom" (7:15). The wisdom that Pseudo-Solomon is granted includes some elements that were associated with Solomon in the book of Kings ("the species of plants, and the virtues of roots"). But the configuration of the whole has overtones of Hellenistic philosophy. It entails "unerring knowledge of existent being, to know the structure of the universe and the operation of the elements; the beginning,

2. *SVF* 2.1027; Long and Sedley, *The Hellenistic Philosophers,* 1.275.
3. *SVF* 2. 442; 1009; 1027. See H. Hübner, "Die Sapientia Salomonis und die antike Philosophie," in H. Hübner, ed., *Die Weisheit Salomos im Horizont Biblischer Theologie* (Neukirchen-Vluyn: Neukirchener Verlag, 1993) 60.
4. See M. Pohlenz, *Die Stoa* (2d ed.; Göttingen: Vandenhoeck & Ruprecht, 1959) 1.64–75; F. H. Sandbach, *The Stoics* (New York: Norton, 1975) 72–73.
5. H. Kleinknecht, "*Pneuma, pneumatikos* etc." *TDNT* 6 (1968) 354–55.
6. *SVF* 2.439. *SVF* 2.448; Diogenes Laertius 2.439. Winston, *The Wisdom of Solomon,* 104.
7. *SVF* 2.448; Diogenes Laertius 2.439. (Winston, *The Wisdom of Solomon,* 104.) The idea of something holding all things together is found already in Xenophon, *Memorabilia* 4.3.13; *Cyropaedia* 8.7.22. There are also parallels in Philo, *De Conf.* 136; *De Somn.* 1.63–64.
8. Hübner, "Die Sapientia Salomonis," 55–81; H. Engel, "Was Weisheit ist," 94; C. Larcher, *Le Livre de la Sagesse ou la Sagesse de Salomon* (Paris: Gabalda, 1984) 479–518.
9. Greek *harmozousa,* rendering the problematic MT reading *'āmôn.*
10. Diogenes Laertius 7.156. Compare Cicero, *De Natura Deorum* 2.58: "The nature of the world itself . . . is styled by Zeno not merely 'craftsmanlike' but actually 'a craftsman' [*artifex*]." See Winston, *The Wisdom of Solomon,* 176.

and end, and middle of times" (7:17–18). The language echoes Chrysippus, who taught that "the structure of the whole is constituted from the four elements."[11] The understanding to which Pseudo-Solomon aspires has a systematic character that was lacking in the wisdom speculation of Ben Sira.

The echoes of Stoicism continue in the list of the attributes of Wisdom in 7:22b–24.[12] The passage begins: "For in her is a spirit intelligent [*noeron*] and holy." While the text does not say that Wisdom *is* such a spirit, we have already seen that a distinction between Wisdom and spirit cannot be maintained. In Stoic philosophy, God is often called a *pneuma noeron*, an intelligent spirit.[13] Most striking in this passage, however, are the attributes that impart to wisdom a fine physical quality, like the Stoic *pneuma:* subtle (*lepton*), agile (*eukinēton*), lucid (*tranon*)—more mobile than any motion. The Stoic pneuma "consisted of fire and air and pervaded all bodies . . . moved of itself, unto itself."[14] Wisdom "pervades and permeates all things by reason of her pureness" (7:24). For the Stoics, the *pneuma* is that which pervades all things, by which all things are held together.[15] We have already seen that the "spirit of the Lord" is portrayed in similar terms in Wis. 1:7. Yet another similar formulation is found in Wis. 8:1: "She stretches mightily from pole to pole and orders all things well." The way in which Wisdom transforms human beings is also reminiscent of the Stoic Logos: "generation by generation she enters into holy souls and renders them friends of God and prophets" (7:27). Wisdom is able to enter into people because of its fine, subtle quality. People are transformed to the degree that the spirit of God is in them.

The Stoic Logos/Pneuma is an immanent deity, identical either with the world itself or with the active force within it.[16] The Wisdom of Solomon, like Ben Sira and the entire Jewish tradition, insisted on a transcendent creator God, who "created the world out of formless matter" (11:17). This is not yet the idea of creation out of nothing, an idea that was only dubiously attested in ancient Judaism. (Second Maccabees 7:28, in the course of an argument on resurrection, says that God made heaven and earth and all that is in them "out of things that did not exist" *ex ouk ontōn*).[17] But the idea of creation requires a clear distinction be-

11. *SVF* 2.555. Both Wis. Sol. and Chrysippus use the Greek words *systasis* and *stoicheia*.

12. See E. des Places, "Epithètes et attributs de la 'Sagesse' (Sg 7, 22–23 et SVF 1 557 Arnim)," *Bib* 57 (1976) 414–19.

13. *SVF* 2.310, 1009. Engel, "Was Weisheit ist," 74. Compare Posidonius, frags. 100–101 (ed. Kidd): "an intelligent spirit pervading all being." See Winston, *The Wisdom of Solomon*, 180.

14. *SVF* 2.442. See Hübner, "Die Sapientia Salomonis," 61. For further parallels see Winston, *The Wisdom of Solomon*, 181.

15. *SVF* 2.416.

16. On the ambiguity of Stoicism in this respect, see Sandbach, *The Stoics*, 73. Chrysippus called the whole world "God" (Cicero, *De Natura Deorum* 1.39).

17. Cf. also Job 26:7, where God "hangs the earth upon nothing," but Job does not envisage creation out of nothing.

tween God and the world, which is closer to Platonism than to Stoicism. The formulation of Wis. Sol. is close to that of Philo, who interpreted Genesis in the light of Plato's *Timaeus*. It is uncertain whether Philo thought that primordial matter was itself created.[18] The Wisdom of Solomon is likewise unclear on this subject.

Wisdom and the Creator

The relation of Wisdom to the creator God is addressed explicitly in Wis. 7:25–26:

> She is an exhalation from the power of God,
> a pure effluence from the glory of the Almighty;
> therefore nothing tainted insinuates itself into her.
> She is an effulgence of everlasting light,
> an unblemished mirror of the active power of God
> and an image of his goodness.

The language of this passage vacillates between dynamic (effluence, *aporroia*) and passive (mirror) images. The terminology is reminiscent of the Platonic tradition rather than Stoicism, as it implies a God beyond this world.[19] It is not adequately explained by reference to the Glory of God in the Hebrew Bible, which is also said to stream forth like a light.[20] The biblical "Glory," or *Kābôd*, is never given a role in ordering the universe. Rather, this passage stands in the tradition of Sir. 24:3, according to which Wisdom "came forth from the mouth of the Most High, and covered the earth like a mist." (Compare Wis. 9:1–2, where Word [*logos*] and Wisdom are parallel to each other as God's means of creation.) The language of emanation or effulgence, however, suggests an even closer connection between Wisdom and the Deity than was envisaged by Sirach.

The language of emanation later acquires a technical sense in Neo-Platonism, where all modes of being are held to emanate from the One Supreme Being. It does not yet have this sense in Wis. Sol., but it implies more than a simple affirmation of divine origin. Wisdom is an independent entity, which derives from God and reflects the divine glory, but then becomes the means of God's presence in creation. Plato used the analogy of light and the sun to explain the relationship between the good as present in the world and the Idea of

---

18. See H. A. Wolfson, *Philo* (Cambridge, Mass.: Harvard Univ. Press, 1948) 1.295–324; D. Winston, *Logos and Mystical Theology in Philo of Alexandria* (Cincinnati: Hebrew Union College Press, 1985) 47–49.

19. For the parallels, see Winston, *The Wisdom of Solomon*, 184–86; Larcher, *Le Livre de la Sagesse*, 496–505.

20. Hübner, "Die Sapientia Salomonis," 66–71; Larcher, *Études sur le Livre de la Sagesse*, 387–88.

the Good.[21] The term *apaugasma,* effulgence, is also used by Philo to express the relationship between the human mind and divine Logos: "Every man, in respect of his mind, is allied to the divine Logos, having come into being as a copy or fragment or *apaugasma* of that blessed nature,"[22] and he relates this claim to the statement in Genesis that God breathed into Adam the breath of life.[23] In the cosmic analogy, Wisdom is the mind or spirit of the universe. In effect, Wisdom embodies the Stoic concept of the Pneuma or Logos, but subordinates it to a transcendent God, who is affirmed as its source.

The Philosophical Context

The question arises, then, whether the author had really understood and assimilated his philosophical sources, or whether he was attempting to combine contradictory systems by superficial rhetoric. Chrysostom Larcher, one of the most learned modern commentators on Wisdom, emphasized the diversity of philosophical doctrines that can be seen to be reflected in the book. Larcher concluded that the author had read a little of everything but had failed to grasp the totality of any philosophical system, or to appreciate the differences between the various schools.[24] In this judgment, Larcher followed in the footsteps of Paul Heinisch, who characterized the philosophical knowledge of the author as "very superficial," and saw no evidence that he had ever studied a major philosopher at first hand.[25] More recently, however, David Winston has pointed out that the background of the book should not be sought in classical Platonism or Stoicism, but in "the philosophical sphere of Middle Platonism, whose boundaries stretch from ca. 80 B.C.E. to ca. 220 C.E."[26] The trademark of this school was the combination of Stoic and Platonic ideas. In the words of John Dillon, "Antiochus [of Ascalon, c. 130–68 B.C.E.] . . . had a coherent view of how philosophy had developed, and that view may not have been quite as perverse as it now appears to us. He and his successors felt justified in appropriating from the Peripatetics and the Stoics such doctrines and formulations as seemed to them to express better what Plato had really meant to say. At most, they were 'modernizing' Plato. The rationale of their procedure was clear and consistent, and it does not seem to me to be profitable to character-

---

21. *Republic* 508. See H. Lyttkens, *The Analogy between God and the World* (Uppsala: Lundequist, 1953) 26.

22. *De Opif.* 146.

23. *De Spec. Leg.* 4.123. On the *apaugasma* in Philo, see E. R. Goodenough, *By Light, Light: The Mystic Gospel of Hellenistic Judaism* (New Haven, Conn.: Yale Univ. Press, 1935) 11–47.

24. Larcher, *Études,* 235–36.

25. P. Heinisch, *Die Griechische Philosophie im Buche der Weisheit* (Münster: Aschendorff, 1908) 155.

26. Winston, *The Wisdom of Solomon,* 33.

ize it as eclectic."[27] Other Middle Platonists, after Antiochus of Ascalon, included Eudorus of Alexandria, who flourished about 30 B.C.E. and wrote a commentary on Plato's *Timaeus,* and Arius Didymus, who was Augustus's court philosopher in the late first century B.C.E. "Timaeus Locrus," an interpretation of Plato's *Timaeus* from the late first century B.C.E., was also representative of this philosophical school. Typical of Middle Platonism was the affirmation of a transcendent deity, and of an intermediate realm mediating between the highest deity and the visible world.[28] Also typical was the formulation of the goal of life as *homoiōsis theō,* becoming like God.[29]

Conversely, Middle Stoicism, in the same period, increasingly gave God "a real place in the Stoic system over against the cosmos."[30] Posidonius distinguished between God and nature in a way that earlier Stoics had not.[31] The notion of an effluence (*aporroia*) from God was probably developed by the Middle Stoics. Cicero wrote that "if mankind possesses intelligence, faith, virtue and concord, whence can these things have flowed down upon the earth if not from the powers above?"[32] It is likely then that the combination of Platonic and Stoic ideas in Wis. Sol. did not result from the superficiality of the author, but reflected the philosophical tendencies of his day. The basic Platonic, rather than Stoic, structure of his thought is shown by the importance he attaches to the immortality of the soul in chaps. 1–5, and also by the insistence on a transcendent creator.

The closest parallels to Wisdom, as we might expect, are not found in Cicero or Antiochus but in the author's Jewish compatriot, Philo of Alexandria.[33] Of primary importance in the present context is Philo's doctrine of the *Logos,* which he identifies with Wisdom in several places.[34] The Logos is an intermediate reality between the transcendent God and the universe.[35]

27. J. Dillon, *The Middle Platonists: A Study of Platonism 80 B.C. to A. D. 220* (London: Duckworth, 1977) xiv. See also his essay, "'Orthodoxy' and 'Eclecticism': Middle Platonists and Neo-Pythagoreans," in J. M. Dillon and A. A. Long, eds., *The Question of 'Eclecticism': Studies in Later Greek Philosophy* (Berkeley: Univ. of California Press, 1988) 103–25. For a defense of the category "eclecticism" in the case of Philo, see J. Mansfeld, "Philosophy in the Service of Scripture: Philo's Exegetical Strategies," in ibid., 70–102.

28. T. H. Tobin, *The Creation of Man: Philo and the History of Interpretation* (Washington: Catholic Biblical Association, 1983) 10–19; Dillon, *The Middle Platonists,* 136–37.

29. Dillon, *The Middle Platonists,* 43–44; Tobin, *The Creation of Man,* 18. The formula was derived from Plato's *Theaetetus* 176b and is found in a fragment from Eudorus. This formula was also used by later Stoics.

30. E. R. Dodds, *Proclus: The Elements of Theology* (Oxford: Oxford Univ. Press, 1963) 214.

31. J. M. Rist, *Stoic Philosophy* (Cambridge: Cambridge Univ. Press, 1969) 202–18.

32. *De Natura Deorum* 2.79. See Winston, *The Wisdom of Solomon,* 185.

33. For a detailed listing of parallels, see Winston, *The Wisdom of Solomon,* 59–63.

34. *Leg. All.* 1.65; *De Fug.* 97; *De Somn.* 2. 242. See L.K.K. Dey, *The Intermediary World and Patterns of Perfection in Philo and Hebrews* (SBLDS 25; Missoula, Mont.: Scholars, 1975) 8.

35. See T. H. Tobin, "Logos," *ABD* 4:350–51; Wolfson, *Philo,* 1.226–82; Winston, *Logos and Mystical Theology,* 9–25.

It resembles the Stoic Logos or Pneuma insofar as it is a principle of ratio-
nality pervading the universe, but as an intermediate being it conforms
rather to the pattern of Middle Platonism. The Logos was a metaphysical reality distinct from God, but it still participated in the reality of God. It was
the image and reflection of God, the model for the rest of creation, but it was
also the power through which the universe was ordered and continued to be
ordered.[36] The Logos was the paradigm for the creation of humankind. The
human mind was to the rest of the human being as the Logos was to the cosmos as a whole: "It is in respect of the mind, the sovereign element of the
soul, that the word 'image' is used; for after the pattern of a single mind,
even the mind of the universe as an archetype, the mind in each of those who
successively came into being was moulded. It is in a fashion a god to him
who carries and enshrines it as an object of reverence; for the human mind
evidently occupies a position in men precisely answering to that which the
great ruler occupies in all the world."[37] The mind was a part or emanation
of the divine Logos.[38] Finally, the Logos was the guide of the human soul
in its mystical ascent, in the process of becoming like God, "showing, as it
does, the way to the things that are best, teaching, as it does, such lessons
as the varying occasions require. For God, not deeming it meet that sense
should perceive him, sends forth his words to succour the lovers of
virtue."[39] In all of this, Philo's Logos is similar to Wisdom in the Wisdom
of Solomon, although it is more elaborately conceived. Philo's Logos could
also be represented as an angel.[40] In Wis. 18:15 the all-powerful Logos leaps
from heaven like a mighty warrior.

The author of Wis. Sol. was not a philosopher, and his thought is far less
complex than that of Philo. Plato's theory of Ideas plays no significant part in
his book, and he makes no mention of God's Powers. He does not develop the
idea of the ascent of the soul. Nevertheless there is enough correspondence
with Philo to debunk the idea that he was an idiosyncratic amateur making his
own superficial use of philosophical terms. He had evidently had a good education, although his inclination was to rhetoric rather than to philosophy. His
concept of Wisdom is developed far beyond that of Ben Sira, and is intelligible in the context of the Middle Platonic philosophy of his day.

36. Philo distinguished between the Creative Power and the Ruling Power, and associated them
with the names Elohim and Lord, respectively (*De Vita Mos.* 2.99–199).

37. *De Opif.* 69.

38. *De Opif.* 146 (cited above); *De Spec. Leg.* 4.123.

39. *De Somn.* 1.68–9, 86; *Leg. All.* 3.169–78; Winston, *Logos and Mystical Theology,* 9–25. Cf.
Solomon's prayer in Wis. Sol. 9, where he confesses that human beings cannot find their way to
God without the aid of Wisdom.

40. Dey, *The Intermediary World,* 8–9.

Wisdom and Isis

Thus far we have emphasized the philosophical affinities of the concept of Wisdom. Many scholars, however, have argued for influences of a more mythological character, specifically from the cult of the Egyptian goddess Isis.[41] This thesis carries a measure of a priori plausibility. A connection between Isis and Wisdom has also been argued with reference to Proverbs 8 and Sirach 24.[42] Several epithets and characteristics of Wisdom are also predicated of Isis.[43] For example, an aretalogy (self-praise) of Isis from Cyme in Asia Minor credits her with much of the work of ordering the universe, and says that she is in the rays of the sun.[44] Many of these epithets, however, are not peculiar to Isis. The motif of ordering the universe was more strongly associated with the Stoic Logos, and the imagery of light had a central role in the Platonic tradition since Plato's Allegory of the Cave in the *Republic*. Despite occasional claims to the contrary, the form of the aretalogy, or self-praise, that is reflected in Sirach 24 is not found in Wis. Sol.[45] There are, however, resemblances of a more general nature between Wisdom and Isis that would have been apparent to any Hellenistic reader. While Wisdom is not closely or primarily modeled on Isis, these resemblances are undoubtedly significant for the rhetorical impact of the book.

There are three general points of similarity between Wisdom and Isis.

First, and most obvious, is the depiction of Wisdom as a feminine figure, whom the devotee can pursue for a bride (Wis. 9:2). This trope is already found in Proverbs and Sirach, but it is reminiscent of the goddess nonetheless. Wisdom is depicted as living both with God (8:3; 9:4) and Solomon (8:9) and as the beloved of each. Isis was wife of Osiris but also spouse of the king. (For this reason several Ptolemaic queens identified themselves with Isis.) Conversely, the name Isis was suggestive of wisdom in Greek. So Plutarch speaks of her as "one who is exceptionally wise and devoted to wisdom. Her name certainly seems to imply that to her more than anyone belong knowledge and understanding."[46]

---

41. Reese, *Hellenistic Influence*, 40–52; B. L. Mack, *Logos und Sophia: Untersuchungen zur Weisheitstheologie im hellenistischen Judentum* (Göttingen: Vandenhoeck & Ruprecht, 1973); idem, "Wisdom Myth and Mythology," *Interpretation* 24 (1970) 46–60; J. S. Kloppenborg, "Isis and Sophia in the Book of Wisdom," *HTR* 75 (1982) 57–84. Kloppenborg reviews the older literature.

42. On Proverbs, C. Kayatz, *Studien zu Proverbien 1–9* (Neukirchen-Vluyn: Neukirchener Verlag, 1966); on Sirach, Conzelmann, "The Mother of Wisdom."

43. Reese, *Hellenistic Influence*, 48–49, although some of his parallels are questionable.

44. F. C. Grant, *Hellenistic Religions* (Indianapolis: Bobbs-Merrill, 1953) 131–33. On the Isis aretalogies, see J. Berman, *Ich Bin Isis* (Uppsala: Almquist & Wiksells, 1968).

45. Contra Reese, *Hellenistic Influence*, 45.

46. Plutarch, *On Isis and Osiris*, 2.

Second, the entire Wisdom of Solomon is presented as an address to the kings of the earth, and the benefits of Wisdom are presented in relation to kingship: "The desire for Wisdom leads to a kingdom. . . . Honor Wisdom so that you may reign forever" (6:20–21). Isis boasts that it is by her that kings reign, and she is depicted as nurse and counselor of the king.[47] She is also the giver of life. The theme of kingship is suggested in Wis. Sol. by the persona of Solomon, but the prominence of the theme may well be suggested by the association of Isis with the kingship.

Finally, Isis is frequently called "savior," and she is acknowledged as such in several dedicatory inscriptions. An inscription from Medinet Madi reads:

> As many as are in prison, in the power of death,
> and as many as are in pain because of long, troubled sleepless nights,
> all who wander in foreign lands,
> and as many as sail on the Great Sea in winter
> when men are destroyed, their ships broken and sent below,
> all these are saved when they pray that you be present.[48]

In Wis. Sol. 10, Wisdom takes over the saving role that is reserved to the Lord in the Hebrew Bible. The hazards from which she saves are of the same kind as those from which Isis rescues: water, fire, imprisonment, and so on. Of course the list of saving actions is determined by the biblical narrative, but as Kloppenborg has pointed out, other paraphrases of salvation history only rarely attend to such matters as the guidance of the ark and the imprisonment of Joseph.[49] It is reasonable, then, to assume that the model of Isis has had some influence on the formulation of Wis. Sol.

Some scholars attribute this influence to the author's "conscious effort to offset the appeal of the literature of the revived Isis cult."[50] It is difficult, however, to see any apologetic polemic at work in the tacit allusions to Isis. When Wis. Sol. wants to oppose a pagan cult, it does so openly and with vigor in chapters 13–15. It is true that the book offers Jews an alternative to Isis in the figure of Wisdom, but there is no hint here, or anywhere else in Jewish literature of the time, that Jews found the cult of Isis especially attractive or tempting. Rather, the tacit allusions to Isis are taken up into the complex picture of Wisdom to enrich it and make it more attractive and satisfying to a hellenized Jewish readership. The allusions to Isis are not essentially different in function from the more overt allusions to Greek philosophy: they make the figure of Wisdom intelligible by depicting it in terms that were familiar and well respected in the Hellenistic world.

47. Kloppenborg, "Isis and Sophia," 75. Mack, *Logos und Sophia,* 90–95.
48. Kloppenborg, "Isis and Sophia," 68.
49. Ibid., 71.
50. Reese, *Hellenistic Influence,* 40.

The Knowledge of God

It is because of the connections established through Wisdom that humanity can arrive at the knowledge of God. Solomon's prayer for wisdom in chap. 9 disparages human ability in this regard:

> For what man can comprehend the plan of God,
> or who can grasp what the Lord wills?
> The reasonings of mortals are wretched
> and our devices precarious;
> for a perishable body weighs down the soul,
> and this tent of clay encumbers a mind full of cares.
> We barely make inferences concerning what is on earth,
> and laboriously discover what is at hand;
> who, then, has tracked out what is in the heavens?
> Who was privy to your design, unless you gave him Wisdom,
> and sent your holy spirit from on high?
> Thus it was that the paths of earthlings were set aright,
> and men were taught what pleases you,
> and were saved by Wisdom.
>
> (Wis. 9:13–18)

The limitations of human knowledge are frequently noted in ancient Jewish, and more generally Near Eastern, literature. The famous question of Agur in Prov. 30:4: "Who has ascended to heaven and come down?" implies that no one has. Some things are simply inaccessible to humanity. The same inference can be drawn from the speeches of God at the end of the book of Job. In the Hellenistic period, however, such an admission of limitation is often the preface to an apocalyptic revelation.[51] Enoch asks, "Who is there who can look at all the works of heaven? and how should there be anyone who could understand the works of heaven?" (*1 Enoch* 93:12–13), and the angel Uriel bombards Ezra with impossible questions (4 Ezra 4). Enoch, of course, claims to have been shown all the works of heaven, and 4 Ezra concludes with a series of apocalyptic visions. In Wis. Sol. there is no recourse to such supernatural revelations. Wisdom is of supernatural, divine origin, but it transforms human understanding from within. It is the complement and fulfillment of the natural human state, which compensates for the shortcomings of bodily existence.

The Wisdom of Solomon vacillates as to whether human beings are culpable if they fail to arrive at the knowledge of the true God:

---

51. M. E. Stone, "Lists of Revealed Things in the Apocalyptic Literature," in F. M. Cross et al., eds., *Magnalia Dei: The Mighty Acts of God* (New York: Doubleday, 1976) 414–52.

Vain by nature were all who were ignorant of God and were unable to know the Existent One [*ton onta*] from the good things that are seen, or to recognize the Craftsman through attention to his works. But either fire, or breath, or swift air, or starry heaven, or torrential water or the celestial lights they accounted gods, cosmic lords. If through delight in the beauty of these things they took them to be gods, let them know how much superior is the Master of these things, for it was the primal author of beauty who created them. If it was through amazement at their dynamic operations, let them apprehend from these how much more powerful is he who shaped them. For from the greatness and beauty of created things is their author correspondingly [*analogōs*] perceived. Yet little blame attaches to these, for they too perhaps err in spite of their search for God and their desire to find him. For they are engaged in searching out his works, and are persuaded by visual impressions, since what they see is beautiful. Yet even they are not to be excused, for if they were so resourceful as to be able to infer the "Universe," how is it they did not sooner discover the master of these things?

(Wis. 13:1–9)

The notion that "the heavens tell forth the glory of God" (Ps. 19:1) has honorable precedents in the Hebrew Bible.[52] Since the reality and primacy of the God of Israel are almost universally taken for granted in the Bible, however, the problem of arriving at a knowledge of God is never addressed. When the rival claims of different deities are assessed in Second Isaiah, the appeal is to history as the arena of vindication. It is only when Jewish tradition comes in contact with Greek philosophy that the possibility of a systematic theology based on the study of nature arises. Wisdom of Solomon 13 must be viewed in the context of Hellenistic philosophical debates and of the contemporary Jewish reasoning of Philo of Alexandria.

The Greek debate about the relation of God or the gods to nature and the cosmos had its origin in the rise of naturalistic philosophy in the fifth century.[53] At the extreme of this development, the atomists Leucippus and Democritus found no role for gods in the workings of the universe or in human life. A more reverential but related attitude is attributed to Socrates by Xenophon:

He that orders and holds together the whole universe in which are all things beautiful and good, and who preserves it for us to enjoy always unimpaired, undisordered and undecaying, obeying his will more swiftly than thought and with all regularity, is manifest himself only in the performance of his mighty works, being invisible to us while he controls them.

(*Memorabilia* 4.3.13; cf. 3.3–15)

52. J. Barr, *Biblical Faith and Natural Theology* (Oxford: Clarendon, 1993) 81–101. Barr discusses elements of natural theology in Pss. 19, 104, and 119, the Wisdom literature, the Prophets, and the Law. On the relevance of the earlier Wisdom literature to this discussion see also J. J. Collins, "The Biblical Precedent for Natural Theology," *JAAR* 45/1 Supplement (1977) 35–67.

53. For a concise summary see M. R. Wright, *Cosmology in Antiquity* (London: Routledge, 1995) 166–75.

Plato, in the *Laws*, took issue with those who found the sources of being in the natural elements and regarded the gods as existing not by nature but by convention and law (*Laws* 10 [890]). He argued that the soul was prior to the body, and that the souls of the planets and such were gods "whether as living beings inside bodies arranging the whole universe or in some other way" (*Laws* 898b). In the *Timaeus*, he envisaged a craftsman or Demiurge who was responsible for the construction of the universe after a perfect atemporal model. This craftsman was the maker and father of the cosmos and could be referred to as god. Aristotle reasoned from the universality of motion that there must be a first Mover, which is unmoved (*Physics* 258b), but this Prime Mover is a force within the world. Again, the Stoics use much of the same terminology as Plato, but their God is immanent and even part of the physical universe. God is identified as the active principle in the universe, the Logos inherent in matter.[54] He is

> the artificer [demiurge] of the universe and, as it were, the father of all, both in general and in that particular part of him which is all-pervading, and which is called many names according to its various powers. They give the name Dia because all things are due to him; Zeus pervades all life; the name Athena is given, because the ruling part of the divinity extends to the aether; the name Hera marks its extension to the air; he is called Hephaestus since it spreads to the creative fire; Poseidon, since it stretches to the sea; Demeter, since it reaches to the earth.[55]

God may even be identified with the cosmos itself, or with its commanding faculty or mind.[56]

Despite the immanence of God in Stoic theology, the manner of argumentation is rather similar to what we find in Wis. Sol. Cleanthes saw the chief cause of belief in God as

> the regularity of the motion, the revolution of the heavens, and the individuality, usefulness, beauty and order of the sun, the moon, and all the stars. The mere sight of these things . . . was proof enough that they are not products of accident. Just as, if someone enters a house, a gymnasium or a forum, when he sees the controlled methodical pattern of all that goes on he cannot think that these things happen without cause, but understands that there is someone in charge who is obeyed, much more must he, in the case of these great motions and phases and of the orderings of things so numerous and immense . . . conclude that it is by some mind that these great motions of nature are controlled.[57]

Or again: "We alone of living creatures know the risings and settings, and the courses of the stars . . . and contemplating the heavenly bodies the mind arrives at a knowledge of the gods."[58]

54. Diogenes Laertius 7.134.
55. Diogenes Laertius 7.147; *SVF* 2.1021.
56. Diogenes Laertius 7.148; Cicero, *De Natura Deorum* 1.39; *SVF* 2.1077.
57. Cicero, *De Natura Deorum* 2.12–15.
58. Ibid., 2.253.

The closest parallels to Wis. Sol. are found, as usual, in the works of Philo. In his treatise on the Decalogue he writes:

A great delusion has taken hold of the larger part of mankind in regard to a fact which properly should be established beyond all question in every mind to the exclusion of, or at least above, all others. For some have deified the four elements, earth, water, air and fire, others the sun, moon, planets and fixed stars, others again the heaven by itself, others the whole world. But the highest and the most august, the begetter, the Ruler of the great World-city, the Commander-in-Chief of the invincible host, the Pilot who ever steers all things in safety, Him they have hidden from sight by the misleading titles assigned to the objects of worship mentioned. Different people give them different names: some call the earth Kore or Demeter or Pluto, and the sea Poseidon. . . . They call air Hera and fire Hephaestus, the sun Apollo, the moon Artemis . . .[59]

It is clear from the passages cited above that Philo here is taking issue with Stoicism. The issue is the distinction between the cosmos and God, and the consequent contingency of creation:

For the world has become what it is, and its becoming is the beginning of its destruction, even though by the providence of God it be made immortal, and there was a time when it was not. But to speak of God as "not being" at some former time, or having "become" at some particular time and not existing for all eternity, is profanity.[60]

Although both Philo and Wis. Sol. make extensive use of Stoic concepts and arguments, their biblical heritage lent itself more readily to rapprochement with the Platonic tradition. The possibility of knowledge of God *kata analogian* was also affirmed by the Middle Platonic philosopher Albinus.[61]

Wisdom of Solomon clearly regards those philosophers who worship the creation rather than the creator as culpable to some degree. This implies that at least some knowledge of God is attainable in principle by human reason. The same implication is found, more carefully nuanced, in Rom. 1:19–20: "For what can be known about God is plain to them, because God has shown it to them. Ever since the creation of the world his eternal power and divine nature, invisible though they are, have been understood and seen through the things he has made. So they are without excuse." In view of the disparagement of human reason in Wis. 9:14–17, success would seem to be unlikely without the divine gift of Wisdom, but the possibility is nonetheless affirmed.

The reluctance of Wis. Sol. to condemn those who deify the cosmos can be clarified by another parallel passage in Philo's *De Decalogo:*

59. Philo, *De Decal.* 52–54; cf. *De Spec. Leg.* 1.13–20. Winston, *The Wisdom of Solomon,* 248.
60. *De Decal.* 58.
61. Winston, *The Wisdom of Solomon,* 253. On the Greek tradition, especially the usage in Neo-Platonism, see further Lyttkens, *The Analogy Between God and the World,* 15–110.

But while all who give worship and service to sun and moon and the whole heaven and universe or their chief parts as gods most undoubtedly err by magnifying the subjects above the ruler, their offence is less than that of the others who have given shape to sticks and stones and silver and gold and similar materials, each according to their fancy, and then filled the habitable world with images and wooden figures and the other works of human hands fashioned by the craftsmanship of painting and sculpture, arts which have wrought great mischief in the life of mankind.[62]

The philosophers who seek the true God and fall short deserve respect. Those who engage in mere idolatry receive nothing but contempt.

The Polemic against Idolatry

The Wisdom of Solomon also follows its digression on the knowledge of God with a lengthy polemic against idolatry in 13:10–14:31 and 15:7–19.[63] Jewish opposition to idol worship can be traced back to the Decalogue, although its ultimate origin remains mysterious. It is widely attested in the Second Temple period.[64] The most elaborate denunciation in the Hebrew Bible is found in several passages in Second Isaiah.[65] In Isa. 44:9–20, the prophet derides those who take part of a piece of wood to make a fire and cook food, and bow down before the other part as the image of a god. Other notable biblical passages are found in Jeremiah 10; Hab. 2:18–19, and Pss. 115:4–8 and 135:15–18. Polemic against idols becomes more common in the Hellenistic period. Extended examples are found in the Letter of Jeremiah and in the story of Bel and the Dragon, appended to the Greek translation of Daniel.[66] Denunciation of idolatry is a common theme in Jewish literature written in Greek from the Egyptian Diaspora, such as the *Letter of Aristeas* and the *Sibylline Oracles*.[67] The closest parallels to Wis. Sol. are found in Philo, although the similarities are not so close as to require interdependence.[68]

62. *De Decal.* 66.

63. M. Gilbert, *La Critique des Dieux dans le livre de la Sagesse* (AnBib. 53; Rome: Pontifical Biblical Institute, 1973).

64. W.M.W. Roth, "For Life, He Appeals to Death (Wis 13:18): A Study of Old Testament Idol Parodies," *CBQ* 37 (1975) 21–47; H. D. Preuss, *Verspottung fremder Religionen im Alten Testament* (Stuttgart: Kohlhammer, 1971); G. von Rad, *Wisdom in Israel* (Nashville: Abingdon, 1972) 177–85.

65. These passages are probably secondary insertions into the exilic oracles. Roth, "For Life," 22.

66. See Collins, *Daniel*, 405–19.

67. *Ep. Arist.* 134–38; *Sib. Or.* 3:29–35; Gilbert, *La Critique des Dieux*, 262. Goodman, *Mission and Conversion*, 55–56, argues that Wis. Sol. and the *Sibylline Oracles* were exceptional in their hostility to idols, but while they are exceptionally vehement, they are not exceptional in their disapproval.

68. Philo, *De Decal.* 52–81; *De Vita Cont.* 3–9; *De Spec. Leg.* 1.13–29; 2.255; Larcher, *Études*, 162–66.

The polemic against idols in Wis. Sol. begins with a lengthy discourse on the making of wooden images. The first part (13:10–19) closely resembles the polemic of Second Isaiah. A man uses part of a piece of wood to make an everyday vessel and to prepare his food, and then makes an idol from the remainder. "For health he invokes that which is feeble; for life he prays to a corpse" (v. 18). The second part of this discourse (14:1–11) mocks the sailor who appeals for aid "to a piece of wood more unsound than the craft that carries him." The ship is a product of "Wisdom the artificer" and is steered by divine providence. The Stoics spoke of the guiding power of the Logos as a kind of steering (*kybernaō*), and Philo used the same verb for both human reason and divine providence.[69] The author is careful to distinguish between the proper use of wood and the abuse of the idolator.[70] The polemic against clay figurines (15:7–13) is in a similar vein, but here the potter is accused of acting in bad faith: for one must make a living, he says, from whatever source, even an evil one. For this man knows more than any other that he sins, fabricating from earthen stuff frail vessels and carved images.

But Wis. Sol. also offers a more philosophical explanation of idolatry, in 14:12–31. Two illustrative instances are cited: the father who makes an image of a dead child, and the ruler who commands that his statue be worshiped in his absence. The first instance finds an interesting parallel in the work of the fourth-century convert to Christianity, Firmicus Maternus, *De errore profanarum religionum,* who drew on ancient sources. According to Firmicus, Dionysus was the son of a Cretan king named Jupiter. Since he was the product of an adulterous union, the king's wife, Juno, had him murdered by the Titans. When the father discovered this he had an image made in the likeness of the son and instituted a cult.[71] Several other parallels can be cited, notably the cult of Hadrian's favorite Antinous, who drowned in Egypt in 130 C.E.[72] The tendency toward a cult of the dead, involving the erection of statues, could probably have been observed in Roman Egypt. The author's explanation of idolatry may also be indebted to the theories of Euhemerus of Messene, who wrote about 300 B.C.E. Euhemerus claimed that Cronos and Zeus were great kings of the past who were worshiped as gods by grateful people. His theory was taken up by Diodorus Siculus in his world history, in the middle of the first century B.C.E. It is also reflected in Hellenistic Jewish writings. *Sibylline Oracles* 3:110–55 tells the story of Cronos and the Titans as an early phase of

69. Winston, *The Wisdom of Solomon,* 214; *SVF* 3.390; Philo, *De Opif.* 88, 119; *De Abr.* 84; *De Decal.* 155.

70. It is difficult, nonetheless, to see 14:7 ("Blessed is the wood through which righteousness comes") as anything but a Christian interpolation. Winston avoids this conclusion by translating "through which righteousness survives" (*ginetai*). See Gilbert, *La Critique des Dieux,* 114–24.

71. Gilbert, *La Critique des Dieux,* 153–55; J. Geffcken, "Der Bilderstreit des heidnischen Altertums," *ARW* 19 (1919) 292–93.

72. Gilbert, *La Critique des Dieux,* 146–57.

human history. The *Letter of Aristeas* (135–37) argues that it is foolish to deify people because they invented things, as they only demonstrated the usefulness of things that were already created. Wisdom of Solomon does not engage in a full Euhemeristic critique of polytheism, but the critique of idols reflects a similar mentality. The idea that idolatry was not practiced from the beginning, but was a product of human history, is commonplace in Jewish literature, where it is often associated with the generation of Enosh in the antediluvian period.[73]

The worship of images to honor absent rulers was characteristic of the Roman era. The attempt of Caligula to install his statue in the Jerusalem Temple comes to mind.[74] Josephus reports that Herod erected temples and statues in the cities he built, although not in Jewish territory: "To the Jews he made the excuse that he was doing these things not on his own account but by command and order, while he sought to please Caesar and the Romans by saying that he was less intent upon observing the customs of his own nation than upon honoring them."[75]

Finally, Wis. Sol. adds a caustic comment on animal worship, which was especially characteristic of Egypt: "Moreover, they worship the most hateful beasts, who compared for brutishness are worse than all the rest" (15:18). Philo similarly castigated the Egyptians:

> But the Egyptians are rightly charged not only on the count to which every country is liable, but also on another peculiar to themselves. For in addition to wooden and other images, they have advanced to divine honours irrational animals. . . . But actually the Egyptians have gone to a further excess, and chosen the fiercest and most savage of wild animals, lions and crocodiles and among reptiles the venomous asp.
>
> (*De Decal.* 76–78)

Josephus questioned whether the Egyptians deserved to be called "men," because they worshiped animals hostile to humanity (*Ag. Ap.* 2.66). Artapanus, who wrote in the second century B.C.E., rings a peculiar change on this polemic when he claims that Moses actually founded the Egyptian animal cults, judging the animals in question to be useful![76] But for most Hellenistic Jewish writers the worship of animals typified the abysmal character of the Egyptians.[77]

---

73. S. Fraade, *Enosh and His Generation* (Chico, Calif.: Scholars, 1984) 174, 226–27; P. Schäfer, "Der Götzendienst des Enosch: Zur Bildung und Entwicklung aggadischer Traditionen im nachbiblischen Judentum," in idem, *Studien zur Geschichte und Theologie des Rabbinischen Judentums* (Leiden: Brill, 1978) 134–52.

74. *J. W.* 2.184–87.

75. *Ant.* 15.330.

76. Collins, *Between Athens and Jerusalem*, 35.

77. *Ep. Arist.* 138; *Sib. Or.* frag. 3; 3:30; Gilbert, *La Critique des Dieux*, 239–40.

While the polemic against idolatry was obviously directed at pagan practice, the Jewish apologists could hope to find a sympathetic hearing among
some Greek philosophers. There had been a growing tendency toward
monotheism in Greek philosophy since the fifth century B.C.E.[78] The oldest critiques of idolatry in this tradition can be found in the fragments of Heraclitus
and Xenophanes.[79] Antisthenes, a pupil of Socrates and teacher of Diogenes,
taught that there were many conventional gods, but only one by nature.[80]
Clement of Alexandria claims that "Zeno, the founder of the Stoic sect, says in
the book on the state that it is necessary to make neither temples nor statues,
for no contrivance is worthy of the gods."[81] According to St. Augustine, the
Roman antiquarian Varro (first century B.C.E.) claimed that "for more than one
hundred and seventy years the ancient Romans worshipped the gods without
an image. 'If this usage had continued to our own day,' he says, 'our worship
of the gods would be more devout.' And in support of his opinion he adduces,
among other things, the testimony of the Jewish race."[82] Strabo also expresses
admiration for Judaism in this respect, in a passage that is thought to derive
from Posidonius: "[Moses] taught that the Egyptians were mistaken in representing the Divine Being by the images of beasts and cattle, as were also the
Libyans; and that the Greeks were also wrong in modelling gods in human
form; for, according to him, God is this one thing that encompasses us all."[83]
Plutarch complains that "then again such persons give credence to workers in
metal, stone, or wax, who make their images of gods in the likeness of human
beings, and they have such images fashioned, and dress them up and worship
them. But they hold in contempt philosophers and statesmen, who try to prove
that the majesty of God is associated with goodness, magnanimity, kindliness,
and solicitude."[84] Numerous other examples can be cited from the writings of
Stoics and Cynics around the turn of the era.[85]

It is clear, then, that the critique of idolatry in Wis. Sol. does not represent
an unqualified opposition to the Gentile world.[86] Rather, the author was attempting to make common cause with enlightened Greeks who would share
his contempt for popular superstition, and especially for the crass forms of

78. M. P. Nilsson, *Geschichte der Griechischen Religion. 2. Die hellenistische und römische
Zeit* (Munich: Beck, 1974) 569–78.
79. B. de Borries, *Quid veteres philosophi de idolatria senserint* (Göttingen: Dieterich, 1918).
80. Cicero, *De Natura Deorum* 1.32.
81. Clement, *Strom.* 5.11.76.
82. Augustine, *De Civitate Dei* 4.31.
83. Strabo 16.2.35.
84. Plutarch, *De superstitione,* 167 D.
85. See H. W. Attridge, *First-Century Cynicism in the Epistles of Heraclitus* (Missoula, Mont.:
Scholars, 1976) 13–23.
86. *Pace* Barclay, *Jews in the Mediterranean Diaspora,* 186–88, who misses both the philosophical context of the polemic and the parallels in Philo.

idolatry practiced in Egypt.[87] Moreover, he lumps together with idolatry all manner of abuses associated with "secret mysteries" and "strange laws" of which cultured Greeks and Romans would disapprove (14:23–28). This strategy had implications that were social as well as theological. Jews of the kind represented by Wis. Sol. and by Philo of Alexandria desperately sought acceptance by the cultured Greeks of Alexandria and sought to distance themselves from the Egyptians, who were barbarians and, besides, were subject to the hated Roman poll tax. Unfortunately for their purpose, not all the Greeks of Alexandria were cultured, and those of whom we have any knowledge were more concerned with preserving their privileged status than with advancing notions of human solidarity.

We should not, however, think of Wis. Sol.'s polemic against idolatry as merely part of the social strategy of Alexandrian Judaism. It was one of the aspects of the book that had deepest roots in Jewish tradition. It was also part of a coherent theology that was founded in the understanding of Wisdom as a universal spirit that bound the universe to the creator God.

Cosmos and History

The relations between Judaism and the Gentile world constitute the central issue in the long paraphrase of biblical history in chaps. 10–19.

The reading of biblical history in Wis. Sol. is quite different from what we found in Ben Sira, although both books have in common an interest in the characterization of individuals rather than narrative sequence. Both books are presumably influenced by the Hellenistic convention of listing examples (*Beispielreihen*).[88] Ben Sira's stated purpose is to sing the praises of pious men, and to hold them up as models to be imitated. This is also true of the appeal to paradigmatic figures in 1 Maccabees 2; 4 Maccabees 16 and 18; and Hebrews 11. In Wis. Sol., however, Wisdom rather than human beings is the subject of praise. The encomium has clear implications for human behavior, but there is a greater sense here of a pattern in history than was the case in Sirach. Consequently, there is also some resemblance to apocalyptic summaries of history, which often show a pattern of sin, punishment, and salvation.[89]

---

87. M. Görg, "Die Religionskritik in Weish 13,1f. Beobachtungen zur Entstehung der Sapientia-Salomonis im späthellenistischen Alexandria," in G. Hentschel and E. Zenger, eds., *Lehrerin der Gerechtigkeit* (Leipzig: Benno, 1991) 13–25, argues that the polemic is primarily against Egyptian religion.

88. See the literature cited in Chap. 6 above. On Wis. Sol. 10 as a "Beispielreihe," see A. Schmitt, "Struktur, Herkunft und Bedeutung der Beispielreihe in Weish 10," *BZ* 21 (1977) 1–22.

89. On the treatment of history in apocalyptic literature, see in general R. G. Hall, *Revealed Histories: Techniques for Ancient Jewish and Christian Historiography* (Sheffield: JSOT Press, 1991).

The most interesting comparative reviews of history are provided by the *Apocalypse of Weeks* in *1 Enoch* 93:1–10 and 91:11–17 and the Damascus Document (CD) 2:14–3:11. The Apocalypse of Weeks resembles Wis. Sol. 10 insofar as no names are named, although the characters of biblical history (Noah, Abraham, etc.) are easily recognizable. There is a dialectic of righteousness and iniquity, with a recurring pattern of salvation, and those who are saved are righteous, at least implicitly. There is, however, a fundamental difference between the two texts. In the Apocalypse of Weeks, history moves inexorably toward a predetermined goal. The decisive turning point comes in the seventh "week," or period, and thereafter comes the judgment and a new creation. Historical progression has no significance in Wis. Sol. 10, nor indeed in Wis. Sol. as a whole.

Unlike the Apocalypse of Weeks and Wis. Sol. 10, CD 2:14–3:11 mentions names. In some respects, it is the inverse of Wis. Sol. 10. It narrates the effects of the evil inclination, the antithesis of Wisdom. Because of it, the Watchers and the sons of Noah fell. But CD also narrates a history of salvation, which comes to fruition at a specific point in time with a new revelation to "those who remained steadfast." While CD provides a series of moral examples as does Wis. Sol., it also resembles the Apocalypse of Weeks in identifying a turning point in history and a movement toward a goal.

There is no turning point in Wis. Sol., and the goal is accessible irrespective of chronological progression. Noah, Abraham, Lot, Jacob, and Joseph all serve as types of "the righteous man." Israel in Egypt is "a holy people and a blameless race," and Moses is "the servant of the Lord." While the identifications are transparent to anyone who is familiar with biblical narrative, they are never made explicit. The implication is that the specific historical figures are only significant as examples of a type. The story of Israel is viewed as a cosmic allegory, that could in principle be appropriated by any righteous people, if any other should ever exist.[90]

This manner of treating the early history is related to Philo's allegorical treatment of the patriarchs. For Philo, the patriarchs were animated laws (*empsychoi nomoi*). Seven are singled out, two triads and then Moses, who stands alone. In the first triad, Enosh symbolizes hope, Enoch repentance, and Noah justice. In the second, Abraham represents virtue derived from instruction, Isaac virtue from natural endowment, and Jacob virtue achieved by effort. The figure of Moses is more complex, representing the perfect man, who can even be called a god.[91] Philo's allegories are much more complex than the

---

90. See B. L. Mack, "Imitatio Mosis: Patterns of Cosmology and Soteriology in the Hellenistic Synagogue," *Studia Philonica* 1 (1972) 27–55. This point is in no way negated by the observation that "it is a stylistic and rhetorical device, in the Alexandrian tradition of literary allusion" (*pace* Barclay, *Jews in the Mediterranean Diaspora,* 190).

91. See Goodenough, *By Light, Light,* 121–234.

treatment we find in Wis. Sol., where each of the patriarchs uniformly represents "the righteous man."[92] In both cases, however, historical particularity is disregarded and primary importance is attached to representative type.

Wisdom of Solomon 10 emphasizes that each of the patriarchs in question is saved by Wisdom. The hazards from which they are delivered are clear enough, even if they involve some surprising assessments. (Abraham was kept strong against pity for his child.) But in what does their salvation consist? On the surface, it would seem that it consists in rescue from the danger of the moment. There are two passages in the book, however, that seem to speak of judgment and salvation in more definitive terms.

The first of these passages is found in Wis. 5:15–23, and we have touched upon it at the end of Chapter 10. There we are told explicitly that "the righteous live forever and their reward is with the Lord." But the passage goes on to speak of a transformation in terms reminiscent of Isa. 59:16–17. In the Isaian text, God "put on righteousness like a breastplate, and a helmet of salvation on his head; he put on garments of vengeance for clothing, and wrapped himself in fury as in a mantle." In Wis. Sol., "he will put on righteousness as a breastplate, and wear impartial justice as a helmet; he will take holiness as an invincible shield, and sharpen stern wrath for a sword." But Wis. Sol. adds another motif: "He will arm all creation to repel his enemies," and "the cosmos will fight with him against the madmen." There are biblical precedents for the cooperation of nature in the wars of the Lord. Judges 5:20 says that the stars fought from heaven for Israel against Sisera. There is no apocalyptic new creation here, however, no transformation of nature such as we know from Isaiah 11. It is not even clear that the cosmos reaches a final state. The promise is rather that it will be consistently subservient to the purposes of God in a way that is not apparent in the present.

The manner in which the cosmos is harnessed for the divine purposes is illustrated in the second passage that suggests a definite salvation and judgment, the account of the exodus in Wis. Sol. 16–19.[93] The whole story of the exodus is taken to show that "creation, serving you who made it, exerts itself to punish the unrighteous, and in kindness relaxes on behalf of those who trust in you" (16:24). Wisdom of Solomon draws here on a Stoic theory whereby the elements admit of different degrees of tension or relaxation.[94] The idea is that elements are modified or interchanged. Nothing new is created. So in 19:6 we are told that "the whole creation in its nature was fashioned anew, complying

92. Again there are seven, culminating in Moses, but the figures chosen are different from those in Philo because of the emphasis on deliverance from some predicament. See Winston, *The Wisdom of Solomon*, 211–12.
93. P. Beauchamp, "Le salut corporel des justes et la conclusion du livre de la Sagesse," *Bib* 45 (1964) 491–526.
94. Winston, *The Wisdom of Solomon*, 300.

with your commands, so that your children might be kept unharmed." In 19:18 the process is explained: "For the elements changed places with one another, as on a harp the notes vary the nature of the rhythm, while each note remains the same." The cosmos is a closed entity, although it admits of internal variation.[95] The goal of history is to illustrate the workings of God. There is no movement toward ultimate transformation. Philo also uses the idea of tension and slackening to explain changes in nature. The bow that God sets in the clouds after the flood indicates that "in the laxness and force of earthly things there will not take place a dissolution by their being completely loosened to the point of incongruity nor will there be force up to the point of reaching a break" (*Quaest. Gen.* 2.64). God also provided the manna by "changing round the elements" (*De Vita Mos.* 2.266–67).

Philo at least retains a glimpse of traditional Jewish national eschatology. In the treatise on Rewards and Punishments (*De Praemiis et Poenis*) he entertains the possibility that the Jewish people will convert in a body to virtue, and thus strike awe into their masters, who will set them free. "When they have gained this unexpected liberty, those who but now were scattered in Greece and the outside world over islands and continents will arise and post from every side with one impulse the one appointed place, guided in their pilgrimage by a vision divine and superhuman" (*De Praem.* 165). Then, "everything will suddenly be reversed, God will turn the curses against the enemies of these penitents, the enemies who rejoiced in the misfortunes of the nation." (169). Harry Wolfson concluded from these passages that "the solution found by Philo for the Jewish problem of his time was the revival of the old prophetic promises of the ultimate disappearance of the Diaspora,"[96] but he has been justifiably criticized for reading Philo in the light of an overly harmonistic picture of "native Judaism."[97] Philo's nationalism must be modified. Even Wolfson grants that "the depiction of the Messianic Age in Philo is quite evidently colored with Stoic phraseology," although he contends that it is nonetheless opposed to the Stoic ideal of a universal polity. Philo's eschatological vision entails harmony with the animal world, as prophesied in Isaiah 11, peace, and prosperity. His God is the One "to whom all must belong who

95. Cf. J.P.M. Sweet, "The Theory of Miracles in the Wisdom of Solomon," in C.F.D. Moule, ed., *Miracles* (London: Mowbray, 1965) 115–26; J. J. Collins, "Cosmos and Salvation: Jewish Wisdom and Apocalyptic in the Hellenistic Age," *HR* 17 (1977) 127–28.

96. Wolfson, *Philo*, 2.407.

97. R. D. Hecht, "Philo and Messiah," in J. Neusner, W. S. Green, and E. S. Frerichs, eds., *Judaisms and Their Messiahs at the Turn of the Christian Era* (Cambridge: Cambridge Univ. Press, 1987) 139–68. Hecht argues that messianic hope is consistently dehistoricized in Philo. Cf. also U. Fischer, *Eschatologie und Jenseitserwartung im Hellenistischen Diasporajudentum* (BZNW 44; Berlin: de Gruyter, 1978) 184–213.

follow truth unfeigned instead of mythical figments" (*De Praem.* 162), not just the God of Israel. He repeatedly defines the antithesis in terms of the virtuous and the wicked rather than in national or ethnic terms. Those who are destined for destruction in the messianic war are "some fanatics whose lust for war defies restraint or remonstrance" (94). The beneficiaries of eschatological prosperity are "those who follow God and always and everywhere cleave to His commandments" (98). Moreover, *De Praemiis* is exceptional in the Philonic corpus in its lack of allegorical interpretation. Elsewhere, Philo typically reads the biblical text in terms of the spiritualized experience of the individual. Nonetheless, we know that Philo was an advocate for his community in the time of the emperor Caligula, and that he insisted on the literal observance of the laws in addition to the spiritual interpretation. It is likely, then, that he retained a literal messianic hope, even though he emphasized its symbolic significance for humankind as a whole.[98] In the words of Peder Borgen, "the literal and allegorical interpretations are interwoven, and the concrete national and 'messianic' eschatology and the general, cosmic principles belong together."[99] In the case of Wis. Sol., however, there is no overt messianic eschatology. The hope of national restoration might be inferred from the pattern of the exodus, but the book never addresses the question of a final resolution of history.

The understanding of nature and history that we find in Wis. Sol. is very close to what we found earlier in Ben Sira. Sirach also envisaged the cosmos as the implement of God. He speaks of "winds created for vengeance" and claims that wild animals and even "the sword that punishes the ungodly" never disobey the divine command (Sir. 39:28–31). Sirach, however, recognizes the ambivalence of nature: "All these [elements] are good for the godly, but for the sinners they turn into evils" (Sir. 39:27). The claim is that people experience nature, and history, differently in accordance with their characters. The claim of Wis. Sol. in the account of the exodus is similar: "For through the very things by which their enemies were punished, they themselves received benefit in their need" (Wis. 11:5). So the elements were consistently destructive to the Egyptians but protective toward the Israelites. The claim of Wis. Sol. is that nature is ever thus protective of the righteous and destructive toward the wicked. We might infer from this that the righteous ultimately prosper and the wicked are punished. When Wis. Sol. addresses the issue of ultimate reward and punishment, however, in chapters 1–5, the reward takes the form of everlasting life for the individual rather than communal vindication.

---

98. See Collins, *Between Athens and Jerusalem,* 116.

99. P. Borgen, "'There Shall Come Forth a Man': Reflections on Messianic Ideas in Philo," in J. H. Charlesworth, ed., *The Messiah* (Minneapolis: Fortress, 1992) 360.

Universalism
and Particularism

Unlike Sirach, Wis. Sol. uses the story of the exodus to illustrate the contrasting fates of righteous and wicked, and thereby seems to identify the Israelites with the righteous and their enemies with the wicked. Consequently, many commentators speak of "undisguised particularism" in this part of the book, and find that God is partial to the Jews and inimical to their enemies."[100] Israel is never mentioned by name. Instead it is called "a holy people and blameless race" (10:15), but also "your people" (12:19; 16:2, 3, 5, etc.), "your children" (16:10, 21, 26; 18:4), "the holy children" (18:9), "the holy nation" (16:2), "your holy ones" (18:2), and even "the son of God" (18:13). The last-mentioned title, which has its biblical basis in Exod. 4:22–23, echoes Wis. 2:13–20, where the righteous man claims to be son of God and that God is his father. But ethnic continuity is also a factor. Wisdom of Solomon 18:6 refers to the Israelites of the exodus as "our ancestors."

The question is, then, how far has the exodus story been reduced to an allegory of the righteous and the wicked, and how far does it reflect the ethnic antagonisms not only of Israelite history but also of Roman Alexandria? Winston is surely right that "the ancient Egyptians and Canaanites . . . served the author as symbols for the hated Alexandrians and Romans of his own day."[101] The primary sins of which the Egyptians are accused, idolatry and infanticide, were common reproaches in Hellenistic Jewish polemic. Winston also notes that Philo, the most universalistic of all Jewish writers, also entertains a fantasy of nationalistic triumph in *De Praemiis et Poenis*. In both Wis. Sol. and Philo, however, the occasional nationalistic notes clash with the philosophy of *philanthrōpia* that both writers explicitly endorse.

The adjective *philanthrōpos* occurs three times in Wis. Sol. It is used twice to characterize Wisdom (1:6; 7:23). In 12:19, the mercy of God is cited as evidence that the righteous ought to be philanthropic. God's mercy is grounded in creation: "For you love all things that exist, and detest none of the things that you have made, for you would not have made anything if you had hated it. . . . You spare all things, for they are yours, O Lord, you who love the living. For your imperishable spirit is in all things" (11:24–12:1). By this logic, God should love the Egyptians as well as the Israelites.

The notion of *philanthropia* was a Stoic concept, grounded in the affinity between the divine and the human established by the Logos. "The world is, as it were, the common dwelling-place of gods and men, or the city that belongs

---

100. J. Reider, *The Book of Wisdom* (New York: Harper, 1957) 41; Barclay, *The Jews in the Mediterranean Diaspora,* 181–91, takes Wis. Sol. as a whole as an example of "cultural antagonism."

101. Winston, *The Wisdom of Solomon,* 45.

to both; for they alone have the use of reason and live by justice and law."[102] Among human beings, there should be no division: "The much admired Republic of Zeno . . . is aimed at this one main point, that our household arrangements should not be based on cities or parishes, each one marked out by its own legal system, but we should regard all men as our fellow-citizens and local residents, and there should be one way of life and order, like that of a herd grazing together and nurtured by a common law."[103] Seneca recognized that "there are two communities—the one, which is great and truly common, embracing gods and men, in which we look neither to this corner nor to that, but measure the boundaries of our state by the sun; the other, the one to which we have been assigned by the accident of our birth."[104] For Philo, "All we men are kinsmen and brothers, being related by the possession of an ancient kinship, since we receive the lot of the rational nature from one another."[105] But even the Stoics did not think that universalism eliminated all need for discrimination. Zeno, "making an invidious contrast, declares the good alone to be true citizens or friends or kindred or free men; and accordingly in the view of the Stoics parents and children are enemies, not being wise."[106] Later Stoics modified this view, but a distinction between righteous and wicked, wise and foolish, remained essential. For the Stoics and the Cynics, however, there could be no assumption that these distinctions coincided with ethnic lines.

For Jews in the Hellenistic world, in contrast, such an assumption was part of their cultural heritage, and not easily discarded. Jews were often accused of an antisocial and misanthropic way of life, even by people who were not ill-disposed to them.[107] Hecataeus comments on their "unsocial and intolerant mode of life" (*apanthrōpon tina kai misoxenon bion*), although his account was generally positive.[108] Diodorus Siculus attributed the intervention of Antiochus Epiphanes in Jerusalem to advice that he should wipe out the Jews, "since they alone of all nations avoided dealings with any other people and looked upon all men as their enemies."[109] These charges were amplified in anti-Jewish polemics of Alexandrian Greeks in the Roman period.[110] In large part, these charges arose from the impression of exclusiveness created by dietary laws, and by refusal to intermarry and to worship the same gods as

102. Cicero, *De Natura Deorum* 2.154.
103. Plutarch, *On the Fortune of Alexander* 329 A-B; *SVF* 1.262.
104. Seneca, *On Leisure* 4.1.
105. *Quaest. Gen.* 2.60.
106. Diogenes Laertius 7.33.
107. See Feldman, *Jew and Gentile,* 125–31.
108. Diodorus Siculus 40.3.4.
109. Ibid., 34/35.1.1.
110. See J. N. Sevenster, *The Roots of Pagan Anti-Semitism in the Ancient World* (Leiden: Brill, 1980). J. G. Gager, *The Origins of Anti-Semitism* (New York: Oxford, 1983) 39–54. The charges are recorded and answered in Josephus' tract *Against Apion.*

everyone else. Apologists for Judaism such as Philo labored to explain, both to the Jews themselves and to any Gentile who might listen, that these Jewish practices were really in the best interests of humanity and served the purpose of *philanthrōpia*.[111] Philo devoted a lengthy exposition to the *philanthrōpia* of Moses and his laws in *De Virtutibus* 51–174. Yet even the argument for the *philanthrōpia* of Judaism often entails a claim of Jewish superiority.[112] "The Jewish nation," writes Philo, "is to the whole inhabited world what the priest is to the State,"[113] and in an ideal world "each nation would abandon its peculiar ways, and throwing overboard its ancestral customs, turn to honouring our laws alone."[114] True, ethnic affiliation alone did not qualify anyone as righteous, and conversion was certainly possible. "In reality," wrote Philo, "the proselyte is one who circumcises not his uncircumcision but his desires and sensual pleasures and the other passions of the soul. For in Egypt, the Hebrew nation was not circumcised."[115] Philo might have agreed with Paul that "he is not a real Jew who is one outwardly, nor is true circumcision something external and physical. He is a Jew who is one inwardly, and real circumcision is a matter of the heart, spiritual and not literal" (Rom. 2:28–29). Yet Philo, unlike Paul, was unwilling to dispense with literal circumcision, or with the special importance of "Israel according to the flesh."

The same is most probably true of the author of Wis. Sol. His intentions were indeed universalist, and his God hated none of the things that he had made. The High Priest is able to intercede for humanity, "for on his long robe the whole world was depicted" (Wis. 18:24).[116] For a Jew in first-century Alexandria, however, this was a difficult ideal to maintain. Custom and tradition led him to associate righteousness with the observance of the Jewish law, however modified. Conversely, the enemies of the Jews were "an accursed race from the beginning," and their wickedness was inbred (12:10–11). The pagan world offered few if any exemplars of virtue. When the Jewish community came increasingly under attack, the inclination to draw the lines between the holy people and the accursed foreigners was irresistible.

The fact that ethnic animosities surface in his work should not, however, detract from the sincerity or admirable character of the author's humanistic ideal.[117] At no point does he fault the Gentiles for failing to observe peculiarly

---

111. See A. Mendelson, *Philo's Jewish Identity* (Atlanta: Scholars, 1988) 103–13.
112. Ibid., 128–29.
113. *De Spec. Leg.* 2.163.
114. *De Vita Mos.* 2.44.
115. *Quaest Exod.* 2.2.
116. Compare Philo, *De Spec. Leg.* 1.66–97, where the truest temple of God is the whole universe.
117. Barclay, *The Jews in the Mediterranean Diaspora,* 190, misses the complexity of the book when he characterizes its primary tone as one of "cultural antagonism."

Jewish customs, or hold them to ideals that were not shared by some Gentile philosophers. The sins for which the Gentiles are condemned are idolatry and infanticide; they are not reproached for dietary observances or sabbath violation. The insistence that Egyptians deserved their fate is ultimately a reaction to *their* hostility to the Jews: "for they practiced a more bitter hatred of strangers. Others had refused to receive strangers when they came to them, but these made slaves of guests who were their benefactors" (Wis.19:13–14). The ancient story of captivity in Egypt was all too applicable to Jews who were faced with the hostility of Greeks and Egyptians in Roman Alexandria. It was a story of deliverance, not of conquest. The destruction of the enemy takes place because of their aggression toward the Israelites. Unlike other biblical stories and prophecies, it does not represent the establishment of Israelite rule over the Gentiles. It may well be that the Stoic ideal of *philanthrōpia* was ultimately incompatible with the Jewish claim to be God's chosen people, but the ethnic hostility that seeps through in Wis. Sol. 11–19 was a reflection of historical circumstances rather than a logical consequence of the author's ideology.

Chapter 12.
Epilogue: From Hebrew Wisdom
to Greek Philosophy

At the beginning of this book we noted that the category "wisdom literature" was not identified by systematic literary analysis but was prompted by the frequency of words meaning "wisdom" in certain books, and then extended by analogy to other books of similar content. The principle of analogy would certainly permit us to include a much larger corpus of literature than what we have considered here.[1] There is certainly merit in an inclusive approach, but there is also some danger that the concept of wisdom may become so broad as to cease to become useful. In this book we have chosen a narrower focus, by concentrating primarily on the two major wisdom books, the book of Ben Sira and the Wisdom of Solomon, with supplementary discussions of the Dead Sea Scrolls and Pseudo-Phocylides to fill in the context. Even with such a limited corpus, however, the variety that we have found is remarkable.

It is clear that wisdom literature is not held together by a single literary genre. Certain literary forms are characteristic of this literature and appear repeatedly, such as the gnomic sentence, the wisdom instruction, and poems in praise of wisdom. Even these forms take on different colorings when we move from Hebrew to Greek material and the conventions of Greek rhetoric come into play. At most we may speak of a macro-genre that encompasses various literary forms on a fairly high level of abstraction. Wisdom literature is primarily instructional literature, characterized by second-person forms of address. The classic form of this instruction is cast as the advice of a father to his son, but variations are possible. The second-person speech of Wis. Sol. 11–19 is addressed to God, although the passage is homiletic in character and has clear didactic implications. Wisdom also includes a significant amount of reflective material, in the form of assertions in the third person. This material may be considered "the expression of the actual," in von Rad's phrase,[2] but the expression can be highly tendentious. (Consider Ben Sira's "factual" statement that "from a woman sin had its beginning.") It is better regarded as a construction or construal of reality, and is often an expression of the conventional

---

1. See the inclusive survey of M. Küchler, *Frühjüdische Weisheitstraditionen* (OBO 26; Göttingen: Vandenhoeck & Ruprecht, 1979).

2. G. von Rad, *Wisdom in Israel* (Nashville: Abingdon, 1972) 115.

wisdom of the author's time and place. The hymnic and encomiastic praises of Wisdom are also reflective, and may be taken as attempts to construct a metaphysical view of reality. The praises of Wisdom are couched in more philosophical language in the Wisdom of Solomon than in Sirach.

While wisdom literature is thus a loose category, it is still possible to distinguish it from other forms of biblical and parabiblical writing. It is not narrative in form. When narrative elements are subsumed into these books (e.g., Wis. Sol. 10–19), they serve the purpose of illustrations. Wisdom does not claim to be inspired speech in the manner of prophecy (even though Ben Sira claimed to pour forth teaching like prophecy). Neither does it have the force of law, even though it often takes the form of commands and prohibitions. While the poems in praise of wisdom resemble hymns, this literature was not composed for liturgical use, and the wisdom poems are only subordinate elements within the whole. Wisdom literature sometimes approximates to philosophy, especially in the Wisdom of Solomon, but on the whole it does not pursue its analyses in a rigorous or sustained way. It generally avoids the abstract reasoning of the philosophers. So while wisdom literature does not constitute a very satisfactory literary genre, it has recognizable parameters, and the category is not arbitrary.

The Wisdom Tradition

The Jewish wisdom books may be considered to constitute a tradition that is held together by certain family resemblances rather than by a single literary form. Both Ben Sira and the Wisdom of Solomon draw heavily on Proverbs. Wisdom of Solomon also draws on Sirach, and the incorporation of Israelite history in the older wisdom book was an important precedent for the Alexandrian author.[3] Pseudo-Phocylides stands more directly in the tradition of Greek gnomic poetry, but has extensive parallels with Ben Sira in the area of social ethics. All of these books are in continuity with aspects of the book of Proverbs. But all of them also reflect the new environments in which they were written, and, they depart from the older biblical wisdom in significant ways.

In his excellent introduction to *Old Testament Wisdom,* James Crenshaw suggests that wisdom involves "a marriage between form and content."[4]

> Formally wisdom consists of proverbial sentence or instruction, debate, intellectual reflection; thematically, wisdom comprises self-evident intuitions about mastering life for human betterment, gropings after life's secrets with regard to innocent suffering, grappling with finitude, and quest for truth concealed in the created order and manifested in Dame Wisdom.

3. C. Larcher, *Études sur le Livre de la Sagesse* (Paris: Gabalda, 1969) 101.
4. J. L. Crenshaw, *Old Testament Wisdom: An Introduction* (Atlanta: John Knox, 1981) 19.

He suggests that "wisdom is a particular attitude toward reality, a world view."[5] The worldview consists in a way of looking at things that "begins with humans as the fundamental point of orientation. It asks what is good for men and women. And it believes that all essential answers can be learned in experience."[6] It is apparent that Crenshaw has only the wisdom books of the Hebrew Bible in mind in all of this, and is not reckoning with the new developments of the Hellenistic period. His usage, however, is typical of Old Testament scholarship, and he is certainly right that the wisdom books of the Hebrew Bible share a worldview as well as particular literary forms. This worldview involves more than a point of orientation. It also involves a set of assumptions about the universe. It affirms a world where there is an organic connection between cause and effect, where human fulfillment, such as it is, is to be found in this life, and where wisdom can be attained from accumulated experience without recourse to special revelations. This worldview is found primarily in Proverbs and is already called into question to some extent in Job and Qoheleth, but it undergoes more fundamental transformations in the Hellenistic age.

In the biblical context, the most distinctive feature of the wisdom books is their avoidance of the specific traditions of Israel. The wisdom they transmit is potentially available to any wise and righteous person, regardless of ethnic affiliation. It does not derive its authority from any special revelation of God to Israel. In this respect, the biblical wisdom books may be said to constitute an incipient form of natural theology, in the broad sense of the term—the idea that "just by being human beings, men and women have a certain degree of knowledge of God . . . or at least a capacity for such an awareness; and this knowledge or awareness exists anterior to the special revelation" to Israel.[7] This is not to suggest that wisdom teaching was based on reason alone, or that it attempted to prove the existence of God.[8] The Hebrew sages were not philosophers. Still less should they be considered secular. While they make no reference to the exodus or Sinai, their worldview is profoundly religious. It is oriented to creation rather than to the history of Israel, and so it might equally well be called creation theology.[9]

While they occasionally appeal to personal experience (primarily in the cases of Qoheleth and Job), the wisdom books are, for the most part, compendiums of traditional opinions. The strategy of the sages is well articulated by Bildad, in Job 8:8–10:

5. Ibid., 17.
6. Ibid., 18.
7. J. Barr, *Biblical Faith and Natural Theology* (Oxford: Clarendon, 1993) 1. Cf. J. J. Collins, "The Biblical Precedent for Natural Theology," *JAAR* 45/1 Supp. B (1977) 35–67.
8. These are other understandings of "natural theology" acknowledged by Barr, *Biblical Faith*, 2.
9. Leo G. Perdue, *Wisdom and Creation: The Theology of the Wisdom Literature* (Nashville: Abingdon, 1994), esp. 77–122.

> For inquire, I pray you, of bygone ages,
> and consider what the fathers have found;
> for we are but of yesterday, and know nothing,
> for our days on earth are a shadow.

The sages do not aspire to originality. Rather they reflect the consensus of their culture, and pass on the commonly accepted assumptions about reality. The biblical wisdom books do not give us the full range of ancient Israelite ideas about reality. They pay little attention to mythological beliefs, although the author of Job, at least, was familiar with them. They virtually ignore the cult. It is reasonable to believe, however, that what they give us was widely shared in Israelite society.

Sirach and the
Wisdom Tradition

The wisdom of Ben Sira is not greatly at variance with the worldview of Proverbs, despite the fact that it equates wisdom with the book of the Torah and draws its examples of great and famous men from the history of Israel. Sirach reads the Torah through the lens of Deuteronomy. He pays virtually no attention to the Priestly laws of Leviticus. Deuteronomy itself was heavily influenced by the older wisdom tradition,[10] and had already suggested the identification of wisdom and the Law. Apart from its focus on Israel, the worldview of Deuteronomy has much in common with that of Proverbs. The commandment is not something that has to be brought down from heaven, but is in your mouth and heart for you to observe it (Deut. 30:11–14; cf. Prov. 30:4). Deuteronomy assumes the same chain of act and consequence that is operative in Proverbs. One course of action leads to life, another to death (Deut. 30:19). Nonetheless, Deuteronomy differs radically from the wisdom tradition preserved in Proverbs in assuming a qualitative difference between Israel and the other nations.

The position of Ben Sira on the relation between Israel and the nations is open to dispute, but we have argued for a universalist interpretation. The Torah is the supreme manifestation of wisdom, but wisdom can also be found elsewhere. The law of Sinai is only a concretization of the wisdom implanted in the world at creation. In this respect, the Jerusalem sage anticipates Philo, the Jewish philosopher of Alexandria, who held that "the world is in harmony with the Law and the Law with the world" (*De Opif.* 3). But the idea that the Jewish Torah is identical with the best in human wisdom inevitably gives rise to tensions. These tensions barely become evident in Sirach. The Stoic-sounding

---

10. M. Weinfeld, *Deuteronomy and the Deuteronomistic School* (Oxford: Oxford Univ. Press, 1972); *Deuteronomy* (AB 5; New York: Doubleday, 1991) 62–65.

phrase "He is the all" (Sir. 43:27) is logically incompatible with the transcendence of God, which Sirach otherwise maintains. The notion that God's creation is made up of complementary opposites (33:15) entails divine responsibility for evil in a way that the sage is reluctant to endorse. If these tensions do not become more apparent in Sirach, it is only because he fails to explore the implications of his identification of Wisdom and the Law. His use of the history of Israel remains unproblematic, because he draws from it examples of glorious and distinguished men, with virtually no philosophical reflection.

In addition to the difficulties posed by incorporating Israelite history into wisdom teaching, another set of problems arises from the changing worldviews of the Hellenistic age. Wisdom teaching tended to reproduce conventional beliefs. Some of the beliefs that were conventional in the time of Proverbs were undergoing change by the time Ben Sira wrote. Hellenistic ideas play only a modest role in Sirach. The Stoic ideas cited above are cases in point. The increased importance of honor and shame in the sage's ethical teaching also betrays the Hellenistic context, but these ideas were not completely alien to Israelite tradition. Sirach stood firm in rejecting the belief in retribution after death that was gaining ground in his time, and consequently he continued to view the context of human decision making in terms very similar to those of Proverbs or Deuteronomy.

That context changes, however, in the text called Sapiential Work A, from Qumran. Here ethical decisions are informed by "the mystery that is to be" (*raz nihyeh*), which includes the prospect of eschatological judgment. Even though the actual ethical advice given in this document is paralleled in Sirach at many points,[11] its presuppositions are different in two crucial respects. First, the "mystery" is not accessible to everyone, but presupposes a special revelation to a select group. Second, the notion of eschatological judgment radically alters the this-worldly perspective of Proverbs. On both of these points, the text from Qumran is influenced by another tradition that emerges in the Hellenistic period, that of apocalypticism.

Wisdom and Apocalypticism

The apocalypses of *Enoch* and Daniel in the early second century B.C.E. introduce a view of the world that is sharply at variance not only with the biblical wisdom books, but with the Hebrew Bible as a whole.[12] This new worldview is distinguished primarily by the increased importance attached to

11. D. J. Harrington, "Wisdom at Qumran," in E. Ulrich and J. VanderKam, eds., *The Community of the Renewed Covenant* (Notre Dame, Ind.: Univ. of Notre Dame Press, 1994) 137–52.

12. See my essay, "The Place of Apocalypticism in the Religion of Israel," in P. D. Miller, P. D. Hanson, and S. D. McBride, eds., *Ancient Israelite Religion: Essays in Honor of Frank Moore Cross* (Philadelphia: Fortress, 1987) 539–58.

supernatural agents and a world beyond this one, and by the hope for judgment and vindication beyond death. Of course, belief in the supernatural world was commonplace in antiquity. What was novel was the degree to which this world was thought to impinge on human affairs and the belief that human beings could have access to it. This novelty is readily evident if we compare the various components of *1 Enoch* with Ben Sira.

The relations between wisdom and apocalypticism have been the subject of two distinct debates in recent biblical scholarship. In the context of the Hebrew Bible, the debate has centered around the controversial claim of Gerhard von Rad that wisdom is "the real matrix from which apocalyptic literature originates."[13] This claim has not been accepted, but it has contributed to a tendency to refer to the content of apocalyptic revelations as a kind of wisdom, although a very different kind from that which we find in Proverbs and Qoheleth.[14] In New Testament scholarship the debate has centered on the mixture of apocalyptic and sapiential material in the sayings source Q. Some scholars have argued that these two kinds of material represent different redactional layers, with the wisdom sayings constituting the older stratum.[15] Burton Mack has argued that this conclusion "turns the tables on older views of Jesus as an apocalyptic preacher and brings the message of Jesus around to another style of speech altogether."[16] There is an implication here that there is some inherent incompatibility between sapiential sayings and apocalypticism.

The Sapiential texts from Qumran throw some new light on both of these debates. Sapiential Work A shows close parallels both with the antiapocalyptic wisdom of Ben Sira, on the one hand, and the quintessentially apocalyptic Instruction on the Two Spirits, on the other. It lends credence to the view that there was continuity between the sages of Qumran, who attached great importance to the Torah, and the kind of wisdom school represented by Ben Sira.[17] It does not, however, throw any light on the origins of apocalypticism in Judaism.[18] The oldest apocalypses, in *1 Enoch* and Daniel, are not characterized by reflection on the Torah, and are far more likely to have influenced the

---

13. G. von Rad, *Old Testament Theology* (New York: Harper, 1965) 2.306.

14. E.g., Küchler, *Frühjüdische Weisheitstraditionen*, 62–87 ("Die Weisheit der Apokalyptiker").

15. H. Koester, "GNOMAI DIAPHOROI: The Origin and Nature of Diversification in the History of Early Christianity," in J. M. Robinson and H. Koester, eds., *Trajectories through Early Christianity* (Philadelphia: Fortress, 1971) 138; J. S. Kloppenborg, *The Formation of Q: Trajectories in Ancient Wisdom Collections* (Philadelphia: Fortress, 1987) 317.

16. B. L. Mack, *A Myth of Innocence: Mark and Christian Origins* (Philadelphia: Fortress, 1988) 59.

17. J. J. Collins, "Wisdom, Apocalypticism and the Dead Sea Scrolls," in A. A. Diesel et al., eds., *"'Jedes Ding hat seine Zeit . . .': Studien zur israelitischen und altorientalischen Weisheit* (BZAW 241; Berlin: de Gruyter, 1996) 19–32.

18. *Pace* A. Lange, *Weisheit und Prädestination* (Leiden: Brill, 1995) 301–6, who argues that the Qumran texts support the thesis of von Rad.

sapiential texts from Qumran than vice versa. The apocalyptic elements in Sapiential Work A testify to the influence of apocalypticism on the wisdom schools rather than to the influence of wisdom on apocalypticism.

The Sapiential Work from Qumran should give pause to those who take wisdom and apocalypticism as mutually incompatible forms of discourse. Even before this text became available, there was ample evidence that the two kinds of material could be combined in various ways.[19] The apocalyptic belief in eschatological judgment provided a frame for ethical exhortation, by holding out the prospect of everlasting reward or punishment. In many apocalypses, the exhortation is implicit,[20] but it is sometimes spelled out in forms that resemble those of the wisdom literature. Perhaps the clearest use of a sapiential instruction in an apocalyptic context is found in the second *Sibylline Oracle,* a Christian adaptation of a Jewish oracle, probably from the second century C.E.[21] The Jewish oracle was organized around the familiar Sibylline schema of ten generations. At the end of the description of the tenth generation, the Christian redactor inserted a passage about "a great contest for entry to the heavenly city. It will be universal for all men, holding the glory of immortality" (*Sib. Or.* 2:39–55). At this point there is inserted a lengthy extract from the sayings of Pseudo-Phocylides. At the end of the extract the Sibyllist resumes, "This is the contest, these are the prizes, these the awards" (2:149). The extract from Pseudo-Phocylides is evidently meant to supply the rules for the contest, the criteria for the apocalyptic judgment. This is clearly a secondary usage of the sapiential material. The sentences are inserted intact, and not redacted. (There are a few omissions.) There is none of the eschatological urgency here that is typical of apocalyptic material. Rather, we find the typical sapiential ethic of moderation: "Do not gain wealth unjustly, but live from legitimate things" (v. 56); "Do not damage your mind with wine or drink to excess" (v. 95). The sayings represent everyday wisdom, and are not materially altered by their new context. While this text is exceptional in many respects, it may serve as a warning that ancient writers could sometimes juxtapose materials that seem ideologically incompatible to us.

In other cases, the content of the wisdom is integrally related to the apocalyptic context. The Epistle of Enoch (*1 Enoch* 91–104) is the last major section of the collection we know as *1 Enoch.* The affinity of the Epistle with wisdom instructions is apparent from the exordium: "Hear my children, all the words of your father and listen properly to the voice of my mouth" (91:3). The ensuing instruction distinguishes repeatedly between the wise and the foolish. The typical form con-

---

19. J. J. Collins, "Wisdom, Apocalypticism and Generic Compatibility," in L. G. Perdue et al., eds., *In Search of Wisdom: Essays in Memory of John G. Gammie* (Louisville, Ky.: Westminster John Knox, 1993) 165–85.

20. E.g., the wise in Daniel 11 are said to instruct the *rabbim,* but the actual instruction is not recorded.

21. J. J. Collins, "The Sibylline Oracles," in *OTP* 1.345–53.

sists of an exhortation or admonition, followed by a short motivation clause (e.g., 94:1: "And now I say to you my children, love righteousness and walk in it; for the paths of righteousness are worthy of acceptance, but the paths of iniquity will quickly be destroyed and vanish"). The subject matter of Enoch's instruction is quite traditional and is primarily concerned with the exploitation of the poor by the rich. It differs from other sapiential instructions in two respects. First, the authority to which he lays claim derives from his knowledge of the heavenly tablets. His utterances, therefore, have the quality of revelation, and give his instruction a prophetic as well as a sapiential tone. Second, the primary motivating factor is the expectation of judgment, and the assurance for the righteous that they "will shine like the lights of heaven and will be seen, and the gate of heaven will be opened to you" (104:2). As a corollary of this, it is a premise of the apocalyptic worldview that earthly wealth is fleeting, and this conviction strengthens the woes against the wicked. Unlike the sayings of Pseudo-Phocylides in *Sibylline Oracles* 2, the words of Enoch are thoroughly permeated with an apocalyptic worldview.[22]

The Sapiential Text from Qumran shows an even closer fusion of wisdom forms and apocalyptic worldview. Formally, this text is a wisdom instruction. Much of the practical wisdom it inculcates is similar to what we find in Ben Sira. But the presuppositions of this author about the nature of the world and human destiny are very different from those of Sirach, since they are predicated on a mystery and expect an eschatological judgment. This text shows that the form of the wisdom instruction was not inherently wedded to the kind of worldview that we find in Proverbs, but could just as well be used in the service of an apocalyptic worldview.

The Sapiential text from Qumran also shows that wisdom forms are not inherently wedded to natural theology. The *raz nihyeh* is not available to humanity at large, but presupposes a special revelation, just like the instruction of Enoch. The Qumran sage can draw on common wisdom about honoring parents and wealth and poverty, just as the Sibyl can draw on the sayings of Pseudo-Phocylides. But in each case the "natural" wisdom is subordinated to the revelation or inspiration to which the writers lay claim.

Wisdom and Hellenistic Philosophy

The Wisdom of Solomon is also influenced by apocalyptic traditions in its depiction of the judgment of the dead.[23] It also speaks of "the mysteries of God" (Wis. 2:22). In this case, however, the apocalyptic elements are recast in

---

22. Compare also the combination of sapiential instruction and eschatology in the *Testaments of the Twelve Patriarchs* and in *2 Enoch* 39–66; Collins, "Wisdom, Apocalypticism and Generic Compatibility," 177–79.

23. J. J. Collins, "Cosmos and Salvation: Jewish Wisdom and Apocalyptic in the Hellenistic Age," *HR* 17 (1977) 121–42.

the language of Greek philosophy, by adapting the Platonic notion of the immortality of the soul. Despite the allusion to "mysteries," Wis. Sol. continues the search of the sages for a natural theology, antecedent to special revelation. The Alexandrian author was considerably more sophisticated philosophically than Ben Sira, but for that very reason his book exposes the tensions and difficulties of trying to combine natural theology with biblical revelation.

The key passage on natural theology in Wis. Sol. is found in 13:1–9, and we have discussed it in Chapter 11 above. The author vacillates as to whether Gentiles (more specifically Gentile philosophers) are culpable for failing to reach the knowledge of the true God, and he acknowledges that human reason can hardly guess at what is on earth, much less what is in heaven. Yet he does hold them responsible, for if they had power to know so much, why did they fail to discover the Lord of all? The argument assumes that philosophical reasoning should lead to the conclusion that one God has created the world. While Wis. Sol. can scarcely be said to have supplied the necessary arguments, the author could claim adequate support for this position among the philosophers of his day. It seems clear, however, that the author's own belief is not the fruit of philosophical reasoning, but of the faith inherited from his religious tradition. His use of philosophy seems to be rhetorical rather than constructive, but it does attest to his conviction that the truth is one, and is accessible in principle to Greek as well as Jew.

A more severe difficulty attends the attempt of Wis. Sol. to incorporate the history of Israel into the author's universalist theology. Ben Sira's use of biblical history was relatively unproblematic. He used the great figures of the Bible as exemplars of civic accomplishment. Wisdom of Solomon, however, attempts to glean a more profound moral, and even cosmological, lesson by using the story of the exodus as a paradigm of virtue and wickedness. Consequently, Israel becomes "a holy people and a blameless race," while the Egyptians are "a nation of oppressors" and the Canaanites were deservedly punished because of their idolatry. Wisdom of Solomon does not name names, and so leaves open the possibility that there may be other holy peoples and nations of oppressors. The author appears to be interested in the type rather than in the historical particulars. Nonetheless, many commentators have found here "undisguised particularism," and undoubtedly the book reflects the animosities of Roman Egypt in the first century C.E. There is an undeniable tension between the avowed universalism, according to which the creator loves all things that exist "for they are yours" (11:26), and the identification of the author's own ancestors as God's people and children in a special sense.

In the case of both Philo and the Wisdom of Solomon, the use made of Greek philosophy was selective. The Jewish authors made much use of Stoic concepts, but ultimately the structure of their thought was Platonic. Platonism allowed them to affirm the transcendence of God, as opposed to the immanent

deity of the Stoics. The doctrine of immortality of the soul was acceptable because the belief in a significant afterlife had been popularized in Judaism by the apocalyptic writers. Nonetheless, the biblical tradition was greatly altered when it was interpreted through Platonic lenses. The emphasis on immortality leads to the reversal of much of Ben Sira's value system and opens the way for an ascetic view of life, where childlessness and early death can be viewed positively. The claim that God did not make death also bespeaks a view of the universe that is far removed from that of the Hebrew sage. Still, Pseudo-Solomon believed that he was affirming the essentials of his tradition in affirming the one creator God and rejecting idolatry, infanticide, and sexual perversions. On each of these points he was taking a stand against Greek popular culture but could claim the support of the more enlightened philosophers.

The attempt to combine natural theology, through the medium of Greek philosophy, with biblical revelation set the tone for much of Western theology down to modern times. In his great opus on Philo of Alexandria, Harry Wolfson argued that it was Philo who inaugurated medieval philosophy, by insisting that "since God is the author both of the truths made known by revelation and of the truths made known by reason, there can be no conflict between them."[24] In fact, this principle is already implicit in Sirach's identification of Wisdom and the Torah, but Sirach lacks stature in the history of philosophy. There were other antecedents in Hellenistic Judaism, notably the second-century philosopher Aristobulus,[25] but it is Philo who first explores this principle at length and in depth. The Wisdom of Solomon comes from the same world as Philo, but presents its argument in rhetorical form rather than through philosophical analysis. Because of its stature as scripture in the Catholic Church, Wis. Sol. arguably had greater influence than the Jewish philosopher.

Neither Wis. Sol. nor Philo wished to assert (or even conceived of) the autonomy of reason. Both insisted on the need for divine assistance, through Wisdom or the Logos. But both also insisted on the ability of human reason to arrive at some apprehension of God, and both saw the work of Wisdom as complementary to human inquiry, in no way antithetical to it.

The understanding of natural theology that was inaugurated by the Wisdom of Solomon and Philo received an influential endorsement in the epistle to the Romans, where Paul asserted that "what can be known about God is plain to them [the Gentiles], because God has shown it to them. Ever since the creation of the world his eternal power and divine nature, invisible though they are, have been understood and seen through the things he has made" (Rom. 1:19–20). Again, in Rom. 2:14, Paul allows that the Gentiles who do not have

24. H. A. Wolfson, *Philo* (Cambridge, Mass.: Harvard Univ. Press, 1947) 2.447.
25. See C. R. Holladay, *Fragments from Hellenistic Jewish Authors,* vol. 3, *Aristobulus* (Atlanta: Scholars, 1995).

the Law may "do by nature [*physei*] the things of the law." The relation of Paul
to natural theology is complex, and cannot be adequately discussed here. In 1
Cor. 1:22 he sets Christ crucified, the foolishness of God, over against "the wisdom of the Greeks," as if these were antithetical. But whatever the place of natural theology in Paul's thought as a whole, he at least makes passing use of it
in formulating his argument in Romans 1 and 2, and he is also credited with an
appeal to natural theology in the speech on the Areopagus in Acts 17:16–31.[26]
By virtue of these passages, Paul lent a powerfully authoritative voice to natural theology in the Christian tradition.

That tradition received its classic formulation from Thomas Aquinas in the
Summa Theologica, First Part, Article 12. Thomas cites Romans 1, but the discussion seems closer to the formulation of Wis. Sol. 13:

> Our natural knowledge takes its beginning from sense. Hence our natural knowl-
> edge can go as far as it can be led by sensible things, but our mind cannot be led
> by sense so far as to see the essence of God, because the sensible effects of God
> do not equal the power of God as their cause. Hence from the knowledge of sen-
> sible things the whole power of God cannot be known; nor therefore can His
> essence be seen. But because they are His effects and depend on their cause, we
> can be led from them so far as to know of God whether He exists, and to know
> of Him what must necessarily belong to Him as the first cause of all things, ex-
> ceeding all things caused by Him.

Neither Thomas nor any authentic "natural theologian" suggested that God
can be fully or adequately known by human reason, but he affirmed that natural human knowledge has its fulfillment and goal in the knowledge of God.
In this he continued an approach to theology that had its roots in the Jewish
wisdom writings of the Hellenistic age.

26. See Barr, *Biblical Faith and Natural Theology,* 21–57; G. Bornkamm, "Gesetz und Natur:
Röm 2, 14–16," in idem, *Studien zu Antike und Urchristentum* (Munich: Kaiser, 1959) 111, 117.

Abusch, T., "Gilgamesh's Request and Siduri's Denial," Part One in M. E. Cohen et al., eds., *The Tablet and the Scroll: Near Eastern Studies in Honor
of W. W. Hallo* (Bethesda, Md.: CDL Press, 1993) 1–14; Part Two in
JANESCU 22 (1993) 3–17.

Adkins, A. W. H., *Moral Values and Political Behavior in Ancient Greece*
(London: Chatto & Windus, 1972).

Alexander, P. S., "Incantations and Books of Magic," in Schürer, *The History
of the Jewish People*, 3.342–79.

Allegro, J. M., "The Wiles of the Wicked Woman, a Sapiential Work from
Qumran's Fourth Cave," *PEQ* 96 (1964) 53–55.

———, *Qumrân Cave 4.1 (4Q158–4Q186) (DJD* 5; Oxford: Clarendon,
1968).

Alon, G., "The Halakah in the Teaching of the Twelve Apostles," in idem, *Studies in Jewish History in the Times of the Second Temple, the Mishnah and
the Talmud* (Jerusalem: Hakibbutz Hameuchad, 1957) 1.274–94 (Heb.).

Amir, Y., "The Figure of Death in the 'Book of Wisdom,'" *JJS* 30 (1979)
154–78.

Applebaum, S., "Jewish Urban Communities and Greek Influences," in *Judaea
in Hellenistic and Roman Times* (Leiden: Brill, 1989) 30–46.

———, "The Legal Status of the Jewish Communities in the Diaspora," in
S. Safrai and M. Stern, eds., *The Jewish People in the First Century* (CRINT
1/1; Assen: Van Gorcum/Philadelphia: Fortress, 1974) 420–63.

———, "The Organization of the Jewish Communities in the Diaspora," in
S. Safrai and M. Stern, eds., *The Jewish People in the First Century* (CRINT
1/1; Assen: Van Gorcum/Philadelphia: Fortress, 1974) 464–503.

Archer, L. J., *Her Price Is Beyond Rubies: The Jewish Woman in Graeco-
Roman Palestine* (Sheffield: JSOT Press, 1990).

Argall, R. A., *1 Enoch and Sirach: A Comparative Literary and Conceptual
Analysis of the Themes of Revelation, Creation and Judgment* (Atlanta:
Scholars, 1995).

Attridge, H. W., *First-Century Cynicism in the Epistles of Heraclitus* (Missoula, Mont.: Scholars, 1976).

Baillet, M., J. T. Milik, and R. de Vaux, *Les 'Petites Grottes' de Qumrân (DJD 3*; Oxford: Clarendon, 1962).

Balch, D. L., *Let Wives Be Submissive: The Domestic Code in 1 Peter* (SBLMS 26; Chico, Calif.: Scholars, 1981).

Balch, D. L., "Household Codes," in D. E. Aune, ed., *Greco-Roman Literature and the New Testament: Selected Forms and Genres* (Atlanta: Scholars, 1988) 25–50.

Barclay, J. M. G., *Jews in the Mediterranean Diaspora, from Alexander to Trajan (323 BCE – 117 CE)* (Edinburgh: T. & T. Clark, 1996).

Barr, J., *Biblical Faith and Natural Theology* (Oxford: Clarendon, 1993).

Barrett, C. K., *The New Testament Background: Selected Documents* (San Francisco: Harper & Row, 1987).

Barton, J., *Oracles of God: Perceptions of Ancient Prophecy in Israel after the Exile* (Oxford: Oxford Univ. Press, 1986).

Bauckmann, E. G., "Die Proverbien und die Sprüche des Jesus Sirach: Eine Untersuchung zum Strukturwandel der israelitischen Weisheitslehre," *ZAW* 72 (1960) 33–63.

Bauer, J. B., ed., *Memoria Jerusalem* (Jerusalem/Graz: Akademische Druck- und Verlagsanstalt, 1977).

Baumgarten, J., "On the Nature of the Seductress in 4Q184," *RevQ* 57 (1991) 133–43.

Baumgartner, W., "Die literarischen Gattungen in der Weisheit des Jesus Sirach," *ZAW* 34 (1914) 161–98.

Beauchamp, P., "Le salut corporel dans le livre de la Sagesse," *Bib* 45 (1964) 491–526.

Beentjes, P. C., "'Full Wisdom Is Fear of the Lord.' Ben Sira 19, 20–20, 31: Context, Composition and Concept," *Estudios Bíblicos* 47 (1989) 27–45.

Begg, C. R., "Ben Sirach's Non-Mention of Ezra," *BN* 42 (1988) 14–18.

Berman, J., *Ich Bin Isis* (Uppsala: Almquist & Wiksells, 1968).

Bernays, J., *Über das phokylideische Gedicht: Ein Beitrag zur hellenistischen Literatur* (Berlin, 1856); reprinted in Bernays's *Gesammelte Abhandlungen* (Berlin: Hertz, 1885) 192–261.

Betz, H. D., *The Sermon on the Mount* (Hermeneia; Minneapolis: Fortress, 1995).

Bickerman, E. J., "La Charte séleucide de Jérusalem," in idem, *Studies in Jewish and Christian History* (Leiden: Brill, 1980) 2.44–85.

———, "Une question d'authenticité: les privilèges Juifs," in idem, *Studies in Jewish and Christian History* 2.24–43.

———, *The Jews in the Greek Age* (Cambridge, Mass.: Harvard Univ. Press, 1988).

Bizzetti, P., *Il Libro della Sapienza* (Brescia: Paideia, 1984).

Blenkinsopp, J., *Ezra-Nehemiah: A Commentary* (OTL; Philadelphia: Westminster, 1988).

Bloch, A., and C. Bloch, *The Song of Songs* (New York: Random House, 1995).

Boccaccini, G., "The Preexistence of the Torah: A Commonplace in Second Temple Judaism or a Later Rabbinic Development?" *Henoch* 17 (1995) 329–48.

Bohlen, R., *Die Ehrung der Eltern bei Ben Sira* (Trier: Paulinus, 1991).

Borgen, P., " 'There Shall Come Forth a Man': Reflections on Messianic Ideas in Philo," in J. H. Charlesworth, ed., *The Messiah* (Minneapolis: Fortress, 1992) 341–61.

Bornkamm, G., "Gesetz und Natur: Röm 2,14–16," in idem, *Studien zu Antike und Urchristentum* (Munich: Kaiser, 1959) 2.93–118.

Borries, B. de, *Quid veteres philosophi de idolatria senserint* (Göttingen: Dieterich, 1918).

Box, G. H., and W. O. E. Oesterley, "Sirach," in *APOT* 1.298–303.

Braun, R., *Kohelet und die frühhellenistische Popularphilosophie* (BZAW 130; Berlin: de Gruyter, 1973).

Brooten, B. J., *Love between Women: Early Christian Responses to Homoeroticism* (Chicago: Univ. of Chicago Press, 1996).

Bryce, G. E., *A Legacy of Wisdom: The Egyptian Contribution to the Wisdom of Israel* (Lewisburg, Pa.: Bucknell Univ. Press, 1979).

Büchler, A., "Ben Sira's Conception of Sin and Atonement," *JQR* 13 (1922/23) 303–35.

Budge, E. A. Wallis, *Facsimiles of Egyptian Hieratic Papyri in the British Museum with Descriptions, Summaries of Contents, Etc.* (Second Series; London: Harrison & Sons, 1923).

Burgmann, H., "The Wicked Woman: Der Makkabäer Simon?" *RevQ* 8 (1974) 323–59.

Camp, C., "Understanding a Patriarchy: Women in Second Century Jerusalem Through the Eyes of Ben Sira," in A. J. Levine, ed., *"Women like This": New Perspectives on Jewish Women in the Greco-Roman World* (Atlanta: Scholars, 1991) 1–39.

———, "Woman Wisdom as Root Metaphor: A Theological Consideration," in Hoglund et al., eds., *The Listening Heart,* 45–76.

Caquot, A., "Ben Sira et le Messianisme," *Semitica* 16 (1966) 43–68.

Carmignac, J., "Poème allegorique sur la secte rivale," *RevQ* 5 (1965) 361–74.

Ceresko, A. R., "The Sage in the Psalms," in Gammie and Perdue, eds., *The Sage in Israel and the Ancient Near East,* 217–30.

Charlesworth, J. H., ed., *The Old Testament Pseudepigrapha* (2 vols.; New York: Doubleday, 1983, 1985).

Clarke, M. L., *Higher Education in the Ancient World* (London: Routledge, 1971).

Clifford, R. J., "Proverbs IX: A Suggested Ugaritic Parallel," *VT* 25 (1975) 298–306.

Cohen, S. J. D., "Crossing the Boundary and Becoming a Jew," *HTR* 82 (1989) 13–33.

————, " 'Those Who Say They Are Jews and Are Not': How Do You Know a Jew in Antiquity When You See One?" in S. J. D. Cohen and E. S. Frerichs, eds., *Diasporas in Antiquity* (Atlanta: Scholars, 1993) 1–45.

Collins, J. J., "Apocalyptic Eschatology as the Transcendence of Death," *CBQ* 36 (1974) 21–43.

————, "Cosmos and Salvation: Jewish Wisdom and Apocalyptic in the Hellenistic Age," *HR* 17 (1977) 121–42.

————, "The Biblical Precedent for Natural Theology," *JAAR* 45/1 Supp. B (1977) 35–67.

————, "The Root of Immortality: Death in the Context of Jewish Wisdom," *HTR* 71 (1978) 177–92.

————, "Proverbial Wisdom and the Yahwist Vision," *Semeia* 17 (1980) 1–17.

————, *Between Athens and Jerusalem: Jewish Identity in the Hellenistic Diaspora* (New York: Crossroad, 1983).

————, "A Symbol of Otherness: Circumcision and Salvation in the First Century," in J. Neusner and E. S. Frerichs, eds., *To See Ourselves as Others See Us: Christians, Jews, "Others" in Late Antiquity* (Chico, Calif.: Scholars, 1985) 179–85.

————, "The Biblical Vision of the Common Good," in O. F. Williams and J. W. Houck, eds., *The Common Good and U. S. Capitalism* (Lanham, Md.: University Press of America, 1987) 50–69.

————, "The Place of Apocalypticism in the Religion of Israel," in P. D. Miller, P. D. Hanson, and S. D. McBride, eds., *Ancient Israelite Religion: Essays in Honor of Frank Moore Cross* (Philadelphia: Fortress, 1987) 539–58.

————, *Daniel* (Minneapolis: Fortress, 1993).

————, "Wisdom, Apocalypticism, and Generic Compatibility," in Perdue et al., eds., *In Search of Wisdom,* 165–85.

————, "Before the Canon: Scriptures in Second Temple Judaism," in J. L. Mays et al., eds., *Past, Present and Future: Essays in Honor of Gene M. Tucker.* Old Testament Interpretation (Nashville: Abingdon, 1995) 225–41.

————, "The Origin of Evil in Apocalyptic Literature and the Dead Sea Scrolls," in J. A. Emerton, ed., *Congress Volume: Paris* (Leiden: Brill, 1995) 25–38.

————, *The Scepter and the Star: The Messiahs of the Dead Sea Scrolls and Other Ancient Literature* (New York: Doubleday, 1995).

————, "Wisdom, Apocalypticism and the Dead Sea Scrolls," in A. A. Diesel et al., eds., *"Jedes Ding hat seine Zeit . . ." Studien zur israelitischen und altorientalischen Weisheit: Diethelm Michel zum 65. Geburtstag* (BZAW 241; Berlin: de Gruyter, 1996) 19–32.

————, *Apocalypticism in the Dead Sea Scrolls* (London: Routledge, 1997).

————, "Marriage, Divorce, and Family in Second Temple Judaism," in L. G. Perdue et al., *Families in Ancient Israel* (Louisville, Ky.: Westminster, 1997) 104–62.

Conzelmann, H., "The Mother of Wisdom," in J. M. Robinson, ed., *The Future of Our Religious Past* (New York: Harper, 1971) 230–43.

Couard, L., *Die religiösen und sittlichen Anschauungen der alttestamentlichen Apokryphen und Pseudepigraphen* (Gütersloh: Mohn, 1907).

Cowey, J., "Zwei Archive aus dem zweite Jahrhundert vor Christus," a paper presented to the Twenty-First International Congress of Papyrology in Berlin in August 1995.

Crenshaw, J. L., "The Problem of Theodicy in Sirach: On Human Bondage," *JBL* 94 (1975) 47–64.

————, *Old Testament Wisdom: An Introduction* (Atlanta: John Knox, 1981).

————, "The Shadow of Death in Qoheleth," in Gammie, ed., *Israelite Wisdom*, 205–16.

————, "Wisdom and Authority: Sapiential Rhetoric and Its Warrants," in J. A. Emerton, ed., *Congress Volume: Vienna, 1980* (VTSup 32; Leiden: Brill, 1981) 10–29.

————, ed., *Theodicy in the Old Testament* (Philadelphia: Fortress, 1983).

————, "Education in Ancient Israel," *JBL* 104 (1985) 601–15.

————, "The Wisdom Literature," in D. A. Knight and G. M. Tucker, eds., *The Hebrew Bible and Its Modern Interpreters*, 369–407.

————, *Ecclesiastes* (OTL; Philadelphia: Westminster, 1987).

————, "The Sage in Proverbs," in Gammie and Perdue, eds., *The Sage in Israel and the Ancient Near East*, 205–16.

Cross, F. M., "Papyri of the Fourth Century B.C. from Dâliyeh," in D. N. Freedman and J. C. Greenfield, eds., *New Directions in Biblical Archaeology* (New York: Doubleday, 1969) 41–62.

Crouch, J. E., *The Origin and Intention of the Colossian Haustafel* (Göttingen: Vandenhoeck & Ruprecht, 1972).

Dalbert, P., *Die Theologie der Hellenistisch-Jüdischen Missionsliteratur unter Ausschluss von Philo und Josephus* (Hamburg: Reich, 1954).

Davies, P. R., *In Search of Ancient Israel* (JSOTSup 148; Sheffield: Sheffield Academic Press, 1992).

————, "Scenes from the Early History of Judaism," in D. V. Edelman, ed., *The Triumph of Elohim: From Yahwisms to Judaisms* (Kampen: Kok, 1995) 145–82.

Day, P. L., ed., *Gender and Difference in Ancient Israel* (Minneapolis: Fortress, 1989).

Delcor, M., "L'immortalité de l'âme dans le livre de la Sagesse et dans les documents de Qumrân," *NRT* 77 (1955) 614–30.

Delia, D., *Alexandrian Citizenship during the Roman Principate* (Atlanta: Scholars, 1991).

Delorme, J., *Gymnasion* (Paris: Boccard, 1960).

Denis, A.-M., *Les thèmes de connaissance dans le Document de Damas* (Studia Hellenistica 15; Louvain: Leuven Univ. Press, 1967).

Derron, P., *Pseudo-Phocylide: Sentences* (Paris: Société d'Édition "Les Belles Lettres," 1986).

des Places, E., "Epithètes et attributs de la 'Sagesse' (Sg 7,22–23 et SVF 1 557 Arnim)," *Bib* 57 (1976) 414–19.

Deutsch, C., "The Sirach 51 Acrostic: Confession and Exhortation," *ZAW* 94 (1982) 400–409.

Dey, L. K. K., *The Intermediary World and Patterns of Perfection in Philo and Hebrews* (SBLDS 25; Missoula, Mont.: Scholars, 1975).

Dihle, A., "Ethik," *RAC* 6 (1966) 667–68.

DiLella, A. A., *The Hebrew Text of Sirach* (The Hague: Mouton, 1966).

———, "The Meaning of Wisdom in Ben Sira," in Perdue et al., eds., *In Search of Wisdom*, 133–48.

Dillon, J. M., *The Middle Platonists: A Study of Platonism 80 B.C. to A.D. 220* (London: Duckworth, 1977).

———, "'Orthodoxy' and 'Eclecticism': Middle Platonists and Neo-Pythagoreans," in J. M. Dillon and A. A. Long, eds., *The Question of "Eclecticism": Studies in Later Greek Philosophy* (Berkeley: Univ. of California Press, 1988) 103–25.

Dimant, D., "Pseudonymity in the Wisdom of Solomon," in N. Fernández Marcos, ed., *La Septuaginta en la investigación contemporánea (V Congreso de la IOSCS)* (Madrid: Instituto "Arias Montano" C.S.I.C., 1985) 243–55.

Dodds, E. R., *The Greeks and the Irrational* (Berkeley: Univ. of California Press, 1951).

———, *Proclus: The Elements of Theology* (Oxford: Oxford Univ. Press, 1963).

Doran, R., "Jason's Gymnasion," in H. W. Attridge et al., eds., *Of Scribes and Scrolls: Studies on the Hebrew Bible, Intertestamental Judaism and Christian Origins* (Lanham, Md.: University Press of America, 1990) 99–109.

Dover, K. J., *Greek Homosexuality* (London: Duckworth, 1978).

———, *Greek Popular Morality* (Indianapolis: Hackett, 1994).

Dupont-Sommer, A., "Les 'impies' du Livre de la Sagesse ne sont-ils pas des Épicuriens?" *RHR* 111 (1935) 9–109.

Edersheim, A., "Ecclesiasticus," in H. Wace, ed., *The Holy Bible According to the Authorised Version: Apocrypha* (London: Murray, 1888) 2.1–239.

Eisenman, R. H., and M. Wise, *The Dead Sea Scrolls Uncovered* (Rockport, Mass.: Element, 1992).

Elgvin, T., "Admonition Texts from Qumran Cave 4," in M. O. Wise et al., eds., *Methods of Investigation of the Dead Sea Scrolls and the Khirbet*

Qumran Site: Present Realities and Future Prospects (New York: New York Academy of Arts and Sciences, 1994) 179–94.

———, "4Q423," *DJD* 20 (forthcoming).

———, "Early Essene Eschatology: Judgment and Salvation According to Sapiential Work A," in N. Reynolds and D. Parry, eds., *Proceedings of the Judaean Desert Scrolls Conference at Brigham Young University, 1995* (Leiden: Brill, forthcoming).

———, "The Mystery to Come: Early Essene Theology of Revelation," in T. L. Thompson, and N. P. Lemche, eds., *Qumran Between the Old and the New Testament* (Sheffield: Sheffield Academic Press, forthcoming).

———, "Wisdom, Revelation and Eschatology in an Early Essene Writing," in E. H. Lovering, ed., *SBL Seminar Papers* (Atlanta: Scholars, 1995) 440–63.

Ellis, E. E., *The Old Testament in Early Christianity* (WUNT 54; Tübingen: Mohr, 1991).

Engel, H., " 'Was Weisheit ist und wie sie entstand, will ich verkünden': Weish 7,22–8,1 innerhalb des *egkōmion tēs sophias* (6,22–11,1) als Stärkung der Plausibilität des Judentums angesichts hellenistischer Philosophie und Religiosität," in G. Hentschel and E. Zenger, eds., *Lehrerin der Gerechtigkeit* (Leipzig: Benno, 1991) 67–102.

Englund, G. "Gods as a Frame of Reference: On Thinking and Concepts of Thought in Ancient Egypt," in idem, ed., *The Religion of the Ancient Egyptians: Cognitive Structures and Popular Expressions* (Stockholm: Almqvist & Wiksell, 1989) 7–28.

Fang Che-yong, M., *Quaestiones theologicae selectae libri Sira ex comparatione textus graeci et hebraici ortae* (Rome: Pontifical Biblical Institute, 1964).

Feldman, D. M., *Birth Control and Jewish Law* (New York: New York Univ. Press, 1968).

Feldman, L. H., *Jew and Gentile in the Ancient World* (Princeton, N.J.: Princeton Univ. Press, 1993).

———, "The Omnipresence of the G-d Fearers," *BAR* 12 (1986) 58–69.

Fichtner, J., *Die altorientalische Weisheit in ihrer israelitischjüdische Ausprägung* (BZAW 62; Berlin: de Gruyter, 1933).

———, *Weisheit Salomos* (HAT 2/6; Tübingen: Mohr, 1938).

Fischer, U., *Eschatologie und Jenseitserwartung im Hellenistischen Diasporajudentum* (BZNW 44; Berlin: de Gruyter, 1978).

Fitzmyer, J. A., "The Matthean Divorce Texts and Some New Palestinian Evidence," in idem, *To Advance the Gospel: New Testament Studies* (New York: Crossroad, 1981) 79–111.

———, *Romans* (AB 33; New York: Doubleday, 1993).

Flint, P. W., *The Psalters at Qumran and the Book of Psalms* (Leiden: Brill, 1997).

Focke, F., *Die Entstehung der Weisheit Salomos* (Göttingen: Vandenhoeck & Ruprecht, 1913).

Fontaine, C. R., *Traditional Sayings in the Old Testament: A Contextual Study* (Sheffield: Almond, 1982).

———, "The Sage in Family and Tribe," in Gammie and Perdue, eds., *The Sage in Israel and the Ancient Near East*, 155–64.

———, "Wisdom in Proverbs," in Perdue et al., eds., *In Search of Wisdom*, 99–114.

Fox, M. V., *The Song of Songs and the Ancient Egyptian Love Songs* (Madison: Univ. of Wisconsin Press, 1985).

———, *Qoheleth and His Contradictions* (JSOTSup 71; Sheffield: Sheffield Academic Press, 1989).

———, "Wisdom in Qoheleth," in Perdue et al., eds., *In Search of Wisdom*, 115–31.

———, "Wisdom in Proverbs," a paper read to the International Organisation for the Study of the Old Testament at Cambridge (July 1995).

Fraade, S., *Enosh and His Generation* (Chico, Calif.: Scholars, 1984).

Fraser, P. M., *Ptolemaic Alexandria* (3 vols.; Oxford: Clarendon, 1972).

Freedman, D. N., ed., *The Anchor Bible Dictionary* (6 vols.; New York: Doubleday, 1992).

Freund, R., "The Ethics of Abortion in Hellenistic Judaism," *Helios* 10 (1983) 125–37.

Friedländer, M., *Geschichte der jüdischen Apologetik* (Zurich: Schmidt, 1900).

Fuchs, A., *Textkritische Untersuchungen zum hebräischen Ekklesiastikus* (BibS(F) 12,5; Freiburg im Breisgau: Herder, 1907).

Gager, J. G., *The Origins of Anti-Semitism* (New York: Oxford Univ. Press, 1983).

Gammie, J. G., and L. G. Perdue, eds., *The Sage in Israel and the Ancient Near East* (Winona Lake, Ind.: Eisenbrauns, 1990).

Gammie, J. G., ed., *Israelite Wisdom: Theological and Literary Essays in Honor of Samuel Terrien* (Missoula, Mont.: Scholars, 1978).

———, "Wisdom in Sirach," in Gammie and Perdue, eds., *The Sage in Israel and the Ancient Near East* (Winona Lake, Ind.: Eisenbrauns, 1990) 355–72.

Gaventa, B. R., "The Rhetoric of Death in the Wisdom of Solomon and the Letters of Paul," in Hoglund et al., eds., *The Listening Heart*, 127–45.

Gazov-Ginzberg, A. M., "Double-Meaning in a Qumran Work: The Wiles of the Wicked Woman," *RevQ* 6 (1967) 279–85.

Geffcken, J., "Der Bilderstreit des heidnischen Altertums," *ARW* 19 (1919) 286–315.

Gentili, B., and C. Prato, *Poetarum Elegiacorum testimonia et fragmenta* (Leipzig: Teubner, 1979).

Georgi, D., "Der vorpaulinische Hymnus Phil 2, 6–11," in E. Dinkler, ed., *Zeit und Geschichte: Dankesgabe an R. Bultmann* (Tübingen: Mohr, 1964) 263–93.

————, *Weisheit Salomos* (JSHRZ 3/4; Gütersloh: Mohn, 1980).

————, *The Opponents of Paul in Second Corinthians* (Philadelphia: Fortress, 1986).

Gerstenberger, E., *Wesen und Herkunft des sogennanten 'apodiktischen Rechts' im Alten Testament* (WMANT 20; Neukirchen-Vluyn: Neukirchener Verlag, 1965).

————, *Psalms, with an Introduction to Cultic Poetry* (FOTL 14; Grand Rapids: Eerdmans, 1988).

Gilbert, M., *La Critique des Dieux dans le livre de la Sagesse* (AnBib 53; Rome: Pontifical Biblical Institute, 1973).

————, "L'éloge de la Sagesse (Siracide 24)," *RTL* 5 (1974) 326–48.

————, "Ben Sira et la femme," *RTL* 7 (1976) 426–42.

————, ed., *La Sagesse de l'Ancien Testament* (BETL 51; Louvain: Leuven Univ. Press, 1979).

————, "Wisdom Literature," in Stone, ed., *Jewish Writings of the Second Temple Period,* 283–324.

————, "Il giusto sofferente di Sap 2:12–20," in G. de Gennaro, ed., *L'antico testamento interpretato dal nuovo: il messia* (Naples: Edizioni Dehoniane, 1985) 193–218.

————, "Sagesse," *DBSup* 11 (1986) 77–87.

————, "Gn 1–3 dans le livre de la Sagesse," LD 127 (1987) 323–44.

Gilmore, D. G., ed., *Honor and Shame and the Unity of the Mediterranean* (Washington, D.C.: American Anthropological Association, 1987).

Ginzberg, L., *Legends of the Jews* (7 vols.; Philadelphia: Jewish Publication Society, 1925).

Golka, F. W., *The Leopard's Spots: Biblical and African Wisdom in Proverbs* (Edinburgh: T. & T. Clark, 1993).

————, "The Israelite Wisdom School or 'The Emperor's New Clothes,'" in idem, *The Leopard's Spots,* 4–15.

Goodenough, E. R., *By Light, Light: The Mystic Gospel of Hellenistic Judaism* (New Haven, Conn.: Yale Univ. Press, 1935).

Goodman, M., *Mission and Conversion: Proselytizing in the Religious History of the Roman Empire* (Oxford: Clarendon, 1994).

Gordis, R., "The Social Background of Wisdom Literature," *HUCA* 18 (1943/44) 77–118.

Görg, M., "Die Religionskritik in Weish 13, 1f.: Beobachtungen zur Entstehung der Sapientia-Salomonis im späthellenistischen Alexandria," in G. Hentschel and E. Zenger, eds., *Lehrerin der Gerechtigkeit* (Leipzig: Benno, 1991) 13–25.

Grant, F. C., *Hellenistic Religions* (Indianapolis: Bobbs-Merrill, 1953).

Gregg, J. A. F., *The Wisdom of Solomon* (Cambridge: Cambridge Univ. Press, 1909).

Grelot, P., "L'eschatologie de la Sagesse et les apocalypses juives," *À la Rencontre de Dieu: Mémorial Albert Gelin* (Le Puy: Mappus, 1961) 165–78.

Gressman, H., "Die neugefundene Lehre des Amenemope und die vorexilische Spruchdichtung Israels," *ZAW* 42 (1924) 272–96.

Grimm, C. L., *Das Buch der Weisheit* (Leipzig, 1860).

Habel, N. C., *The Book of Job* (OTL; Philadelphia: Westminster, 1985).

Hadot, J., *Penchant Mauvais et Volonté Libre dans La Sagesse de Ben Sira
(L'Ecclésiastique)* (Brussels: University Press, 1970).

Hall, R. G., *Revealed Histories: Techniques for Ancient Jewish and Christian
Historiography* (Sheffield: JSOT Press, 1991).

Harrill, J. A., *The Manumission of Slaves in Early Christianity* (Tübingen:
Mohr, 1995).

Harrington, D. J., and J. Strugnell, "Qumran Cave 4 Texts: A New Publication," *JBL* 112 (1993) 491–99.

Harrington, D. J., "Wisdom at Qumran," in E. Ulrich and J. C. VanderKam,
eds., *The Community of the Renewed Covenant* (Notre Dame, Ind.: Univ. of
Notre Dame Press, 1994) 137–52.

————, *Wisdom Texts from Qumran* (London: Routledge, 1997).

Harris, William V., *Ancient Literacy* (Cambridge, Mass.: Harvard Univ. Press,
1989).

Harvey, J. D., "Toward a Degree of Order in Ben Sira's Book," *ZAW* 105
(1993) 52–62.

Haspecker, J., *Gottesfurcht bei Jesus Sirach* (AnBib 30; Rome: Pontifical Biblical Institute, 1967).

Hays, R., "Relations Natural and Unnatural: A Response to John Boswell's
Exegesis of Romans 1," *JRE* 14 (1986) 184–215.

Heaton, E. W., *The School Tradition of the Old Testament* (Oxford: Oxford
Univ. Press, 1994).

Hecht, R. D., "Philo and Messiah," in J. Neusner, W. S. Green, and E. S.
Frerichs, eds., *Judaisms and Their Messiahs at the Turn of the Christian Era*
(Cambridge: Cambridge Univ. Press, 1987) 139–68.

Heinemann, I., "Die griechische Quelle der Weisheit Salomos," in idem,
Poseidonios' Metaphysische Schriften (reprint; Hildesheim: Olms, 1968)
136–53.

Heinisch, P., *Die Griechische Philosophie im Buche der Weisheit* (Münster:
Aschendorff, 1908).

————, *Das Buch der Weisheit* (Münster: Aschendorff, 1912).

Hengel, M., *Judaism and Hellenism* (2 vols.; Philadelphia: Fortress, 1974).

Herford, R. Travers, *The Ethics of the Talmud: Sayings of the Fathers* (New
York: Schocken, 1962).

Hermisson, H. J., *Studien zur Israelitischen Spruchweisheit* (WMANT 28;
Neukirchen-Vluyn: Neukirchener Verlag, 1968).

Hirzel, R., *Agraphos Nomos* (Leipzig: Teubner, 1900; reprint, Hildesheim:
Olms, 1979).

Höffken, P., "Warum schwieg Ben Sira über Ezra," *ZAW* 87 (1975) 184–202.

Hoglund, K. G., et al., eds., *The Listening Heart: Essays in Wisdom and the Psalms in Honor of Roland E. Murphy, O. Carm.* (JSOTSup 58; Sheffield: Almond, 1987).

Holladay, Carl R., *Fragments from Hellenistic Jewish Authors* (4 vols.; Atlanta: Scholars, 1983, 1989, 1996).

Honigmann, S., "The Birth of a Diaspora: The Emergence of a Jewish Self-Definition in Ptolemaic Egypt in the Light of Onomastics," in Cohen and Frerichs, eds., *Diasporas in Antiquity* (Atlanta: Scholars, 1993) 93–127.

Horbury, W., "Jewish Inscriptions and Jewish Literature in Egypt, with Special Reference to Ecclesiasticus," in J. W. van Henten and P. W. van der Horst, *Studies in Early Jewish Epigraphy* (Leiden: Brill, 1994) 9–43.

———, "The Christian Use and the Jewish Origins of the Wisdom of Solomon," in J. Day, ed., *Wisdom in Ancient Israel: Essays in Honour of J. A. Emerton* (Cambridge: Cambridge Univ. Press, 1995) 182–96.

Horbury, W., and D. Noy, *Jewish Inscriptions of Graeco-Roman Egypt* (Cambridge: Cambridge Univ. Press, 1992).

Horsley, R. A., "The Law of Nature in Philo and Cicero," *HTR* 71 (1978) 35–39.

Horst, P. W. van der, *The Sentences of Pseudo-Phocylides* (Leiden: Brill, 1978).

———, "Pseudo-Phocylides Revisited," *Journal for the Study of the Pseudepigrapha* 3 (1988) 3–30; reprinted in idem, *Essays on the Jewish World of Early Christianity* (Göttingen: Vandenhoeck & Ruprecht, 1990) 35–62.

———, *Ancient Jewish Epitaphs* (Kampen: Kok Pharos, 1991).

Hübner, H., "Die Sapientia Salomonis und die antike Philosophie," in idem, ed., *Die Weisheit Salomos in Horizont Biblischer Theologie* (Neukirchen-Vluyn: Neukirchener Verlag, 1993) 55–81.

Hughes, H. M., *The Ethics of Jewish Apocryphal Literature* (London: Culley, 1910).

Humbert, P., *Recherches sur les sources égyptiennes de la littérature sapientiale d'Israel* (Mémoires de l'Université de Neuchatel 7; Neuchatel: Secrétariat de l'Université, 1929).

Ilan, T. *Jewish Women in Greco-Roman Palestine* (Tübingen: Mohr, 1995).

———, "Notes and Observations on a Newly Published Divorce Bill from the Judaean Desert," *HTR* 89 (1996) 195–202.

Jacob, E., "L'Histoire d'Israel vue par Ben Sira," in *Mélanges bibliques rédigés en l'honneur de André Robert* (Paris: Bloud et Guy, 1957) 288–94.

Jansen, H. Ludin, *Die spätjüdische Psalmendichtung: Ihr Entstehungskreis und ihr 'Sitz im Leben'* (Oslo: Dybwad, 1937).

Janssen, E., *Das Gottesvolk und seine Geschichte. Geschichtsbild und Selbstverständnis im palästinensischen Schrifttum von Jesus Sirach bis Jehuda ha-Nasi* (Neukirchen-Vluyn: Neukirchener Verlag, 1971).

Jeremias, J., *The Prayers of Jesus* (Philadelphia: Fortress, 1967).

Jones, A.H.M., *The Greek City from Alexander to Justinian* (Oxford: Clarendon, 1940).

———, *The Cities of the Eastern Roman Provinces*, 2d ed. (Oxford: Clarendon Press, 1971).

Juster, J., *Les Juifs dans l'empire romain* (2 vols.; Paris: Geuthner, 1914).

Kaiser, O., "Die Begründung der Sittlichkeit im Buche Jesus Sirach," *ZTK* 55 (1958) 51–63 = *Der Mensch unter dem Schicksal* (Berlin: de Gruyter, 1985) 63–90.

Kasher, A., *The Jews in Hellenistic and Roman Egypt* (Tübingen: Mohr, 1985).

———, "The Civic Status of the Jews in Ptolemaic Egypt," in P. Bilde et al., eds., *Ethnicity in Hellenistic Egypt* (Aarhus: Aarhus Univ. Press, 1992) 100–121.

Kayatz, C., *Studien zu Proverbien 1–9* (Neukirchen-Vluyn: Neukirchener Verlag, 1966).

Kearns, C., "The Expanded Text of Ecclesiasticus: Its Teaching on the Future Life as a Clue to Its Origin" (Diss., Pontifical Biblical Institute; Rome, 1951).

———, "Ecclesiasticus, or the Wisdom of Jesus the Son of Sirach," in R. C. Fuller, ed., *A New Catholic Commentary on Holy Scripture* (London: Nelson, 1969) 541–62.

Kieweler, H. V., *Ben Sira zwischen Judentum und Hellenismus* (Frankfurt am Main: Lang, 1992).

Kister, M., "On a New Fragment of the Damascus Covenant," *JQR* 84 (1993/94) 249–52.

Kleinknecht, H., "Nomos," *TDNT* 4 (1967) 1032–33.

———, "Pneuma, pneumatikos etc.," *TDNT* 6 (1968) 354–55.

Kloppenborg, J. S., "Isis and Sophia in the Book of Wisdom," *HTR* 75 (1982) 57–84.

———, *The Formation of Q: Trajectories in Ancient Wisdom Collections* (Philadelphia: Fortress, 1987).

Klostermann, A., "Schulwesen im alten Israel," *Theologische Studien Th. Zahn* (Leipzig: Deichert, 1908) 193–232.

Knight, D. A., and G. M. Tucker, eds., *The Hebrew Bible and Its Modern Interpreters* (Philadelphia: Fortress, 1985).

Koch, K., "Gibt es ein Vergeltungsdogma im Alten Testament?" *ZTK* 52 (1955) 1–42 (English translation: "Is There a Doctrine of Retribution in the Old Testament?" in J. L. Crenshaw, ed., *Theodicy in the Old Testament* (Philadelphia: Fortress, 1983) 57–87.

———, "Is Daniel Also among the Prophets?" *Int* 39 (1985) 117–30.

Koester, H., "Nomos Physeos: The Concept of Natural Law in Greek Thought," in J. Neusner, ed., *Religions in Antiquity: Essays in Memory of E. R. Goodenough* (Leiden: Brill, 1970) 521–41.

————, "*Gnomai Diaphoroi:* The Origin and Nature of Diversification in the History of Early Christianity," in J. M. Robinson and H. Koester, eds., *Trajectories through Early Christianity* (Philadelphia: Fortress, 1971) 114–57.

————, "*physis*, etc." *TDNT* 9 (1974) 264–66.

Kolarcik, M., *The Ambiguity of Death in the Book of Wisdom 1–6* (AnBib 127; Rome: Pontifical Biblical Institute, 1991).

Koole, J. L., "Die Bibel des Ben-Sira," *OTS* 14 (1965) 374–96.

Kraabel, A. T., "The Disappearance of the 'God-Fearers,' in Overman and MacLennan, eds., *Diaspora Jews and Judaism*, 119–30.

Küchler, M., *Frühjüdische Weisheitstraditionen* (OBO 26; Göttingen: Vandenhoeck & Ruprecht, 1979).

Kuhn, K. G., and H. Stegemann, "Proselyten," *PWRE* Sup 9 (1962) 1260.

Kuhrt, A., and S. Sherwin-White, *Hellenism in the East* (Berkeley: Univ. of California, 1987).

Lang, B., *Frau Weisheit* (Düsseldorf: Patmos, 1975).

————, "Schule und Unterricht in Israel," in Gilbert, ed., *La Sagesse de l'Ancien Testament*, 192–99.

————, *Wisdom and the Book of Proverbs: An Israelite Goddess Redefined* (New York: Pilgrim, 1986).

Lange, A., *Weisheit und Prädestination: Weisheitliche Urordnung und Prädestination in der Textfunden von Qumran* (Leiden: Brill, 1995).

Lapidge, M., "Stoic Cosmology," in J. M. Rist, ed., *The Stoics* (Berkeley: Univ. of California Press, 1978) 161–85.

Larcher, C., *Études sur le Livre de la Sagesse* (Paris: Gabalda, 1969).

————, *Le Livre de la Sagesse ou la Sagesse de Salomon* (3 vols.; Paris: Gabalda, 1983–85).

Lee, T. R., *Studies in the Form of Sirach 44–50* (Atlanta: Scholars, 1986).

Leiman, S. Z., *The Canonization of Hebrew Scripture: The Talmudic and Midrashic Evidence* (Hamden, Conn.: Archon, 1976).

Lemaire, A., *Les écoles et la formation de la Bible dans l'ancien Israel* (Göttingen: Vandenhoeck & Ruprecht, 1981).

————, "The Sage in School and Temple," in Gammie and Perdue, eds., *The Sage in Israel and the Ancient Near East*, 165–81.

Levenson, J. D., "Who Inserted the Book of the Torah?" *HTR* 68 (1975) 203–33.

————, "The Theologies of Commandment in Biblical Israel," *HTR* 73 (1980) 17–33.

Levine, A. J., ed., "*Women like This*": *New Perspectives on Jewish Women in the Greco-Roman World* (Atlanta: Scholars, 1991).

Levison, J. R., "Is Eve to Blame? A Contextual Analysis of Sirach 25:24," *CBQ* 47 (1985) 617–23.

————, *Portraits of Adam in Early Judaism from Sirach to 2 Baruch* (Sheffield: JSOT Press, 1988).

Lewis, N., *The Documents from the Bar-Kochba Period in the Cave of the Letters* (Jerusalem: Israel Exploration Society, 1989).

Licht, J., *The Rule Scroll: A Scroll from the Wilderness of Judaea, 1QS, 1QSa, 1QSb: Text, Introduction and Commentary* (Hebrew; Jerusalem: Bialik, 1965).

Lichtenberger, H., "Eine weisheitliche Mahnrede in den Qumranfunde (4Q185)," in M. Delcor, ed., *Qumrân: Sa piété, sa theologie et son milieu* (BETL 46; Louvain: Leuven University Press, 1978) 151–62.

Lichtheim, M., *Ancient Egyptian Literature*, vol. 1 (Berkeley: Univ. of California Press, 1973).

————, *Late Egyptian Wisdom Literature in the International Context: A Study of Demotic Instructions* (OBO 52; Fribourg: Fribourg University, 1983).

Lindenberger, J. M., *The Aramaic Proverbs of Ahiqar* (Baltimore: Johns Hopkins Univ. Press, 1983).

Long, A. A., and D. N. Sedley, *The Hellenistic Philosophers* (Cambridge: Cambridge Univ. Press, 1987).

Lüderitz, G., "What Is the Politeuma?" in J. W. van Henten and P. W. van der Horst, eds., *Studies in Early Jewish Epigraphy* (Leiden: Brill, 1994) 183–225.

Lumpe, A., "Exemplum," *RAC* 6 (1966) 1229–57.

Luyten, J., "Psalm 73 and Wisdom," in Gilbert, ed., *La Sagesse de l'Ancien Testament*, 59–81.

Lyttkens, H., *The Analogy Between God and the World* (Uppsala: Lundequist, 1953).

Mack, B. L., "Wisdom Myth and Mythology," *Int* 24 (1970) 46–60.

————, "Imitatio Mosis: Patterns of Cosmology and Soteriology in the Hellenistic Synagogue," *Studie Philonica* 1 (1972) 27–55.

————, *Logos und Sophia: Untersuchungen zur Weisheitstheologie im hellenistischen Judentum* (Göttingen: Vandenhoeck & Ruprecht, 1973).

————, *Wisdom and the Hebrew Epic: Ben Sira's Hymn in Praise of the Fathers* (Chicago: Univ. of Chicago Press, 1986).

————, *A Myth of Innocence: Mark and Christian Origins* (Philadelphia: Fortress, 1988).

MacLennan, R. S., and A. T. Kraabel, "The God-Fearers—A Literary and Theological Invention," in Overman and MacLennan, eds., *Diaspora Jews and Judaism* (Atlanta: Scholars, 1992) 131–43.

Maertens, T., *L'Éloge des pères* (Ecclesiastique XLIV–L; Bruges: Abbaye de Saint-André, 1956).

Maier, G., *Mensch und Freier Wille* (Tübingen: Mohr, 1971).

Malherbe, A. J., *Moral Exhortation; A Greco-Roman Sourcebook* (Philadelphia: Westminster, 1986).

Mansfeld, J., "Philosophy in the Service of Scripture: Philo's Exegetical Strategies," in J. M. Dillon and A. A. Long, eds., *The Question of "Eclecticism": Studies in Later Greek Philosophy* (Berkeley: Univ. of California Press, 1988) 70–102.

Marböck, J., *Weisheit im Wandel: Untersuchungen zur Weisheitstheologie bei Ben Sira* (Bonn: Hanstein, 1971).

———, "Gesetz und Weisheit: Zum Verständnis des Gesetzes bei Jesus Sira," *BZ* 20 (1976) 1–21.

———, "Das Gebet um die Rettung Zions Sir 36, 1–22 (G:33, 1–13a; 36, 16b–22) im Zusammenhang der Geschichtsschau Ben Siras," in J. B. Bauer, ed., *Memoria Jerusalem* (Jerusalem/Graz: Akademische Druck- und Verlagsanstalt, 1977) 93–116.

Marrou, H. I., *A History of Education in Antiquity* (London: Sheed & Ward, 1956; reprint: University of Wisconsin, n.d.).

Martin, D. B., "Slavery and the Ancient Jewish Family," in S. J. D. Cohen, ed., *The Jewish Family in Antiquity* (Atlanta: Scholars, 1993) 113–29.

Martin, J. D., "Ben Sira—A Child of His Time," in J. D. Martin and P. R. Davies, eds., *A Word in Season: Essays in Honour of William McKane* (Sheffield: JSOT Press, 1986) 141–61.

———, "Ben Sira's Hymn to the Fathers: A Messianic Perspective," in A. S. van der Woude, ed., *Crises and Perspectives* (Leiden: Brill, 1986) 107–23.

Martínez, F. García, *The Dead Sea Scrolls Translated* (Leiden: Brill, 1994).

Mays, J. L., "The Place of the Torah-Psalms in the Psalter," *JBL* 106 (1987) 3–12.

McKane, W., *Prophets and Wise Men* (London: SCM Press, 1965).

———, *Proverbs: A New Approach* (Philadelphia: Westminster, 1970).

McKnight, S., *A Light among the Gentiles: Jewish Missionary Activity in the Second Temple Period* (Minneapolis: Fortress, 1991).

Mendelson, A., *Secular Education in Philo of Alexandria* (Cincinnati: Hebrew Union College Press, 1982).

———, *Philo's Jewish Identity* (Atlanta: Scholars, 1988).

Meyers, C., *Discovering Eve* (New York: Oxford Univ. Press, 1988).

Michaelis, D., "Das Buch Jesus Sirach als typischer Ausdruck für das Gottesverhältnis des nachalttestamentlichen Menschen," *TLZ* 83 (1958) 601–8.

Middendorp, Th., *Die Stellung Jesu Ben Siras zwischen Judentum und Hellenismus* (Leiden: Brill, 1973).

Mitsis, P., "Natural Law and Natural Right in Post-Aristotelian Philosophy: The Stoics and Their Critics," *ANRW* 2.36.7 (1994) 4812–50.

Modrzejewski, *The Jews of Egypt: From Ramses II to Emperor Hadrian* (Philadelphia: Jewish Publication Society, 1995).

Moore, C. A., *Daniel, Esther, and Jeremiah: The Additions* (AB 44; New York: Doubleday, 1977).

Moore, G. F., *Judaism in the First Centuries of the Christian Era* (3 vols.; New York: Schocken, 1975).

Moore, R. D., "Personification of the Seduction of Evil: The Wiles of the Wicked Woman," *RevQ* 10 (1981) 505–19.

Mowinckel, S., "Psalms and Wisdom," in *Wisdom in Israel and the Ancient Near East* (Fs. H. H. Rowley; VTSup 3; Leiden: Brill, 1955) 205–44.

Moxnes, H., "Honor and Shame," *BTB* 23 (1993) 167–76.

Muenchow, C., "Dust and Dirt in Job 42:6," *JBL* 108 (1989) 597–611.

Muraoka, T., "Sir 51:13–30: An Erotic Hymn to Wisdom?" *JSJ* 10 (1979) 166–78.

Murphy, R. E., "*Yeṣer* in the Qumran Literature," *Bib* 39 (1958) 334–44.

————, "A Consideration of the Classification, 'Wisdom Psalms,'" *Congress Volume: Bonn, 1962* (VTSup 9; Leiden: Brill, 1963) 156–67.

————, *Wisdom Literature: Job, Proverbs, Ruth, Canticles, Ecclesiastes and Esther* (FOTL 13; Grand Rapids: Eerdmans, 1981).

————, "Wisdom and Creation," *JBL* 104 (1985) 3–11.

————, "The Sage in Ecclesiastes and Qoheleth the Sage," in Gammie and Perdue, eds., *The Sage in Israel and the Ancient Near East*, 263–71.

————, *The Tree of Life: An Exploration of Biblical Wisdom Literature* (New York: Doubleday, 1990).

————, "Wisdom in the OT," in D. N. Freedman, ed., *ABD* 6 (1992) 920–31.

————, *Ecclesiastes* (WBC 23; Dallas: Word, 1992).

Newsom, C. A., *Songs of the Sabbath Sacrifice: A Critical Edition* (Atlanta: Scholars, 1985).

————, "4Q370: An Admonition Based on the Flood," *RevQ* 13 (1988) 23–43.

————, "Woman and the Discourse of Patriarchal Wisdom: A Study of Proverbs 1–9," in P. L. Day, ed., *Gender and Difference in Ancient Israel* (Minneapolis: Fortress, 1989) 142–60.

————, "The Sage in the Literature of Qumran: The Functions of the Maskil," in Gammie and Perdue, eds., *The Sage in Israel and the Ancient Near East*, 373–82.

————, "'Sectually Explicit' Literature from Qumran," in W. Propp et al., eds., *The Hebrew Bible and Its Interpreters* (Winona Lake, Ind.: Eisenbrauns, 1990) 167–87.

Nickelsburg, G. W., *Resurrection, Immortality and Eternal Life in Intertestamental Judaism* (Cambridge, Mass.: Harvard Univ. Press, 1972).

————, "The Apocalyptic Message of 1 Enoch 92–105," *CBQ* 39 (1977) 309–28.

————, "Riches, the Rich, and God's Judgment in 1 Enoch 92–105 and the Gospel according to Luke," *NTS* 25 (1979) 324–44.

————, *Jewish Literature between the Bible and the Mishnah* (Philadelphia: Fortress, 1981).

Niebuhr, K. W., *Gesetz und Paränese* (Tübingen: Mohr, 1987).

Nilsson, M. P., *Geschichte der Griechischen Religion, 2: Die hellenistische und römische Zeit* (Munich: Beck, 1974).

Noy, D., "The Jewish Communities of Leontopolis and Venosa," in J. W. van Henten and P. W. van der Horst, eds., *Studies in Early Jewish Epigraphy* (Leiden: Brill, 1994) 162–82.

O'Fearghail, F., "Sir 50, 5–21: Yom Kippur or The Daily Whole Offering?" *Bib* 59 (1978) 301–16.

Ogden, G. S., "The 'Better'-Proverb (Tôb-Spruch), Rhetorical Criticism, and Qoheleth," *JBL* 96 (1977) 489–505.

Olyan, S., "Ben Sira's Relationship to the Priesthood," *HTR* 80 (1987) 261–86.

———, "And with a Male You Shall Not Lie the Lying Down of a Woman": On the Meaning and Significance of Leviticus 18:22 and 20:13," *Journal of the History of Sexuality* 5 (1994) 179–206.

Overman, J. A., and R. S. MacLennan, eds., *Diaspora Jews and Judaism: Essays in Honor of, and in Dialogue with, A. Thomas Kraabel* (Atlanta: Scholars, 1992).

Paul, S., "Heavenly Tablets and the Book of Life," *JANESCU* 5 (1973) 345–53.

Pautrel, R., "Ben Sira et le stoicisme," *RSR* 51 (1963) 535–49.

Perdue, L. G., *Wisdom and Cult* (SBLDS 30; Missoula, Mont.: Scholars, 1977).

———, *Wisdom in Revolt: Metaphorical Theology in the Book of Job* (JSOT-Sup 112; Sheffield: Sheffield Academic Press, 1991).

———, *Wisdom and Creation: The Theology of Wisdom Literature* (Nashville: Abingdon, 1994).

Perdue, L. G., and W. C. Gilpin, eds., *The Voice from the Whirlwind: Interpreting the Book of Job* (Nashville: Abingdon, 1992).

Perdue, L. G., B. B. Scott, and W. J. Wiseman, eds., *In Search of Wisdom: Essays in Honor of John G. Gammie* (Louisville, Ky.: Westminster John Knox, 1993).

Peters, N., *Das Buch Jesus Sirach oder Ecclesiasticus* (Münster: Aschendorff, 1913).

Peterson, E., *Heis Theos* (Göttingen: Vandenhoeck & Ruprecht, 1926).

Pfann, S., "4Q298: The Maskil's Address to All Sons of Dawn," *JQR* 85 (1994) 203–35.

Philonenko, M., "Mythe et histoire qoumrânienne des deux Esprits: Ses origines iraniennes et ses prolongements dans le judaïsme essénien et le christianisme antique," in G. Widengren et al., *Apocalyptique Iranienne et Dualisme Qoumrânien* (Paris: Maisonneuve, 1995) 163–211.

Ploeg, J. P. M. van der, "Le Psaume 119 et la sagesse," in M. Gilbert, ed., *La Sagesse de l'Ancien Testament*, 82–87.

Pohlenz, M., *Die Stoa: Geschichte einer geistigen Bewegung* (2d ed.; Göttingen: Vandenhoeck & Ruprecht, 1959).

Pohlmann, K. F., *Studien zum Dritten Esra* (Göttingen: Vandenhoeck & Ruprecht, 1970).

Pomykala, K., *The Davidic Dynasty Tradition in Early Judaism: Its History and Significance for Messianism* (Atlanta: Scholars, 1995).

Porten, B., *Archives from Elephantine: The Life of an Ancient Jewish Military Colony* (Berkeley: Univ. of California Press, 1968).

Porter, F. C., "The Yeçer HaRa: A Study in the Jewish Doctrine of Sin," in *Biblical and Semitic Studies* (New York: Scribners, 1901) 93–156.

Prato, G. L., *Il Problema della Teodicea in Ben Sira* (AnBib 65; Rome: Pontifical Biblical Institute, 1975).

Preuss, H. D., *Verspottung fremder Religionen im Alten Testament* (Stuttgart: Kohlhammer, 1971).

Pritchard, James E., *Ancient Near Eastern Texts Relating to the Old Testament* (3d ed., Princeton, N.J.: Princeton Univ. Press, 1969).

Prockter, L. J., "'His Yesterday and Yours Today' (Sir 38:22): Reflections on Ben Sira's View of Death," *Journal for Semitics* 2 (1990) 44–56.

Puech, E., "Ben Sira 48:11 et la Résurrection," in H. Attridge et al., eds., *Of Scribes and Scrolls, Studies on the Hebrew Bible: Intertestamental Judaism and Christian Origins* (Lanham, Md.: University Press of America, 1990) 81–90.

———, "4Q525 et les péricopes des béatitudes en Ben Sira et Matthieu," *RB* 98 (1991) 80–106.

———, *La Croyance des Esséniens en la Vie Future: Immortalité, Résurrection, Vie Éternelle?* (Paris: Gabalda, 1993).

Purvis, J. D., "Ben Sira and the Foolish People of Shechem," in *The Samaritan Pentateuch and the Origin of the Samaritan Sect* (Cambridge, Mass.: Harvard Univ. Press, 1968) 119–29.

Qimron, E., and J. Strugnell, *Qumran Cave 4. V. Miqsat Maʿaśê HaTorah* (*DJD* 10; Oxford: Clarendon, 1994).

Rackman, H., *Aristotle: The Athenian Constitution, The Eudemian Ethics, On Virtues and Vices* (LCL; Cambridge, Mass.: Harvard Univ. Press, 1961).

Rad, G. von, "Life and Death in the OT," *TDNT* 2 (1964) 843–49.

———, *Wisdom in Israel* (Nashville: Abingdon, 1972).

Rajak, Tessa, "Was There a Roman Charter for the Jews?" *Journal of Roman Studies* 74 (1984) 107–203.

Rankin, O. S., *Israel's Wisdom Literature* (Edinburgh: T. & T. Clark, 1936).

Reese, J. M., "Plan and Structure in the Book of Wisdom," *CBQ* 27 (1965) 391–99.

———, *Hellenistic Influence on the Book of Wisdom and Its Consequences* (AnBib 41; Rome: Pontifical Biblical Institute, 1971).

Reider, J., *The Book of Wisdom* (Dropsie College series; New York: Harper, 1957).

Reiterer, F. V., ed., *Freundschaft bei Ben Sira* (Berlin: de Gruyter, 1996).

Reynolds, J., and R. Tannenbaum, *Jews and God-Fearers at Aphrodisias* (Suppl. 12; Cambridge: Cambridge Philological Society, 1987).

Rickenbacher, O., *Weisheitsperikopen bei Ben Sira* (Göttingen: Vandenhoeck & Ruprecht, 1973).

Riesner, R., *Jesus als Lehrer* (Tübingen: Mohr, 1981).

Rist, J. M., *Stoic Philosophy* (Cambridge: Cambridge Univ. Press, 1969).

Roth, W. M. W., "For Life, He Appeals to Death (Wis 13:18): A Study of Old Testament Idol Parodies," *CBQ* 37 (1975) 21–47.

———, "The Gnomic-Discursive Wisdom of Jesus Ben Sirach," *Semeia* 17 (1980) 35–79.

Rüger, H. P., *Text und Textform in Hebräischen Sirach* (BZAW 112; Berlin: de Gruyter, 1970).

Ruppert, L., *Der leidende Gerechte* (Würzburg: Katholisches Bibelwerk, 1972).

———, "Gerechte und Frevler (Gottlose) in Sap 1, 1–6, 21: Zum Neuverständnis und zur Aktualisierung alttestamentlicher Traditionen in der Sapientia Salomonis," in Hübner, ed., *Der Weisheit Salomos,* 1–54.

Safrai, S., "Education and the Study of Torah," in Safrai and Stern, eds., *The Jewish People in the First Century,* 945–70.

Safrai, S., and M. Stern, eds., *The Jewish People in the First Century* (CRINT 1/2; Assen: Van Gorcum, 1976).

Saldarini, A. J., *Pharisees, Scribes and Sadducees in Palestinian Society* (Wilmington, Del.: Glazier, 1988).

Sandbach, F. H., *The Stoics* (New York: Norton, 1975).

Sanders, E. P., *Paul and Palestinian Judaism* (Philadelphia: Fortress, 1977).

Sanders, J. A., *The Psalms Scroll of Qumran Cave 11 (11QPsᵃ)* (DJD 4; Oxford: Oxford Univ. Press, 1965).

———, *The Dead Sea Psalms Scroll* (Ithaca, N.Y.: Cornell Univ. Press, 1967).

Sanders, J. T., "Ben Sira's Ethics of Caution," *HUCA* 50 (1979) 73–106.

———, *Ben Sira and Demotic Wisdom* (Chico, Calif.: Scholars, 1983).

Saracino, F., "Risurrezione in Ben Sira?" *Henoch* 4 (1982) 185–203.

Scaliger, J., "Animadversiones in Chronologia Eusebii," in idem, *Thesaurus Temporum* (London, 1606).

Schäfer, P., "Der Götzendienst des Enosch: Zur Bildung und Entwicklung aggadischer traditionen im nachbiblischen Judentum," in idem, *Studien zur Geschichte und Theologie des Rabbinischen Judentums* (Leiden: Brill, 1978) 134–52.

Schechter, S., "The Quotations from Ecclesiasticus in Rabbinic Literature," *JQR* 3 (1890/91) 682–706.

Schechter, S., and C. Taylor, *The Wisdom of Ben Sira: Portions of the Book of*

Ecclesiasticus from Hebrew Manuscripts in the Cairo Genizah Collection Presented to the University of Cambridge by the Editors (Cambridge: Cambridge Univ. Press, 1899).

Schiffman, L. H., "4QMysteries^b, A Preliminary Edition," *RevQ* 16 (1993) 203–23.

———, *Reclaiming the Dead Sea Scrolls* (New York: Jewish Publication Society, 1994).

———, "4QMysteries^a: A Preliminary Edition and translation," in Z. Zevit et al., eds., *Solving Riddles and Untying Knots: Biblical, Epigraphic, and Semitic Studies in Honor of Jonas C. Greenfield* (Winona Lake, Ind.: Eisenbrauns, 1995) 207–60.

Schmid, H. H., *Wesen und Geschichte der Weisheit* (BZAW 101; Berlin: de Gruyter, 1966).

Schmitt, A., "Struktur, Herkunft und Bedeutung der Beispielreihe in Weish 10," *BZ* 21 (1977) 1–22.

———, *Das Buch der Weisheit* (Würzburg: Echter, 1986).

Schnabel, E. J., *Law and Wisdom from Ben Sira to Paul* (Tübingen: Mohr, 1985).

Schneider, C., "Eros," *RAC* VI, 309.

Schökel, L. A., S.J., "The Vision of Man in Sirach 16:24–17:14," in Gammie et al., eds., *Israelite Wisdom*, 235–60.

Schürer, E., *The History of the Jewish People in the Age of Jesus Christ* (3 vols. Rev. and ed. G. Vermes et al.; Edinburgh: T. & T. Clark, 1979–86).

Schuller, E., "4Q372 1: A Text about Joseph," *RevQ* 14 (1990) 349–76.

Segal, M. H., *Sēper ben Sîrâ haššālēm* (Jerusalem: Bialik, 1958).

Sevenster, J. N., *The Roots of Pagan Anti-Semitism in the Ancient World* (Leiden: Brill, 1980).

Sheppard, G. T., *Wisdom as a Hermeneutical Construct* (BZAW 151; Berlin: de Gruyter, 1980).

Shupak, N., "The 'Sitz im Leben' of the Book of Proverbs in the Light of a Comparison of Biblical and Egyptian Wisdom Literature," *RB* 94 (1987) 98–119.

———, *Where Can Wisdom Be Found? The Sage's Language in the Bible and in Ancient Egyptian Literature* (OBO 130; Fribourg: Fribourg University, 1993).

Siebeneck, R. T., "May Their Bones Return to Life! Sirach's Praise of the Fathers," *CBQ* 21 (1959) 411–28.

Skehan, P. W., and A. A. DiLella, *The Wisdom of Ben Sira* (AB 39; New York: Doubleday, 1987).

Smallwood, E. Mary, *The Jews under Roman Rule* (Leiden: Brill, 1976).

Smend, R., *Die Weisheit des Jesus Sirach erklärt* (Berlin: Reimer, 1906).

Smith, D. E., and H. Taussig, *Many Tables: The Eucharist in the New Testament and Liturgy Today* (Philadelphia: Trinity, 1990).

Soll, W., *Psalm 119: Matrix, Form and Setting* (CBQMS 23; Washington, D.C.: Catholic Biblical Association, 1991).

Stadelmann, H., *Ben Sira als Schriftgelehrter* (Tübingen: Mohr, 1980).

Stern, M., *Greek and Latin Authors on Jews and Judaism* (2 vols.; Jerusalem: The Israel Academy of Sciences and Humanities, 1976).

Stone, M. E., "Lists of Revealed Things in the Apocalyptic Literature," in F. M. Cross et al., eds., *Magnalia Dei: The Mighty Acts of God* (New York: Doubleday, 1976) 414–52.

————, *Jewish Writings of the Second Temple Period* (CRINT 2/2; Philadelphia: Fortress, 1984).

————, M. E., *Fourth Ezra* (Hermeneia; Minneapolis: Fortress, 1990).

Stone, M. E., and D. Satran, eds., *Emerging Judaism: Studies on the Fourth and Third Centuries B.C.E.* (Minneapolis: Fortress, 1989).

Striker, G., "Origins of the Concept of Natural Law," in J. J. Cleary, ed., *Proceedings of the Boston Area Colloquium in Ancient Philosophy* (Lanham, Md.: University Press of America, 1987) 79–94.

————, "Following Nature: A Study in Stoic Ethics," *Oxford Society for Ancient Philosophy* 9 (1991) 1–73.

Strotmann, A., *"Mein Vater Bist du!" (Sir 51:10)* (Frankfurt am Main: Knecht, 1991) 59–97.

Strugnell, J., "Notes en marge du volume V des 'Discoveries in the Judaean Desert of Jordan,'" *RevQ* 7 (1970) 163–276.

Stuart, G. H. Cohen, *The Struggle in Man between Good and Evil: An Inquiry into the Origin of the Rabbinic Concept of Yeser Haraʿ* (Kampen: Kok, 1984).

Sweet, J. P. M., "The Theory of Miracles in the Wisdom of Solomon," in C. F. D. Moule, ed., *Miracles* (London: Mowbray, 1965) 115–26.

Tanzer, S. J., "The Sages at Qumran: Wisdom in the *Hodayot*," (Ph.D. Diss., Harvard Univ., 1987).

Taubenschlag, R., *The Law of Greco-Roman Egypt in the Light of the Papyri* (2 vols.; New York: Herald Square, 1944).

Taylor, R. J., "The Eschatological Meaning of Life and Death in the Book of Wisdom I–V," *ETL* 42 (1966) 102–13.

Tcherikover, V., "Jewish Apologetic Literature Reconsidered," *Eos* 48 (1956) 169–93.

Tcherikover, V., and A. Fuks, *Corpus Papyrorum Judaicarum* (Cambridge, Mass.: Harvard Univ. Press, 1957).

————, *Hellenistic Civilization and the Jews* (New York: Jewish Publication Society, 1959; reprint, New York: Atheneum, 1970).

Tennant, F. R., "The Teaching of Ecclesiasticus and Wisdom on the Introduction of Sin and Death," *JTS* 2 (1900/01) 207–23.

Thomas, J., *Der jüdische Phokylides* (Göttingen: Vandenhoeck & Ruprecht, 1992).

Thompson, D. J., *Memphis under the Ptolemies* (Princeton, N.J.: Princeton Univ. Press, 1988).

Thompson-Crawford, D. J., "The Idumaeans of Memphis and the Ptolemaic Politeumata," in M. Gigante, ed., *Atti del XVII Congresso Internazionale di Papirologia* (Naples: Centro Internazionale per lo Studio dei Papiri Ercolanesi, 1984) 3.1069–75.

Thyen, H., *Der Stil der Jüdisch-Hellenistischen Homilie* (Göttingen: Vandenhoeck & Ruprecht, 1955).

Tobin, T. H., *The Creation of Man: Philo and the History of Interpretation* (Washington, D.C.: Catholic Biblical Association, 1983).

———, "4Q185 and Jewish Wisdom Literature," in H. W. Attridge, et al., eds., *Of Scribes and Scrolls: Studies on the Hebrew Bible, Intertestamental Judaism and Christian Origins* (Lanham, Md.: University Press of America, 1990) 145–52.

———, "Logos," *ABD* 4:348–56.

Toorn, K. van der, *From Her Cradle to Her Grave: The Role of Religion in the Life of the Israelite and the Babylonian Woman* (Sheffield: JSOT Press, 1994).

Tov, E., "Biblical Texts as Reworked in Some Qumran Manuscripts with Special Attention to 4QRP and 4QParaGen-Exod," in Ulrich and VanderKam, eds., *The Community of the Renewed Covenant*, 111–34.

Trenchard, W. C., *Ben Sira's View of Women* (Chico, Calif.: Scholars, 1982).

Ulrich, E., "An Index of the Passages in the Biblical Manuscripts from the Judean Desert (Part 2: Isaiah–Chronicles)," *Dead Sea Discoveries* 2 (1995) 86–107.

———, "The Bible in the Making: The Scriptures at Qumran," in E. Ulrich and J. VanderKam, eds., *The Community of the Renewed Covenant*, 77–93.

Ulrich, E., and J. VanderKam, eds., *The Community of the Renewed Covenant* (Notre Dame, Ind.: Univ. of Notre Dame Press, 1994).

Urbach, E. E., *The Sages: Their Concepts and Beliefs* (2 vols.; Jerusalem: Magnes, 1975).

Vawter, B., "Intimations of Immortality and the Old Testament," *JBL* 91 (1972) 158–71.

———, "Proverbs 8:22: Wisdom and Creation," *JBL* 99 (1980) 205–16.

———, *The Path of Wisdom* (Wilmington, Del.: Glazier, 1986).

Vermes, G., "Genesis 1–3 in Post-Biblical Hebrew and Aramaic Literature before the Mishnah," *JJS* 43 (1992) 221–25.

———, *The Dead Sea Scrolls in English* (4th ed.; London: Penguin, 1995).

Wacholder, B. Z., and M. G. Abegg, *A Preliminary Edition of the Unpublished Dead Sea Scrolls* (Washington, D.C.: Biblical Archaeology Society, 1992).

Waert, P. van der, "Zeno's Republic and the Origins of Natural Law," in idem, ed., *The Socratic Movement* (Ithaca, N.Y.: Cornell Univ. Press, 1994) 272–308.

Walter, N., *Poetische Schriften* (JSHRZ 4.3; Gütersloh: Mohn, 1983).

Watson, G., "The Natural Law and Stoicism," in A. A. Long, ed., *Problems in Stoicism* (London: Athlone, 1971) 216–38.

Weinfeld, M., *Deuteronomy and the Deuteronomic School* (Oxford: Oxford Univ. Press, 1972).

————, *Deuteronomy* (AB 5; New York: Doubleday, 1991).

Wernberg-Møller, P., "A Reconsideration of the Two Spirits in the Rule of the Community (1Q Serek III, 13–IV, 26)," *RevQ* 3 (1961) 413–41.

Westermann, C., *Roots of Wisdom* (Louisville, Ky.: Westminster John Knox, 1995).

Whybray, N., *The Intellectual Tradition in the Old Testament* (BZAW 135; Berlin: de Gruyter, 1974).

————, "Slippery Words, IV: Wisdom," *Expository Times* 89 (1978) 359–62.

Wilcken, U., *Grundzüge und Chrestomathie der Papyruskunde* I.1 (Leipzig & Berlin: Teubner, 1912).

Williams, R. J., "The Sage in Egyptian Literature," in Gammie and Perdue, eds., *The Sage in Israel and the Ancient Near East*, 19–30.

Wilson, G. H., *The Editing of the Hebrew Psalter* (SBLDS 76; Chico, Calif.: Scholars, 1985).

————, "The Qumran Psalms Scroll Reconsidered: Analysis of the Debate," *CBQ* 47 (1985) 624–42.

Wilson, W. T., *The Mysteries of Righteousness: The Literary Composition and Genre of the Sentences of Pseudo-Phocylides* (Tübingen: Mohr, 1994).

Winston, D., *The Wisdom of Solomon* (AB 43; New York: Doubleday, 1979).

————, *Logos and Mystical Theology in Philo of Alexandria* (Cincinnati: Hebrew Union College Press, 1985).

————, "Theodicy in Ben Sira and Stoic Philosophy," in R. Link-Salinger, ed., *Of Scholars, Savants, and Their Texts* (New York: Lang, 1989) 239–49.

Wischmeyer, O., *Die Kultur des Buches Jesus Sirachs* (BZNW 77; Berlin: de Gruyter, 1995).

Wise, M. O., *A Critical Study of the Temple Scroll from Qumran Cave 11* (Chicago: The Oriental Institute, 1990).

Wolfson, H. A., *Philo* (2 vols; Cambridge, Mass.: Harvard Univ. Press, 1948).

Wright, A. G., "The Structure of the Book of Wisdom," *Bib* 48 (1967) 165–84.

Wright, B. G., *No Small Difference: Sirach's Relationship to Its Hebrew Parent Text* (SCS 26; Atlanta: Scholars, 1989).

Wright, M. R., *Cosmology in Antiquity* (London: Routledge, 1995).

Yadin, Y., *The Scroll of the War of the Sons of Light against the Sons of Darkness* (Oxford: Oxford Univ. Press, 1962).

————, *The Ben Sira Scroll from Masada* (Jerusalem: Israel Exploration Society, 1965).

Zenger, E., "Die späte Weisheit und das Gesetz," in J. Maier, ed., *Literatur und Religion des Frühjudentums: Eine Einführung* (Gütersloh: Mohn, 1973) 43–56.

Ziegler, J., *Sapientia Jesu Filii Sirach* (Septuaginta 12/2; Göttingen: Vandenhoeck & Ruprecht, 1965).

Zuckerman, Constantine, "Hellenistic Politeumata and the Jews: A Reconsideration," *Scripta Classica Israelica* 8–10 (1985–88) 171–85.

INDEX OF PASSAGES

INDEX OF AUTHORS